# Does the Village Still Raise the Child?

SUNY series, Early Childhood Education:
Inquiries and Insight

Mary A. Jensen, Editor

# Does the Village Still Raise the Child?

## A Collaborative Study of Changing Child-rearing and Early Education in Kenya

Beth Blue Swadener
with
Margaret Kabiru and Anne Njenga

State University of New York Press

Published by
State University of New York Press, Albany

For information, address State University of New York Press
90 State Street, Suite 700, Albany, NY 12207

Production by Michael Haggett
Marketing by Anne M. Valentine

**Library of Congress Cataloging-in-Publication Data**

Swadener, Beth Blue.
    Does the village still raise the child? : a collaborative study of changing childrearing
and early education in Kenya / Beth Blue Swadener with Margaret Kabiru and Anne Njenga.
        p.    cm. — (SUNY series, early childhood education)
    Includes bibliographical references (p. ) and index.
    ISBN 0-7914-4757-X (alk. paper) — ISBN 0-7914-4758-8 (pbk. : alk. paper)
    1. Early childhood education—Kenya.    2. Child care—Kenya.    3. Education,
Rural—Kenya.    I. Kabiru.    II. Njenga.    III. Title.    IV. Series.

    LB1139.3.K4 S92 2000
    372.21'096762—dc21                                                        00-026955

10 9 8 7 6 5 4 3 2 1

# Contents

*Acknowledgments*                                                          ix

Introduction: Decolonizing Research, Deconstructing Change                  1

Part I   Multiple Contexts for the Study                                   13
  1  Child-rearing and Early Education in a Changing Kenya                 17
  2  A Collaborative Study                                                 35

Part II   Traditional Communities in Transition:
          Narok and Samburu                                               45
  3  Narok District: It Takes Grandmothers
     to Raise a Maasai Child                                              49
  4  Samburu District: It Takes a Clan to Raise a Child                   79

Part III   Tea and Coffee Plantations: Kericho and Kiambu                107
  5  Kericho Tea Estates: It Takes Child Care Centers
     and Older Siblings to Raise a Child                                 113
  6  Kiambu Coffee and Tea Estates: It Takes a
     Weighing Station and Supportive Manager to Raise a Child            141

Part IV   Rural/Agricultural Contexts: Embu and Machakos                 167
  7  Embu District: It Takes Tradition and Intergenerational
     Support to Raise a Child                                            171
  8  Machakos District: It Takes Preschool Teachers
     As Health Workers to Raise a Child                                  193
Part V   Urban/High Population Density: Nairobi and Kisumu               213
  9  Nairobi: It Takes Money and Partners to Raise a Child               219

10  Kisumu Municipality: It Takes *Ayahs* and Preschools
    to Raise a Child                                                    239

Part VI   Conclusions, Recommendations, and Reflections              263
11  Making Meaning: Does the Village Still Raise the Child?            265

*Epilogue: Methodological Reflections*                                287
*Appendix A: List of Local Collaborators*                             293
*Appendix B: Research Questions*                                      295
*Appendix C: Research Methodology and Description of Procedures*       297
*References*                                                          307
*Index*                                                               313

# List of Figures

Fig. 1     District Map of Kenya                                              xiii
Fig. 2     Research Collaborators                                              10
Fig. 1.1   Kenya Preschool Growth                                             28
Fig. 2.1   Maasai Local Collaborator with Children                           36
Fig. 3.1   Maasai Grandmothers Singing
           Traditional Lullabies to Under Threes                             50
Fig. 4.1   Samburu Parents with DICECE Trainer
           and NACECE Driver                                                 80
Fig. 5.1   Mothers Making Toys for Plantation Preschool                      114
Fig. 5.2   Kericho Mothers and Children in
           Tea Plantation Preschool                                         127
Fig. 6.1   Naptime at Child Care Center in
           Kiambu Coffee Plantation                                         142
Fig. 7.1   Embu Primary School Boys Dancing
           Curing Cooking Demonstration                                     172
Fig. 7.2   Cooking Demonstration of
           Traditional Weaning Foods                                        181
Fig. 8.1   Preschool Teacher in Machakos District
           Demonstrating Oral Rehydration Therapy to Parents                194
Fig. 8.2   Preschool Children Walking Home in Wamunyu                        202
Fig. 9.1   Preschool Teacher in Nairobi Slum                                 220
Fig. 10.1  Kisumu Parents During Interview                                   240
Fig. 11.1  Visiting Researcher with Members of
           Oloototo Women's Group, Narok District                           286

# Acknowledgments

The collaborative research upon which this book is based is the result of the contributions of many colleagues and supported financially by both the Fulbright African Regional Research Program and the World Bank through the Kenyan Ministry of Education ECD (Early Childhood Development) Initiative. The roots of the study were two collaborative seminars that brought together early childhood professionals from the United States and Kenya at the National Centre for Early Childhood Education (NACECE) in Nairobi in 1992 and 1994. These seminars were planned by Ms. Diane Adams (USA), Mrs. Margaret Kabiru (NACECE), and Mrs. Anne Njenga (NACECE). The original Fulbright proposal, to study ways in which rapid social and economic change are affecting child-rearing and community involvement in early childhood education and care in Kenya, was written in consultation with Mrs. Kabiru and Mrs. Njenga, who also helped refine it upon my arrival for the 10-month visiting researcher appointment at the NACECE. Both colleagues have provided various kinds of support, from logistical (e.g., arranging for transportation and recruitment of local collaborators) to conceptual (e.g., active involvement in refining the study and later in coding and analyzing the large data set). They also have been involved in disseminating the findings of our study in Kenya and in Africa.

Special appreciation must be expressed to the 21 local DICECE (District Centre for Early Childhood Education) collaborators, without whom the study would not have been possible. Their vital roles in the recruitment of local samples, their arranging for interview venues, their active participation in interviews (as translators and co-researchers), and their role in data analysis and interpretation were all critical to the authenticity of the findings and the relevance of our recommendations. These colleagues are listed by location and position in Appendix A and included the following people: Mrs. Gladys Mugo, Mr. S.A. Nyaga, and Mr. J.J. Karunyu (Embu DICECE); Mr. Philip Cheruiyot, Mr. Ezekiel Mutai (Kericho DICECE), Mr. Njuguna Wangunya, and Mr. Joseph Gitua (Kiambu DICECE); Mr. Hesbon Ogalo (Kisumu DICECE), the late Mrs. Susan Ouko (Kisumu MUCECE), and Mr. Eliud Onyango Owino (Kisumu Municipality); Mr. Nelson Mulinge and Mrs. Jane Mutingau (Machakos DICECE); Mrs. Mary Ngugi, Mrs. Lois Wanoike, and Mrs. Bernadette Nzoi (Nairobi CICECE); Mr. David ole Sadera, Mr. Paul Kishoyian, and Mr. Santau Kamwaro (Narok DICECE); and Mr. George Lenaseiyan, Mr. Peter ole Kashira, and Mrs. Beatrice Waraba (Samburu DICECE).

I also would like to thank the Kenya Institute of Education and the National Centre for Early Childhood Education in Nairobi for hosting me for the academic year 1994–95 and for making available to me many resources that enhanced my understanding of early childhood care and education in Kenya. My many dynamic colleagues and friends at NACECE, including Mrs. Margaret Kwame, Mrs. Mercy Berichi, and the late Mrs. Catherine Kamau, will continue to be professional colleagues in the coming years. The very capable and patient professional drivers for NACECE also must be acknowledged—as I became "Mama Safari" and made weekly trips to different districts, my journeys were safe and enjoyable, largely due to the drivers' skill and camaraderie. I would be remiss not to express my gratitude for the gracious hospitality of Mr. Francisco Villasenor, who provided for my housing during follow-up visits in 1996 and 1999, and who showed me that an agricultural estate can be a nurturing place for families. I also deeply appreciate the support and encouragement from my husband Daniel and daughter Rachel while we lived in Kenya and during my several years of work on this book.

For their thorough feedback and editorial assistance, we thank the anonymous reviewers of the manuscript and SUNY Press staff members Jennie Doling, Michael Haggett, and Michele Lansing.

Finally, particular thanks go to the many parents, preschool teachers, primary students, local leaders, and other participants in the study. It is *their voices* that must be heard, or the study will not have achieved a primary goal—to better understand the perspectives of those most affected by change in Kenya and to foreground their needs and suggestions in planning expanded services for children—especially children under age three in Kenya.

We dedicate this book to our friends and colleagues, Mrs. Catherine Kamau and Mrs. Leah Kipkorir, who are deeply missed and fondly remembered at the National Centre for Early Childhood Education and in many Kenyan communities.

Does the Village Still Raise the Child?

# Map of Kenya

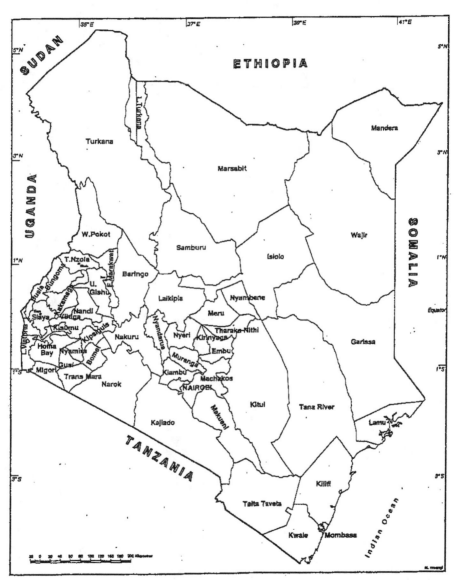

Fig. 1   District Map of Kenya

# Introduction:
# Decolonizing Research,
# Deconstructing Change

In many societies, experiences of childhood that have remained relatively stable for countless generations are now being transformed within a generation, and for many children, even within the span of their own childhoods

—Woodhead, *In Search of the Rainbow*

As the winds of rapid change have blown across much of the world in the latter part of the twentieth century, they have swept across the literal cradle of humanity—the Great Rift Valley—and have touched the many cultures of contemporary East Africa. Some of these changes have been largely the result of the unfolding of sociopolitical events, often with violent and unpredictable consequences; other changes reflect a legacy of colonization, neocolonialism, and a global recession and debt crisis, with associated rises in unemployment, overurbanization, and delocalization. Other changes are more subtle, happening within families, communities, and the changing cultural landscape of day-to-day experience and struggle. This book draws from the narratives of parents, children, grandparents, teachers, and community leaders, using child-rearing, early education practices, and community mobilization as lenses through which to deconstruct and, hopefully, to better understand the dynamics of social, cultural, and ideological change on indigenous and blended cultures in Kenya. It represents a sustained, six-year collaboration of the co-authors, and it draws largely from interviews collected in the year during which the first author lived in Kenya (1994–1995), with follow-up data for the book collected during the summers of 1996 and 1999.

1

The title of this book emerged at a time when the African proverb "It takes a village to raise a child" was in widespread use and gaining semiotic meaning on new levels in the United States. During the 1996 U.S. presidential election year, for example, Hillary Rodham Clinton's book, *It Takes a Village to Raise a Child*, was published. The metaphor of the village raising the child was called into question when Republican presidential candidate Bob Dole responded, "It doesn't take a village to raise a child—it takes a family!" During the same period of time, welfare reform was being signed into law by President Clinton, ending a national entitlement program for children and families and causing many child advocates to ponder why the village would further penalize the poor instead of doing more to empower parents to raise their children.

One pervasive assumption, implicit in the many uses—and misuses—of this proverb, is that the African "village," whether defined as extended family, larger community, or nation-state, continues to raise its children collectively and responsibly, as it traditionally has for generations. This book represents, in part, an interrogation of the widespread assumption that the contemporary African village (and nation-state) continues to share responsibility for raising its children in "traditional" ways. It raises several questions, including the following: What challenges does the village face in raising its children? Are there children the village no longer raises? How do stakeholders in contrasting settings and circumstances view the process of child-rearing and early education? This book also raises issues of relevance to the planning of services and support for Kenyan (and other East African) families with young children. We join Kilbride and Kilbride (1990), in addressing the increasing threat to East African children that "comes from the human social environment, primarily from their parents and other relatives who are reacting to threats to their own economic and social well-being" (p. 1), as well as more external threats to family well-being. This book also attempts to contextualize quality-of-life issues for children and families—particularly children under age three.

Much like the Kilbrides'work (Kilbride & Kilbride, 1990, 1997) and other ethnographic and cross-cultural studies (Tsing, 1993; Wallman, 1996; Weisner, Bradley, & Kilbride, 1997) that have sought to foreground the voices and life experiences of those who function at the margins while leading dynamic lives and engaging in creative forms of daily resistance and persistence, we have struggled to avoid essentializing or overgeneralizing the Kenyan child-rearing and early education experience. Recognizing the unlimited and divergent experiences echoed in the realities of families with young children, we have sought to capture the perspectives of a few of these and to interpret them in ways that can inform both "insider" and "outsider" audiences, recognizing that these are problematic terms and false dichotomies. The overarching research question, concerning ways in which rapid social and economic change have affected child-rearing, appeared to cut across age, gender, ethnicity, religion, and setting in its power to evoke stories and an array of concerns. In giving titles to the chapters that summarize the findings, we returned to these concerns—using a synthesis of participants' descriptions of what was needed for that community to successfully raise its children. For our purposes, this meant spending many hours with those most closely tied to child-rearing and early education in Kenya—parents, grandparents, siblings, elders, community leaders, and teachers of young children.

We grappled with issues common in cross-cultural, particularly anthropological, research, including the tendency to exoticize or romanticize the "Other." We are aware of the potential, as Michelle Fine (1994) has described it, for the ethnographer to play "ventriloquist" and to highlight those quotes or retell the stories of the Other that best reflect the particular biases and ideology of the researcher(s). One way in which we attempted to cross cultural borders with sensitivity and maximize insider interpretation was the active participation of local collaborators who shared cultural background and language with the participants in each district, discussed in greater depth in both chapter 2 and Appendix C. We have attempted to take advantage of the insider/outsider nature of the collaborative research team while moving beyond essentializing and simplistic dichotomies to better understand our divergent and convergent global imaginations (Tsing, 1993). We also have attempted to frame our findings in culturally relevant ways and disseminate them in East Africa. In other words, we sought to achieve a "bidirectional" collaboration, "in which Western researchers come to learn Kenyan research goals, questions, and methods, and Kenyans learn those of the West" (Whiting & Whiting, 1997, p. xiv).

Although we could never fully bridge the borders of the complex cultural differences inherent among our large and diverse research team and study participants, we attempted to engage with marginalized or "out-of-the-way" groups in relational and mutually meaningful ways. We contrast this to Tsing's (1993) observation that

> [I]n describing out-of-the-way places, the more common strategy has been to cordon off local perspectives from those of the writer and his or her readers, who are, thus, to represent a unified, cosmopolitan modern world. In this strategy, marginal groups speak to the modern imagination only from the outside—as the wise, innocent, savage, or exotic Other. As experts on the "Primitive," anthropologists have often deployed this strategy; but it extends far beyond the discipline in the international imagination. (p. 289)

We attempted, during field work and later in data analysis and various phases of our writing project, to describe the "everyday spaces" of these "out-of-the-way places." In fact, few acts embody as much "everyday-ness" as child-rearing and family life. Child-rearing reflects implicit as well as explicit social and cultural assumptions, and it is a significant barometer when measuring impacts of social and economic change. It also was critical to our study to capture intergenerational perspectives. In many communities we interviewed participants representing three to four generations, or age sets. We also sat with women's self-help groups, which included the perspectives of two to three generations of mothers discussing issues pertaining to changing child-rearing patterns and practices. Such conversations were particularly rich and informative.

This book represents, in part, the culmination of a collaboration between an early childhood researcher from the United States (Beth Blue Swadener) and two Kenyan early childhood leaders and researchers (Margaret Kabiru and Anne Njenga). This collaboration, like any complex research and writing process, has moved through many spaces—from our initial meeting at a Kenya–U.S. Early Childhood Collaborative Training Seminar in 1992, through conceptualization of the research reported in this volume, to the fine-tuning of the research design and interview protocols, and through data analysis and various dissemination activities in Kenya and the United States.

The study reflects a combination of existential and instrumental perspectives on child and family experiences (Polakow, 1993), early education and care trends, and implications for policy and practice. On the instrumental side, our data has been utilized in making recommendations to the Kenyan Ministry of Education and Human Resource Development (MOEHRD) and the World Bank, as well as informing the local technical assistance process through District Centers for Early Childhood Education and a number of nongovernmental organizations (NGOs). On the existential side, we have all learned from each other, and many local collaborators commented on the value of open-ended discussions, in which listening to parents, children, and teachers was at the forefront of our agenda. We also learned about ourselves and our visions for the future as we reflected on parents' and community leaders' visions for the future of their children and for the mobilization of their community to better meet children's needs.

## Decolonizing Cross-cultural Research: Ethical and Methodological Issues

Urban schools in the United States, where the majority of students are poor and often are children of color, have been referred to as "data plantations" in which researchers collect data without forming genuine relationships with teachers and students or contributing to the life of the school. Similarly, doing cross-cultural work in neocolonial settings presents many ethical and methodological dilemmas, particularly when there is a conscious attempt to decolonize the research (Gandhi, 1998; Harrison, 1991; Sibley, 1995; Smith, 1999; Willinsky, 1998). A number of such ethical, ideological, and methodological issues were—and continue to be—present in our work. This section highlights some of these concerns, several of which are revisited in greater depth in chapter 2 and the epilogue.

Among the dilemmas with which we have grappled were the different priorities each of us had for this project. In other words, while this study was at the foreground of the visiting researcher's professional priorities, it was one of many field-based initiatives and grant-funded projects involving the Kenyan collaborators or research "hosts." The sense of urgency that the first author often experienced did not, at times, appear to be shared by her Kenyan collaborators; yet, when we look back, it would have been premature to collect data before the visiting researcher gained more cultural familiarity and local credibility. (This sense of urgency also was observed by street children with whom the visiting researcher volunteered, who nicknamed her "Mama Harakisha," or "Mrs. In-a-Hurry.") The in-country collaborators were more cognizant of what was involved in data collection, including competing, time-consuming activities involving local collaborators. Kenyan collaborators also were in key leadership positions (i.e., coordinator and deputy coordinator of the NACECE) during a period of time in which the World Bank had "discovered" and prioritized early childhood development issues in Kenya, a process that involved the coordination of needs assessment and planning studies and countless hours of meetings. The demands on their time and emotional energy, particularly during 1995 and 1996, were phenomenal.

Another challenge faced in different ways by members of the national research team involved our attempts to "decolonize" the work and move beyond still-dominant paradigms in cross-cultural/cross-national research. For the cultural outsider/non-Kenyan, this meant interrogating the unearned power and privilege of being European American in a former British colony that still had persistent neocolonial patterns, influenced not only by colonization but by pervasive missionary-convert and donor-recipient dynamics. This observation was underscored by a visiting African-American friend and colleague, who was struck by the pervasiveness of missionary influence, or the Christianization of Kenya, as well as by many obvious manifestations of "internalized oppression" among Kenyan people. This refers to the internalization of myths regarding the "superiority" of the oppressor and contributes to a sense of powerlessness and dependency.

Other unequal power dynamics that needed decolonization included the power of the national collaborators over the local collaborators, in that they were national leaders to whom district leaders (i.e., local collaborators) reported. To their credit, the national collaborators (Margaret Kabiru and Anne Njenga) brought collegiality, humility, and an attitude of genuine caring and partnership to their fieldwork. This was particularly evident on the occasions when we were in rural areas together, including Baragoi in the Samburu District, Oloototo in Narok, and Runyenjes in Embu. Local collaborators, on rare occasions, expressed more privileged views than national collaborators (e.g., being charmed by the earnestness of the lives of the "simple peasant" parents we had interviewed in a rural area, or commenting on the lack of awareness of basic hygiene and the neglectful behavior of parents in both rural and urban contexts).

A third arena of challenge was related to decolonizing the study through striving for authentic collaboration in as many ways as possible, with the roles of local collaborators going beyond that of translators or research assistants to participating as co-constructors of the study and meaning makers with the data. Local DICECE colleagues recruited the interview participants, arranged for the observation sites and interview venues, and often conducted the interviews, adapting questions in culturally and locally appropriate ways. Making the interview questions culturally relevant was particularly challenging, since much of the project design was established before the visiting researcher's arrival in Kenya, as necessitated by the writing of funding proposals. The research questions and methodology were subsequently modified, both in collaboration with the two national collaborators and with 19 of the 21 local collaborators during an orientation session in Nairobi in October 1994.

Even with these collaborative efforts and collegial field interactions, power and privilege patterns needed to be constantly interrogated. One example of this was many participants' initial assumption that the visiting researcher worked for a nongovernmental organization (NGO) or other charity and was conducting a needs assessment for a future funded project in that location. So pervasive was this assumption that it became part of the introduction to the study for local collaborators to explain to participants that this was solely a research project and that the visiting researcher was "one of us!" The DICECE collaborators clarified the purpose of the project, edited the typed transcripts of all interviews for accuracy, and occasionally provided cultural interpretation of the emergent findings from our shared interviews.

Another dilemma involved the struggle to move the book beyond an earlier "final report," in format and intone, in which personal stories, contradictory findings, and discrepant evidence were not interrogated. During the visiting researcher's return visits to Kenya, the three co-authors and several local collaborators discussed this issue at some length. These discussions, along with follow-up interviews, also helped move this volume beyond a research report. Consistent with the emphasis on authentic collaboration, several of the local collaborators had an opportunity to edit the final draft of the chapter representing their district.

As discussed earlier, there are a number of ways in which the notion of insider/outsider can be constructed as it applies to this research endeavor. Although the visiting U.S. researcher was a cultural and linguistic outsider, so too were the national collaborators, in that, while they were clearly insiders to Kikuyu culture (and to their ageset, class, and gender identities and their experiences as Kenyan professionals), they were virtual "outsiders" to several of the cultures that were represented in the study. The ethnicity, cultural identity, and languages of the local collaborators, however, reflected the local cultures and thus facilitated not only the mother tongue/local language interviews but also the cultural interpretations available to the team. It was particularly interesting to be in the field with ethnically diverse Kenyan colleagues who openly shared cultural insights from their different experiences, customs, and vernacular. At such times, the study became a catalyst for cross-cultural dialogue, including the naming of myths and stereotypes as well as the cultural clarification of child-rearing customs and sharing of amusing anecdotes of cross-cultural misunderstandings observed or experienced by colleagues. Some of the most humorous stories had to do with linguistic and cultural conversations in which key information became "lost in translation," particularly between indigenous Kenyans and Europeans. These conversations were not limited to this project, however, but were reflected in the proceedings of several NACECE-sponsored conferences that included information on different Kenyan ethnic groups' customs pertaining to pregnancy, pre- and post-natal care of mother and child, and child-rearing and cultural socialization. Projects such as the Mother Tongue Storybook series (researched and published by the NACECE) and the Islamic Integrated Early Education project also represented attempts to support culture maintenance during this time of rapid change, movement, and Westernization.

One of the most unique cross-cultural opportunities presented itself during one of the visiting researcher's follow-up visits to Kenya (in July 1996), when Margaret Kabiru joined her in a return to Oloototo in the Narok District. We were excited upon our return to see a completed preschool where we had earlier viewed young children cared for in an open-air setting ("under threes under trees"), but we noticed that the older mothers were not present. When we inquired, our Maasai collaborators learned that most of the women had gone a few kilometers away to an annual fertility ceremony and invited us to join it as observers.

Our different positions as research collaborators, as well as our multiple identities, were particularly vivid that day—Maasai women who had participated in all stages of the earlier research were now fully immersed in the intensive three-day ceremony; Maasai (DICECE) collaborators were performing an informant or a bicultural role, interpreting for the true "outsiders." Margaret Kabiru and the driver of our vehicle, who were Kikuyu and not Maa speakers, watched as wide-eyed and with arguably as much intrigue as the U.S. researcher. A further observation that week was that the U.S. researcher was familiar with small local hotels, places to take tea, and other aspects of the Narok community, having stayed there several times during fieldwork in previous years, and acted in some ways as an informant to the Kenyan national collaborator. Examples such as these highlight the complexities of multiethnic collaborative research teams and their potential to provide multiple perspectives on phenomena of shared interest. They also help illuminate the different affinity groups to which research team members belonged.

Another opportunity to better understand the cultural backgrounds of collaborators and to further contextualize the data being collected came during visits to the rural homes, or shambas, of several NACECE and DICECE collaborators. Such visits provided opportunities for the visiting researcher to be with colleagues in their homes and meet extended family members, some of whom were informally interviewed for the study. These visits also led, in some cases, to unique interview opportunities, such as a women's self-help group near Mrs. Gladys Mugo's shamba (in the Embu District), in which three generations of mothers were interviewed following their meeting in a member's home. Other opportunities included participation in two weddings (one traditional Samburu and one in a Nairobi church), a visit to a traditional Maasai *manyatta*, where over 1,000 *morans* (warriors) would be making their rite of passage to the first level of elderhood in a matter of weeks, and attendance of a regional dance and drama competition in Kisumu, where a number of traditional Dholuo songs and dramas were presented. Other, more frequent opportunities for the visiting researcher to experience local culture included trips to markets, staying in local hotels and homes, and frequent visits to preschools and primary schools.

## MULTIPLE READINGS/FRAMINGS OF THE STUDY

The data collected, as well as the research process described in this volume, can be framed and analyzed from a number of different theoretical, as well as applied, perspectives. One of the possible readings of the texts of this project is a study in marginality, reflecting intersections of class, neocolonialism, and gender, within nested contexts of marginality. This analysis is especially relevant, given the sample (e.g., plantation and rural laborers, urban slum dwellers, and pastoralists, with fewer urban or rural middle-class persons interviewed).

The data also can be read as comprising a qualitative study of the impacts of "children in debt" (UNICEF), given the documented impacts of structural adjustment programs (SAPS) and related austerity measures on families raising children in Kenya in a time of rapid change and globalization. This relates directly to a third reading—a "ground-up" contextualized examination of changes in land tenure and similar family structure patterns—particularly in the two pastoralist/traditional districts and in the tea and coffee plantations. In many Samburu and Maasai settings, for example, families were being forced (or, in some cases, were choosing) to move away from communally held land and extended family child-rearing to private ownership and subdivision of land. This, combined with limited grazing corridors and an increase in the number of nuclear families, no longer benefiting from child care provided by the grandmother, contributed to gradual changes in childrearing patterns. In plantation settings, laborers lacked the land to grow even a kitchen garden, and they often lived far from any extended family support for child care and rearing.

Still another reading of this study, and one through which both the World Bank and a number of local participants viewed it, was a needs assessment of "clients" or stakeholders in early care and education, including families with young children, early childhood educators, technical assistance personnel, and local leaders across contrasting settings. Another related reading of the study was in the sociology of early education as it interfaces with child-rearing, continuing in the tradition of O. N. Gakuru, Barbara Koech, and other Kenyan researchers who have examined issues of stratification, access, and quality of early childhood services and have recently worked on contextualized case studies of children's lives.

This study and book also can be cast as a series of conversations across different languages, cultures, life experiences, agendas, and assumptions that served very different purposes for those involved. Indeed, the research that forms the foundation for this book reflects multiple agendas and goals for disseminating and using our findings. It was viewed by some as one of a series of data collection exercises and likely an imposition for many. The study provided an opportunity to collaborate across literally worlds of difference, yet with a shared vision for the possibilities of children and early care and education, and it became a personally and professionally consuming project for the first author. Perhaps this can be said for virtually all collaborative, cross-national studies. It is our intention, however, that through this interrogration of our methodology and the dynamics of our collaboration, new spaces and possibilities can be opened for longer-term collaborative inquiry that will foreground the genuine interests and perspectives of children and families.

We join Tsing (1993) in pursuing the promise of a postcolonial anthropology "that goes beyond the re-analysis of its own problematic past" to engage with "the questions and challenges raised by those concerned with cultural heterogeneity, power, and marginality" (p. 14). From a practical perspective, we wanted this study to make a small difference in the lives of children and families in Kenya, and not merely contribute to another document on Ministry of Education or library shelves. We wanted the hours of time that DICECE collaborators committed to this project to contribute to their ability to understand and act upon grassroots needs and opinions in some way, and not be merely another data collection "exercise," with local collaborators having little stake or agency in the process. Cultural relevance, integrity, and authentic collaboration were all shared values that, we hope, will also form a foundation for this volume. It is our strong desire that this book be used in East Africa to inform policy, practice, and the urgently needed support of families.

Finally, a word about ethnographies and interpretive case studies. Although our study was not a true ethnography, it did employ many ethnographic methods, and we faced similar issues to those described in the anthropological literature. To again quote Tsing (1993):

> Ethnographies are messy; like novels, they tend to include an over-abundance of detail, much of it extraneous to the main argument. Rather than condemn this messiness as boring (Pratt, 1986, p. 33) or outdated (Fox, 1991), I prefer to build from it as a source of analytic heterogeneity and promise. In this messiness, for example, there is room for elements that simultaneously draw readers into projects of cultural comparison, regional cultural history, and local/global positionings. (p. 290)

We too have attempted to build upon the details embodied in discussions with the participants in the study and visits to many communities, schools, and homes in ways that promote both analytic and perspectival heterogeneity and reflect the promise of Kenyan children and families.

## Organization of The Book

This book is organized into six sections. Part I is comprised of chapters 1 and 2, which are intended to provide multiple contexts for the reader and to clarify the nature of early education and care in Kenya, as well as the study upon which the book is based. Parts II through V summarize the data from the contrasting settings (e.g., traditional/pastoralist, plantation, rural, and urban contexts) and present the overall findings. Each of these sections begins with a background description of the demographics, environmental characteristics, and health and nutrition factors affecting families and young children in the two districts intended to represent that type of setting. The findings chapters are organized around the major research questions guiding the study and include portraits of family members and other stakeholders in early education and care from each district. They also include both a summary of responses by issue or category as well as narrative, interpretive sections intended to provide a more dynamic or multidimensional constructed portrait of critical issues in raising children in the various contexts and settings.

Part II, comprised of chapters 3 and 4, discusses the findings from "Traditional and Pastoralist" settings, specifically the Narok (Maasai) and Samburu districts, respectively. Part III, comprised of chapters 5 and 6, describes rural settings of varying agricultural productivity, representing primarily Kiembu and Kikamba (and some Kikuyu) families. Chapter 5 focuses on the findings in the Embu District, and chapter 6 focuses on the Machakos District. Part IV, which includes chapters 7 and

Fig. 2    Research Collaborators

8, concentrates on more densely populated urban contexts, including Nairobi and Kisumu, respectively. Both urban samples included ethnic, religious, and linguistic diversity, with the Nairobi sample comprised primarily of Kikuyu and Luhya families and the Kisumu sample comprised primarily of Dholuo families. The Kisumu sample varied most by class and income background, and it also included both Asian and European (ex-patriot) families. Part V is comprised of chapters 9 and 10, which focus on families living and working on tea and coffee plantations in the Kericho and Kiambu districts. Given the nature of migratory labor patterns in the plantations, a number of ethnic groups were represented in these samples, including Kisii, Luo, Luhya, and Kipsegis in Kericho and Kikuyu, Kiembu, and Kimeru in the Kiambu District (which is considered a peri-urban setting and is located adjacent to Nairobi).

The final section of this book, Part VI, including chapter 11 and the epilogue, offers a discussion of the findings and frames some of the potential meanings of the study in terms of implications for policy, practice, and collaborative research. We draw from postcolonial theory and cultural geography, particularly Soja's (1996) notion of "thirdspace," in imagining spaces of possibility for Kenya's families, and we advocate listening carefully to the parents and community leaders so that the contemporary "village" can be supported in continuing to raise its children.

# Part I

Multiple Contexts for the Study

# Multiple Contexts for the Study

Part I provides background information regarding early childhood issues in Kenya and a brief description of the collaborative study upon which this book is based. Chapter 1 includes background and contextual information for an initial viewing of the Kenyan early childhood care and education (ECCE) landscape through the lenses of history, policy, cultural practices, and highlights from relevant studies. Beginning with the global backdrop of societal and economic change, the first chapter focuses primarily on the history of ECCE in Kenya and discusses the types of changes experienced by families across different social strata and regions of Kenya, particularly the eight districts included in our study. Chapter 2 provides an overview of the research design and raises concerns related to authentic cross-national collaborative research. (A more detailed description of the research methodology, procedures, and sample is found in Appendix C.)

# Chapter 1

# Child-rearing and Early Education in a Changing Kenya

The day will come when nations will be judged not by their military or economic strength, nor by the splendor of their capital cities and public buildings, but by the well-being of their people: by their levels of health, nutrition and education; by their opportunities to earn a fair reward for their labors; by their ability to participate in the decisions that affect their lives; by the respect that is shown for their civil and political liberties; by the provision that is made for those who are vulnerable and disadvantaged; and by the protection that is afforded to the growing minds and bodies of children.

—UNICEF, *The Progress of Nations*

Kenya is, in many ways, a model for early childhood care and education for other African nations. Yet like many countries that have complied with structural, adjustment-related austerity requirements, Kenya has passed the debt burden along to its families—and its children. As we listened to the many stories of parents, grandparents, and teachers about how child-rearing had changed in less than one generation, we were reminded of James Grant's admonition that "debt restructuring has a human face" (Grant, 1993). The globalization of economics, the AIDS crisis, political instability and corruption, and other macro-level problems directly impact the micro level or everyday lives of families. This chapter provides macro-level contexts for the later examination, in far greater detail, of those everyday lives of

17

families with children under age three. It also offers a brief overview of the collaborative research design and methodology employed in the study, which is supplemented with a detailed methodological appendix.

## Global Context: Rapid Social and Economic Change

In the slums there are mothers with no economic means. Homelessness is caused largely by urban migration, and the children have no resources . . . we urbanize, but with no direction.

—Embu, parent and community leader

Though the current public culture and the world economy seem to conspire against its practice, shared family support for children remains a deep influence in Kenyan society.

—Thomas S. Weisner,
*African Families and the Crisis of Social Change*

Parents and other family members in Kenya, as elsewhere in the world, have traditionally been the primary caregivers and educators of their children—particularly children from birth through ages three to four. Parents and other primary caregivers, therefore, have the greatest potential for influencing the future of their children and are critical stakeholders in both local services and larger policies and initiatives designed to benefit young children and their families. Bledsoe (1980) and Weisner, Bradley, and Kilbride (1997) have described features of "socially distributed support" of children and families in Kenya. As Weisner et al. (1997) observe, "Any support system for children, whether based on shared caretaking or not, has certain features recognizable around the world. . . . The African cultural complex of socially distributed social support attempts to meet these needs for children and families while responding to other, cultural, economic, and institutional constraints and opportunities in the region" (p. 23). Child-rearing in Kenya, as in other African contexts, remains a complex, collective activity, traditionally involving siblings, grandparents, and extended family in shared management, caretaking, and support. Our study sought to explore the ways in which such traditional, socially distributed support for child-rearing, particularly for children under age three, has been affected by rapid social and economic change.

In Kenya, early childhood care and education services, including feeding or nutrition programs (where they exist) and the majority of nursery schools, are funded primarily by parents and the local community. Thus, households are the largest investors in ECCE services. Therefore, it is important to understand the dynamic and changing child-rearing issues facing contemporary Kenyan families, particularly the ways in which parents and grandparents frame the needs of their family and community, the aspirations for their children, and the nature of services they desire. The lived experiences of families and communities can serve as a valuable mirror for the health of any nation, and the care of the youngest children can serve as a barometer for the future.

Few would dispute that the past two decades have been a period of rapid social, economic, ideological, and political change in much of the world, including the shift from centrally planned to market economies in Eastern Europe and the former Soviet Union, the official ending of apartheid in South Africa, and widespread austerity measures and other structural adjustment policies associated with Third World debt and global recession (Swadener & Bloch, 1997). There also have been significant population shifts across borders and increased "Balkanization," as well as increasing ethnic and religious violence, including civil war and resulting refugee crises—particularly in Africa and Eastern and Central Europe. The World Summit for Children in 1990, sponsored by the United Nations and attended by over 70 heads of state, brought attention to the impact of many of these changes on children and the need to ensure the basic rights of children worldwide. This summit built upon the United Nations (UN) Convention on the Rights of the Child, a document that was ratified by Kenya but had still not been ratified by the United States at the time of this book's publication.

On the positive side, increased childhood immunization rates and better use of primary health measures have led in many nations to substantial decreases in infant and child mortality rates, and more attention is being paid to the critical nature of the first years of life. UNICEF estimates that since 1985, 2.5 million young lives have been saved each year through low-cost health programs (UNICEF, 1997). Since 1985, Kenya's under-five mortality rate has decreased by 20% and its birthrate, among the highest in the world, began to level off. These trends, unfortunately, have reversed in recent years.

Although increased attention has been paid to the importance of early childhood care and education worldwide, the past decade has been worse rather than better for many of the world's children. More children and families are living in poverty or homeless (UNICEF, 1997) than 10 years ago. The number of children engaged in labor has increased worldwide, with the UN Labor Organization estimating that 250 million 5- to 14-year-olds are employed, half of them full time, and increasing numbers of children are living and working on the street (Aptekar, 1994; Kilbride & Kilbride, 1990; Kilbride & Njeru, 1995; Kilbride, Suda, Njeru, and Kariuki, 2000). Similarly, the number of children and families hurt by warfare, chronic undernutrition, or famine has continued to be high, particularly in Africa and Eastern Europe, and worldwide, 35,000 children die every day of largely preventable causes related to chronic undernutrition, infection, and diarrheal disease, all of which are associated with poverty (UNICEF, 1995).

## "Children in Debt"

The relationship between structural adjustment programs and a rise in child mortality and malnutrition rates in some parts of Kenya is noted by long-time early childhood sociologist Octavian N. Gakuru, who states that, "The child mortality rate is reported to be on the increase since implementation of the structural adjustment programmes. Furthermore, malnutrition is prevalent in many communities" (1995, p. 8). Gakuru and his colleagues further report that in a rural community in the Machakos District, they "found that the population of children in especially difficult situations is increasing," including "orphans, street children, and over-exposed children" (Gakuru & Koech, 1995). Similar to the United States and many other African nations, Kenya has also experienced an increase in the number of female-headed households. Over one-third of households in Kenya are headed by women (Central Bureau of Statistics), which has adversely affected the care of young children, as these women are often quite poor (Government of Kenya and UNICEF 1998). As documented by Kilbride and Kilbride (1990), the majority live in urban slum areas. This means that single mothers typically cannot benefit from the little available family child care support, as their extended families remain in the rural areas.

Most nations have experienced rapid change in the past decade, and Kenya is no exception (cf. Kilbride & Kilbride, 1990, 1997; Gakuru, Koech, & Nduati, 1995; Swadener, Kabiru, & Njenga, 1997). The impact, at the level of family existence and economics, of global recession and the related debt crisis is unevenly documented (Bradshaw, Noonan, Gash, & Sershen, 1993). Associated policies such as structural adjustment and debt restructuring schemes have led to the introduction of greater community cost sharing, higher prices to consumers, and often increased unemployment (Hancock, 1989) and dislocation (Kilbride, 1996; Kilbride & Kilbride, 1997). As previously discussed, these macroeconomic policies and related local dynamics have a "human face" (Grant, 1993) and are directly linked to the quality of life experienced by families and the opportunities afforded their children. In fact, UNICEF has for several years used the phrase "children in debt" to convey the strong correlation between Third World debt, structural adjustment policies, and children's increased risk. Thus one goal of our year-long study was to systematically document the nature and impact of different types of change experienced by families raising young children in Kenya.

## The State of Kenya's Children

The under-five mortality rate, or proportion of children who do not reach their fifth birthday, is "one of the most fundamental indicators of a country's concern for its people" (UNICEF, 1997, p. 28). Kenya's under-five mortality rate at the time of this study (1994–1995) was 90 (per 1,000 live births), comparable to the world average of 89. The under-five mortality rate in Kenya decreased by 20% in one decade (from 1985 to 1995). Such progress is typically associated with a number of factors, including more adequate nutrition, availability of primary health care, access to safe water and improved sanitation, families' economic conditions, and the health and status of women in the community. Yet a demographic and health survey conducted in 1999 found that, in terms of health issues, "The country is performing much worse as we enter the new millennium than we did in the 1970s and 1980s" (Daily Nation, 1999). This recent survey found that infant deaths increased by 24% in the 1990s, compared to the previous two decades. Although statistics vary, this survey reported an under-fiive mortality rate of 103, compared to 90 in the late 1980s and early 1990s. The rate of immunization also is down from 80% in the 1980s to only 65%, although settings in which we collected data had achieved nearly universal immunization by the mid-1990s.

These statistics, however, often mask the actual experience of families and children who can get lost in national statistics that take an instrumental rather than an existential view (Polakow, 1993) of child-rearing and early education. In other words, macro-economic analyses and even national child health statistics may miss critical information regarding the lived experiences of parents and young children. It is these experiences and narratives that this book seeks to capture and share.

The AIDS/HIV crisis and persistent warfare and refugee situations on the African continent have taken a toll on young lives and have left many children orphaned, disabled, and malnourished, with burdens placed on grandparents and struggling mothers (cf. Wallman, 1996). AIDS has afflicted an estimated 2 million patients, leaving many children orphaned and/or HIV-positive. Diseases such as typhus, malaria, and hepatitis B increased in the late 1990s. The bombing of the U.S. Embassy in Nairobi in August 1998 affected thousands of families who lost providers, children, or who have family members who became disabled as a result. Diarrhea and acute respiratory infections continue to take many children's lives, and it is predicted that by 2010, up to 41% of infant mortality in Kenya will be due to AIDS (U.S. Bureau of the Census, World Population Profile, 1996). Other estimates are lower (e.g., 12% estimate from the U.N. Population Division, 1997, cited in GOK/UNICEF, 1998). Yet whether 12% or 40%, the AIDS crisis continues to affect children under age three in Kenya and elsewhere in East Africa. Of the 9 million children worldwide who have lost their mothers to AIDS, 90% live in sub-Saharan Africa, and many have lost both parents. In the most affected countries, it is thought that up to one-third of children will become orphans in the next 10 years (The Guardian, 1997). Thus AIDS continues to be a major threat to children in Kenya, as it is elsewhere on the continent.

## FURTHER CONTEXTS OF THE STUDY

This book builds on the work of Myers (1992), Gakuru and Koech (1995), Weisner, Bradley, and Kilbride (1997), and Woodhead (1996), in its focus on strengthening existing community programs and contextualizing child care and early education in

Kenya. As described in Woodhead's (1996) monograph *In Search of the Rainbow*, "Vast numbers of children, families and communities are caught between the relative stability of tradition and the promise of modernity. Intergenerational continuities are breaking down in the face of rapid social change" (p. 13). In predominantly rural, agrarian societies such as Kenya, children are being raised and are coming of age within a "culture of sponsored development" (Gakuru, 1995), which has promoted patterns of dependence on various external donors (e.g., churches or NGOs) and the government. In Kenya's postcolonial history, however, there is an interesting tension between this cycle of embedded (or entrenched) dependence and the spirit of *Harambee*, or "pulling together," in locally determined self-help initiatives. We would certainly join with Woodhead (1996), Gakuru and Koech (1995), and others in calling for a "negotiated" and more democratic process of community mobilization for children, resulting in the planning and implementation of locally relevant programs and initiatives.

It also is important to understand the reasons that some parents or households are *not* participating in various ECCE programs and services. The most recent statistics, for example, indicate that fewer than 30% of Kenyan children ages three to six attend preschool. Current research, including recent surveys undertaken by the National Centre for Early Childhood Education (NACECE), also show that very few children under age three are cared for in child care centers or preschools. When "under threes" are "served" in preschools, it often is from the backs of their older preschool-attending siblings in programs that are not prepared to meet their unique developmental needs. Preschool teachers often express frustration about this issue and affirm the need for further training in the area of serving under threes, as they wish to provide more than minimal custodial supervision for these younger children. As Gakuru (1995) puts it, "The available evidence indicates that only a minority of children benefit from the formal care and educational programmes, while the informal system is proving severely inadequate for increasing numbers of children" (p. 8).

## National and Historical Contexts: Early Care and Education in Kenya

> We invented the family.
>
> —Ali Mazrui

Kenya remains a predominantly rural, agrarian society, comprised of various ethnic and racial groups, with over 30 distinctive language groups and diverse religious communities, including Christian (with Catholic and assorted Protestant religions, including Anglican, comprising the largest percentage), Islamic, Hindu, and traditional indigenous religions. Until recently, child care and early socialization of preschool-age children have been governed by "powerful family/community structures and traditions, a phenomenon well documented by anthropologists and cross-cultural psychologists" (Woodhead, 1996), including Kilbride and Kilbride (1990, 1997), LeVine and Levine (1974, 1988), Super and Harkness (1997), and Whiting and Edwards (1988), with Kenyan researchers (e.g., Kipkorir, 1994; Bali & Kabiru, 1992; Gakuru & Koech, 1995; Wandibba, 1997). Although these traditions remain deeply entrenched in the values of Kenyan families, few communities have been unaffected by the types of rapid social and economic change previously discussed. Eighty-eight percent of women live in rural areas (Woodhead, 1996). In their traditional roles, they take the major responsibility for cultivating subsistence and cash crops, and patterns of shared child care among relatives, particularly among female siblings, have been the norm (Kipkorir, 1993; Weisner, 1997).

As discussed throughout this book, however, family lifestyles are changing, with the loss of many informal child care support systems. Many traditional approaches to child-rearing are being challenged by recent trends in employment/ unemployment in a cash economy associated with urbanization, dislocalization (see Kilbride & Kilbride, 1990; Kilbride, 1986), and other pervasive patterns in Kenya and rapidly changing political economies and nations. The traditional caregivers of young children—extended family members, particularly grandmothers, older siblings, and certainly mothers—are simply not available in many cases. More mothers are in paid employment and various informal market activities that take them away from their families for long hours each day. Others are laborers on tea, coffee, sisal, and other plantations and leave home before dawn, usually returning late, with few breaks to nurse babies or see to the needs of their other children. Similar to many countries in the latter twentieth century, the growth of early childhood care and education programs has simply not kept pace with the need for expanded child care and early education—a theme that was reinforced virtually by every parent and preschool teacher interviewed in this study.

## Demographic and Economic Change

One of the most striking aspects of change in Kenya is demographic—with the population growing from 16 million to 24 million between 1980 and 1992 (UNICEF, 1992). Until recently, Kenya has had one of the fastest-growing populations in the world. This rapid population growth rate has had some of its most negative effects in urban areas and in some rural and peri-urban locations, with expanded pressures on the already stretched, underfunded infrastructure of services and limited land and housing. Another manifestation of the pressure of rapid population growth, coupled with a greater emphasis on privatization (including individual versus collective ownership and increased subdivision of land), is found in rural areas. This has led to the creation of a growing, rural, landless class, due to the subdivision of family plots to the point of nonviability, even for subsistence—affecting some 20% of rural households (Woodhead, 1996, p. 26). The effects of the increase in rural, landless families were frequently the subject of discussion in interviews with parents, and many drew direct correlations between this pattern and the breakdown in a number of traditional child-rearing practices (ranging from extended breast-feeding and healthier weaning practices to the availability of traditional child care providers, particularly grandmothers).

Other frequently documented changes include the shift to a wage and cash economy, the migration of parents, particularly fathers, and increasingly mothers (as previously discussed), away from their families in search of work, and the rapid urbanization/overurbanization at the end of the twentieth century. Again, all of these trends take place against a backdrop of structural adjustment programs (SAPS), including austerity measures intended to address the economic crisis (Woodhead, 1996). In the short term, such SAPS have placed additional pressures on the unskilled urban and rural poor, through a sort of "trickle down" of cost sharing, cutbacks in services provided by the government in the past (e.g., health care, home visitors, and medications). Forty-seven percent of the rural population lives in poverty, and 29% of Kenyans in urban areas are described as "absolutely poor," (Government of Kenya and UNICEF, 1998). Thirty percent of children are described by UNICEF as "economically active" or involved in child labor (GOK/UNICEF, 1998).

One of the things that distinguishes Kenya from other sub-Saharan African countries is its well-established system of early education and care, which continues to grow and provide leadership on the continent. Preschools were introduced in Kenya as early as the 1940s, mainly in the large plantations and in several larger towns. During colonial rule, and persisting into present-day Kenya, the educationally segregated nation also was reflected in the different types of preschools—for children of British and Asian families, mission programs which often included feeding programs for children in some rural areas, and the early custodial day care centers of the plantations. A larger number of day care centers opened during the Mau Mau wars of independence (1953–1960), with activities for children such as singing and dancing (Kabiru, 1993). In the 1950s, during the Mau Mau struggle for independence, the preschool education program greatly expanded nationwide. These centers provided custodial care to children while their mothers were involved in forced labor.

## Independence and the *Harambee* Movement

The greatest expansion in early childhood programs came shortly after Kenyan independence in 1963, in response to the late President Jomo Kenyatta's call for *Harambee*, or community participation for accelerated education development (Kabiru, 1993). This large increase was in response to the intensification of socioeconomic changes and other forces of development. The motto of *Harambee*, or "pulling together" for a common goal, has been visible ever since the development of many self-help projects, including community-funded, community-built preschools and other services. Such community-supported preschools still far outnumber those built by the government or donors. A remarkable feature of preschools in Kenya is that they serve virtually the entire spectrum of social, economic, cultural, and geographic background of the society, with rapidly growing enrollment over the past 30 years. Whether held in open-air settings in isolated rural areas or in well-equipped, staffed urban settings, preschool education is obviously an "idea whose time has come" in Kenya.

The spirit of *Harambee*, however, is not without grounds for critique, nor is it a panacea for the lack of greater government and other support of ECCE programs. The growing uses—and abuses—of the *Harambee* movement can be critically analyzed from several perspectives. One critique relevant to families with young children is the pressure on parents and other consumers to provide their own services and for parents to donate, sometimes beyond their financial means, to their children's schools and other local services. Indeed, children are routinely sent home and cannot reenter their school or preschool until fees and "mandatory" contributions are paid. The disruption in learning and continuity of care and education is apparent, not to mention the stigma and emotional stress of being sent home for lack of payment of fees, proper uniform, or textbooks and other supplies. Some children, for example, complete primary school through Standard 8, for example, and they do not have funds to pay for their examination fees and, thus, they do not earn their Kenya Primary School Certificate.

There also have been growing calls for the government, through the Ministry of Education and Human Resource Development, to provide salaried preschool teachers to communities, just as it pays the salaries of primary school teachers. Although the idea of greater government support for preschool—particularly in the form of paying teacher salaries, as it does for primary school teachers—has enjoyed growing support, it has been resisted by the national government (Ministry of Education and Resource Development) on the grounds that there are insufficient funds to provide preschool teachers to all communities requesting them and that preschool education is the responsibility of the community (Swadener, Kabiru, & Njenga, 1997, p. 289). This latter argument is a familiar one in the United States and in other Western countries, where the "public versus private" responsibility for preschool and other early childhood services is still being debated. By 1999, county councils were funding fewer preschool teachers, the early childhood education section of the budget had been cut further, and there was little hope for putting preschool teachers on the national teacher service payroll.

Initially, the preschools for African children were intended to be nonacademic, nonteaching, child care settings. This view persisted until the early 1970s. Many parents, however, favored academic instruction and school preparation in the nursery school (Herzog, 1969), and a rapid expansion of preschool education was brought about by the joint efforts of communities, the government, welfare organizations, and private enterprise. The first survey to document the number of children enrolled in preschool was carried out in 1969 through the University of Nairobi, showing that 200,000 children were enrolled in 4,800 centers nationally. Most of the 5,000 teachers were untrained. By 1973, preschool enrollment had risen to nearly 300,000, with 6,326 teachers.

The services provided for young children prior to 1970 in Kenya have been described in Kenyan publications as "very poor" (see, e.g., Kabiru, 1993). This was mainly attributed to a lack of adequate government intervention and coordination. As a result, the curriculum content and methodology used in preschools differed greatly and often was unsuitable or inappropriate for young children (NACECE News, 1995). There also were no properly organized training programs for the teachers, hence the majority of preschool teachers were untrained. A survey done by the Ministry of Cooperatives and Social Services in 1971 revealed that out of 5,000 teachers, only 400 had received basic training in aspects of preschool education. The untrained teachers lacked adequate knowledge and skills for providing stimulating learning experiences for the children. The classrooms typically had no learning and play materials and, hence, used rote and "chalk and talk" teaching methods.

## The Preschool Education Project and Founding of NACECE/DICECE

Faced with this reality, in 1971 the Kenya government, through the Ministry of Education and Human Resource Development and with the assistance of the Bernard van Leer Foundation, initiated the Preschool Education Project, based at the Kenya Institute of Education (KIE). The main objective of the project was to improve the quality of preschool education through the development of viable training models for early childhood care and education (ECCE) personnel and curriculum and other support materials for use by the children, teachers, and trainers. As a result of increased awareness of preschool education, the Ministry of Education (MOE) established a preschool section at KIE. This section assumed all responsibilities of the project, although, up to 1979, the Ministry of Culture and Social Services was responsible for preschool education in Kenya. In 1980, this responsibility was transferred to the Ministry of Education and Human Resource Development, and a preschool section was created at MOE headquarters and the Inspectorate.

In 1982, a national preschool seminar was held to discuss the experiences and outcomes of the Preschool Education Project. One of the recommendations made during this seminar was the establishment of a national center for early childhood education and a network of subcenters at the district level. These were expected to facilitate the dissemination of the project's experiences and outcomes. The MOE responded to this recommendation by establishing the National Centre for Early Childhood Education (NACECE) in 1984 and the District Centres for Early Childhood Education (DICECE) in 1985.

At the time of its founding through the time this book was completed, NACECE's responsibilities have included: (1) training of ECCE personnel; (2) development and dissemination of the curriculum for ECCE programs; (3) identifying, designing, undertaking, and coordinating research in ECCE; (4) offering services and facilitating interaction between agencies and sponsors; and (5) coordinating and liaising with external partners and informing the public on the needs and developments of the ECCE program. The establishment of the DICECE facilitated the decentralization of the ECCE program to the district level. The functions of the DICECE are: (1) training of preschool teachers and other personnel at the district level; (2) supervision and inspection of district preschool programs; (3) mobilization of communities, through the preschool, to improve the care, health, nutrition, and education of young children; (4) development of preschool curriculum; and (5) participation in the evaluation of preschool programs and carrying out of basic research on the status of preschool-age children in and out of school.

## Community Mobilization and Collaboration in ECCE

One of the strengths of the ECCE program in Kenya is its partnership policy, which encourages the participation of various partners, including parents and local communities, local authorities, voluntary organizations, religious bodies, employers, the Ministry of Education, and other ministries and NGOs, several of which have sponsored a number of early childhood initiatives (e.g., the Bernard van Leer Foundation, UNICEF, and the Aga Khan Foundation). Parents and local communities are the most important partners in the ECCE program in Kenya. They have started— literally from the ground up—and manage over 75% of the preschools in the country. As discussed earlier, these schools are typically started on a *Harambee* basis. Through *Harambees*, the parents and local communities provide land and funds for the construction and maintenance of physical facilities. They also provide furniture, materials, and labor and pay teachers' salaries. In addition, they furnish food and labor toward a morning snack, if provided, and they may even donate a *"Harambee* cow," which provides milk for the program.

It is important, however, to point out that the preschools managed by parents experience more financial and organizational problems than those funded either by local authorities or private agencies or entrepreneurs. This is due to several factors, some rather obvious, including the competing economic needs of families and the lack of awareness of the importance of early childhood care and education, as well as a lack of management skills among the parents forming the school committee. Consequently, the facilities in these preschools often are poor, and the teachers are paid low and irregular salaries. Once trained, the majority of the teachers paid by the parents attempt to leave the community-based or *Harambee* preschools or employment with either the local authority or private sector, as these often have better terms and conditions of service.

Thus there are concerns about the limits of building an early childhood infrastructure based primarily on local, private support. Parents are typically more than willing to support preschool education with their time, materials, labor, and money,

## Kenya Preschool Growth:
## Centers, Enrollments, Teachers (trained, not yet trained)

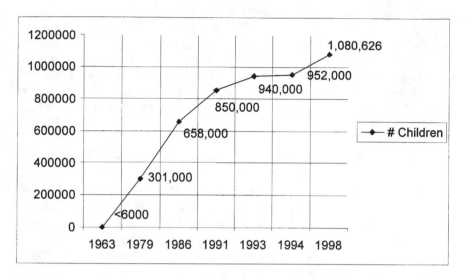

Fig. 1.1     Kenya Preschool Growth (based on Adams & Kabiru, 1995 and Adams & Swadener, in press)

| 1963 | 1979 | 1986 | 1991 | 1993 | 1994 | 1998 |
|------|------|------|------|------|------|------|
| <18 centers mostly in Nairobi | 6,000 centers | 12,182 centers | 17,650 centers | 18,400 centers | 19,083 centers | 24,127 centers |
| NA | NA | 16,182 teachers (68% untrained) | 24,809 teachers (65% untrained) | 25,300 teachers (63% untrained) | 27,829 teachers (62% untrained) | 37,979 teachers (57% untrained) |

but these resources are often limited—especially compared to the rising demand for services and the associated costs. A frequent alternative to preschool, especially for children to age three, has been the use of an *ayah,* or child minder, who typically has many responsibilities for cooking and cleaning and often is young and untrained in basic child development and safety. The role of *ayahs* in the child care and early education "puzzle" in Kenya is discussed in more depth through the perspectives of parents, as reported in later chapters. It is evident, however, from both of our observations, personal experience, and the limited literature on child minders, that many of the girls serving as *ayahs* are emotionally immature and overworked with other domestic chores, making it difficult for them to provide infants and toddlers with much-needed emotional support and physical security (A. Njenga, personal communication June 12, 1998).

In some of the preschools, parents and local communities have initiated community-based feeding programs and growth monitoring and promotion (CBGMP) activities. For feeding programs, the parents contribute the ingredients and the cooking and eating utensils. They also either hire a cook or take turns preparing the food for the children. In addition, the parents participate in weighing the children and plotting the measurements on the chart, assisted by teachers trained as primary health workers (by the Ministry of Health, through local health officers and rural clinics). Some parents and preschool teachers also act as resource persons in parental educational programs as part of the growth monitoring and promotion activities. More recently, parents and other family members have been involved in material-making activities or have gathered recycled materials (e.g., sticks, boxes, sisal, scraps of material, etc.), which preschool teachers have used to make toys, charts, and other learning materials.

## Growth in Preschool Enrollment

Enrollment in preschool programs continues to grow in Kenya. In 1973, preschool enrollment was recorded at nearly 300,000, with 6,326 teachers. By 1979, enrollment in preschools had risen to 400,000 children attending some 8,000 preschools, and the number of teachers had grown to over 10,000. More recent statistics (Ministry of Education and Human Resource Development, 1994) indicate that 951,997 children are enrolled in over 19,083 centers. Still, only about one-third of Kenya's preschool-age (3 to 6 years) children are enrolled in a nursery school. There are a number of reasons children do not participate in preschools, despite their growing availability and the pressure to have at least one year of preschool prior to entering primary school (Standard 1). A sizable number of children are retained in the extended family child care system (Kabiru, 1993), that is, they are needed to provide care to younger siblings and other relatives. It is most typically economic factors that mitigate against enrolling children in preschools, particularly the cost of fees, uniforms (as most preschools require), and other related expenses. Children born earlier in the birth order also may be more likely to have access to preschool, and gender also may affect which children are sent to both preschool and primary school (e.g., girls are more likely to be kept home to care for younger siblings). These issues were discussed in depth with parents interviewed in the study and will be elaborated upon in later chapters. However, more and more families are finding ways to send their children to preschool during the year preceding entry to primary school, as the Standard 1 interviews often are competitive, especially in "better" schools, and there is great pressure on parents to do so.

Unlike many sub-Saharan countries, Kenya has little disparity in urban and rural school attendance. The *Progress of Nations* (1997) report noted that rural school attendance was actually slightly higher than urban attendance, with 83% attendance in urban Kenya and 84% in rural Kenya. The *Harambee* movement has been credited for some of the emphasis on access to education in rural Kenya. Issues facing many urban families also have recently decreased the likelihood that all children will attend primary school. These issues are described, in various stakeholders' words, in chapters 9 and 10.

## Why Focus on Under Threes?

Several Kenyan studies (e.g., Gakuru & Koech, 1995; Kabiru & Njenga, 1997, 1999; Kipkorir, 1994; NACECE, 1994; Swadener, Kabiru, & Njenga, 1995, 1997; NACECE/Aga Khan, 1994; NACECE/UNICEF, 1995) have begun to document a demand for expanded and appropriate services for children under three. Extrafamilial care for the youngest children is particularly urgent in urbanized and agricultural areas, including plantations, where mothers are working long hours, and traditional caregivers (e.g., grandmothers and older siblings) are unavailable to care for young children.

The most common child care arrangements for children under three involve child minders, or *ayahs,* who are typically young girls themselves, and who lack education, such as information on child development, nutrition, and other relevant issues. They serve not only as child minders, but as maids, and they are expected to cook, clean, do laundry, and care for children. As such, they are typically the first to rise (well before dawn), heating the bath water and bathing and dressing the children, making tea, cooking the *uji* (porridge) or other breakfast and lunch to send with school-going children, and then, after a full day of chores, cooking, and child minding, are typically the last to bed, as they clean up after the family has retired for the night. (For a more in-depth description of *ayahs'* daily lives and their critical role in child care in Kenya, see Kipkorir, 1994, or Maillu, 1986). Some readers may imagine that such house help or maids are only employed by middle-class families, but this is not the case in Kenya. Working-class and even some low-income families also employ "house girls," often an uneducated rural relative or a neighbor's child. In our fieldwork in Narok, for example, some of the better-off Maasai families had employed *ayahs* to assist in the care of the children, as further described in chapter 3.

A type of care for under threes, which is only infrequently seen in Kenya, however, is home-based or family child care, in which a neighbor or other hired care provider cares for a small number of children in her home, or a home-like setting, sometimes with an assistant (e.g., a child minder). Many of the parents interviewed in our study supported this idea, as did the local research collaborators. The settings that most resembled family child care homes were found in Nairobi, where some families (both fathers and mothers) were providing group care for children as young as age one or two.

## "Under Three" Initiatives in Kenya

Returning to conferences and national studies of the needs of children under age three in Kenya, the recommendations made by the interdisciplinary group of participants at the "Partnership and Networking in the Care and Development of Under Threes" conference held at Nyeri (Kenya) in October 1993 were of direct relevance to the current study and helped shape its design. The following were of particular relevance, in recommending that: (1) parents and local communities be mobilized to provide services for the under threes in existing programs; (2) traditional knowledge and skills be tapped to enrich the programs on survival, development, and early stimulation; (3) awareness programs be mounted to enlighten parents and other caregivers on the importance of providing quality care for under threes; and (4) research on the care of under threes be intensified, particularly as it relates to early stimulation and conditions under which under threes live.

Another conference that was extremely relevant to the present study was the 1992 Kakamega Seminar on the Care and Educational Needs of Under Threes: Building on People's Strengths. This UNICEF- and Bernard van Leer-supported conference served as an initial "think tank" for academics and NACECE/DICECE leaders to frame policy and practice directions for the nation. The seminar papers emphasized the importance of strengthening and building upon cultural traditions and the role of parents and other family members as children's primary care providers and first teachers, underscoring the importance of parental awareness and education. After discussion of broad areas of developmental need in the first three years (e.g., health, nutrition, safety, stimulation, and growth within all of the developmental domains), the sessions addressed specific issues, including children in difficult circumstances, children on the agricultural plantations, and health risks and primary prevention approaches. In the papers making recommendations for early stimulation in all of the developmental domains, various changes in the family were noted. These included several observations concerning issues affecting children under three, such as the multiplicity of mothers' roles, which often necessitates leaving children on their own for extended periods of time; absent fathers; poverty, and related concerns such as crowding, poor health conditions, and lack of sanitation; and large families, resulting in part from lack of birth spacing and family planning (Bali & Kabiru, 1992).

A number of recommended supportive roles for the community to play were made in the seminar report and particular paper (Bali & Kabiru, 1992), which emphasized the theme of the village raising the child, in that they underscored the importance of all community members in the nurturance of children. "The community is also the custodian of culture. There are many child-rearing practices that can be used to enhance child growth and development (e.g., storytelling). Elders, young people, both male and female, can all play their role in education young children" (Bali & Kabiru, 1992, p. 48). The report advocated community mobilization in the provision of a safe and health environment for children, including provision of water, playgrounds, toys, and so on and through the support of community-based groups, such as women's self-help and youth groups. It also urged the funding of community-based services to support families with young children, for example, child care centers, health care programs, and income-generating groups.

One final aspect of this 1992 (NACECE) report deserves mention—namely, its emphasis on the strengths of families and communities in Kenya, including suggesting strategies for identifying traditional strengths and assessing how these might be "recaptured" in contemporary circumstances. This section also made recommendations regarding the need for greater gender equity, respect of elders, and appropriate participation of children in family and community cultural activities. In addition, it emphasized the care and support of pregnant and lactating mothers. In the section in which Bali and Kabiru provide advice to early childhood colleagues on identifying community strengths, a combination of observing, listening, and engaging in dialogue with community members is advocated. They also state that "the community has to learn to identity its own strengths. The outsider can only serve to trigger the process" (1992, p. 50). They further recommend that it is the community that must decide what it can afford in terms of time, labor, expertise, and other resources, and the community must also make decisions regarding the best way to use these resources. The participatory approach to community empowerment in areas related to child-rearing, early care, and education was pervasive in NACECE and DICECE documents and, more importantly, practices. This approach, as reflected in the Bali and Kabiru (1992) paper, informed our study on multiple levels.

## EVOLUTION OF THE COLLABORATIVE STUDY

Relatively few researchers have focused on child care and preschool education in sub-Saharan Africa, and even fewer have disseminated their findings (Adams, 1983; Gakuru, 1992; Gakuru & Koech, 1995; Kamerman, 1989; Kipkorir, 1994; Kipkorir, Mwaura, Kabiru, & Njenga, 1988). Others have provided ethnographic accounts of child-rearing and child care (e.g., Harkness & Super, 1985, 1992; Kilbride, 1986, 1990; Levine & Levine, 1974, 1988; Swadener, Kabiru, & Njenga, 1997; Tronick, Morelli, & Winn, 1987; Varkevisser, 1973; Weisner et al., 1997; Whiting, 1977; Whiting & Edwards, 1988), or autobiographical accounts (Gatheru, 1981; Nyarango, 1994). The work of the National Centre for Early Childhood Education in Kenya has been significant in increasing the flow of information, resources, and support among early childhood programs and personnel, not only in Kenya but in several African nations, and it served as the host institution for this research project.

Before data collection began, the first author had made six previous trips to Africa for early childhood pilot studies and to participate in the first two U.S.–Kenyan Early Childhood Collaborative Training Seminars, held in Nairobi in 1992 and 1994. Participation in these conferences and further correspondence with the leadership of the NACECE led to the formulation of the current study and development of the Fulbright African Regional Research Program proposal. The study sought to pursue issues of direct, local relevance and to build upon existing Kenyan scholarship in the areas of early childhood education—particularly as applied to children under age three and their families.

A critical aspect of the study and its various forms of dissemination and application has been its emphasis on collaboration. Authentically collaborative research must be based on mutually defined goals and the stated needs of indigenous people, actively seeking to improve the conditions of people—in the present case, young people and their primary caregivers in Kenya. Two levels of collaboration took place during the stay of the researcher. At the national level, the coordinator and deputy coordinator of the NACECE were directly involved in the refinement of the research questions, the selection of districts to be sampled, and the overall design of the study. They were also given transcripts of all of the interviews and took part in the data coding and analysis phase of the project.

At the district/local level, two  DICECE colleagues were nominated to participate in the data collection process. All collaborators, national and local, came to Nairobi for an orientation session in which the interview protocols were further revised and a schedule for data collection generated. This is described in more depth in the following chapter, which focuses on the research design and methodology. Local collaborators also piloted the proposed interview instruments prior to the formal start of the study and served as co-interviewers and translators during periods of data collection in their districts. All interviews were typed and mailed to the collaborators for corrections and other input, thus the project sought to be actively collaborative at every stage and culminated in several co-authored presentations and publications. Likely of more importance or relevance to children and families in Kenya is the ongoing attempt at the district and national levels to utilize findings from this study to enhance preschool education and services to families at the local level and to increase funding of initiatives that parents and community leaders identified as areas of greatest need. We also recognize the limitations of any piece of research to make a difference in the lives of families and the challenges of cross-cultural collaborative research, as briefly discussed in the preface.

## Purpose and Goals of the Study

The focus of the project was threefold. First, the study examined the nature and impacts of recent social and economic change on child-rearing practices and pre-school programs. Second, community views of the nature and potential of early childhood care and education services were examined, including the issue of the cultural relevance of preschool education to families maintaining "traditional" lifestyles. The study also examined ways in which traditional support systems contributed to effective child-rearing and care and how these systems could be supported and enhanced. Finally, the study examined the role and effectiveness of intersectoral collaboration in the provision of services to young children and their families. This focus was added after the visiting researcher arrived in Kenya and had completed background reading of reports, several of which raised issues regarding intersectoral collaboration.

Thus the purpose of the study was to document the impact of social and economic change on child-rearing in Kenya, with an emphasis on parent and community involvement/mobilization and the care and early education of children under age three. The more specific goals of the study were: (1) to examine the impact of social and economic change on child-rearing practices, early childhood services, and related policies; (2) to describe representative types of early childhood care and education, particularly for under threes, and to analyze participation patterns in contrasting ECCE programs; (3) to ascertain the relevance of "formal" early childhood education to families maintaining traditional lifestyles; (4) to examine ways in which traditional support systems and child-rearing practices contribute to effective care of young children, and how this could be strengthened; (5) to better understand the process and significance of community mobilization and parental involvement in early childhood care and education; (6) to formulate policy and programmatic recommendations in terms of more effective services for young children and their families, with an emphasis on capacity building at the community level, and targeting those of greatest need; and (7) to examine the nature and effectiveness of intersectoral collaborations as they pertain to services for young children and their families. (A detailed listing of the research questions and methodology is found in Appendix B and Appendix C.)

The following chapter provides a brief overview of our research design and data collection procedures and draws implications for cross-cultural collaborative research in the context of "decolonizing" research. It also offers an introduction to the settings and families whose stories form the substance of this book.

# Chapter 2

# A Collaborative Study

The promise of a postcolonial anthropology that goes beyond the re-analysis of its own problematic past depends upon engagement with the questions and challenges raised by those concerned with cultural heterogeneity, power and "marginality."
—Anna Lowenhaupt Tsing,
*In the Realm of the Diamond Queen*

## MULTIPLE CONTEXTS: "AFRICANIZING" RESEARCH

This study reflected, in many ways, the changing nature of fieldwork in a postcolonial and postmodern world (Reed-Danahay, 1997) and sought to transcend, wherever possible, the colonial exoticizing of the "Third World Other." In our case, the personal narratives of parents, grandparents, preschool teachers, primary school children, and community leaders were used to decode a number of issues related to changes in child-rearing and early education in Kenya. As discussed earlier, the collaborators strove to design and carry out a study that would have cultural capital and relevance both to Kenyans working with children and families and to larger scholarly audiences interested in cross-cultural research, early childhood education, and social policy affecting children and families. Our work clearly built upon previous studies carried out by Kenyans, including national collaborators Margaret Kabiru and Anne Njenga.

Fig. 2.1    Maasai Local Collaborator with Children

We further sought to involve local collaborators in a number of ways that tran-scended, for the most part, the "traditional" role of informant, cultural guide, or interpreter. As we describe in more detail in this chapter, the local collaborators actively coconstructed the study with us, from the refinement and piloting of potential interview questions to recruiting the sample to cultural interpretation of the data and consultation on the emerging findings. We were, in many senses of the phrase, "to-gether in the field" as research partners and as child advocates.

Although this is not a full-blown ethnographic account by any means, it does reflect the insider knowledge and interpretations of local collaborators, which far exceed the visiting researcher's limited time in any particular setting. The balancing of a national perspective on issues of changing child-rearing with the more in-depth, richly contextualized data available from more extensive ethnography was a source of concern for the first author on many occasions. The need identified by the Kenyan collaborators, however, was to have profiles of families with young children from many contrasting settings in the service of better program planning for children under age three. Thus much of the data reported in this book reads as summaries of themes from multiple interviews with local stakeholders in early childhood care and education, in contrast to in-depth case studies or narratives of a more limited number of participants more typical in ethnographic accounts.

Our study employed a collaborative, micro-ethnographic design, drawing heavily from interview data and repeated observations in eight districts of Kenya, which represented four types of settings. The sample included an array of over 460 local stakeholders in early childhood care and education, including children. As a research team, we attempted to go beyond collection, tabulation, and summary of interview responses and field observations, although these activities also were critical to the study. We utilized a qualitative, constant comparison method in which differences and similarities among groups and across settings were used to generate grounded inferences or hypotheses throughout the study, particularly at the conclusion of the study (Glaser & Strauss, 1967).

In encouraging stories that narrated the impacts of social and economic change on families with young children, we share with White and Epston (1990) the view that narratives not only describe lived experience but shape our lives and relationships. As Linde (1993, p. 3) states, "Stories express our sense of self; who we are and how we got that way. They are also one very important means by which we communicate this sense of self and negotiate it with others." In African contexts, stories often are expressed collectively, thus our study tended to use small group versus individual interviews.

Personal and family narratives also are shaped by the nested contexts (Lubeck, 1987) within which people are socialized, raise their children, and live. The impact of culture, social and environmental context, and personal history should not be underestimated—particularly in African contexts, in which one's history and relationship with one's ancestors play a vital role in collective identity and personal narrative. White (1992, p. 122) suggests that, "Persons are shaped by the meaning that they ascribe to their experience, by their situation in social structures, and by the language and cultural practices of self and of relationship." Kilbride and Kilbride (1990), drawing from their nearly 30 years of fieldwork with families in Uganda and Kenya, affirm the importance of history and social or collective environment to an African identity, stating, "The East African behavioral environment is . . . socially constructed such that the person cannot be separated from a social context" (p. 85). They contrast this collective identity to the Eurocentric and American value of individualism, using examples of speaking in the "we" versus the "me." In other words, the connection of many African people to both their ancestors and future generations is virtually inseparable from personal identity.

## RESEARCH DESIGN AND METHODOLOGY

The study employed multiple, qualitative field-based methods of data collection, including: (1) structured and semistructured (individual and small group) interviews with parents, grandparents, preschool teachers, and caregivers; professionals working with children and families; children who were older siblings of under threes; and community leaders; (2) focus group discussions with professionals (e.g., community health workers, Teacher Assistance Centre (TAC) tutors, adult educators, social workers, community development assistants, head teachers, and DICECE staff) and community leaders (e.g., chiefs, counselors, other elected officials, leaders of women's self-help groups, religious leaders); (3) review and content analysis of reports (e.g., monthly and annual DICECE reports, Ministry of Education and local statistics on preschool enrollments, and relevant research reports and publications); conference proceedings; related studies in family sociology and anthropology; and project reports (e.g., UNICEF, AMREF, Aga Khan Foundation, Bernard Van Leer Foundation, etc.); and (4) observations in homes, preschools, markets, *shambas* (farms), informal child care settings, plantations, and other settings related to the care and early education of young children, as well as parent and community meetings in which child-rearing and early education issues were addressed.

Data collection was divided into two phases: Phase 1 consisted of a full week of interviews with parents, grandparents, children (older siblings of under threes), preschool teachers, and some community leaders. These were structured and semistructured interviews (varying in formality by context, time constraints, etc.), typically conducted individually (especially for teachers) or in small groups. Interviews were interspersed with participant observations in preschools, homes, and various community settings (e.g., markets, health clinics, or canteens on plantations).

Phase 2 consisted of return visits to the sampled communities in which focus groups with community leaders and professionals working with parents and young children participated in a one-to-two-hour discussion of 10 questions, all related to the research questions, often including themes that had been identified from the first round of interviews in their community. DICECE trainers also participated in these discussions, particularly in the professionals focus groups, where English was typically used, thus freeing local collaborators from needing to translate. In other words, the direct input of most DICECE staff in the sampled districts was obtained in Phase 2. (The research methodology and procedures are described in detail in Appendix C.)

## Sampling Procedure

After the participating districts were identified and the orientation was complete, local collaborators, generally two DICECE trainers, set about identifying the local sample. Consistent with purposive sampling, their guidelines were to select areas that offered contrasts, as discussed above, yet were not so far apart that travel time would become problematic (i.e., we wanted to have more time for interviewing and to spend less time traveling to distant locations in the district).

Once such sublocations were identified, the local collaborators visited key sites and individuals (e.g., head teachers, TAC tutors or zonal preschool supervisors, and chiefs) to seek permission to conduct the study in their community. Head teachers and sometimes preschool teachers were instrumental in identifying participants for the study. DICECE trainers tended to select the preschools and teachers to be interviewed, although the majority of teachers interviewed in most districts were not DICECE trained. Responding to the request to interview parents, a number of head teachers recruited one or two members of the school committee to be part of the interview. As previously discussed, gender balance also was sought, where possible (e.g., our request was to interview both fathers and mothers and a smaller number of grandparents, if available).

## RESEARCH SITES

The following is a list of the research sites sampled in the study, organized by category. Note that the settings are described in greater detail at the beginning of each of the four results sections, and samples are described in detail at the beginning of chapters 3 through 10. Readers also should note that the management of the tea and coffee estates we visited requested that their names and specific locations remain confidential. This had not been stipulated by the other locations sampled. In fact, in a number of places we visited, local participants were anxious for the needs and issues of their specific location to become part of our documentation.

### Pastoralist, Semi-arid, Traditional

The most "traditional" communities we sampled were in the Samburu and Narok districts. The specific locations in the Samburu District included the Kisima area (20 kilometers south of Maralal town), including Loltulelei, Baawa, Lchorolelerai, Lkiloriti, and Naiborkeju. In the Narok District, the Maasai communities we visited were in Oloototo, Olopito, Olmukonko, and Inaaisuya/Naisoya, which represented a cross section of lifestyles and contrasting agricultural productivity within the district.

### Rural, Agricultural, Productive and Marginal

Our rural sample included the Embu and Machakos districts. In Embu, local collaborators again selected contrasting local settings, which varied greatly by agricultural productivity. The communities included Runyenjes (town and rural locations), the town of Embu, Ishiara, Machan'ga, and Mwenendega. In the Machakos District, the areas sampled included Wamunyu, Masii, Embuii, Makutano, Mwaasua, and Kawaa, all of which were rural communities of varying agricultural productivity.

### Plantation, Tea and Coffee Estates

Our plantation samples were drawn from two districts known for tea and coffee production, Kericho and Kiambu. In the Kericho District, in western Kenya, we visited larger tea estates and stayed on a plantation where the driver's son labored during our fieldwork there. Data was collected in four selected tea plantation sites, covering approximately a 30 kilometer radius of the town of Kericho. Data was typically collected in the estate preschool/day care center or social hall. In the Kiambu District, we visited two coffee estates and one tea plantation, representing geographically contrasting parts of the district and size of the estates.

## Urban, Slum/High Population Density

The urban samples were drawn from Nairobi (the city) and Kisumu (the municipality). The communities visited in Nairobi included Lunga Lunga and Mukuru (industrial area sublocations), Kariobangi South, Civil Servants, and Kawangwari. The visiting researcher also spent time in various settings of Uthiru and Kangemi, high-popuation density peri-urban areas just outside of Nairobi.

The Kisumu sample included all five municipal zones: Northern, Eastern, Southeastern, Southern, and Western, and sites included Manyatta (the largest slum area of Kisumu). Again, interviews were generally conducted in preschools, TAC centers, or other community settings. The Kisumu sample was one of the largest and also the most diverse in terms of income levels and ethnicity, as it included Asian, European, and American expatriate families.

## RESEARCHERS' BACKGROUNDS

In this final section, we share brief personal narratives in order to situate ourselves, as co-researchers and co-authors, into the study. Beth Blue Swadener is a European American, raised in a working-class neighborhood in northern Indiana, who has been interested in Africa since primary school. During her doctoral work, she pursued her interests in early childhood care and education in sub-Saharan Africa, with a focus on West Africa. Her first trip to Africa was to Senegal and The Gambia as part of a youth cultural exchange program. This led to several short-term projects in the same countries from 1987 through 1990 (in collaboration with Marianne Bloch from the University of Wisconsin and the Ministries of Education in Senegal and The Gambia). In 1992, Swadener made her first trip to Kenya to participate in the first Collaborative Kenyan–U.S. Early Childhood Collaborative Training Seminar. As described in the introduction, it was during this conference and the associated visits to rural preschools throughout Kenya that the seeds for this study were sown. As she states:

> Since I was young I have had an interest in Africa with particular focus on children's health and education. Going to Africa became, for me, a "dream deferred," for many years. I have had close friends from several African nations since high school and have served as a childbirth coach for three African friends living in the U.S. who were having babies far from the reassuring guidance of traditional birth attendants.
>
> After doing several pilot studies on pre-primary education in Senegal and The Gambia in the late 1980's, I was delighted for an opportunity to share that work with early childhood colleagues in Kenya through a conference organized by my long-time friend Diane Adams and the National Centre for Early Childhood Education in Nairobi. We traveled together

throughout Kenya during summer, 1992, and the ideas for this collaborative study began to take root. I quickly came to admire the professional commitment, strong leadership, and energy of two national leaders in early care and education—Margaret Kabiru and Anne Njenga. I was delighted that they were willing to collaborate on a study of changing child-rearing in Kenya and that NACECE was willing to host its first Fulbright visiting researcher. I have learned a great deal about cross-cultural research, Kenyan family life, and child advocacy from Mrs. Kabiru and Mrs. Njenga, and have been thrilled that our collaboration has extended to the completion of this book.

At the time of the study, Margaret Kabiru was coordinator of the National Centre for Early Childhood Education and Anne Njenga was deputy coordinator. Since that time, both have retired from their leadership positions in the Kenya Institute of Education (NACECE) and are continuing their work in related areas. Kabiru founded a child development research and advocacy foundation, Mwana Mwende Child Development Trust, and she has been completing longitudinal research with adolescent mothers and their children in the Machakos District, as well as doing consulting work in a number of African settings, such as UNICEF in South Africa. Njenga is currently a lecturer at Kenyatta University in Nairobi and is working with a new degree program in early childhood education, which has enrolled a number of DICECE trainers, including some of the local collaborators in this study. Both women are Kikuyu and grew up in rural areas. They experienced the Mau Mau struggle for independence and pursued careers in education. Kabiru described some of her life experiences and how they prepared her to lead the national program (*NACECE News*, 1995, p. 7).

> I was born to a family where boys and girls were encouraged to take on all roles—schooling, farming, animal care and so forth, and my mother has always been a church and community leader. My mother . . . had great faith in people and in her beliefs. She lived by her principles, and still does community and church work. She influenced me a lot.
>
> I think I am basically a teacher. I admired my eldest brother, Asaph. Although he stopped school at standard eight, he developed himself a lot, first as a teacher, then as a journalist. My brother was somebody able to take on challenging tasks. He loved people and brought us together as a family.
>
> I've also had a very supportive husband—we practice democracy in our home. I have often left young babies with him. When I started this work, our first daughter was only 18 months old. He has willingly shared in child-rearing.

In terms of critical incidents in her work with the NACECE, Kabiru recounted the following experiences and impressions:

From the time we started working in the rural areas and saw the type
of life some preschool teachers experienced, it had a great impact on
me. For example, in the plantations there were so many children but
very few resources. If they led committed whole lives under those conditions, it was very touching. They were happy in their work with
children. Then, seeing the change that the little we've given them in
training has made in terms of their growth . . . that has also been in-
spiring to me. Working with rural teachers and parents brought humility to my outlook on life.

Similarly, Njenga recalled the influences that her family had on her later career
aspirations.

Mrs. Kabiru and I come from similar backgrounds. I grew up in
Muran'ga and my mother had also been to school. My mother was the
first to go to school in our locality and one of the few to have gone to
church. My mother is still well known as a community and church
leader. I admired my mother, but I always wanted to be better off than
her. I didn't like farm work. I also had an older brother I admired, and
he paid my school fees once.
    I became a teacher, although to begin with I never wanted to be
one . . . I began to appreciate the teaching profession more when I got my
masters degree and began teaching at Kenya Science Teachers College. I
found that I had something to offer to teachers, including those who came
from the rural areas. I counselled them and found I could be useful. This
was a turning point—discovering that I had something to offer to others.

Njenga also reflected on her entry into the field of early childhood education.

Before joining NACECE I had done quite a bit of work with children,
but never thought of them the way I did when I came to work here.
The impact of rural field work also made a deep impression on me. For
example, seeing teachers who were happy to give basic care to children
in difficult circumstances and settings. From then, I realized that one
can be happy with very little. Our problems should be surmounted and
not allowed to destroy us. My work also influenced my understanding
of my own children.

Turning to a discussion of their professional activities at NACECE and in the
community, Njenga continued:

Both of us are professionals—we write, participate in workshops, and
try to keep up with reading. We also do a great deal of editing. We

collaborate with many different agencies. We are not purely an educational organization. We interact with parents, health professionals, and other sponsors dealing with children's needs, because we view children and families in holistic terms. We need expertise to complement our activities and need other sponsors to realize our activities. It is good to call on others, and also to avoid competition. We want to complement each other, not compete!

This spirit of collaboration was truly experienced in the study reported in this volume. Throughout this project and its various dissemination activities, the sense of complementing the interests and perspectives of "insider" and "outsider" researchers has been vital. In the epilogue, we each provide reflective commentary on the process of completing this study together.

We invite the reader to engage with the multiple voices and perspectives of participants found in the following sections. They are the voices of the "village," reflecting on issues related to raising their children and grandchildren in the face of rapid social, cultural, and economic change.

# Part II

Traditional Communities in Transition:
Narok and Samburu

# Traditional Communities in Transition: Narok and Samburu

This section of the book, comprised of chapters 3 and 4, presents and discusses the findings from the two districts that were selected to represent the more "traditional" lifestyles of the Maasai and Samburu. Each chapter begins with basic information about the district, including demographic, agricultural, health, and nutritional facts. This is followed by a description of the sample of parents, teachers, children, and community leaders and includes a summary of responses related to the research questions, combining sampled groups in some cases but clarifying the "voices" of different groups interviewed. Portraits of daily life, drawn from longer narratives, represent typical child-rearing related activities for each group. Given the complexity of the data, findings are organized, in part, around the research questions.

## TRADITIONAL/PASTORALIST: NAROK AND SAMBURU

The Samburu and Narok districts were selected for several reasons. Both include relatively large numbers of traditional pastoralists, many of whom represent families who face hardships inherent in arid and semi-arid settings and have lower rates of participation in formal education. The Maasai and Samburu share common *Maa* languages, and the separation of these two communities/ethnic groups is fairly recent—since the turn of the century, when the central Rift Valley was taken over by the expatriate farmers. Traditional ways of socialization are fairly intact in both the Samburu and Maasai communities, and both emphasize cohesion, cooperation, and preservation of the pastoral way of life. As the chapter titles that follow reflect, both communities have strong extended family systems, with grandmothers often available for child care and early socialization. Grandmothers are still knowledge-able in the use of herbs for treating both humans and animals and are responsible in a number of ways for culture maintenance in families and clans.

Both districts also had a history of strong DICECE collaborative potential to carry out the interviews and micro-ethnographic observations and had participated in other related projects with NACECE in recent years. These projects were conducted in collaboration with the Bernard van Leer Foundation, UNICEF, and the Aga Khan Foundation (e.g., the Samburu Community-Based Early Childhood Care and Education Project and the Care of Under Threes Project in Narok). These districts also were recommended by the two national collaborators in the study. The three national collaborators had visited both districts before formal data collection began, and entry was easily achieved. The visiting researcher had visited both districts in 1992 and 1994, before the start of this project. Finally, these districts represented more sparsely populated settings, where transportation and communication were challenging. Yet we frequently encountered evidence of an intricate local communication system, with, for example, information on ceremonial dates and places effectively communicated.

# Chapter 3

# Narok District:
# It Takes Grandmothers to
# Raise a Maasai Child

Mamas and grannies look after young children so that at no time are young children left alone!

—Preschool teacher, Oloototo

## DESCRIPTION OF SETTING

The Narok District covers an area of 18,531 square kilometers and is the fourth largest district in the Rift Valley Province. According to the 1989 population census, the district had 398,272 people, with a projected population of 474,481 at the time of data collection (1994–1995). Children in the age cohort of birth through age four account for approximately 20% of the total population (NACECE/UNICEF, 1995, p. 11). Narok was divided into two districts, Narok and Trans Mara, shortly before this study began.

In terms of land potential and general environment, the Narok District has varied land potential, ranging from the highland region with good rainfall and fertile soils to the semi-arid lowland regions of the south. Interviews were conducted in both regions, particularly in the south. The high potential region of the south is mainly used for agriculture, with crops grown such as wheat, barley, pyrethrum, maize, sunflowers, and sorghum. This region also is good for sheep and dairy farming. A small section of this land is forested and protected, as it is the main water catchment area for the district. However, charcoal making has contributed to the deforestation of this area.

Fig. 3.1    Maasai Grandmothers Singing Traditional Lullabies to Under Threes

The lowlands of the Narok District are mainly used for pastoral farming and are the primary grazing lands in Kenya for the Maasai, who are traditionally pastoral nomads. A small section of this land is used for growing drought-resistant varieties of maize, sorghum, millet, and sweet potatoes. The Maasai Mara game reserve occupies the biggest portion of this land. When we visited a number of the interview settings, we traveled off road on paths used by the Maasai to reach the main Narok road, often going as many as 15 to 20 kilometers to reach the *N'kang* or *boma* (cluster of homes), where our interviews took place.

Turning to health facilities, the Narok District has 2 hospitals, 10 health centers, and 45 dispensaries. Most of these facilities are unevenly distributed, resulting in some areas being far away from any health facility. This, coupled with a poor transport network, makes it very difficult for people, particularly those living in the semi-arid region, to benefit from existing facilities. This became vividly obvious to us on several occasions, for example, when we were asked to help take a young girl and her grandmother to a local clinic. The girl's condition was beyond treatment at that ill-equipped rural clinic, so we took her to Narok Hospital, where we were told that if she had arrived even hours later her life could not have been saved. The Maasai, however, have great faith, knowledge, and skills regarding traditional medicine, and the majority of people still depend upon traditional medicine for the prevention and treatment of various ailments (NACECE/UNICEF, 1995, p. 12).

Turning to health and nutrition, high rates of malnutrition are found among the pastoral communities due to sporadic drought resulting in famine. Growing cash crops such as wheat and barley takes up most of the fertile land and reduces production of food in the district. As some participants in the study reported, it also was difficult to successfully grow even kitchen gardens due to the wild animals (e.g., elephants) that came at night and trampled their plants. The traditional Maasai diet is meat, blood, and milk, with poultry, *ugali,* and vegetables introduced only relatively recently. Traditional eating habits and weaning foods are sometimes cited as reasons for the high incidence of malnutrition.

The disease incidence also is high. The main causes of morbidity include respiratory infections, malaria, skin and eye diseases, intestinal worms, and diarrheal diseases. Poor personal and environmental hygiene, lack of adequate water, especially in the semi-arid region, and lack of awareness of basic hygiene are the main causes of diseases. Despite these health and nutrition problems, however, the Narok District has a relatively low infant mortality rate of 90 per 1,000.

## NAROK SAMPLE

Five locations of the Narok District were sampled. Two were considered "medium potential," in terms of agricultural productivity, with more cultivation of wheat, maize, beans, and other vegetables. Three were considered "low potential" and were primarily areas where animals grazed and where limited cultivation of beans and maize had begun.

A total of 20 parents and grandparents were interviewed during Phase I, including 9 mothers, 5 fathers, 5 grandmothers, and 1 grandfather. In terms of the ages of the parents' first-born children, the range was from 2 to 15 years, and the mean age was 8 years. In terms of their last born children, the range was 2 to 36 months, and the mean was 14.6 months. It should be noted that several of the parents interviewed also had a second child under age four.

When asked about their roles in the community, six fathers stated that they served on the school or preschool committee, three of whom were officers; six women were active in a women's self-help group, two fathers were active in the ruling KANU (Kenyan African National Union political party) branch committee or youth group, and one described himself as an elder in the community.

In terms of work, as self-described, nine women stated that they were housewives, which was typically mixed with farming or animal tending and child care. Five parents described themselves as involved in farming and five in farming and livestock. Two women were involved in beekeeping, including one grandmother who kept bees and oxen for a women's group.

When asked about their length of time in the community, 18 had lived in their present location since birth, and 2 had lived there for 9 to 10 years. Five men and all of the women interviewed did not have any formal education or training; one father had gone through Standard 7, and another father had some adult education.

Six female preschool teachers were interviewed. Preschools in the Narok District typically had one teacher, although one preschool had four teachers and another had two. In terms of teachers' education, three had completed Standard 7 and two had completed Standard 8. One teacher was a primary school leaver who did not state the last class level attended. One teacher was new in the term in which interviews took place, two had been in their position for one year, one had been in the same job for seven years, and two had taught for nine years. Four teachers had only taught at their current preschool, one had three years of previous teaching experience, and another had six years' experience.

In terms of training, two teachers interviewed were DICECE trained (in 1987 and 1992), and four teachers were untrained. Five teachers were married, and one was single. The average age of the preschool teachers was 24.5 years, and the mean age of first-born children was 9 years, with a range of 8 to 16 years. The mean age of last-born children was 17 months, with a range of 6 months to 3 years.

When asked who paid their salary, four teachers replied that they were employed by the Narok County Council and two were paid by the parents. As in other districts, when a preschool had more than one teacher, the head teacher was typically paid by the council and the other teacher or teachers were paid by the parents. When asked about other income sources, two responded "none," three responded, "husband," and two responded "shamba cultivation."

Nine primary school children, with siblings ages three years and younger (five girls and four boys) were interviewed. Eight were in Standard 3 and one was in Standard 4. Their age range was approximately 8 to 10 years, although children typically did not know their age, or they were unsure of it. This was similar to the responses of the mothers when asked about the ages of their first-born and last-born children.

Two focus group interviews were held in Narok in May 1995. The first was comprised of professionals working with children and families (including a preschool inspector, four DICECE trainers, a health officer, a primary school teacher, and an NGO staff member) and the second was comprised of local leaders, including an elected councillor, community elders, women leaders, and a deputy headmaster of the local primary school. (Note that a councillor is a member of the local county council, the local governing body.) Margaret Kabiru and I returned to the town of Narok and Oloototo settlement in June 1996 and found that a preschool had been completed. We also conducted follow-up interveiws with a number of local leaders and DICECE personnel at that time.

## Portrait: A Maasai Grandmother

*I get up early and prepare breakfast, then I get the babies from neighbors who are going out (to get water and firewood or to go to market). The mothers bring food for the children and then children are left with me all day, or until the mother comes back. I sing lullabies, give them small sticks and beads to play with, and they eat and take a nap. In the evening, I prepare an evening meal and go to bed. I am related to most of the children I care for, but not all.*

## Portrait: A Maasai Mother

*I wake early, do the milking, prepare tea and nurse my son. Then I get the milk from the animals, and sometimes I boil it. Then, I go to the shamba (kitchen garden) and after working in the garden, return to prepare lunch for the school children. I take the baby with me and I work in the garden or shed . . . sometimes I have time to play with him and nurse him. He cries a lot, because I am often unable to nurse, but I try to nurse him as often as I can.*

*After lunch I go back to the garden or go for firewood; then I get water. To do that, I load the donkey with jerry cans and go to the river, about 5 kilometers away. When I go to gather water and firewood I leave the baby with his older sister—or take him along if there's nobody to watch him. In the late afternoon, I return to cleaning, sweeping, washing clothes, and even milking. Then I prepare for the evening meal and go milking, assisted in taking the calves into their pen by my children and husband. Then, I feed my family and go to bed.*

The above quotes were quite representative of the three generations of Maasai mothers we interviewed in the Narok District. The older mamas, now unable to walk long distances to gather firewood or to carry water, stayed home and cared for the babies and young children, while the younger mamas went for water, for wood, to market, and worked in their kitchen gardens. It also appeared that many more of the younger mothers were involved in cultivation than their mothers had been, reflective of the mixed farming/herding in the area. Although threatened with destruction by wild animals, more Maasai families were observed planting maize, beans, and—in one of the areas sampled—wheat.

## Portrait: A Primary Student in Narok

*I wake up, light the fire, eat breakfast (ugali and vegetables) and come to school. After school, I draw water and accompany some ladies and other girls to fetch firewood—far from home. When I come home, I light the fire and wash the utensils, then I assist my mother in caring for the baby by playing with him so he doesn't cry and giving him toys (a ball or some lids to play with) and I sing lullabies and giggle to the baby. I also give him milk and other food, but the baby is still too small for ugali and potatoes. After eating, I go outside to play with my friends and then I sleep in my grandmother's house with other age-mates. At my grandmother's we sing and make plays and my grandmother tells stories.*

The above account of "everything I did yesterday," as given by a girl in Standard 3, captures the multiple role Maasai children—particularly girls—have in contributing to the functioning of the household. In the area of child care, older siblings are involved in most aspects of daily caregiving, with the exception of washing the baby, which a couple of children reported was done by the mother. "Only the mama washes the baby, but I do everything else," a child related.

It should be noted, in terms of a sampling limitation, that all of the children interviewed in both Narok and Samburu were still in primary school. The study worked with local head teachers in recruiting the children's sample, therefore it did not sample out-of-school children.

Although experiencing many changes overall, the Maasai (similar to the Samburu parents in the study) had not lost their traditional support systems for child care—the grandmothers. Similarly, these older mamas were continuing to teach many aspects of traditional Maasai culture through songs, stories (told in the evening only), and daily routines in the compound. That many more children were attending nursery school, usually by age four or five and sometimes younger, did not appear to be affecting the traditional care provided to the under threes by the grandmothers. Had we sampled the town of Narok, we would likely have found a different story—perhaps a more transitional one, with families living in a more nuclear and less extended family setting. The five locations sampled, however, were all rural, and many found families living in versions of the traditional Maasai home in an *En'kang*—a group of houses with an animal crawl in the middle, surrounded by a protective fence (to keep out wild animals) made of tree branches with thorns. Land was beginning to be subdivided, however, and several people pointed out that the current extended family system of under three care could not continue indefinitely, as families moved to land separate from their extended families.

We conducted the first round of interviews in late January, still early in the new school year. Thus several of the nursery schools visited were underenrolled—that is, they had not reached nearly the number of children they had served the previous year. We found a "preschool," with a teacher provided by the local county council, meeting under a tree in January ("under threes under trees"), then visited again in May and found that a school building was being completed on the compound of a councillor. Another preschool visited in October and again in January did not have a teacher. By February, a teacher had been hired, and we met her during our May visit. Thus change in early childhood education in these Maasai communities can be rapid and positive. Life remains difficult for many Maasai families, however, with fewer animals—the source of much of the traditional Maasai diet (milk, meat, and blood)—drought, and the impacts of "development" affecting daily life in numerous ways.

The following sections discuss the findings framed by each of the research questions. Relevant responses of parents, grandparents, teachers, and children are summarized, foregrounding quotes from participants and synthesizing their perspectives.

## Major Challenges or Problems Facing Families with Young Children

The most frequently mentioned problems concerned both food and water. Underfeeding was a problem, with grandmothers and some mothers reflecting, "We have fewer animals now, and less milk is available, so we have to buy food now." Many parents also complained about water shortages and the distance to the closest source of water. Two of the locations sampled had wells attached to windmills, so this was apparently helping to address the water problem. Also mentioned as a problem was the frequent occurrence of wild animals ruining crops. Some of the mothers interviewed had replanted vegetables several times, only to have them eaten or trampled at night. (In fact, one primary school had recently received funding from the Kenya Wildlife Service to erect an electric fence around the school compound to protect the school's kitchen garden from animals at night.)

The distance mothers had to travel for a variety of needs was a central theme of our discussions. The hospital and market in the town of Narok were far, with a *matatu* (public transport mini-van) only serving some of the outlying areas on market days, or two days a week. Women also walked quite far to gather firewood, and they commented that there was a private clinic closer than the hospital in town, but that the clinic was too expensive.

Several health problems were discussed. Aside from the distance to more affordable health care, parents described the common illnesses of young children. These included eye and skin problems, malaria, diarrhea, and upper respiratory problems, including pneumonia. Malnutrition and underfeeding also were both visible problems in some children and were parental concerns.

The cost of living had gone up, and with fewer animals, this created many financial hardships for Maasai families. As one mother stated, "The flow of money is not continuous. Husbands only have money when animals are sold, and this is not a steady income. When fathers take the herds to graze far away, they may not leave enough for the family to live on." The rising cost of school and book fees was named several times as a problem. Some parents felt forced to choose which of their children to educate, due to their inability to afford school-related costs for all of their children. In these cases, they tended to favor their sons (who would remain in the family even after marriage and could help support the family).

Finally, younger mothers stated that they sometimes lacked assistance with child care and needed better care of their youngest children—especially when going for water and firewood. Some of the older mamas, however, felt that younger mothers did not care for their children as well as the older ones had. This is discussed in more detail in the next section, addressing change.

Many of the problems discussed in the focus groups concerned the rising cost of living and families' inability to provide for their often large families. As one participant summarized, "The high cost of living has eroded the purchasing power of families, hence, many cannot provide adequately for basic needs such as food, clothing, and health." Another stated, "The cost of education has also escalated, resulting in some families being unable to educate their children."

Issues of family change also were raised, including teenage mothers who might lack adequate knowledge of child care, and more single-parent families. Increased conflicts in families were noted, particularly by the professional focus group, in reference to divorces and separations, "all of which affect child-rearing."

The problems most frequently mentioned by teachers were related to nutrition and health, such as lack of proper diet, not enough food, and childhood disease. The most common diseases or health problems listed by preschool teachers were malaria, the common cold, measles, and eye and skin problems. Teachers also raised concerns, as parents had, regarding the distance of homes from both clinics/hospitals and schools. The issue of distance is compounded by the dangers when children are walking—particularly the dangers posed by wild animals.

Other problems named by teachers were the cost of health care, particularly at the newer private clinics, which were closer to families but not affordable to most, the lack of access to water, and the lack of good hygiene. Teachers also mentioned that some parents had problems paying school fees; this was particularly true of fees for older children, but it was also true of preschool fees, even when they were nominal (e.g., 5/= Kshs. per month) and for purchasing school uniforms.

## How Are Families Coping?

In response to the question "How are families coping with these problems?" teachers answered that, "Some families have tried to sell maize to get money," and "Other families sell an animal when they need other kinds of food." They also commented that parents now take children to the hospital or clinic much more frequently than before. As parents and children had indicated, however, taking children to the clinic often follows attempting to cure them using local herbs and other traditional health practices. For eye problems, parents wash children's eyes with salt water.

In terms of how parents have coped with the long distances from home to school, one teacher said, "They coped by starting this preschool, as the closest one was too far and dangerous for young children to walk." This was the preschool in which the research team found many "under threes under trees," as a building had not yet been constructed. As previously mentioned, a building was nearly completed by May 1995, when the team returned to this sublocation, and it was in full use during a follow-up visit in 1996.

Other teachers said that they called on parents in their homes when there were problems, and that discussing the problems sometimes helped parents cope. Others simply indicated that they sent children home from school until the funds for a uniform or fees could be found. "Some parents find a way to get the uniform after the children are sent home for about two weeks." Still other parents were apparently defeated in their attempts to cope with the many problems they faced, as reflected in the following quote: "I can't really tell how they cope—a parent may just say, 'I have no way!'"

## Effects of Problems on Children

When teachers were asked about how the previously discussed problems and related family stress affected children in their care, the most common response was that when "children are cold or hungry, this affects their learning very much." Other similar responses included, "Children are tired or sleepy in class," "Children are uneasy in learning," and "Children are uncomfortable if they don't have warm clothes."

Two teachers addressed the issue of children being sent home for funds: "When they're at home, due to lack of fees, etc., they don't get training in a school routine, and they will be delayed in moving on with education in primary school." In other words, if "those sent home lag behind," the financial burden was not only a hardship for parents but could contribute to children's later difficulties in school.

## Good Things the Community Is Doing

In response to the question, "What good things is your community doing for young children?" a number of traditional—and some newer—practices were named. A quote that particularly captured this was, "Mamas and grannies look after young children so that at no time are young children left alone!" As previously discussed, the availability of grandmothers to provide child care was clearly a community asset and a source of pride. Other traditional practices, such as extended breast-feeding, also were mentioned. As one mother stated, "Children are breast-fed until the child is able to walk." Others said, "They are breast-fed for two to three years."

In terms of more recent contributions to the care of young children, parents mentioned the provision of better clothing and warmer shelter. "Before, many children would be naked—now we are giving them warm clothing." They also had constructed preschools and added additional rooms when needed, and they had raised money to hire the teachers. As several parents stated, "We are now taking our children to school," and this started with preschool for more and more Maasai families in our sample.

Clinics also were mentioned as having "improved children's health as more mothers use the services," and access to water had also improved. For example, a windmill and a water pump, donated by Child Care International and on the grounds of a primary/preschool compound, now provided the immediate community with a much better water source—directly benefitting young children. Previously, mothers and older children had walked many kilometers, through quite unsafe areas (i.e., where wild animals were frequently found) to obtain river water. The well water was closer and cleaner as well.

When asked what some of the good things their communities were doing for children, focus group participants responded similarly to the parents interviewed. The continuation of some positive traditional child-rearing practices was the most frequently mentioned contribution. These included "many children still being breast-fed for up to two years, and some longer" and "grandparents and other elders still available in most areas to provide care and support to parents."

Other, more recent practices that were recognized as contributing to young children included "communities putting up preschools and primary schools for their children," "community-based feeding programs, usually preparing uji and milk, and some schools contributing to better nutrition of children," and "more varieties of good foods available for families." Other improvements in the area of parental awareness included "increased awareness on the importance of both parents participating in the rearing of their children, including fathers being more involved" and "parents being more aware of the importance of good health and taking their children for immunization, growth monitoring, and treatment when sick." Improved, warmer clothing for children was mentioned, as was the provision of more and better care given to expectant mothers. As previously mentioned, families now prepare for babies even before they are born, and this was seen as a positive contribution.

## How Life has Changed in the Past Ten to Fifteen Years

Before moving into more specific areas of change, we posed this question in an open-ended way. Grandmothers in one location responded, "The love of children was greater then!" and in another location they stated, "Children are not as healthy now." Otherwise, the general changes were subsumed under housing, food, and lifestyle, among other topics to follow.

### Food

Many changes in the area of family diet were named, often beginning with a parent, particularly a grandmother, saying, "Milk and meat and fat were the major foods, but now there is much greater variety!" or "Porridge with milk used to be taken, but now we eat *ugali* with vegetables and a much more diverse diet." Many more mothers were cultivating kitchen gardens, and more fathers, who formerly would have kept animals as their exclusive livelihood, were now turning to increasingly large-scale farming (especially in the wheat-growing parts of the district).

Also cited under changes related to food were the many new ways of preparing food and greater use of food bought in various markets. Finally, the use of drying racks for utensils and other improved hygiene in food preparation also were mentioned (e.g., boiling milk before using it, especially for children).

The focus groups also noted many of the same changes in the local diet. Previously, the main foods were milk, blood, and meat (as the earlier parent interviews had indicated). Currently, a greater variety of foods includes rice, beans, maize, potatoes, vegetables, sorghum, and other animal products. Some of these foods are grown, while others are bought from the shops or the Narok market (on its two market days).

In addition, more cultivation is now taking place in the Narok District, with more families planting kitchen gardens and other parts of the district growing maize and wheat on a fairly large scale. Wild animals still present a threat to many efforts at cultivation, but more people are now showing a strong interest in growing food as well as in raising animals. People have begun crop cultivation to supplement their access to food and, in some cases, their income.

## Housing

The quote that we heard many times in regard to the often dramatic changes in housing was, "Before, people built with mud and dung, then used thatch and mud, and now they use iron sheets." The housing often appeared quite "traditional," but it could be described as "improved," with more ventilation and light (e.g., more windows), more permanent building materials, and higher ceilings. Such improved homes often were found side by side the more traditional homes. It also should be noted here that women continued to build many of the houses, particularly those in the more traditional style.

As parents had told us in the earlier interviews, housing styles in the Narok District had undergone many changes: from traditional houses made of mud and cow dung to thatched roofs and then to corrugated iron sheet roofs in some areas. The new houses also have more windows, and in areas where land has been demarcated, people no longer live on communal space but on individually owned land (in nuclear, versus extended, family settings).

## Cost of Living

Everyone interviewed agreed that the cost of living, in general, was higher now. As one mama put it, "It is hard now—many families go without tea and even food—especially during drought." Again, parents mentioned that they now have fewer animals or other sources of income. This, combined with higher school fees and the cost of food, clothing, and so on, makes the economic hardships on families quite pervasive.

## Health

One of the first and most frequently mentioned changes in terms of health was the fact that there were now many more hospitals and clinics and more mothers taking their babies to the clinics for immunization, growth monitoring, and other health services. As one father said, "All mothers are now encouraged to take babies for immunization." Only two of the mothers interviewed, in fact, had not taken their children to a clinic—one said that she feared what would be done there and did not trust it. This attitude was clearly exceptional among our sample, however.

Again, parents mentioned that government hospitals and clinics still tended to be further away, and that closer, private ones were unaffordable. In terms of specific health problems, eye and skin afflictions (some of which are made worse by the flies in the family compounds and other environmental hygiene issues) continued to be common. Parents mentioned, though, that more diseases are now preventable—both by immunization and through better personal and environmental hygiene practices.

In terms of child birth, one mother said, "We used to have only traditional doctors and traditional birth attendants, but now the younger mamas are told to have their babies in the hospital." (A later section will report the data on home versus hospital births, but mothers here still tended to have home births, especially for the second pregnancy and subsequent ones.) Improvements in child feeding also were noted, including the attempt to provide a more balanced and varied diet.

The major changes discussed in relation to health factors and care included the introduction of modern medicine. In the past, people relied wholly on traditional medicine. Herbs were used for the treatment of diseases. These days, although sometimes after first treating in traditional ways, sick people, including children, are taken to health centers or even the hospital some distance away (in the town of Narok).

Mothers also are much more likely to take their children to clinics for immunization and growth monitoring. In addition, there is also increased parental education on health. Mothers are taught, for example, how to make and use oral rehydration therapy solutions, which is important for a persistent problem, diarrhea.

Additionally, the focus group participants felt that personal and environmental hygiene had also improved. Access to water was still a problem in some areas, but wells and other water schemes had helped many communities.

## Clothing

Clothing also was an area of great change. Children are now dressed more warmly, and are clothed from infancy on in more families. Most parents stated that clothing was now much warmer and more varied. This was true of adult's, as well as children's clothing. For example, some mothers mentioned that they used to have just one type of clothing, but now, "We have a change of clothes for farming, going to market, visiting, and other activities!" In terms of babies and young children, another mother said, "Children are now clothed and they weren't before." They also commented that clothing was becoming expensive now—particularly school uniforms for their children.

## Family Size

Although there was not a general consensus on whether families were larger or smaller than 15 years earlier, several mothers thought that they were somewhat larger now, primarily due to more children surviving. Several mothers in one setting agreed that, "Before, mamas had 2 to 5 children and now they have 4 to 10."

In terms of family composition, several parents—both mothers and fathers—noted that men are no longer marrying as many women. As one older mama put it, "Now the younger men are only marrying one wife, versus 3 to 6 wives as in my time."

Participants in both focus groups agreed that families were now larger, in part, because both mothers and children are healthier. Lower infant and child mortality rates, combined with better maternal health practices, including moving away from some taboo food for pregnant women, have led to an increase in children in local communities.

Men also have fewer wives that in the past, due, according to the focus group participants, to economic strains. As previously mentioned, men were seen now as being more involved in parenting and more responsible for their family's well-being. One possible contradiction to this, however, was the statement that, "New modes of occupations in business and other paid employment have emerged, keeping men away from home for long periods."

A bit more family planning is also practiced and relates at least indirectly to the length of time mothers breast-feed their children. In fact, this was something that the older mamas said would not have been discussed by couples in the past but now is discussed between husband and wife or wives.

## Education

The overriding observations of parents interviewed was that, "There are many more primary schools and nursery schools than before—and more people are sending their children to school, including on to secondary school." Other parents commented that these changes in education were "costly, but important," and one stated, "If I educate my child, he will be a wealthy person." A couple of mothers mentioned that there was now a decrease in the marriage of schoolgirls, which is actually now against the law and is being actively discouraged by local authorities. "Younger people are moving away from traditional ways of life, and more are going to school," one grandmother stated.

There was a consensus from both Narok focus groups that there had been significant changes in education in the past 15 years. Going further back in time, in fact, there were no schools in many parts of this district. As one elder put it, "Before, children did not go to school—now many do." Now, according to the focus groups, there are "many nursery schools as well as primary and even secondary schools within our community, and a number of children attend these schools." Over the years, then, both the number of schools and their enrollment has continued to grow.

Participants said that the attitude toward education also has changed markedly. In earlier days, parents did not know the value of education, hence they were forced by the local administration to take their children to school. This is no longer necessary, due to increased parental awareness of the importance of education. Parents, particularly women, have activities that support their schools.

## Child-rearing Practices

A number of hygiene practices were mentioned in response to the question of how child-rearing practices had changed. As one grandmother stated, "Before, soon after birth, we didn't wash the babies with soap—we used fat, but now, we wash children with soap." Clothing was, again, mentioned in this context, "We used not to clothe babies, but now, we heavily clothe them." Similarly, feeding practices had changed (as already discussed): "In the past, we only fed children on milk and meat, but now we also feed them on vegetables or fruit—when we can afford these things."

The older mamas felt that they had "loved their children even more" than the younger mothers loved their children. They felt that marriages, however, were better today, with men having only one or two wives and better communication. They also thought that younger fathers were more willing to help their wives, such as holding a baby while their wives cooked, than their husbands had been.

Again, the discussions tended to focus on pre- and post-natal practices, including foods given to young children. There is now a greater variety of weaning foods, for example, such as eggs, rice, vegetables, milk, and porridge, whereas, before, cow's milk and fat were the major weaning foods. There also are more preparations for the baby. Many mothers now attend antenatal clinic, and some even buy clothes for the baby before birth, which had been taboo in previous times. Today, many fathers and mothers discuss the length of breast-feeding, which in most cases is two years. In fact, some of the older mamas interviewed stated that fathers are generally more involved with child care responsibilities than before—or are at least willing to discuss them, if not play an active role in child care.

Focus group participants stated that there was more awareness of the importance of child care as a result of increased parental education programs presented by the Ministry of Health officers. Where mobile clinics had been established, or dispensaries opened closer to people's homes, much better access to antenatal and postnatal care was available.

Although in most locales grandmothers are still available to support mothers in child care, there are reportedly some areas where this system is gradually disintegrating. Particularly where land has been demarcated and families practiced crop farming, the grandmother's child care support is slowly disappearing, along with communal land ownership and extended family living arrangements. Nuclear families are emerging within such settlements, and mothers are left to provide child care support.

With the introduction of Western education and land demarcation, communal discipline of children also has been greatly eroded. Many parents and communities are leaving the discipline of children to teachers, particularly to secondary teachers in boarding school settings. Another side of the complex issue of child discipline and guidance was the fact, according to some participants, that community discipline was no longer acceptable to younger parents in nuclear family situations. That is, parents were assuming exclusive responsibility for disciplining their children, particularly where land had been demarcated, or in town. Whereas, in the past, other community members, elders, or extended family members could discipline children, it was now considered less acceptable to do so. Put yet another way, the village was no longer allowed to raise a child communally.

## Social Structures and Services

The overriding social change noted by the Narok parents was that, "There is much less mobility now." Indeed, the communities visited could be called semi-permanent, if not permanent. Many parents had lived in the area of their present home all or most of their lives. If animals needed better grazing conditions, men and boys would take the animals away, but the women and younger children typically remained behind.

As previously noted, men now have fewer wives, and women do not marry as early as they traditionally had. This point, however, was debated, with participants sharing several examples of primary schoolgirls being engaged or withdrawing from school to marry older men. Such stories were frequently found in the popular media as well, including the role of teachers in trying to keep Maasai girls in school when they were getting married during puberty or early adolescence.

Another interesting change was noted by a father and school committee member: "There are so many leaders now—at all levels! Every area has someone in control." Along with this change, the trend toward individual/family ownership of land versus communal clan sharing of land was also noted—mainly by the fathers interviewed. Such subdivision of land was actually a visible change over the six trips the researcher made to Narok (between July 1992 and July 1996).

Both focus groups discussed the increase in the number of groups, particularly self-help and women's groups in their locations. Participants reported that other community services had increased in the past 10 to 15 years. They stated that there were now more businesses, larger markets, more organizations, more schools, and more churches.

## Farming

Most parents interviewed were in agreement that, although Maasai families continued to herd animals, there were many more farms and many more people cultivating. Also, the size of farms had grown: "There are more farms, and farms are bigger now." Parents often mentioned that, "We are still having problems with wild animals ruining our crops and kitchen gardens," but they were persistent in trying to protect gardens and to continue cultivation.

## Relevance of Preschool Education to Families Maintaining "Traditional" Lifestyles

In response to the question, "Is preschool education relevant to traditional families?" five out of six teachers interviewed answered "yes." In terms of why preschool was relevant, one teacher said, "It's good. Children won't develop or progress in education if they are at home until primary school." Another teacher appeared to understand the issue of cultural relevance better, as she responded, "Preschool prepares children for school, but it is still relevant to children's traditions, language, and home life!"

Several teachers felt that local traditions had not "grown" to include preschool education as being quite acceptable and desirable. For example, a teacher stated, "Life has changed and more children have now gone to nursery school. The elders, for the most part, now support the building of nursery schools and school attendance, in general." Finally, another teacher put it this way: "Nursery school provides an orientation to the formal learning done in school, and those lacking it will be perceived as 'dull' by primary school teachers." In other words, something that is perceived as positive preparation for success in primary school cannot be dismissed as "culturally irrelevant"—at least in the opinion of the (Maasai) teachers interviewed. When asked whether any parents had raised the issue of the cultural relevance of preschool, all said, "No parents have discussed this with us."

A related question was, "What activities have you used to support children's home culture?" Teachers most frequently responded, "Teaching traditional songs and stories and doing news-telling, which is similar to sharing information at home." Other preschool teachers who had a larger number of children (up to 40) reported that they played "home games" or used pretend play, such as "nursing a baby," making dolls, cooking, and so on to keep children involved and happy while at preschool. Another teacher said, "In free choice, children like cooking, modeling, and dramatic play—all these things remind them of home."

Another bridge between home and preschool was the feeding program—where one existed. In the feeding program observed, food was similar to what children would be fed at home. Also, teachers sometimes asked children to bring in food from home, and the snacks they carried in tins also were from home. A particularly powerful quote came from a teacher who said, "Parents' and teachers' love and care is similar—we try to be free with the children and encourage them to communicate—just like at home!"

## Contributions of Traditional Practices to Effective Child-rearing

All of the teachers interviewed felt that traditional child-rearing methods were, on the whole, effective. When asked why, the most common responses had to do with feeding practices. For example, "they're fed regularly," "feeding may be better than some of the other foods given to children now," and "they're breast-fed for a long time," were among the responses given.

Other responses related more to the positive socialization of young children when raised with traditional caregivers at home. As one teacher said, "It helps children grow quickly—by talking to children so that they may learn to talk." Another stated, "Children become social with others—they become free to one another when they are in a group and well cared for."

Teachers also mentioned some positive changes in child-rearing, including the much more frequent practice of immunizing children and taking them to the clinic or hospital both for preventive measures and when they were sick.


## FAMILY AND COMMUNITY INVOLVEMENT IN EARLY CARE AND EDUCATION

Parents provided everything when the preschool was built!

—Preschool teacher, Naisoya

The most frequent parental response to the question—"How are you involved in your child's early education and care?" was in reference to making or providing materials for the preschool and making toys for children to use at home. Second to this was the provision of materials, labor, and funds for building preschools. "We provided building materials and labor for building the preschool" was a common response, particularly from fathers and community elders.

The mothers' most frequent response was "helping with the feeding program," such as bringing food and doing the cooking. We were also told of a feeding program in which parents took turns cooking (with two mamas a day preparing the food). The program had not started up again, as the funding of the food was tied to an earlier drought response project of an NGO, but mothers wanted it to start and expressed their willingness to again volunteer their time to cook. Another related form of parent involvement was the provision of water for the preschool. Other parents who were interviewed, primarily fathers who also were members of the school committee, said that they provided leadership and led in fund-raising efforts. They also were involved in planning for new or expanded preschool buildings and hiring teachers.

Another category of responses to this question of involvement related to doing things at home that supported the child's successful preschool experience. These included: (1) enrolling the child in the preschool and sending him or her most days; (2) buying soap and bathing the child before sending him or her to school; (3) feeding the child well in the morning so that he or she was not hungry during the day (the morning preschool class); and (4) sending materials with the child for the teacher to use.

When asked about the importance of being involved in their children's early education and care, one father's response was, "We like it very much, because we come here and plan the future of our children!" Parents liked to "give guidance to the teacher" and "like very much to be involved in things which affect our children." They saw being involved in their children's early care and education as literally shaping the future of their family and community, and they considered it their duty to be involved.

Finally, parents were asked where they had received most of their information on child development and child-rearing. Some parents responded that they "observed as they grew up." Most parents said that they had learned from their parents, usually their "own mothers," and some said that they had learned from their neighbors. One mother replied, "I have learned on my own through determination!" Another mother agreed that she too had learned very much on her own. Other parents reported learning what they knew about child-rearing from TBAs (Traditional Birth Attendants), older sisters, and their grandmothers.

Turning to teachers' responses, the most frequently mentioned ways in which parents were involved in supporting preschool education were: (1) the provision of materials, both for building schools and making toys and learning materials, and (2) willing participation in parent meetings. Parents were described as being very willing to help, literally from the ground up, as this teacher conveys: "Parents came to clear the tree stumps and build the preschool—they brought timber and other building materials and even donated their labor." A teacher in another location stated, "Parents provided everything when the preschool was built—materials, labor, and even the land or compound was donated by parents!"

Parents also were described as "coming to meetings when called—especially when contacted by the primary school headmaster, school committee chairman, and/or the councillor. In terms of what topics were discussed at such meetings, examples included school fees, the need for improving the preschool or putting up a building, starting a feeding program, and the problem of low enrollment—particularly early in the new term or school year. Two teachers also stated that parents served on the preschool committee.

Regarding feeding programs, teachers reported that parents came to prepare food at one preschool with two at a time working in shifts. Mothers also brought water for cooking *uji* (millet porridge) and maize and beans to be prepared for the children.

Only two teachers stated, "In general we don't involve parents—we do things ourselves." Another stated, "We have little parent involvement or support, beyond sending their children to preschool." Both teachers were encouraged at the end of the interview to take a more active role in parental involvement, and they agreed that this would help mobilize their communities.

Eight of the questions asked in the children's interviews related directly or indirectly to this research question. Beginning with an account of their daily activities, particularly as they pertained to the caregiving of younger siblings, the most common task reported by children was to "stay with the small ones" while the mother cooked, sold in shops, went for water or firewood, or milked animals. Second was "play with the baby so she doesn't cry," which included making toys and finding small objects for the baby to play with.

Other ways children reported helping with the baby included singing to it, feeding it, and walking nursery children to school. Other tasks that related to children's personal and environmental hygiene included cleaning the compound and washing the baby's clothes. When playing with younger siblings, children reported that they made "small houses and used small tins to cook" and role-played other activities of daily life. (When asked if they liked to cook, the girls said yes and the boys said no.) We also observed the child-built houses, which were rather complex constructions, some large enough for small children to play inside. They were made from sticks and often constructed in the traditional Maasai manner, although not filled in with mud but left as open frameworks.

As in other districts, children reported that they taught younger siblings things that they had learned in school, including the alphabet and numbers. When asked in what languages they taught these young ones, they responded with Maasai and Kiswahili. Kiswahili was thought to be helpful when going to both nursery and primary school.

## Identifying and Treating Sick Children

When asked how to tell if the baby was sick, the children's most frequent response was that the child is unhappy and "cries a lot." Other symptoms were diarrhea and fever, or "the baby is hot." They also noted that when a baby was hungry, they tried to feed her to "keep her quiet," and they also noted that loss of appetite was a sign of a health problem. Finally, two children noted that they could "see that the baby's weak" and probably sick.

When asked what they did when the baby was sick, the most frequent response (as in other districts) was "take him to the mother and tell her he's sick." Others said they first "make him stop crying," and then they "take him to the mother." When left alone with the baby and the mother was not available, children reported that they gave the baby boiled (and cooled) water.

Next children were asked what parents do when the baby is sick. The most frequent response was "prepare traditional roots and herbs," and, if the baby gets worse or does not respond to traditional treatment, "Take the baby to the hospital." It should be noted that "hospital" also referred to the local clinic or dispensary.

## TYPICAL CHILD CARE ARRANGEMENTS FOR CHILDREN UNDER THREE

The most common child care arrangements for children under three involved family members—typically the grandmother or an older sister. As discussed earlier, children frequently were left with older mamas when the mother was away getting water or firewood. In such cases, the mother would typically feed the baby when she returned mid-morning—or she would leave supplementary food with the grandmother or other caregiver.

Often, too, children were cared for by their own mothers. As this mother stated, "I stay with the baby when I'm not too busy and sing lullabies, feed her, and teach her the names of things." Often mothers took young children with them to the *shamba* (similar to those in the rural/agricultural areas sampled). One mother described her routine as follows: "I put up a temporary shed where the baby can play and where I can nurse the baby and also play with him from time to time."

Fathers helped some of the younger mamas by holding the baby while the mother was busy. Older siblings, particularly sisters, also were quite involved in child care and in assisting their mothers in a number of ways, discussed in more detail in the following section that presents findings from the children's interviews.

Several other questions dealt with the youngest children's early health and care histories, beginning with the question, "Where is your youngest child during the day?" The response to this question was, "All under threes are at home with the mama, older sister, or grandmother." Very few under threes were reported to be in group care at a nursery school, although in the open-air nursery in particular there were many under threes, mostly on the backs of their older sisters.

In terms of where the youngest children at been born, eight mothers reported that all of their children had been born at home, and three (younger) mothers reported that their children were born in the hospital. An interesting discussion of the differences in home and hospital births ensued during one group interview, in which some mothers speculated that children who were not kept in the dark the first several days after birth (as they traditionally would be at home) but were under bright lights (as they were in the hospital) might have better vision and be less afraid of strangers from an early age.

The majority, but not all, of the mothers took their children for regular clinic visits. Although there were occasionally mobile clinics closer to home, most mothers reported that they had to go into the town of Narok for clinic services. Only one mother said that she did not believe in immunizing her children and had never been inside of a clinic.

In terms of their children's health, most parents reported that their children were "generally healthy" and that the most common illnesses were skin and eye diseases, malaria, diahrrea, and colds. All children were all taken to the hospital when seriously ill, and they also were often treated with traditional herbs when in the early stages of a common illness.

As previously discussed, most mothers reported breast-feeding their children for two to three years. Common weaning/supplement foods were cow's milk, rice, mashed bananas or potatoes, *ugali*, and mashed beans. Toileting was described as "children help themselves around—we usually show them a place away from the house." Several of the compounds visited did not appear to have a latrine.

When asked about any problems with services, many parents responded, "There are *no services* except for minimal extension services in this location!"

When asked, "What activities do you provide to make your youngest child(ren) happy?" the most common response was "give them materials to play with." This included making toys for children. The second most frequent response was feeding them, including breast-feeding. Other responses included: (1) making faces, tickling, and smiling; (2) singing lullabies and cuddling; (3) playing with the child; (4) talking to the child; and (5) "taking them out to see the light." In terms of the specific toys and materials parents used with their youngest children, a few reported that they bought toys, while others made balls, dolls, shakers, and so on.

When asked what they liked most about being a parent, similar to the other districts sampled, the most common responses of the mothers were "getting children," "giving birth" (in reference to motherhood, not merely the act of childbirth), and "getting my name from my children" (e.g., "Mama____"). For fathers, "being a father" and "getting recognition and respect as a father" were the most common responses.

Persons who did not have children were not fully part of the Maasai community. As one mother put it, "Being barren is a great burden!" A young father said, "If I don't have a family, nobody will recognize me as a part of the community!" On motherhood, another parent said, "It is a *must* that you become a mother! You're initiated and there is no way to escape it."

In response to the question, "What is the hardest thing about being a parent?" the most frequent response was, once again, the failure to provide for children's basic needs—particularly food and medical care. "When the children don't get enough to eat," "When the child gets sick," and "When you cannot afford school uniforms, medical treatment, or clothing" were also some of the responses. One mother pointed out that, "Since women have no say over property in the home—such as food and animals—we can't clothe children the way we would wish."

One parent summed up the burden of trying to meet the daily needs of her children in the following way: "It is tight work—you can do it from daylight to nighttime, and you can work hard all your life!"

In response to the question, "How are most under threes being cared for?" the consensus of all of the teachers interviewed was "at home—mainly with mothers and grandmothers." Siblings also were mentioned as providing care—particularly older sisters. One teacher put it this way: "At home, children are just around—feeding is done and they're cared for by mothers, fathers, siblings, and grannies—all these people look after the youngest children!" When cared for by grandmothers, most children are in small groups in the compound of the older mama, and mothers bring food for them to eat while the mother is away doing other necessary work.

## Factors Related to Preschool Participation

When asked what factors were most related to which families sent their children to nursery school and which did not, teachers agreed that lifestyle and gender, respectively, were the biggest factors. Five teachers stated different versions of the following quote. "Traditional families may keep 1, 2 or more children home for herding," and "There are still negative attitudes toward education, and that's *the* big factor!" Several teachers also mentioned that more boys than girls attend both preschool and primary, with their numbers decreasing in each grade of primary, particularly once they enter upper primary. "Girls are used for child care, starting from when they are in nursery school themselves." The issue of investing differentially in boys' education, as they would continue to be in the family even after marriage, also was raised.

Other factors were more economic, including the inability of some families to pay for fees, uniforms, or other school-related expenses. For example, one teacher said, "Children are kept home when the parents don't pay the fees." Another teacher said, "Income is the most significant factor." Her colleague disagreed, saying, "No, fees are very low here." Other teachers felt that the combination of gender and income was the major factor in preschool and other educational participation. This view is captured well in the following quote: "One boy is affordable to educate—while girls look after the house and babies."

The other factors some teachers felt were related to preschool participation were the number of children and the birth order. For the latter, teachers agreed that parents were more likely to invest in the education of first-born children, particularly their sons.

Regarding perceptions of (and goals for) preschool, participants felt that preschool "prepares children for formal education and for life." They also felt that a good preschool experience "provides opportunities for children to develop socially (e.g., sharing) and emotionally (e.g., meeting others, adjusting, controlling emotions, and being able to take turns). In terms of nutrition, preschool could "provide a balanced diet when there is a good feeding program."

Needs identified by the two Narok focus groups included the need to continue parent awareness and education on specific aspects of child development and healthy child-rearing, particularly personal hygiene. A health officer related the following story to illustrate this point.

> One mother was told by nurses at our clinic that her baby would not be attended to next time unless she bathed the baby before bringing her to the clinic. The following month, I saw the same mother stop at the river and dip her baby in the cold water to wash her before coming to the clinic! The water was extremely cold and the baby could have gotten sick—in the name of personal hygiene.

This story illustrates the complexities of parental education in the area of health and child development.

Other examples of the need for increased parental education were that "some children are malnourished, and for such children, the mothers need education on how to provide a balanced diet." Generally, training needs for parents were personal and environmental hygiene, nutrition, and child development, including the importance of preschool education. Services also were seen as being sometimes distant from where families lived. More mobile clinics and community-based services were strongly advocated by both focus groups. For example, one person suggested, "We need to initiate community-based growth monitoring and promotion within reach—for example, right in the preschools." In summary, another participant stated, "We need community motivators to create awareness and mobilization on parent education." Such "community motivators" were seen as other parents from the community who were trained and empowered to share their information, similar to the Bamako Initiative, which is not yet practiced in this district.

## Children's Memories of Preschool

All of the children interviewed had attended preschool. When asked what they remembered most about it, the frequent response was "learning the ABCs," followed by "some play" and "seeing the pictures on the walls and the charts."

They also were asked to compare preschool and primary school, to which two boys said there was "not much difference." Others said that there was "more caning in upper primary," and "when you're late, you're not caned in preschool!" Another boy said, "Lessons were easier to follow in nursery school than lessons are now." Other children thought the physical environment of their primary school was better than their preschool had been. As one girl put it, "These rooms are well built, warm, have good seats, and many charts!" At another setting, children felt the preschool was a better place to learn.

All of the children interviewed thought that children should go to nursery school, because it "will help prepare them for primary school." They also felt that primary school would be harder had they not gone to nursery school first.

## Children's Aspirations

The following were the future career aspirations of the children interviewed in the Narok District: teacher, doctor, policeman, farmer, driver, and nurse. Regarding of their predictions about what their younger brothers and sisters would be in the future, several children wanted both to be teachers. Others wanted their brother to be a driver, doctor, or policeman. When asked what he wanted his sister to be someday, one boy answered, "married."

The other projective questions related to children's own future families. In general, girls wanted fewer children than boys, with the number of children ranging from ages two to seven. Children also tended to want more girls than boys, with the exception of one boy, who wanted to have "four boys and three girls."

## Parental Aspirations for Children

When asked about their "hopes and dreams" for their children's future, most Maasai parents interpreted the question in reference to specific job roles. They also spoke of the need to be well educated for the future, such as the ability to get a good job. The most frequently mentioned profession to which they wanted their children to aspire was "teacher." This was followed by doctor, Minister or M.P. (member of Parliament), and president.

Other potential future careers included a DC/DO (District Commissioner or District Officer), a clerk/secretary, a councillor, and a chief. Parents also expressed the desire for their children—particularly their sons—to obtain wealth to pass on to them, as well as to be leaders in society. The leadership aspiration is clear from the "careers of choice" voiced by these Maasai parents.

When asked how their children's lives would be different from their lives, the most frequent response was, "Due to their education, they will have jobs and different lifestyles." Other responses included, "They may not live on or depend on the land," in reference to anticipated land shortages in the future, and, "They will have better houses," and "They will have cars."

Finally, in response to the question of whether (and how) good early care and education might help children in the future, parents tended to agree that "children who attend preschool will do better in Standard 1," thus in their future education and careers.

The related questions of what the most important factors are in planning for child care and development were frequently responded to with "play materials and toys." This was followed by "warm rooms" and "play equipment" (for both indoors and outdoors), and by "pictures and wall charts." Parents also felt that it was important to give their children food, clothing, and good care, and to cuddle and talk to the youngest ones.

## Teachers' Experience With and Attitudes Toward Under Threes

Of the teachers interviewed, half had taught under threes, and all were willing to teach them. One teacher reported that she used to have under threes, but "no longer—just when we had our feeding program." When asked why they would like to teach under threes, responses included, "The work of the nursery class is meant for small children," "They'd be more free and less afraid," and "They're innocent, and don't have as many disturbances—they're more obedient."

In terms of the question "What is most important in planning for under threes?" teachers' responses included the following: (1) not expecting them to do "everything" (e.g., write well at first); (2) having plenty of materials; and (3) having a feeding program. Preschool was viewed as a morning-only experience for children and not as full-day child care, thus no mention of napping was made.

In response to the related question of what was most important to consider when planning for under threes, teachers responded as follows: (1) poems and stories; (2) music and songs; (3) some counting and letter activities; and (4) outdoor activities, such as jumping and body exercises. They also felt that "easier activities and play materials are appropriate—for example, arranging objects in different ways and modeling."

In response to the question "Where are the needs of under threes best met?" teachers tended to feel that the youngest children were better catered to at home, but the older ones (ages two and up) should be cared for at least part of the day in a preschool. "Children should start out at home, then, as they're a bit older, go to nursery school. At first they're too young for nursery school."

Regarding the advantages of home care, one teacher said, "In order to be fed often, parents give better care than teachers can show them—especially when we have many children." Advantages of nursery school care included, "There can be better care," "They obey the teacher better than their parents," "Children are happy with others, versus isolated in their homes," and "Preschools can offer feeding programs."

Finally, in terms of other needs that teachers had identified for under threes in their locations, the most common response was, "Dispensary services and mobile clinics are needed—much closer to homes." As one teacher stated, "Some children have never been to the clinic—having a mobile clinic here would really help." A related need was for growth monitoring and promotion, which teachers were willing to obtain training in and to provide at the preschool.

Teachers again raised the issue of the need for children to have a more balanced diet and for parents to receive nutrition education. Some teachers wanted to improve the nutrition of younger children with kitchen gardens at the preschools, although some previous attempts had met with destruction from animals. One teacher wanted help in "getting rid of tree stumps and then planting a garden for the school."

Other needs of under threes were the desire for improved sanitation, including the digging of pit latrines. Hygiene was another related issue, as expressed by one teacher. "Families need better access to soap and water—there's such a problem of dirty clothes and lack of personal hygiene for the children."

Finally, teachers expressed the need for children to have more early childhood care and education-"type" activities. In other words, whether cared for by traditional caregivers in their home compounds or in the "baby class" of a nursery school, appropriate activities, stimulation, and materials were needed to enhance the children's growth and development.

Focus group participants agreed with both parents and teachers, that the majority of children under age three were cared for at home, mostly by mothers with the assistance of grandmothers and older sisters. In terms of the setting that was seen to provide the best care for under threes, both groups felt that—assuming the home caregivers were available—the home was the best environment.

## Lack of Intersectoral Collaborations to Benefit Children and Families

Parents' response to the question, "What groups, if any, are working with your community to improve things for children and families?" generally resulted in them saying, "Nobody is working with us," or "Only extension agents—and then only rarely." One setting that is also a project site for a NACECE/DICECE project mentioned this, as a Ministry of Education project, but only after a bit of "prompting." Finally, two sponsoring organizations, the Salvation Army and Child Care International, were named as supporting specific projects (e.g., water schemes and preschools).

Three of the questions in the teachers' interview addressed the issues of sponsorship, collaboration, and better integration of services directed toward children and their families. In reply to the question, "Is your preschool working with other agencies?" two teachers said "No" and "None." All other teachers named at least one agency, including the Salvation Army, Child Care International, the Pentecostal Church of God, and World Vision. Some indicated that their sponsor had been more active in the past, while others were enthusiastic about the level of support provided.

Governmental agencies working with the preschool sampled included the Narok Town Council and County Council (both of which employed head teachers at several preschools), the Ministry of Education, through the Narok DICECE, and—to a limited degree—the Ministry of Health (in reference to growth-monitoring activities and mobile clinics). Most teachers felt that these collaborations were effective but limited by the lack of contact and infrequent visits and so on of resource personnel to their school.

## "Model Programs" for Under Threes and Families

Finally, the last question in the teacher interview asked preschool teachers to design a "model" program for under threes in their community. Teachers in Narok emphasized parent/family education, including providing advice on children's health (e.g., the importance of regular clinic visits) and providing good and frequent feedings. For example, one teacher said, "Parents need to be encouraged to have good feeding habits and may need advice on nutrition." Teachers also felt that families needed greater awareness about personal and environmental hygiene, such as "asking parents to send children to preschool clean."

There was strong support for intersectoral collaboration, not surprisingly, in the professionals focus group (which represented a cross section of different agencies). As one person stated, "Intersectoral collaboration with government departments, NGOs, and communities is essential for development and for improving the lives of people!" Such collaboration can be both formal and informal. For example, "When a family is faced with a serious problem, the father may go to the elders or a neighbor for advice or assistance and may, in turn, be referred to an outside service." Other ways communities were seen as collaborating, at a "grassroots level," included building home-based preschools and starting feeding programs for children.

The health sector was viewed as engaging in such collaborations, including its successful collaboration with the Narok DICECE. Some health facilities also were sponsored by NGOs or churches. Plans for strengthened collaboration included training more preschool teachers in growth monitoring and other primary health practices.

When asked which specific agencies were collaborating with different participants or their agencies, the following were named: Child Care International, local authorities who pay some of the preschool teachers (e.g., the town and county councils), the British government (which had recently agreed to build a boarding primary school in one of the sampled locations), the Salvation Army, Kenya Wildlife Services (which was erecting an electric fence around a school compound to protect the kitchen garden from wild animals at night), the Ministry of Education (through the Narok DICECE), the Ministry of Health (through the hospital and some mobile clinics), and the District Development Committee (DDC).

## EFFECTIVE WAYS OF ENSURING THAT AVAILABLE RESOURCES BENEFIT THE POOREST FAMILIES

When probed on the issue of effective targeting of limited funds intended to benefit poor families, the first response of the professionals focus group was "capacity building. We need to train personnel, including local parents, so that they can provide the required services." Others agreed and also thought that local committees should be formed "with clear terms of services and roles to manage the project, its funds, and to plan *Harambees* to raise additional funds locally."

The notion of building in sustainability was underscored in the following quote: "Cost-sharing must be introduced for all those to benefit, and this can be a cost-sharing of labor, as well as money. For example, taking turns to cook, making toys and other learning materials, providing labor, and also providing some payment can all be viable." Another participant put it in even stronger terms. "Never give free grants or services. You can offer subsidy, but never free! If you give grants, the sellers will hike the prices and people become more dependent."

Their final words of advice regarding any new initiative to benefit children and families were, "Always involve the community in decision-making, planning, and implementation of any project," and "Let communities identify their own needs. Never impose your projects or ideas on them—they will not follow through if it wasn't their idea." "Many projects fail because the donor, and even the local leaders, think they know what the communities need—and don't ask!" An example of a cattle dip project was given. The community was not consulted, and the cattle dip is now an abandoned project. Finally, the groups were probed about the importance of going through the DDC when introducing new initiatives. "For any new project, the DDC must be informed—that is the district clearinghouse for all projects."

## Summary

Among the many themes that can be gleaned from this chapter is that the critical role of the older mamas or grandmothers is one of the most pervasive. Grandmothers in this study were enacting an array of traditional roles in the care of young children—particularly those under age three. While younger women gathered water and wood, maintained the compound, went to market, or performed other communal work, grandmothers cared for the youngest children. Their daily activities included supervising and playing with the children, singing lullabies and feeding the children, and treating childhood illnesses, usually with traditional herbs and other remedies. This vital role of the grandmothers, however, was not viewed as a permanent situation. Even in some of the more isolated, traditional Maasai settings in the Narok District, patterns of land tenure and "development" were affecting clans and families in many often contradictory ways. Grazing corridors for animals were being cut off by increasing agricultural production in the district, and private versus communal land ownership patterns were eroding the communal way of life of the Maasai. With the increasing subdivision of larger plots of land and private ownership of more land, one of the very real and pressing family questions was, "With whom do the elders, particularly grandmothers, live?" Given the many child-rearing roles that the older mamas play, this was a real concern to many of the participants interviewed.

Regarding more formal early childhood education and related services, another impact of social change was that more children were enrolled in local preschools and primary schools. This was generally viewed in positive ways, although problems with having buildings for all of the preschools and paying the teachers' salary were noted, as was the lack of feeding programs in most preschools. Access to maternal and child health services was uneven, with many transportation challenges. A mother wanting to take a sick child to the clinic, for example, had to wait until the next market day, when *matatu*s (mini-vans) would be coming within walking distance of their home. Some areas, notably Oloototo, were served by church- or NGO-sponsored clinics and school compounds. In two of the communities in our sample, the school compound also had a windmill and a well, and women used donkeys or walked to gather water there each day.

Other lifestyle changes included more cultivation and semi-permanent housing. Mothers, grandmothers, and younger children typically stayed in the same area for many years, with men and older boys taking animals for grazing in times of drought. Several parents and teachers reported that the diet had expanded from relying exclusively on animals (e.g., meat, milk, and blood) to including vegetables (particularly "*sukima*" [kale] and pumpkins), raised in kitchen gardens or purchased at market in the town of Narok, as well as *ugali* (a staple food in Kenya, made from corn flour). Many people interviewed described problems with trying to grow kitchen gardens, particularly from wild animals. Parents also commented on the great changes in how children were dressed. Children under three were now clothed, and older children were typically dressed in "European" clothing such as school uniforms.

Health problems, including malnutrition, respiratory illnesses, and eye diseases (often associated with the hygiene issues of sharing living space with animals and a lack of water), were concerns of parents and grandparents. As discussed in the focus groups comprised of local leaders, feeding programs, more consistent growth monitoring, and other health services for children needed to be made more accessible to families. There also were concerns that, although Narok is in many ways a wealthy district (in terms of the value of cattle and some of the agricultural production in the highlands), these resources were not being invested sufficiently in children and families. Creative partnerships and expanded services for children under three were identified as high priorities.

A final note relates to the significant role of male elders in the Maasai community. Many interviewed in our study were serving on school committees for preschools and primary schools or were responsible for funding the building of new preschools. One example, briefly discussed in this chapter, was a councillor who built a small preschool on his own land and found a teacher to staff it. Elders voiced a strong commitment to providing necessary services for their children and maintaining the proud traditions of the Maasai. They were also involved in the socialization of children and youth, and they had strong feelings and beliefs about the importance of children for the future survival of their culture and traditions. In many ways, the Maasai and, as will be evident in the following chapter, the Samburu communities were most actively involved in providing traditional communal care and socialization of children under age three. Although persistent, and far less assimilated into dominant Kenyan culture, these traditions often were described as threatened or diminished as a result of social and economic change and pressures on families to adopt less communal and more nuclear family patterns and roles.

# Chapter 4

# Samburu District:
# It Takes a Clan to Raise a Child

In order to put up a preschool, the parents come together and donate animals to
raise money, find lumber and stones, and provide labor.

—Samburu father

When young children are at home the mother or grandmother oversees their total
welfare, including feeding, washing, and allowing them to play and explore.
Children are nursed for at least 2 years and sometimes longer.

—Samburu mother

## DESCRIPTION OF THE SAMBURU DISTRICT

The Samburu District lies within the semi-arid region of Kenya. It suffers
sporadic droughts that result in serious famines. The district also has very rough
terrain and lacks roads and other transportation infrastructure, making it difficult
for outside services, including health, education, and communication, to reach many
of the communities. This district has been made a priority for the enhancement of
early childhood care and education services due to the adverse effects of these conditions on the community—particularly mothers and children (NACECE, 1993).

The Samburu District is one of 14 districts in the Rift Valley Province, and it
has an area of 20,800 square kilometers. It is bordered by the Baringo and Turkana

Fig. 4.1    Samburu Parents with DICEC Trainer and NACECE Driver

districts to the west and northwest, the Marsabit District to the northeast, the Isiolo District to the east, and the Laikipia District to the south. It is administratively divided into four divisions—Lorroki, Baragoi, Wamba, and Waso. The district's headquarters is at Maralal in the Lorroki division. Visits were made by the visiting researcher to Lorroki, Baragoi, and Wamba, with most of the data collected in the Lorroki division, near Kisima (south of the town of Maralal).

The district lies in the northern interface between the highlands and low-lands. To the west is the Suguta Valley, running from south to north and bordered by fault escarpments on both sides. The floor of this valley experiences very high temperatures (34 to 40 degrees centigrade) and often is flooded during occasional heavy rains. East of the Suguta Valley, the district has high plateaus made of lava. Kirisia hills form the highest part of the plateau, rising to over 2,000 meters (with breathtaking views). The plateau is heavily eroded, therefore, it is unproductive. It is covered with poor (desert-like) vegetation. The higher altitude areas are covered by indigenous forests that are gazetted and grazing controlled. During periods of drought, however, livestock graze in these areas. Some serious fires also have affected the forests, particularly in Lorroki, where cultivation (particularly of wheat) is encroaching on these forests. The plateaus and plains have poor soil and are mainly covered with poor Savannah types of vegetation dominated by acacia trees and tufted grass.

The water resources in the district are poor, given the low and unreliable rainfall. The Ewaso River that forms the boundary between the Samburu and Laikipia districts (in the south) is the only permanent one. The northern tip of the district touches Lake Turkana, a fresh-water lake, but it has not been tapped for improving the water supply in the district.

The land potential in the Samburu district has been classified into three categories: (1) high potential land, with an annual rainfall of over 850mm. This area covers about 140,000 hectares and is mainly in the Lorroki division. Just over one-third of the land is cultivated, mainly with maize and wheat; (2) medium potential land, which receives rainfall between 610mm and 850mm. This area covers parts of the hills in Lorroki, Baragoi, and Wamba; and (3) low potential land, which is estimated at 1.6 million hectares and covers the rest of Lorroki, Baragoi, and Wamba. The annual average amount of rainfall in this large area is less than 610mm. All other land covers 329,000 hectares. This land includes gazetted forests, the Samburu game reserve, and other land set aside for military purposes.

## Land Use

In terms of land use, pastoralism is the most prominent land use in the district, occupying more than 90% of the Samburu people. The Lorroki division is suitable for dairy, beef cattle, sheep, and goats, in addition to crop production. The Baragoi division (where several DICECE projects have been focused) is best suited for goats and camels, since it is drier, rockier, and has poorer vegetation. A few parts of the division have pastures suitable for cattle. The Wamba and Waso divisions are suitable for goats and also have a moderate number of cattle.

The Samburu, like the Maasai, Turkana, and Somalis, base their livelihood on livestock. Their lifestyle is highly influenced by and closely related to livestock herding. During the last decade, their livestock has decreased considerably due to cattle rustlers "ngoroko," diseases, degradation of the environment, and frequent droughts. This has affected people's lifestyles and has eroded their purchasing power and articipation in development activities. Cattle provide most of the meat and milk for the people, which still form the most important part of the diet, even where foodstuff such as maize is gaining prominence. Livestock is used to pay for bride wealth, and it forms part of most ceremonies, such as circumcision, marriage, and fertility. Livestock is the main source of money among the Samburu. A number of livestock improvement projects are sponsored by NGOs, and camel farming is being encouraged in the areas where the study took place. Other related projects include training Samburu youth as paravets to identify, prevent, and treat animal diseases in their communities.

Mixed farming is mainly concentrated in the Lorroki division. At the time of data collection, about 5,000 hectares were under wheat, maize, beans, Irish potato, and vegetable cultivation. Most arable farming started with the Turkana, who had taken refuge around Baragoi, South Horr, and Maralal. Samburu women's groups also have been at the forefront in initiating cultivation. Wheat farming, however (in the highlands north of Maralal), is mainly carried out by outsiders who have leased land from the local people. Often these wheat farmers are not interested in land conservation and leave the land degraded—a persistent neocolonial legacy.

Tourism is another source of income for the district and county council. It is concentrated in the 225-square-kilometer Samburu game reserve in the Wamba and Waso divisions. There also is a small game sanctuary near the town of Maralal (and the Maralal Safari Lodge). Over 90% of the revenue of the county council comes from tourism. Similar to the role of the Maasai Mara in the Narok District, local people sell crafts (beadwork and leather) to tourists and supply livestock for food to the hotels. Tourism also has had negative influences in the erosion of traditional values, particularly in major towns such as Wamba and Maralal.

## Population Profile

The Samburu District was the least densely populated district visited during this study. The estimated population of the district in 1993 was 108,484, an increase from the 1979 population of only 76,908. The population distribution reflects the land potential, rainfall, and economic activities, with shifts in population in times of drought and other nomadic patterns persisting. A striking feature of the population that is particularly relevant to this study is that 61% of the population is below age 19. Most are of school-going age, however, the participation rate in primary education (in 1991) was only 54%.

About 5.5% of the population of the Samburu District is composed of older people (ages 55 and up). This, combined with the high percentage of children and youth, would typically imply a "dependency population" of over 66%. In the Samburu District, much like in Narok, however, most of the children and young people are involved in the economic activity of looking after livestock. This theme will be revisited throughout this chapter, as the tensions between formal education and traditional contributions to the economic viability of the extended family/clan were among the themes of our findings. The relevance of formal education also is an obvious issue facing those who promote greater participation in formal and informal education among indigenous people who are maintaining cultural, centuries-old traditions. This complex issue led, in part, to an innovative project which I had an opportunity to be peripherally part of—the Out-of-School Youth Education Project, sponsored by the NACECE and piloted in Baragoi. Participants in this late afternoon/evening nonformal education project were herd boys and out-of-school girls, and the setting was the local preschool.

As previously noted, population density in this district is low, and the average size of households in the last formal census (1979) was 4.6 members. This is misleading, however, as Samburu families do not typically live in nuclear family configurations. Since Samburu people are pastoralists, the notable migration within the district is rural to rural in the form of nomadism. For example, the district officer in Baragoi told us about losing track of a chief because he led his people to better grazing and, in doing so, he crossed the Somalia national border and was no longer in Kenya. The intradistrict migration is temporary, though frequent, due to dry spells when better grazing and water sources are needed. The majority of Samburu limit their migration to within a clan's collectively owned land. In many cases, in more recent times, families do not move outside of a 10 kilometer radius. In Lorroki, where data for this study were collected, a growing number of people are erecting semi-permanent and permanent buildings. The animal herders, mainly young men, will move the livestock many miles away from home or from clan land, as needed, in times of severe drought.

Finally, there is little migration of people from outside of the district intending to settle in the district, since the land is communally owned by the Samburu people. In the towns are businesspeople, civil servants, and other workers from outside of the district. Some development projects have a distinctively international flavor to them, including the building of houses by Kenyan troops that recently returned from peacekeeping missions in Bosnia and Namibia, in which areas in small towns were called names such as "Little Bosnia." The relative lack of outside influence is one of the reasons often cited for the Samburu people's maintenance of cultural traditions and way of life.

In terms of ethnic groups residing in the Samburu District, in 1993, it was estimated that 75% of the population were Samburu (who inhabit over 90% of the district), 17% were Turkana, and 8% were others (including Kikuyu, Ameru, Rendille, Somali, Dorobo, etc.). The urban centers are small compared to other districts, but they have experienced a rapid growth rate (of 5%) since 1984, due primarily to drought and insecurity. The growth of the town of Maralal also can be attributed to the greater availability of services in the district headquarters.

## Personal Images from the Samburu District

On a more personal level, the Samburu District represented one of the most distant places and realities from Nairobi (and from the daily lives of the researchers) in the study. The visiting researcher had first come to the Samburu District in 1992 and had visited Archer's Post and Wamba, where she met a colleague, George, who later was to become the primary local collaborator in this study. In October 1997, all three national collaborators visited Maralal and Baragoi to conduct workshops for teachers involved with an out-of-school youth initiative and to conduct focus group interviews related to a community mobilization project for children and families. The drive to Samburu from Nairobi goes through Gilgil and Nyahururu (Thompson's Falls) near Laikipia, and the turnoff to the Maralal road came to be known by the visiting researcher as the "place the road ends." Maralal is a frontier town that has experienced some growth in trade and tourism, but it is served by only one bus a day and is isolated in many ways. Samburu *Morans* (warriors) and some Turkana men and women walk the streets, and open markets sell bright red *shukas* (the cloth worn by Samburu men) and household goods. Butcheries, *dukas* (shops or kiosks), and small hotels line the few dusty dirt roads. Several Catholic mission projects, including a large boarding school, are found on the periphery of the town. Interviews for this study were conducted in a region 10 kilometers south of the town Maralal.

When we first came to Maralal in 1994, we traveled a second day from Maralal to Baragoi, where the roads were extremely rocky and were made worse by the beginning of the rainy season with flooding and much mud. Before leaving the Nairobi area, we had stopped to buy vegetables and had also brought several jerry cans of water. When we reached Baragoi, it was evident why we had done so. The out-of-school training was held in an isolated preschool surrounded by a Samburu settlement, with only a nearly dry bore hole for water. Since this area was drought prone (semi-arid), most foodstuffs other than meat needed to be purchased or was in short supply. All of the DICECE and NACECE staff on the trip helped in food preparation for the large evening meal each day, which was amusing, especially since the Samburu men usually would not be caught preparing vegetables or performing other cooking tasks.

The setting was stark, but beautiful. Feathery acacia trees lined the horizons on every side, and huge white clouds drifted across a wide African expanse of blue sky. Goats wandered in and out of the school compound, and the cooing of the laughing dove could be heard, especially in the morning. At night, since there was no electricity where we stayed, the stars of the Southern Hemisphere were breathtaking, and the total darkness of night was peaceful. On a couple of evenings we visited the homes of local families, and the windowless structures revealing a central burning fire created a surreal envrionment in which fellowship could be felt, even when a shared language could not be spoken between us. On the last evening of the workshop, a Samburu girls choir performed against the backdrop of a spectacular sunset.

Teachers had travelled long distances to this training, mostly on foot. Life here was a stark contrast to the urban and peri-urban settings close to Nairobi. Before data collection for this study officially began, the visiting researcher returned to the Samburu District in early January with her daughter and other friends. The view from the high bluffs of the Great Rift Valley was breathtaking, and the title of the book "Craters on the Moon" came to mind. The visiting researcher returned alone, with a NACECE driver, to begin data collection in Samburu during late January 1995 and stayed in a small local hotel in the town of Maralal (the district headquarters). On the first day of data collection, we happened on a traditional wedding. Later that night, one of the local collaborators showed us a videotape of the highlights of the traditional three-day wedding of her niece. This was just one of many unexpected cultural experiences which the visiting researcher enjoyed in the Samburu District. Thus while official (that is, government and donor) portraits of the district typically paint a very marginal picture, it was one of the most strikingly beautiful places visited during this study.

## SAMBURU SAMPLE

A total of 12 parents and grandparents were interviewed, including 6 mothers, 3 fathers, 2 grandmothers, and 1 grandfather. The age range of first-born children was 3 to 30 years, with a mean age of 17.5 (note that two families had a 30-year-old first born and a 2-to 5-year-old last born). Last borns ranged from age 2 to 5, with a mean age of 3.2.

In terms of roles in their communities, three parents (fathers) were members of the school or preschool committee, three women were members of a Women's Development Committee or other women's self-help groups, one father was a local elder who conducted *Harambee*s for school fees and so on, and one father was the chairman of the local KANU (Kenya African National Union, the ruling party) branch.

Work roles included five housewives, also involved in animal tending, and one mother, who was a charcoal burner and firewood seller. Two fathers were livestock farmers, and one mother and one father described themselves as *"shamba* farmers," growing mostly vegetables. Note that everyone interviewed kept animals.

Six of the parents and grandparents interviewed had lived their entire life in their present community, two had lived there for 45 to 50 years, one had lived there for 32 years, one 22 years, and one 12 years. Thus to describe this sample as pastoralist, implying a more nomadic lifestyle, is somewhat problematic. Although men in both the Narok and Samburu districts may leave home to take animals for better grazing during drought and so on, the communities tend to be permanent, even if the housing is still largely "semi-permanent." In terms of education, 11 parents and grandparents had no formal education, and one father had on-the-job training as a civil servant and soldier.

Eight preschool teachers were interviewed. The average number of teachers at preschools was two, although some schools that previously had two teachers only had one at the start of the new term, when interviews were conducted. In terms of teachers' education, one had completed Form 2, six had attained the KCPE (Kenya Certificate of Primary Education), and one had completed Standard 7. Seven of the teachers were DICECE trained, with three completing their training with the Samburu DICECE and four with the Baringo DICECE. One teacher was untrained. No other types of training were mentioned by these teachers.

Regarding years in their current teaching position, one teacher had taught for 15, another for 8, two for 5, one for 4, one for 3, and two for 2. In terms of previous teaching experience, one had taught for 10 years, one for 7, and one for 4. The others had taught only in their present preschool.

Teachers ranged in age from 20 to 33 years, with a mean age of 26.3 years. Five teachers were married, and three were single. Three of the teachers were single mothers. The age range of teachers' first borns was 3 to 12 years, with a mean age of 7.6 years. The range of last borns was 6 months to 4.5 years, with a mean age of 3.6 years.

In terms of who paid their salary, five reported that they were paid by parents, including one where the Christian Children's Fund also provided an allowance to supplement the salary paid by parents. Three teachers were paid by the Samburu County Council. When asked about other income sources, six reported "none," and two said "husband." At least two teachers had small *shamba*s and also were involved in cultivation.

Turning to the primary children sampled, 12 children, 6 boys and 6 girls, were interviewed. Their ages ranged from 8 to 13 years, although some were uncertain of their ages. Their mean age was 9.5 years. Two children were in Standard 2, six were in Standard 3, two were in Standard 4, one was in Standard 5, and one was in Standard 7. This reflects, in part, the wide variation in age in primary school classes and frequency of late school entry. The following sections summarize interview responses based on the research questions guiding the study.

## Portrait: A Mother in Lchorolelerai

*In the morning, I wake up, wash the youngest children, feed the children and then the children help separate the kids from the goats. The youngest child may accompany me to fetch water and firewood, and learn how to do these things, or may be left with older mamas or whoever is there! At times I stay with the children—there are some special occasions within the home. I like to see the children playing with hoops, stones, and playing games. . . . I observe and visit them doing these things when I'm at home. When I'm not at home there are many other mamas to watch the young ones.*

## MAJOR CHALLENGES FACING FAMILIES WITH YOUNG CHILDREN

The most frequently mentioned problem facing families with children under age three was scarcity of food, due to poverty and frequent droughts. The second most frequent problem, as described by parents and grandparents, was the increased incidence of childhood diseases, even though most children are now immunized. This was sometimes mentioned in connection with the lack of clean water and the shared use of water sources (bore holes, etc.) by animals and people. Since animals are still the major livelihood and source of identity and pride among the Samburu, the increase in animal diseases also was seen as a major problem for families. In addition, the distance to the nearest clinic was cited as a problem, with "the long distances to health centers making it difficult for most people to benefit." As discussed in the section on health changes in this chapter, the lack of mobile clinics was cited as a concern—particularly for families with young children.

As discussed in other chapters, the high cost of living, particularly education for the children, was also mentioned. "Some parents cannot afford to pay the school fees and buy uniforms for their children," or at least not for all of their children. Another related problem was the lack of money to build schools and health clinics, and the need for both to be closer to where children lived. This was particularly an issue of safety from wild animals, as children had to walk long distances to school or preschool.

## Ways Families Are Coping

The most frequent response to how families were coping with these challenges to child-rearing was to "do contract labor." As one father put it, "In order to provide food, families do contract labor which earns them little money." However little that money, the growth of a cash economy meant that more ways of earning money needed to be found. Some parents also engaged in small businesses or microenterprise activities, including charcoal burning and selling and hawking foodstuff. In order to get school fees or pay for uniforms, parents reported that they sold animals or worked in contract labor. Others turned to growing more food for their family, although they had problems with wild animals when they tried to grow a kitchen garden. When there was no milk, several mothers reported that they "cooked *uji* without milk and gave it to the baby."

In terms of community mobilization for children, a community elder reported that "in order to build a school for our children, the parents join together and contribute finances (animals) and labor to put up the school." In some cases, parents also joined together to provide finances and labor to supply water to the community.

Finally, several parents reported that they had been fortunate in getting NGO or church sponsorship for their children's school fees, uniforms, and textbooks, from organizations such as Christian Children's Fund, the Catholic Church, and other donors. Some of these organizations also assist communities in constructing schools and clinics. In the case of diseases, parents also reported that some organizations provided medicines, for example, deworming tablets were provided free to children in several communities.

## Good Things the Community Is Doing for Children

The most frequent response to this question was, "People are doing their best to provide adequate food for their children—particularly milk." The second most frequent response related to parents' growing awareness of the importance of education. Responses included, "Parents are taking their children to school," and "The community is putting up preschools for children to learn." When asked why preschool was important, a typical response was, "When children go to school this makes them happy." In addition to the educational role of preschool, parents were initiating feeding programs in some of the preschools and were engaging in growth monitoring and promotion activities encouraged by the preschool teacher or community health worker.

Other health and nutrition examples included families who were growing kitchen gardens, and most mothers reported that they were taking their children to clinics. Parents also were attempting to practice better hygiene and were providing clothing for their children. Children were typically breast-fed for three years, giving them a good nutritional start in life and contributing to birth spacing. Finally, the availability of mothers and older siblings meant that children under age three were well cared for in general and were seldom neglected.

## Relevance of Preschool to Samburu Communities

"Children are happy in preschools—that is all we care about!" This response reflected the views of many Samburu parents and grandparents. The activities that parents felt were most culturally relevant (worded as "pleased them and helped children know about their culture") encompassed telling stories, learning songs, and playing—particularly role-playing traditional activities of the clan and community, including gender-specific roles.

## Parents' Contributions to Preschools

Samburu parents typically generated a fairly long list of ways in which they supported their children's preschool. The most frequent ways had to do with the feeding programs, with activities such as paying the cook to prepare food for the children, providing food and cooking utensils, and fetching water and firewood. Financial contributions included raising funds and contributing money to erect a community preschool, paying the teacher's salary, and contributing money for the preschool teacher to purchase materials such as chalk and exercise books. A variation of this was to contribute goats that were later sold with the money used to build the preschool. Several parents said that they supported the preschool by purchasing their child's uniform and by paying the fees.

Another way in which parents supported preschools was through their time, including serving on the school committee. Many parents also reported gathering materials such as building materials (e.g., collecting stones, water, timber) for putting up the preschool and for making toys and learning materials. Several reported that they had participated in materials making, which they did at home at the request of the teacher and then sent them to the preschool with the children. Finally, a few parents said that they contributed by constructing up the teacher's house.

When asked why parents make these many different types of contributions to their children's preschool, one response said "to ensure sustainability." As one father and school committee member put it, "If the government or donor pulls out, we know that the services provided in preschool will continue." Several parents expressed their concern about feeding programs that had been cut when NGOs or other outside groups no longer funded them. As a community, they were committed to doing all they could to continue feeding programs in the preschools, as they had observed the positive outcomes for their children. The other response was that, "By contributing, we feel that our children will get good services in the preschool."

## Typical Care Arrangements for Under Threes

The most frequent response to this question was that under threes were at home with the mother, who "oversees their total welfare, including feeding, washing, changing, and allowing them to play and explore." The importance of play was emphasized by several mothers, who said that the activities that made their children happy were singing, playing, telling stories, playing with toys, modeling, and playing games. Several parents reported making play materials and toys for their youngest children, as did some of the older siblings.

All of the children in the sampled communities in the Samburu District were cared for within the compound and played in groups, doing role-plays, making constructions, and other performing traditional activities together. This group child-rearing, encouraging strong age cohorts, is well documented in the literature (e.g., Fratkin, 1975; Kilbride & Kilbride, 1990; Spencer, 1973). Age and gender cohorts play a strong role in both Maasai and Samburu socialization of children and youth and form the basis of the elderhood system, described in the Samburu District Socio-Cultural Profile (1986) as follows:

> This informal education is given in the homestead or out in the grazing grounds, for the traditional classroom is wide and open. . . . Most of the games played by the children are more or less a rehearsal for the performance of activities which are the serious business of all members of the Samburu community. The boys hunt butterflies as imaginary lions, since they hunt lions when they in turn become warriors. They play with small wooden spears and shields made of dried cowdung. The girls make houses, practise sewing and clean imaginary calabashes. Whatever else a Samburu might learn cannot easily compare with his knowlege of livestock. The child is taught to recognize the cattle brands and ear marks of the clan and those of other clans. He or she must know all the cattle, sheep and goats. (pp. 41–42)

After the initial period when boys and girls are exposed to more or less the same instruction and experiences, the stage of teaching children to perform the duties relevant to their gender follows. After this period of gender-segregated instruction, initiation into adulthood comes at age 10 to 15 for girls and 15 to 20 for boys. It is still common for Samburu girls to be married as young as age 10 to 12. Female circumcision is still widely practiced and must be done before many traditional Samburu and Maasai girls can be married. Unlike men, Samburu women do not belong to age sets but to two age grades, girlhood and womanhood. Samburu girls' education is typically strict and in the hands of the mothers. An age set is comprised of all men who have been circumcised in youth during a specified period of time, generally every 12 to 14 years. The three principal age grades among Samburu men are boyhood, moranhood (Lmurani or warriorhood), and elderhood.

When asked what the best place was for under threes, however, the consensus among parents was that the preschool would be preferred to at-home care, because "children learn to live with others" and have custodial care from the teacher. As in Narok, several two-and three-year-olds came to preschool with their older siblings. Teachers did not support this as strongly as did the parents, as they did not always feel well equipped to meet the needs of under threes in an academically oriented preschool setting. Yet parents stated that, "Preschool is best, because children learn many things and are happy there," in contrast to Narok, where Maasai families felt that the grandmothers and younger mothers were the best caregivers of under threes and were pleased to send older children to preschool but did not feel that the pre-school was necessarily the most appropriate setting for the youngest children.

## Joys and Difficulties of Being a Parent

> The feeling that one has children is good and satisfying.
>
> —Mother

When asked what they liked most about being a parent, responses were similar to other settings visited in the study. The most typical responses were being called "mother" and "father," emphasizing the importance of parenthood to one's identity and contribution to the clan. The birth of a child seals the legitimacy and stability of a marriage. As Spencer (1965, as cited in Institute of African Studies, 1986) observed:

> The Samburu say . . . children alone can find a man and his wife together . . . a wife without a child has one foot inside the settlement and one outside . . . she is likely to run away from her husband. (p. 46)

Parents in our study also expressed pleasure at being able to educate their children and to provide them with food. Also similar to other settings and districts, Samburu parents saw children as a source of assistance to them. As one mother put it, "We like knowing that you will have someone to help you with chores, including herding, carrying water, and later, making money." Another expressed pride in "knowing that my children will grow up and be able to support their families."

Many parents spoke of their aspirations for their children. As one father put it, "I like knowing that my child may grow up to be an important person!" The most frequent response to the question regarding parental aspirations related to daughters getting married. "We want to see girls married," to which some added, "to get more animals." This relates to the bride price in animals, and increasingly in cash and other gifts, when a daughter is married. As previously mentioned, we encountered a traditional Samburu wedding during Phase 1 data collection, which led to a local collaborator showing the visiting researcher videotapes of a traditional three-day wedding of one of her relatives and explaining the many rituals and customs still practiced. Like the couple we met, many more professional young Samburu couples are married both in a church and in the traditional way, at home. The public presentation of gifts, particularly animals, is widely practiced, and families are literally made richer when a daughter is married.

Parents also emphasized that children should develop skills to become "self reliant." This was considered particularly important for sons. Typical responses were, "Boys should be self-reliant and support themselves," and "Boys should be hardworking." Others anticipated an increasing wage-based economy and a decline in raising animals as the primary source of wealth for Samburu families, stating, "I want my children to get good jobs."

Still other responses included wanting children "to grow up and be married and have families," and "for my children to be able to support me at my old age." Several mothers and fathers stated that they wanted their "children to learn well" so that they could be successful and self-reliant in the future. One parent appeared to sum up the feelings of many others when she said, "I want my children to have a better life than mine!"

Turning to the question regarding the hardest thing about being a parent, the most frequent response was "not having enough food for my children." Several parents expressed this in more general terms, such as, "It is sad when you cannot provide for the needs of children." More specific examples included "not having enough money to pay fees for my child—particularly in secondary school." This related to the fact that preschool and primary schools were generally quite physically and financially accessible to the Samburu families in our study. In fact, the interviews typically took place at either the local preschool or the combined preschool and primary school compound. Secondary schools, however, were usually further from these rural, pastoralist communities and were often boarding schools that were quite expensive for many families, unless they had outside sponsorship for their children. Similar to Narok, several primary schools in the Samburu district were boarding schools, in part, due to the dangers (from wild animals) children encountered while walking long distances to school.

Several parents stated that the hardest thing about being a parent was seeing their child sick or suffering. Others, particularly fathers, commented that it is hardest to be a parent when "one has far too many" to care for. Thus children were highly desirable and treasured. The identity of being a parent was prized, as it was in virtually all of the communities sampled. The greatest frustrations for parents, not surprisingly, came when they could not meet their child(ren)'s needs. It was also interesting to note the age range of children for most mothers interviewed. Although we did not think it was culturally appropriate to ask mothers how many children they had, we did ask them the age or birth year of their first-born and last-born children. It was not unusual for first-born children to be in their 20s and last-born children to be under age three. (We did not learn whether the Samburu culture has a similar fertility rite to the Maasai, such as the one observed in June 1996, but the value placed on having children and the tragedy of being barren came out clearly through the parent and grandparent interviews in both communities/districts.)

# HOW LIFE HAS CHANGED

The following sections address different aspects of change that Samburu families experienced in the past 10 to 15 years.

## Food

The most frequently mentioned change in food by Samburu participants related to the greater variety of weaning foods currently in use. Examples included mashed potatoes, *uji*, and milk. The second change was related to diet and nutrition, since there were fewer animals now, thus less meat and milk in the diet, including milk to give young children. As one father put it, "We have fewer animals, hence the scarcity of food."

In general, food was considered very expensive, and some of the new foods that were bought from shops were not considered nutritious. A few families had tried to grow small kitchen gardens, but the wild animals typically destroyed their crops. Thus they either got food from animals, which was the traditional diet, or they purchased food from shops or in markets in small towns.

## Housing

The most frequently mentioned change in housing was in the size of homes. Although still built in the traditional Samburu style (See Illustration . . . ), several parents said that houses were bigger now, and also better. A greater number of building materials was now available, so, "We do not rely only on thatch and mud for building." In the small towns the sampled areas bordered, more homes were built of corrugated metal with wood frames. Other changes in housing included "more windows" and the construction of latrines. Latrines were seldom found in many of the sampled areas, however, even where families had settled in an area and built permanent or "semi-permanent" housing. The lack of latrines was likely related to toilet-digging cultural taboos as much as it was related to the more "settled" contemporary lifestyle of the Samburu.

## Cost of Living

Parents and teachers concurred that the cost of living had increased and that the "high cost of living makes it difficult for parents to provide for their children." When parents stated that, "People have less money than before," this often meant that they had fewer animals (cattle and goats), as animals are their wealth. This theme echoed the interviews in the Narok District, where land subdivision, droughts, and financial hardships had converged and led to a loss of animals. Also, when economic times were hard, animals were sold. Another loss of animals came through cattle raids. One of the local Samburu collaborators, in fact, lost 73 head of cattle during a raid on his family's farm at the beginning of data collection.

## Health and Nutrition

Although many parents felt that children had poorer health, especially childhood diseases, including diarrhea, several commented that many more children were taken to hospitals or clinics for growth monitoring and promotion (GMP), immunizations, and when sick. The availability of clinics and health outreach activities had, not surprisingly, a high correlation with child health. Poor health was attributed to the relative scarcity of food, particularly due to the semi-arid and drought-ridden setting and to the use of less nutritious foods.

On the positive side, more mothers attend antenatal classes and give birth in hospitals, and experienced traditional birth attendants (TBAs) were present in most communities. One father commented that, "There are no serious health problems because the health clinic is close by." A nutritionist, sponsored by a church mission project, visited families once a week to advise them on a balanced diet, prevention of diseases, making oral rehydration solution, and other important health and nutrition information. Such intensive health outreach services were not reported, however, in other sublocations sampled in the Samburu District. Parents in other communities, in fact, stated that a major problem was the "lack of mobile health clinics which could reach more people wherever they are." Given the nature of the semi-permanent, pastoralist Samburu lifestyle, the need for a mobile, community-based approach to primary health and nutrition education was considered critical by many of the stakeholders interviewed.

## Education

As in the Narok District, most parents and grandparents interviewed stated that there were more schools now and that, "More parents are taking their children to school." Formal, Western education was still a new phenomenon to many Samburu families, but they saw its growth as inevitable and, in most cases, they supported this change. Parents stated that Samburu parents and communities were "more positive about education, hence they take their children to school." As in every location sampled in the study, parents commented on the high—and rising—cost of education, including the expense of books, uniform, and fees. Several were sending only some of their children to school for this reason, while the others were kept home to tend to animals and to assist in the care of younger siblings.

## Family Size and Child-rearing

In discussing family size, an initial response often made reference to the decreasing number of wives that most Samburu men now have. "Life is too expensive to support as many wives and children" was a frequent response among adults and children alike. Declining birthrates were attributed to the rising cost of living. As one mother put it, "Children's needs are many and they all are expensive—including education, clothing, food, and health." Others attributed this to the introduction of family planning information and an increase in birth control practices.

Turning to changes in child-rearing, breast-feeding is widely practiced and considered to help in family planning/child spacing. Breast-feeding also was considered to "keep children healthy," and Samburu children were breast-fed in most cases for three years. This was comparable to Maasai weaning practices and a longer time period than found in any of the other ethnic groups we interviewed.

In terms of toileting, children "helped themselves around [outside] the house," and parents or grandmothers disposed of it. We did not see latrines in the traditional Samburu housing areas, although they were more common in towns such as Maralal or among those working in government positions or with greater education.

## Social Structures

In terms of changes in social structures in the Samburu communities and clans sampled, the first response often was that more children were attending school, thus fewer children were available to tend to the livestock. Another change was that some families engaged in crop farming, unlike before. The fact that cultivation was still considered quite new to the Samburu was underscored by the following anecdote, shared by one of the local collaborators: Her father was Samburu and her mother was Kikuyu. When her mother planted maize, other Samburu women laughed at her and gave her a name that translated to "woman who scratches in the dirt." Her brother was one of the first Samburu to complete a high school and later a college education, and he held a high position in the Ministry of Education. We visited his *shamba*, which had an interesting combination of cultivation (of maize and wheat) and livestock.

In terms of changes in clothing, as with the Maasai sample, Samburu parents stated that young children wore clothing now, and they often wore "European"-style clothing, whereas in the past, young children were not clothed. Children who were sent to school typically had at least parts of the uniform. Preschool children were less likely to wear a uniform, but this varied across the spectrum of families and programs we visited.

## Community Mobilization and Collaboration

Intersectoral collaboration is very important!

—Preschool teacher

Given that it is a semi-arid district that has experienced food shortages, drought, loss of animals, and other significant problems, the Samburu District also has been a "target" district for government and nongovernmental assistance projects of various sorts. In addition, there is a strong Catholic mission presence in many parts of the district, including the towns of Maralal (where a large boarding school, a project for out-of-school girls, a literacy program, and rural outreach projects are based) and Baragoi (where preschool and primary schools and many secondary school sponsorships are provided by the church). Also, several NGOs, including the Christian Children's Fund and Oxfam, have or have had projects in the areas sampled. Thus parents are very aware of many of the "donor-recipient" dynamics of such projects. Yet when asked about intersectoral collaboration, their examples were primarily community self-help ones, as summarized below.

The most frequent examples of collaboration were between parents and teachers, including, "Teachers work with parents to develop materials," and "Parents provide learning and play materials to their children." After meeting the local collaborators and learning more about the role of the DICECE staff, some parents commented that, "Teachers need to work with DICECE to improve services for children." Other examples of parental contributions to early education, as earlier discussed, include building preschools, including fund-raising (*Harambee*), the purchase of building materials, and the provision of labor. Parents also were involved in feeding programs, such as fetching water and firewood and hiring a cook (e.g., an older man at the Baragoi preschool).

## PRESCHOOL TEACHER PERSPECTIVES

Teachers expressed views that differed from parents in a number of ways, but they agreed about the ways in which life had changed and had become even more challenging for many of the families of the children they taught. As described at the beginning of the chapter, preschool teachers were typically from the local community and had little formal education beyond primary school. They were hired by the parents, unless the preschool was church sponsored, and their pay was often unpredictable for this reason. They felt that parents often used the preschool for custodial care and struggled to pay the fees and provide sufficient food for their young children. They also reflected an attitude of collaboration with parents, however, and felt that parent involvement was critical to the success of early care and education in their communities. The following section provides more specific summaries of teachers' responses and includes their recommendations for enhancing care and education—particularly for children under age three.

## Problems Facing Children and Potential Solutions

The most frequently mentioned problem, as perceived by preschool teachers, was the malnutrition and undernutrition. Teachers described the lack of food that faced many families, who were unable to send food to school with their child or contribute food to a feeding program. Drought, poverty, loss of animals, and other problems previously discussed were cited as reasons for this food shortage. Several teachers stated that, "Poverty is the biggest problem facing Samburu families—all the other problems go back to that one." They also described health problems, some of which were related to a lack of water or clean water and poor environmental and personal hygiene. Some teachers felt that parents were unable to provide proper care for their children and used the preschool mainly for custodial care.

In terms of potential solutions to these problems, teachers said that they talked with parents about nutrition and encouraged them to "give children more food." Some teachers felt that more support from organizations such as the Christian Children's Fund (CCF) was needed and stated that, "Money from CCF comes only once a year and is so little compared to the great need of our families." Other teachers said that they had talked to parents about the "proper age to send children to preschool." In other words, parents were anxious to send children to school and had, in some teachers' view, been sending them too young (under age three). At one preschool, both teachers simply stated, "We have not tried" [to work with parents to find solutions].

When asked for their perspective on how parents in these circumstances were coping, the most frequent response was, "They get relief aid and food such as maize." Other responses included, "They move closer to water sources," and "Children are fed at school" (when they cannot be fed well at home). One teacher stated, "Parents sometimes collect food from the school—maybe we feed the whole family." Other teachers stated that parents worked to get money or supplies for their children's preschool. When probed about whether parents utilized them as a resource for information about child care and stimulation, particularly for younger children at home, most teachers said that they had not, or that "only a few" parents had done so.

## Effects on Children

The most obvious effect on children of the problems facing families was that, "Children do not learn well when they are hungry." As other teachers put it, "Children who are hungry look tired and do not concentrate well," and "Children are less healthy when they don't get enough to eat." Finally, one teacher commented on the fact that children's growth was stunted and that there could be longer-term damage as a result of poor nutrition in early childhood.

## Relevance of Preschool to Traditional Samburu Families

Teachers were divided in their opinions about the relevance of preschool education to traditional Samburu families, with the majority feeling that it was important and welcomed by families. Those who thought preschool was culturally relevant stated that, "It reflects the child's home," and "It has many things that they know from home, and the role-plays are similar to what they do in their families." Teachers who felt that it was not relevant gave fewer reasons, often simply stating that, "It is necessary now, but not really relevant to their traditional way of life."

When asked about specific activities to support home culture, the most frequent responses were "stories, poems, and rhymes," "role-plays of family activities," and " traditional songs." Teachers also mentioned the importance of including things brought from home in the classroom environment, learning about animals and their care, playing traditional games, and modeling or other environmental activities that they might also do at home with older siblings or peers.

Reversing the question a bit, when asked whether (and how) traditional systems of care contribute to effective child-rearing, the majority of teachers felt that they did. Examples included extended breast-feeding and food taboos for pregnant and nursing mothers. In general, "care of children is very good," was the response. They also felt that children were watched and treated "safely," and that even young children were provided with some "general knowledge" that was important and relevant to daily life. The teacher who felt that traditional systems of care were not effective again cited problems with food and the potential neglect of some children in her community.

## Parental Contributions and Involvement

Similar to parent responses, and likely reflecting the impact of the DICECE training and workshops for teachers, the most frequently mentioned contribution by parents was "materials making." The second was "parents participating in putting up the school," including bringing building materials and providing their labor. Several responses related to the feeding program, such as fetching water and firewood for cooking, hiring a cook, or having mothers take turns cooking. In one setting, parents had fenced the school, making it safer for children (protecting it from wild animals), and in another, they had planted trees. Several teachers mentioned that an important contribution of parents was paying their fees and sending their child to preschool.

Regarding involvement in the activities of the preschool itself, examples included telling stories to the preschool children, participating in cooking demonstrations (facilitated by the DICECE and local nutritionist), and, as previously mentioned, making learning materials and toys for children. Parents served on the school committee in every preschool we visited, and we often were welcomed by members of the preschool committee (parents and elders), several of whom participated in the small group interviews. Teachers also stated that parents were involved in health clinics, such as taking their children for immunizations and growth monitoring.

We also asked teachers about their efforts to involve parents, and responses offered great contrasts, ranging from, "I have done little to involve parents, as I live far from the school" and "Parents are not willing to attend meetings," to "Parents are very involved through the school committee and in supporting the feeding program." In terms of strategies for involving parents and communicating with them, the following were mentioned: "communicating through the chief's announcements," "participating in religious events which both teachers and parents address," "parents mobilize other parents by calling them for meetings," and "going through the Headmaster of the primary school." These parental involvement strategies were common in many other settings as well and demonstrate a range of ways in which the community is being mobilized for early education and care in the Samburu District. Going through both the chief and the primary school headmaster were among the most typical strategies used for the "village to raise the child" in collaboration with the preschool program and teachers. In one setting, teachers described a women's group that was making home visits and "teaching mamas how to cook and make clothes." This self-help initiative was started by field extension workers. This was one of the few initiatives in the Samburu District that related directly, through its nutrition emphasis, to empowering mothers in the care and provision for under threes.

Turning to problems or challenges in parental involvement, the most frequent response was, "Parents do not involve the teacher or seek advice" regarding child-rearing or other issues affecting their family. When asked why this was the case, one teacher said, "Parents do not take the teacher seriously." The second most frequent response related to the lack of funds and inability of parents to pay. Responses included, "The fees are not always paid," and "The school is closed at times, when the teacher has not been paid." In two schools, preschool teachers reported that few parents were willing or able to serve on the school committee ("Parents are not involved in the school committee"). A variation of this was, "Parents are not willing to participate and attend meetings." In one school, however, the teacher stated, "Parent involvement is not much of a problem, the school committee is active, and the parents are involved."

When asked about parent-teacher conferences or parent meetings, six teachers reported that they held parent conferences, and two said that they did not. When asked about the focus of such parent meetings, responses were divided between funding the program and children's learning and well-being. In the former category, responses included, "discuss the teacher's salary," "discuss construction of a new preschool," and "discuss payment of fees." More child-centered responses included, "discuss children's learning," "parents want to know the problems of their children," and "discuss what is required for preschool enrollment, in terms of fees, materials, and uniform." One teacher said that they discussed the age required to attend nursery school.

Finally, when asked about whether parents sent their younger children (under threes) to preschool, one response was, "Yes, particularly those closest to the preschool." Three teachers said that they had begun to send children at age two, and two teachers said that parents generally waited until age two and a half to send them to preschool. Two other teachers stated that parents had not sent under threes to preschool, and that none had asked about doing so.

## Why Parents Enroll Children in Preschool

Another discussion with teachers focused on the reasons parents send their children to preschool, which included talking about why some families do not participate in the local preschool program. The most frequently stated reason for sending children to preschool was "to learn and get an education," followed by "to prepare for primary school," and "to get food." Other reasons included socialization and custodial services or care. Teachers generally felt that communities and parents were supportive of preschool and saw a need to send children.

When asked why some families did not send their children to preschool, the most frequent response related to the still-persistent nomadic patterns and lifestyle of the Samburu: "The moving of families from place to place is the greatest reason they do not send children." This theme echoed informal (pilot) interviews conducted in 1992 in the Wamba (Archers Post) location of the Samburu District, in which we were shown "ghost preschools"—good structures with paid teachers that were very underenrolled due to drought and many families leaving the area for better grazing of animals in another location. We were told that some preschools stand empty now and that "mobile preschool teachers," who travel with families when they move, were being explored. Other barriers to preschool enrollment were economic ones. Either families could not afford the fees, or they needed to "keep one or two children home to look after animals." When asked which children were typically left at home, teachers agreed that they usually were girls.

## PRESCHOOL TEACHERS' EXPERIENCES WITH UNDER THREES

Five of the teachers interviewed stated that they had worked with under threes, but only two described this as taking place in the preschool. When asked what they liked about working with younger children, responses included, "They have mercy," "They learn quickly," "They are free, not shy," and "They are fun to work with." Three teachers stated that they did not want to work with under threes in the preschool setting. Reasons included, "It is a big problem," "They disturb others," and "They cry and sleep a lot." Four teachers mentioned crying as a problem, and two teachers said that, "There is no morning snack or feeding program in our preschool, and they are too hungry at school." Other concerns about serving under threes included, "They are shy," "They are fearful," "They cannot stay awake long," "They are not toilet trained and cannot control themselves," and "There is a lack of proper-sized furniture, and they are uncomfortable sitting in the desks." It is important to keep in mind the typical preschool environment—long rows of bench seats with attached desks or rows/clusters of tables and chairs, chalk and talk instruction much of the morning, and some time in free play or use of "learning centers" in the room. Thus teachers were quite concerned that preschool was not (developmentally) appropriate for children under three.

When asked what resources they would need to better serve under threes, responses included "a morning snack," "an additional teacher," "assistance from parents at the center," and "appropriate materials and furniture, including napping facilities." Two teachers stated again that they would not like to work with under threes, "not the very young ones," because it was "too difficult when mixed with older ones," and "they are too cumbersome."

When asked about "model services for families of under threes," the most common responses related to nutrition. "A feeding program and varied diet are important." Other responses included, "appropriate clothing for children," "clinic services, including growth monitoring and immunizations," "a safer environment for young children," "materials for children to play with," and "good physical facilities" for an under-three care program. When probed about how to achieve some of these goals, teachers felt that "awareness meetings to give parents advice on good diet, care, and provision of play materials at home" would be an important first step.

Regarding what would be important in planning new initiatives or programs for under threes, the most frequent reply was "appropriate activities." This was followed by "adequate materials." Other aspects mentioned were "oral learning and singing" "regular and frequent food," "supervision—enough adults to work with them," and "appropriate care which meets their needs." When asked to contrast this to priorities for older prechool children (ages 3 to 5), responses related entirely to pre-academic or school-readiness concerns: "reading," "enough books," "writing," "numbers," and "materials for teaching."

## Teacher Perceptions of Under Three Care

Similar to the parents' responses to the same question, preschool teachers' most frequent response was, "Most under threes are at home with older mamas, their own mothers, or siblings." In general, teachers felt that parents "tried to give proper feeding," with three teachers stating that, "Children have little to eat due to lack of money and food." Concerns about undernutrition were again expressed. "Parents with little livestock have difficulty in feeding their children." Two teachers commented that a positive aspect of the lives of under threes at present was that, "Children are allowed to play." One teacher stated that, "Some under threes do go to preschool." Another comment was that the youngest wife and her children typically receive more attention from the husband/father, while other wives and children may be neglected. Another issue was clothing. "Poverty afffected clothing, and many under threes are improperly clothed." One teacher felt that parents had more children than they could support, and that religion (e.g., Catholicism) was encouraging large families, which led to parents being "unable to feed their children."

When asked about where the needs of under threes were best met, teachers were divided in their opinions, with five feeling that preschool was the best setting and three feeling that the home was best. Reasons given in support of the preschool included, "Children can learn," "It is more safe," "Children are better understood," and "They can socialize." Reasons for caring for under threes at home included, "They need the closeness with their family," "Young children cannot cope well in preschools," "Children learn many things at home," and "They can be fed better and more often." Another very real concern was the distance many children traveled to the preschool. "Children are scattered in homes—the walk is too far and too dangerous!"

Finally, when asked about other specific needs identified for young children in their community, preschool teachers listed the following: "more sponsors," "better care for children," "a shorter morning—there is too long a waiting period for lunch for the youngest children," "appropriate materials," and "more parent involvement."

## INTERSECTORAL COLLABORATION AND PLANNING

The preschool teacher interview also included questions designed to help answer the seventh research question, which related to the degree and effectiveness of intersectoral collaboration in the community. When asked whether their preschool was working with other agencies, most teachers described the support their program was receiving from a church or community-based group. One program received "food from the Catholic health worker," while another said "A (Catholic) sister helps with income generating activities such as selling bead work" that benefited families, and still another stated that an "agricultural extension worker gives demonstrations on gardening." The Christian Children's Fund had erected a building, sponsored children for preschool, and paid an allowance to the teacher, and missionaries had helped with the mobile clinic. Finally, a women's self-help group gave some financial assistance to one preschool, and another received food from the Ministry of Education.

When asked whether such collaboration was effective, most teachers agreed that it was. "Parents have become more positive to the preschool and to the mobile clinics," and "Sponsorship has led to retention of children in school." In terms of how collaboration could be enhanced, teachers' responses included the suggestion that, "Mobile clinics could come more often," "Mamas should be more committed to the use of services," and "Sisters should help the women's groups more." In other words, these were good things that could be made better with greater or more sustained support—common themes of capacity building at the sub-location and community levels.

## CHILDREN'S INTERVIEWS

### Portrait of a 10-Year-Old Girl in Loltulelei

*I got up, milked the goats and helped the small goats suckle, went to bathe, then to school—coming with my two younger brothers, both are in nursery school here. After school we went home, brought the kids (goats) home and put them in their pen. Then I fetched water and washed my school clothes, played with the younger children, and ate supper. After supper, I washed the utensils, went to play, and then went to sleep.*

### Portrait of a 9-Year-Old Boy in Naiborkeju

*I got up early and let out the cows; then I came to wash, take tea, and get ready for school. After school, I put the calves in a pen, helped the baby goats suckle, separated the kids from the mother goats, closed the pen, and ate supper. Then I played, danced, and sang and went to sleep.*

### Sibling Care Responsibilities

As in other districts, 12 children (ages 8 to 12) with preschool siblings, particularly under threes, were interviewed at their primary school. Unfortunately, we did not interview any out-of-school children (e.g., young animal herders) during our brief time in the district. We began with a discussion of the various roles that children played in their home and clan—specifically their involvement in the care of their youngest siblings. Eight of the children, including all of the girls and two of the boys, said they helped their parents look after the youngest ones. In terms of the forms that this care took, five children said they stayed with younger children "a long time when the mother goes to fetch firewood and water," and one of them added that she "sometimes stay with the child all day until evening." Two girls said that they bring their younger brothers to nursery school and that they bath them before taking them to school.

When asked what activities they performed while caring for younger siblings, all 12 children said that they gave their sister or brother "materials or a toy" that they had made, including "animals and other things modelled in clay," "a toy car made with wires," and "rattles." Similarly, all children reported that they sang to younger siblings and taught them songs, or told them stories in the evening. (Note that storytelling in the Samburu and Maasai cultures appeared to be an evening activity, whereas singing was used to help children take a nap or to calm them.) When we probed children about telling stories and riddles only at night, they responded that it was taboo to do so during the day, as the cows could eat the maize.

Other ways in which children helped with their younger siblings included assisting in keeping the child clean (including after toileting), playing with the child, and helping to prepare food by boiling milk. Eight Samburu children reported that they taught their younger siblings words in both the mother tongue (Kisamburu) and in Kiswahili or English. When asked why, one child said (through translation) "to acquire knowledge and communicate with someone not knowing Kisamburu." Eight children said that they showed the younger ones how to take care of animals. Two girls reported that they prepared *uji* (porridge) and fed it to younger siblings, and three children said that they made a "play house" for the younger ones. Two boys said that they made "a stick like a warrior's spear" for their little brothers and also made bows and arrows for them.

When asked who cares for their youngest siblings when they are not available, such as when they attend school, three children said that they could leave a young one "with any parent" or "carry the child with them." Two children said that they "use a neighbor boy or older brother who's not in school" to care for younger siblings while they are in school. Other responses were that "an old mama" (grandmother) and "the mother" cared for the baby while they were away.

## Caring for Sick Children

Next we asked children how they could tell when a child was sick. Ten children said, "The child looks dull and doesn't play," and the child "doesn't eat properly" or "lacks an appetite." Nine children said that a sick child was "sleepy" and that the child "had a fever" or "felt hot." Four children stated that a sick child "coughs," and four stated that a child was sick when she had "diarrhea and vomiting."

In response to the question about what they did when a child was sick, 10 children said "inform the mother or the parents." Four children said that they "took care of the baby until the mama comes," two children said that they "looked for herbs to prepare traditional medicine" for a sick child, and two stated that they went to the "shop (chemist) to buy some drugs" for a younger sibling when the parents were not available. When asked what their parents did when a younger sibling was sick, four stated that they took the child to a clinic or hospital, and two said that they "used herbs" and "slaughtered a goat for the sick child to take soup or meat." When asked whether their parents take younger siblings to a clinic for growth monitoring and immunizations, eight children reported that they did, including "for weighing and sometimes to get food." Four stated that their parents did not take children to the clinic. (Samburu colleagues clarified that when children referred to a "hospital," it was likely to mean a clinic or a dispensary, and that a "doctor" was often any man in a clinic and any woman was a "Sister" or a senior nurse.)

When asked how they comforted a crying child, 10 children stated that they "give the child milk or food," nine stated that they "bounced or rocked" the baby, eight said that they carried the child and "sang lullabies," and seven said that they took the baby "to the mother to nurse." In terms of gender roles in play, several children described songs that only girls or only boys sang. Four children said that brothers and sisters did not typically play together. Children also said that boys usually tended the animals, while girls helped more with household chores and child care.

## Children's Nursery School Experiences

It's good for small children to go!

—Primary student

Of the 12 primary school children interviewed, 10 had attended nursery school and 2 had not. When asked what they remembered most about nursery school, five children said "learning the alphabet" and "scribbling on the ground" (free writing in the sand), and four said they remembered counting and numbers. Two children recalled modelling and singing. When asked to compare preschool to primary school, responses included, "In primary school we read and write in books; in preschool, we had no books, pens, or pencils—we scribbled in the dirt," and "In preschool, we didn't have to study so many things." As one child put it, "You learn more in primary, and in nursery school you learn very little." Another said, "In preschool, you can't read, and in primary, you can!" When probed about the importance of preschool, one child put it this way: "In preschool, you start to learn how to write— which is important for Standard 1!"

All children felt that it was good for them to go to school, and that all children should attend nursery school. When asked why preschool was important, children stated, "After preschool, they go to standard one and if they learn this will help them to someday be employed," and "Children will acquire knowledge to help continue learning so they can go on to get a good education." One child said simply, "It's good for small children to go!"

When children were asked, "What is the best place for children under three?" 11 stated that nursery school was best. The one girl who said "home" best put it this way: "It's better for such young ones to be at home." In terms of why nursery school was better than home, responses were similar to those reported above: "Children will learn better in primary school," "They'll be together and learn," and "They can learn language and do well." Another interesting reason was, "Preschool's a good place—when it's hot they can have a shaded place . . . the class can provide shade—outside it's too dusty!" Other children felt that they were safer in nursery school, and were cleaner. "Children can get seats, and outside, children always sit on the ground."

In terms of children's aspirations for future careers for themselves and their siblings, nine stated that they wanted to be a teacher, two (girls) said that they wanted to be nurses, and one boy said that he wanted to be "a senior officer in the army." When asked what their siblings might be when they grew up, six children said that their sister would be a teacher, and two said that their sister would be a nurse. Three children said that their brother would be a teacher, two said a soldier, one said "an education officer," one said "a driver," and one said "a priest."

Turning to their future family, several children said that they did not know how many children they would like to have someday. Two said they wanted three to four children, and one said two to three children. In terms of wives or co-wives, four girls said that they wanted one co-wife, and two wanted to be the only wife. Three of the boys said that they wanted only one wife (to be able to afford to support her and a smaller number of children), and one boy said he wanted four wives. One of the boys who stated that he wanted only one wife said, "I want one wife—my father has four, and there are many children to take care of!"

## SUMMARY

Similar to the Narok District, the persistence of traditional care was evident in the extended family settings we visited. Both grandmothers and mothers were viewed as being the most appropriate caregivers for children under three, with value placed on a nursery school education for older children. Since all preschool teachers we interviewed were Samburu, the cultural continuity from home to school was not a major issue. In fact, both parents and children saw preschool activities as reinforcing Samburu traditions, songs, and lifestyle. The role of the nursery school in supplementing children's food and health needs also was valued, although few programs were providing feeding programs at the time of our visits.

The areas we visited were isolated, starkly beautiful, and vulnerable to drought and poor grazing conditions for animals. Camels were seen in increasing numbers, and some families reported that older sons and fathers had taken animals, particularly cattle, to find better grazing. Similar to some of the Maasai communities that we visited in the Narok District, which could be described as semi-permanent and engaging in agriculture (e.g, maize and wheat farming), a number of the Samburu parents and grandparents that we interviewed had lived their entire lives in their present community. In contrast to a number of wealthier Maasai who owned large wheat farms in the highlands of the Narok District, in the Samburu District, the wheat farming was still mostly in the hands of ex-patriots or wealthier non-Samburu Kenyan farmers (e.g., Kikuyu or Ameru). One exception to this was a large farm that we visited, which was owned by a Samburu elder who had employed a number of Samburu women to process beans. The Samburu could easily be described as "persistently pastoralist," maintaining many of the traditions of their past.

In terms of changes affecting child-rearing and early education, the Samburu families we interviewed exhibited an interesting combination of collective self-reliance and reliance upon various, mostly Christian, donor organizations in the area. The combination of frequent droughts, lack of access to water, and a related scarcity of food were frequently named as problems facing families. Although most children were now being immunized, there was still a high incidence of childhood diseases and chronic undernutrition. The long distances families needed to travel for basic health care services were also a challenge. The preschools we visited were typically attached to or near a local primary school, were community or church sponsored, and served a variety of functions in the community (e.g., feeding children and being involved in primary health promotion activities, including immunization, growth monitoring, and preparing children for primary school).

Although few of the teachers had completed the DICECE training, they were clearly trying to both maintain safe and stimulating environments and prepare children for primary school. Preschool children frequently brought younger siblings (ages two to three) with them to school, as parents encouraged this. The teachers we interviewed did not feel that the preschool was suitable for under threes, but parents felt that children would receive appropriate custodial care from the teacher and would enjoy playing with the other children. Some parents complained that with more children in school, fewer were available to tend to the animals, particularly the small goats.

In terms of changes experienced by Samburu families, many commented on the varying diet and array of weaning foods now used for young children. Again, similar to the Maasai families interviewed, many parents and grandparents discussed the fact they their family and clan had far fewer animals in the past and had supplemented their traditional diet of meat, milk, and blood with *ugali*, potatoes, and *sukuma wiki*. Weaning foods included *uji*, mashed potatoes, and pumpkins (where they were able to grow, as elephants and other wild animals would invade kitchen gardens, drawn to the smell). Families found food quite expensive, and they had trouble growing kitchen gardens. They essentially were being forced into a cash economy when their wealth had been their animals, forcing them to sell more of their animals than they would have in the past. Housing also was changing, from the traditional mud-and-dung construction to the use of wood and tin, as encouraged by the government, with such developments as "Little Bosnia."

Thus although traditions were clearly being maintained by the Samburu, social, economic, and lifestyle changes were affecting daily life in a variety of often contradictory and challenging ways. Although preschool education represented one of these changes from the more informal family child minding of the past, education appeared to be valued and understood as being necessary to children's success in a rapidly changing district and nation. Boarding schools have also, for some time, been one way of addressing the great distances children had to travel to school, and the commitment to at least a basic education for Samburu children was evident in our interviews.

# Part III

Tea and Coffee Plantations:
Kericho and Kiambu

# Tea and Coffee Plantations:
# Kericho and Kiambu

I spend two to three hours a day with my youngest children while they are awake.
—Mother and tea picker in Kericho

When attempting to "decolonize" cross-cultural research, it was ironic yet also critical to the study that we visit some of Kenya's many agricultural plantations or estates. Urban schools in the United States serving primarily poor students, often of color, have been described as "data plantations" for educational researchers who further exploit students and families by collecting data and never returning to or entering the lives of the students in any meaningful way. We clearly hoped that our visits to tea and coffee plantations in the Kericho and Kiambu Districts would not represent such an exploitive or a voyeuristic enterprise. Rather, it was our intent to respect local collaborators' suggestions for which estates to visit. We tended to visit settings where DICECE staff were already working with preschool teachers (as most estates provided at least morning or extended preschool, if not full day care) or hoped to in the future. In fact, several times the opportunity to work with plantation preschools that they had not previously served was given as a rationale for suggesting certain settings. We also had to go through the management of each plantation, and we only met with a clearly negative response on one occasion, near the end of the study.

A number of factors influenced our choice of these districts and of the plantation settings we visited in the study. In contrast to other districts and settings sampled in the study, the plantations provided an opportunity to talk to persons of mixed ethnic backgrounds who were often migrant laborers, and "forced" to coexist. This was particularly true of the temporary or "casual" laborers versus the "permanent" workers, who had more benefits (e.g., free health care and preschool, etc.). Large agricultural plantations in Kenya are owned by corporations (ex-patriot, multinational, Kenyan) or individuals. Many women are employed on the tea and coffee plantations, and they are often single mothers. Thus, similar to the urban sample in some ways, the plantation sample enabled us to better understand the particular child-rearing issues faced by single mothers involved in agricultural paid labor. Also similar to urban contexts, a lack of extended family nearby adds to the problems of child care and culture maintenance. In fact, questions about the "cultural relevance" of preschool education were very confusing to many plantation parents, who stated, "We do little to maintain our culture here, except speak our mother tongue at home." In other words, care was often viewed as custodial and not educational, and people were too busy working to worry about the loss of their traditions and cultural values.

Tea and coffee workers typically live in poverty, with no land on which to plant subsistence crops and very rarely a place to grow a kitchen garden. Children growing up on Kenya's plantations frequently drop out of primary school quite early to work in the fields alongside their parent(s). Thus a study of family life on the estates also involved exposure to child labor patterns.

## PLANTATION PRESCHOOLS: AN OVERVIEW

Preschools or child care centers are owned by the plantation and administered by the management, so there is typically less participation of the community and parents in early childhood centers due to both employment patterns and ownership of the centers. While neighboring rural communities may have a number of *Harambee* or community-sponsored and community-run preschools, the plantations typically provided at least limited preschool programs or child care centers for children but did little to involve parents in these preschools. The following two chapters examine all of these issues in greater depth.

Child care and early education issues in the tea, coffee, sisal, pineapple, flower, and other estates are not a new subject of research in Kenya (NACECE/UNICEF, 1995). In fact, an Aga Khan-sponsored research project completed the year before this study included some of the same Kericho tea plantations in its sample. The lives of families of farm laborers on large estates present some unique, yet widespread, challenges in that parents (increasingly single parents) leave the home early in the morning and return late and tend to leave the youngest children in the care of children only slightly older. Traditional caregivers, including extended family members such as grandparents, are not available on the estates, and parents are encouraged to send older siblings to primary school, making them less available to assist in child care. The other pervasive form of care for under threes, namely the employment of *ayahs* or child minders, was not an option for most families on agricultural estates. They were simply too poor and often lacked room enough even for their own family, without trying to accommodate a live-in maid.

Although preschools are present on most of the plantations, they are typically not staffed adequately for the large number of children who attend—often with younger siblings, including babies, on their backs. Often one teacher is employed with a child minder to assist her; these two adults could be responsible for supervising from 50 to 100 young children. Some plantation preschools, but fewer than in the past according to our study, provide a limited feeding program, serving *uji* in the morning. Older siblings of under threes, particularly sisters, are often held back from enrolling in the primary school in order to care for their younger brothers and sisters, and the instances of child neglect are higher than in many settings in Kenya. It is also quite common to find children of primary school age still in the preschool, in part due to their sibling care roles. The dropout rates from primary school also are high, as children can earn money picking tea or coffee, and families struggle to pay their school-related fees and other expenses.

## THE "PRESSURES OF PICKING"

Another relevant dimension of family life on plantations is the pressure on mothers to stay in the fields and pick their minimum quota for the day, taking very few breaks. Nursing mothers, for example, may take young children to the fields with them on their backs, but may only nurse them at the weighing station, after they have filled their baskets. In some cases (e.g., in Kiambu), under threes were left at the weighing station under the informal supervision of the overseer who weighs the tea leaves. An older child might also be left to play with the babies, but this appeared to be a purely informal arrangement.

As will be evident from the interview summaries, mothers were often hesitant to take babies or young children to the clinic, as this meant that they could not meet the daily minimum "debits" to be picked. We were told in Kiambu that mothers sometimes worked collectively, picking extra tea so that a mother taking her child to the clinic outside the estate would not lose an entire day's pay. To their credit, many of the plantations we visited did have their own clinics, and some of these were better equipped than the public Ministry of Health-sponsored local clinics (e.g., they had good supplies of medicine and refrigeration facilities for immunization serum, etc.). In terms of maternity leave, "permanent" workers were given leaves ranging from six weeks to three months, while casual laborers (the majority of workers on some estates we visited) received no maternity leave and often returned to the field only two or three days after giving birth. It also should be clarified that the majority of women working as casual laborers on estates *are* women, thus greatly limiting their access to "company" policies and benefits.

During the first week of data collection in the Kericho District, the visiting researcher stayed on the grounds of a large tea plantation, in the home of the son of a NACECE driver who was employed there. This provided a rich opportunity to experience life "inside" the estate, although in the home of a "middle manager," not a tea picker. The self-contained nature of the estates, complete with clearly delineated social strata, was apparent, and the daily routines of workers and their families were easily observed. Not surprisingly, there were visibly different standards of living and access to recreational, educational, and health facilities between the workers and the managers. In fact, some of the managers we interviewed stated that they would never send their children to schools or other programs provided for the workers, or exist in the conditions under which their workers did.

Finally, whereas other sections of this book discuss good things the "community" was doing for children and families, this section frames the discussion in terms of what the estate was doing. Again, this relates to the fact that estates in Kenya are self-contained communities that often have minimal contact with outside services. It is management that sets the tone for the "community" of workers and their children. Plantations also represented one of the more ethnically mixed settings visited in our study. In interviews with parents (tea or coffee pickers), for example, it was not unusual to have three or four ethnic groups represented or described as living on that particular estate. The absence of grandparents or "community elders" also was in stark contrast to several of the rural settings included in the study. This was most similar to the urban sample—particularly the Nairobi slum setting, where single mothers often struggled to meet their children's needs without the assistance of either a husband or a grandmother, reflecting the loss of extended family and community support.

# Chapter 5

# Kericho Tea Estates: It Takes Child Care Centers and Older Siblings to Raise a Child

## KERICHO DISTRICT DESCRIPTION

The Kericho District is in the southwestern part of the Rift Valley Province and occupies an area of 2,515 square kilometers. The 1989 census recorded a total of 900,934 people. This population was projected to have reached over 1 million by 1993. About 19% of the population is children ages birth to four years.

In terms of land potential, the district is in the highland region and is endowed with good rainfall and fertile volcanic soils. The low temperatures and low evaporation rates increase the impact of the rainfall. Tea is the main cash crop grown in the district. Large plantations are owned by multinational companies such as Brooke Bond and African Highlands. Small-scale farmers, however, produce the largest amount of tea. Coffee, pyrethrum, and sugarcane also are grown on a small scale. Other crops grown in the district include maize, beans, Irish potatoes, peas, cabbage, onions, tomatoes, millet, and sorghum. Dairy farming also is an important income source in the district. A large tract of land is covered with either natural or planted forests, and wood is used in both tea production and as the primary source of heating and cooking fuel for laborers on the tea plantations and for other rural inhabitants of the district.

Turning to nutrition and health, due to the high food production, increased awareness of proper nutrition, and relatively high standards of living, the nutritional levels in most parts of Kericho District are quite good. However, the children of families working on the tea plantations have a relatively higher incidence of malnutrition and related

113

Fig. 5.1    Mothers Making Toys for Plantation Preschool

problems, due primarily to the fact that these families own little land, if any, for growing crops or planting a kitchen garden, depending on their meager incomes for food and other needs. Most of the tea laborers hail from other districts, primarily Kisii, Nyamira, and Kisumu.

The main causes of morbidity in the district are respiratory infections, malaria, skin diseases, urinary tract infections, ear infections, rheumatism and diarrheal diseases. In 1983, the district had an infant mortality rate of 86 per 1,000. By 1992, this had dropped to 42 per thousand, which is lower than the national average of 74 per 1,000 This dramatic decline is attributed to increased immunization coverage, better food security, higher living standards, increased nutritional and hygiene awareness, and availability of health services. Most of the health facilities are accessible, hence most people make use of them. Tea plantations generally have clinics and employ at least a nurse/nutritionist, making health care more available to laborers.

## KERICHO SAMPLE

Four tea estates in the Kericho District were sampled, representing contrasting levels of commitment of management to their preschool programs (ranging from no feeding program to a hot lunch program for under threes through Standard 8 pupils). Most interviews of both teachers and parents were held in preschools, held outside, or held in the estate's employee canteen.

A total of 29 parents were interviewed, including 27 mothers (of children under age three) and two fathers. No grandparents were interviewed, as estates were populated primarily by younger families who were either casual laborers or permanent employees. First-born children ranged in age from 3 months (an only child) to 18 years, with a mean age of 6.3 years. Last-born children ranged in age from 2 months to 5.5 years, with a mean age of 1.6 years.

When asked about roles in their community or on the estate, most parents reported no specific role beyond their many hours working on the estate. The two fathers interviewed (both of whom were laborers on a tea plantation) were members of the preschool committee, and one mother reported that she was active in a church. No women's self-help groups were reported, with the exception of a women's choir in one tea estate that made and sold baby clothing.

In terms of work roles, as self-described, 13 mothers were homemakers or housewives, sometimes combined with other work. Eight parents were tea pluckers or pruners, five mothers were engaged in small farming or leased shamba cultivation (i.e., they rented land outside of the estate), two mothers reported that they bought and sold vegetables to other families on the estate, and one mother was a tailor.

Turning to the length of time participants had worked on their present estate, five had worked for less than one year, four for one year, six for two years, three for three years, two for four years, two for five years, one for six years, two for seven years, and two parents for 10 years. Thus, approximately half of the sample had worked for two years or less in their current position, and half had worked for up to 10 years on the same estate.

Turning to parents' level of education, only partial information was obtained from this sample, including eight parents who had completed Standard 8, two who had completed Standard 7, five who had completed Standard 6, three who had completed Standard 5, and two who had completed Standard 4.

Twelve female preschool teachers were interviewed in the Kericho District. The average number of teachers/child minders at a preschool was four, with most plantations visited having two separate buildings (either for different age groups or to accommodate large numbers of children—as high as 306 preschool children). Most appeared to have the title "teacher" as compared to their counterparts in Kiambu, who were typically given the title "child minder" or "babysitter." The exception appeared to be those working in under-three child care settings.

The average age of the preschool teachers interviewed was 28.9 years, with a range of 22 to 43 years. In terms of their formal education, six had completed Form 4, one had completed Form 3, and one had completed Form 2; two were Standard 8 leavers, and two were Standard 7 leavers. Seven teachers were trained, and five were untrained. Of the seven trained teachers, five were DICECE trained (1989, 1990, and 1994 graduates), and two had taken the one-year pre-service training.

Years of preschool teaching experience ranged from two months to 26 years, with a mean of 8.8 years. In terms of the number of years teaching at their present school, eight had taught only at their present preschool, and four had taught in two pre-schools before coming here—mostly in rural, non-plantation preschools. Several teachers reported that their salaries were paid by parents, through a payroll deduction each month (sometimes with matching funding from the company), two were paid by the Kericho County Council, and one head teacher was paid by the Kericho Municipality. The two other teachers reported that their salaries were paid by the company, not by parents. Ten teachers reported no other income sources, and two sold vegetables.

Turning to their marital and family status, nine teachers were married and three were single. First-born children of teachers ranged from 2 months to 26 years, with a mean age of 9.8 years, and last-born children ranged from 6 months to 5 years, with a mean age of 3.1 years.

Nine primary children with siblings under age three were interviewed, including five boys and four girls. Their ages ranged from 9 to 14 years, with five children between 11 and 12 years, although they were all drawn from Standard 3 and Standard 4 classes. Again, this reflected the wide age range in any class, which appeared to be exacerbated by the caregiving roles of the older siblings, particularly sisters, of preschool children, who often delayed primary school entry until their younger sibling(s) were more independent. We viewed this as a gender issue that needed to be addressed, as girls typically missed out on educational opportunities, while their brothers did not. By the time most of the girls in plantation settings enroll in primary school, they are well above the required age. They are forced to learn with younger children, which can erode their self-esteem. As we were frequently reminded by primary teachers, these were the pupils who dropped out of school early, as they were not able to fit into the classroom environment. The ages of younger siblings ranged from two months to four years, with seven children having siblings between one to three years of age.

## Portrait: A Tea-Plucker in Kericho

*Mother of 1-year-old tea-picker:*

*I'm up by 4:30 A.M., make uji (porridge), after drinking, I wash utensils, and get ready to pick tea, leaving at 6:30. After I leave, my older nursery school child takes care of the baby, including taking him with her to nursery school (carrying on back). The child taking most care of the baby is 9 years old. By 4 or 5 P.M., I am allowed to come home, but I don't come home for lunch; since I prepare everything early in the morning, the 9-year-old can feed the baby during the day. After work, I look for vegetables and on Sundays I fetch firewood. While the vegetables are cooking I bathe, and by 6 P.M. I cook supper, so that we can eat and go to bed early—by 7:30 P.M. we are all in bed! The younger daughter washes. When there is much tea to be picked, I come back late. I spend about 2-3 hours per day with my youngest children while we are awake.*

This quote is typical of tea pluckers and other casual laborers working on estates in Kericho (and Kiambu). All parents interviewed described a daily routine of rising before sunrise, doing many preparations, often leaving children in charge of younger children, and working 8 to 10-hour days. Many pickers do not have a lunch break during the day, and lunch for their children, particularly if there is not a feeding program in their preschool, is typically cold leftovers from supper the night before (e.g., *ugali* or beans and maize) or bread and tea.

## Portrait: A Primary School Pupil in Kericho

*Mama works at picking tea, and makes tea for us before leaving in the early morning. I wake up with my older brother and wash my face, take tea, and put on my uniform; while I'm getting ready, my 3-year-old sister is still taking tea; I help her wash her feet, use Vaseline, then I give her a pencil and some paper and bring her to nursery school. At lunchtime, my older brother (in Standard 6) is already home and preparing lunch, then I take my younger sister from nursery and we wash and eat lunch. I also have a sister in Standard 1 and she walks home for lunch. After school, we went to go to the forest to fetch firewood with my older brother, but it was late and we were afraid, so we used other wood. My brother cooked and then I watched TV in the canteen hall. When I came home, my brother was still cooking, my mama was resting, and my brother prepared* githeri *(maize and beans). Then, after supper, we went back to watch TV.*

This quote was typical of the children interviewed in the estates. By the time they rise in the morning, their mothers are already heading for the tea fields. They are left with many household and child care responsibilities, which appeared to be delegated far more by age than by gender. When a child is still under two years of age, he or she typically goes to nursery school with an older sibling, tied on his or her back. This also has the effect of postponing primary school entry for older siblings, who act as caretakers of babies. When asked, several parents and teachers observed that when a child is more independent, usually by age three or four, then the older sibling can move on to primary schools. Only the wives of supervisors, managers, and senior factory workers on the estates appeared to be able to afford maids or other in-home child care providers.

Nursing mothers typically are not given time off to breast-feed their infants, and they either carry babies with them to the field, leave them at a tea weighing station (with the overseer) near their picking site, or leave them with a sibling, neighbor, or preschool teacher/child minder, with weaning food for daytime feedings. Many mothers are single parents, often with three or more children. Traditional caregivers, such as grandmothers, are not to be found on plantations, and extended family child care is quite rare.

Certain benefits are provided to the tea pickers if they are permanent employees and not "seasonal" or "casual" laborers. These benefits typically include housing, access to treated tap water (typically with taps outside of homes), a clinic and free medical services within the estate, transportation to the hospital (if an emergency, and if transportation is available), and free or low-cost preschool/child care. Some estates also provide firewood during colder seasons, as most houses on estates use wood for cooking and heating. Several estates in Kericho also provide small kitchen garden plots to permanent employees, to encourage growing more food. Some estates provide recreational activities, particularly sports fields, and may have a canteen for workers' use in the evenings and for purchasing food or other items.

Housing, although free, is very small and crowded—typically one or two rooms and perhaps a store. As workers' families grew, many commented on the crowding that their family experienced. Teachers saw this crowding as having negative social outcomes, and parents saw it as evidence that they were "not able to cater for all their children's needs." Many parents commented on the rising price of food and of educating their children. Poor diet was particularly acute where families did not have access to a *shamba* or a kitchen garden for growing vegetables.

Mobility also was a factor for some, though certainly not all, pickers. Frequent moves to places where the tea picking was good could mean that the benefits of being a "permanent" employee were not available. Another issue on some estates was the large number of out-of-school youth. Although managers attempted to enforce the "all children must go to nursery and primary school" rule, a number of children entered late or left primary school to pick tea or coffee (thus contributing to family income) or to care for younger siblings, or due to a lack of funds for school fees, books, uniforms, building and activity funds, and other costs of education. Most people interviewed expressed concern about the future of such youth, as well as about their current behavior in the estate.

In such a setting, what is the "cultural relevance" of nursery school? When workers and managers are of many different cultural backgrounds/ethnic groups, traditions tend to break down or become assimilated into the dominant culture. The importance of preschool is clearly its child care function, enabling many mothers to become productive tea pluckers. Women who teach in the estate nursery schools tend to have titles such as "child minder," "babysitter," or "caregiver." They often work six days a week and teach year-round, with less than one month's annual leave. They often are untrained, although this varies greatly by company and setting, and they often are not recognized as "real teachers." In one case, parents had voted to cut back on teachers' salaries, as well as terminate a feeding program, when their cost-share became too high, and management proposed sacking (dismissing) one of the four teachers to save money.

Alcohol abuse also was discussed on some of the estates. Even where banned by management, workers were reported to make "home brew" in the woods nearby. The problem of drinking was particularly acute on paydays—on the two Fridays of each month. Another issue related to paychecks concerned the number of items that was typically deducted from the workers' pay, including their union dues, nursery school tuition, contribution to health care costs (insurance), and any money borrowed against future earnings (e.g., for children's school tuition). Many parents interviewed reported that the rapidly rising cost of living, combined with a relatively small and fixed income, made it extremely hard to provide what they knew they should be providing for their children.

## Major Challenges Facing Families with Young Children

Similar to other districts sampled, most of the problems cited by parents related to the high cost of living and their limited resources. The most frequently mentioned (by 16 parents interviewed) problem was improper diet. Among the reasons were food is too expensive, certain foods are not available, or are quite costly, and families tend to be large. A related issue, mentioned second in frequency to food, was lack of access to land on which to grow a kitchen garden. As one mother put it, "We are only provided with very small plots, and these are hard to get." Others were not provided with garden plots, did not have other land in their areas of origin, and were thus completely dependent on purchasing all foodstuff. Many mothers interviewed reported that they bought most food from the market in the town of Kericho, which was some distance from their homes and required the expense of transportation.

The next most frequently mentioned problem was lack of money. As mentioned earlier, this problem was seen as overriding the many other ones discussed by parents working on plantations. Some parents summarized all of their problems with one word—poverty. One aspect of the low income problem that several parents, particularly fathers, raised concerns about was the payroll deductions that were taken out of each paycheck. These included, in the words of one father, "NSSF (social security), health care, municipal service, preschool fees, and union dues." When these were removed, it typically left "less than 1,550/= (Kshs.) per month to support a large family," with no other visible sources of income.

Illness and disease were mentioned by 11 of the parents interviewed. In particular, malaria was listed by many of the mothers, who reported that mosquitoes were a problem due to the amount of rain and bushy areas, and that most of the malaria was not the more deadly "highland malaria." Other health problems included skin diseases, malnutrition, and upper respiratory problems. Parents also complained about both the lack of and high cost of medicine, which used to be more widely available and free.

Another problem cited by several parents concerned the difficulties in obtaining fuel and firewood. One mother said, "As the company uses the closest supply, we have to go far to gather wood." It was observed that much wood from the neighboring reserves was used in many aspects on the Kericho plantations—for both home consumption and running the tea processing factories. In fact, several of the larger estates had sawmills and consumed large quantities of wood.

The lack of time also was named as a problem by several of the parents interviewed. As one mother put it, "There is a great lack of time for working mothers to care for our babies—we are often gone from 6:30 A.M. until nearly 6 P.M.!" Another suggested, "We should be released early. When we work up to 6:00 P.M., there's very little time for our children—even discipline of the child has gone down." They reminded us that they do not get a lunch break and of how hard it is to nurse a young baby when there is no time to leave the tea fields until the end of the work day.

Clothing for children was identified as a problem by several mothers. More specifically, providing warm enough clothing for young children and school uniforms for older, primary, and secondary age children was named as a problem. Again, these difficulties related directly to a family's poverty, combined with the rising cost of living. Such changes are discussed in more detail in the following section.

School-related fees were named next as a problem facing families. The many separate costs of educating children in Kenya (e.g., fees, uniforms, textbooks, activities fees, and building funds) are very hard for plantation workers to afford. In particular, parents commented on how hard this hit families with several school-age children. "You can get some assistance with one child, perhaps, but not with three or four!" was how one father put it.

Mothers in particular frequently lamented over the lack of child care during their long working hours. Many expressed the desire to employ a maid or an *ayah*, but said, "Getting a maid is too expensive for most." Instead, they relied heavily on older siblings, particularly girls, and occasionally on neighbors. They also relied on preschools that were often ill equipped and not well prepared to work with under threes. These younger children often were referred to, particularly by teachers, as "tag-alongs," who were brought to the nursery school each day by their older siblings, remaining there until the younger one was more independent.

Finally, mothers who were the wives of men working in tea factories or middle management/supervisory positions expressed their frustration about being "idle." As one mother put it, "We would welcome training and employment. We are home with our babies, but could be doing some small business or employed part-time on the estate!" They appeared to desire such training and employment for both financial reasons and personal fulfillment.

## PRESCHOOL TEACHERS' VIEWS ON PROBLEMS FACING FAMILIES

Teachers' responses corroborated parents', with the exception of teachers who described essentially forms of parental neglect (e.g., leaving children alone). The two most frequently mentioned family problems were lack of time for child care activities and lack of adequate food for families. Just as both parents and older siblings had told us, "Parents have a very long working day—usually 6:00 A.M. to 6:00 P.M.—hence there is not time to care for their children." Teachers saw these long work hours as defining the purpose of preschool on the estate. "As a result of the lack of time parents have to care for children and their long working day, most children are brought to nursery school for custodial care." They also described food shortages in homes and the lack of time to prepare food for children, resulting in many children carrying a cold lunch in a tin, when there was not a feeding program in the preschool. Frequent illnesses of children also were mentioned by teachers. As one teacher put it, "Under threes are often sick, hence they are always being taken to clinics for treatment."

Another issue raised by both parents and teachers was the combination of the high cost of living and limited incomes, resulting in parents being unable to provide for the basic needs of their children, including food, clothing, and so on. This also was seen as leading many parents to leave children alone. "Children are left in homes when parents go to work—children have no adult to supervise or advise them." To supplement their incomes, some parents operated small businesses, such as selling clothes and vegetables, as their time permitted. Teachers also supported the idea of a "merry-go-round self-help group in which members contribute a small amount of money and give it to one teacher." This was used to help supplement their meager incomes and could also be a model for bringing in additional funds to families on the estate.

## Impact of Problems on Children

When hungry, children tend to drop out of school.

—Preschool teacher on tea estate

The most frequently mentioned effects of the above-mentioned problems on children, as seen in the preschool context, were related to poor nutrition and hunger. "When children are hungry they become dull, sleepy, cry, and do not learn well." This problem also affected children's peer interactions in the preschool. As one teacher put it, "When hungry, some children become aggressive, they may take food (from others' lunches), and they complain." They also discussed the longer-term impact of children being chronically hungry. "When hungry, children tend to drop out of school." By leaving school, some could join their parents in tea-picking or other income-generating activities, as well as provide care for younger siblings.

Other impacts of family problems on children included the effects of neglect. "Due to lack of love and attention, children feel insecure." Problems were viewed as directly affecting children's emotional well-being. "You can tell when a family has problems by children's moods and behavior in preschool . . . children appear frightened." Other examples of the physical impacts on such children were evident. "When there are problems, children may become sick."

Thus children were traumatized by home experiences. This was particularly true for those with single mothers, who had stressful work lives. Under-three programs as such were rarely available, there were frequent food shortages, and the youngest children lacked care for at least part of most work days. These were children at the margins of their parents' employment, which was also the source of their family's survival. Siblings and preschool teachers appeared to provide the most consistent care for the under threes on the estates visited.

## Coping Strategies

Parents also were asked how families coped with the previously mentioned problems. They had little to say about this, basically responding that they have few choices in their lives and learn to appreciate whatever comes their way from the company—which usually was named as the only source that could directly address their problems. One mother said, "We cope by knowing that some things are getting better." Another said, "At least we have free, treated water, small gardens, a dispensary, and a nursery school."

## Good Things the Estate Is Doing

The "good things" paralleled closely the examples given by the mother above. The dispensary or the clinic, staffed by the company, was mentioned by most of the parents interviewed. Free immunizations and growth monitoring, some free drugs, and other health care issues appeared to be a source of satisfaction among many of the workers interviewed. Next most frequently mentioned was water—"free, treated water from taps." The provision of small garden plots to at least some of the workers also was cited by those families who had access to such kitchen gardens.

Seven other issues were mentioned by at least five parents each. These included:

free housing, "even if small";

a free vehicle to take you to the hospital if having a baby or sick in the night;

toilets (latrines) maintained by the estate;

providing good primary classrooms, including permanent buildings;

assistance with school fees, in which management pays the full amount of the fee and then deducts a monthly payment from paycheck (only one site);

free under-three care with *uji* at mid-morning (only one site); and

a growing number of children who go on to primary and "no longer just keep repeating preschool"

## How Life Has Changed

The broad question of how life had changed in the past 10 to 15 years, which typically yielded the most lengthy discussion among parents, was divided into several dimensions of change in specific areas of family life, including housing, food, cost of living, health, clothing, education, family size, social structures, services, and child-rearing practices. A summary of parents' responses in each of these areas follows. It should be noted that the responses of those on plantations tended to be framed more in the "here and now" than in the "change over time." In some cases, it almost appeared that parents lacked a reference point outside of present time—there appeared to be a daily reality of "right now, today" and less of a reflection on both the past and future. This issue will be discussed in more depth in the cross-district comparisons drawn in chapter 11.

## Housing

The most frequently mentioned change in terms of housing on the estates was increased crowding, with parents describing coming to their first estate with only one child or at least much smaller families. As one father put it, "I only had one child when I started to work here—now I have four and we are still in the same small house. It is more crowded now." Most workers described their homes as having one to two rooms. "Laborers have small houses of two rooms, including the kitchen/store and sitting/sleeping rooms, and junior staff have four room, two bedroom homes" one parent said of the different types of housing on the estate.

Some workers who had labored on the same estate for many years stated that they had "moved up" from a one room to a two room house. Yet, "As my home grew, so did my family—and we're still crowded!" When asked what other improvements they had seen in housing, three people responded, "The major improvement in 10 years is to have inside water." This was not available in most of the estates visited, however.

## Food

The majority of parents interviewed were quick to respond that, "Ten years ago, food prices were very low—we could afford quality food and a more balanced diet. Now prices have really grown up!" For example, as one mother told us, "Milk is too much now, and fruit for the children is very rare."

A related concern was that their diets lacked variety and that some kinds of food were not obtainable, either financially or due to shortages. As a mother stated, "Sometimes there is a shortage of vegetables, so we buy fish." In relation to fruit, another said, "We have to buy fruit in town and cannot often afford it."

Transportation to the market in Kericho also was mentioned, as this market was a major food source. Since the market was rather far away from most of the mothers interviewed, several commented on the lack of transportation or the cost of it when it was available to go buy food. In general, the estates appeared to lack many small vendors of vegetables. Again, families fortunate enough to have plots for a kitchen garden did not have to rely on the market in town for all of their foodstuff.

## Cost of Living

The discussion of the cost of living could be fairly well summarized in the following parent's statement. "Before, although the salary appeared small, it was sufficient. Now, it cannot purchase everything a family needs." Six parents expressed the observation that although income was up, prices were also up, and that wages failed to keep pace with such rapidly rising prices.

Others stated simply that, "It is costly and hard to provide for your family here!" The long days, prescribed activities, limited wages, and lack of opportunities to diversify income sources all fed into a concern about the failing of many workers to provide for their families. "Some try to have a small business, but there's so little time for that," said one working mother.

## Health

Health was an area in which most parents agreed that real improvement had taken place. "Children's health has improved—most children are immunized now and are generally healthier." Immunizations in particular were mentioned by a number of parents as an important improvement in health care. However, other drugs, such as anti-malarial medicines, have become drug resistant, creating new health problems. Highland malaria was cited as a very serious problem, because it is resistant to most of the anti-malarial drugs, specifically those that are cheaper and more easily available.

Many mothers mentioned that medicine is less in supply now and that workers tend to be referred to a central hospital which, although partially covered by health insurance, is more costly than before. Thus the familiar combination of a lack of drugs and the more costly alternative of going to either a hospital or a private clinic added to a family's financial burden.

Some parents framed the child health care situation in terms of income and position of the parents. As one mother put it, "It depends on the parents—if you have the money or occupation, you may be OK. Without funds, there are many health problems!"

The issue of child health could be summarized by the following quote. "In comparison to before, children look healthier—people are now tending to have smaller families, clinics are closer, and in general things have improved." In other words, access to the medicine and care needed was still problematic due to poverty, but the overall health of workers' children had apparently improved.

## Clothing

In terms of clothing, one mother stated, "Children are better clothed now, but they need more and warmer clothing." Tea-growing areas such as the highlands of the Kericho District tend to be cold and rainy, particularly during the rainy seasons of the year. Children suffering from exposure also tend to suffer from increased colds and upper respiratory infections, and warmer clothing was seen as protecting them from such problems. Again, the major stumbling block was money. Also mentioned in this regard was the cost of a school uniform and how hard it was to buy uniforms for several children out of a family's small monthly budget.

## Education

The overwhelming response to the question of education was, "Fees have gone up, and the same high fees are here on the plantations as in town or rural schools, including fees for activities, books, registration, and so forth!" Parents expressed the burden they felt at the beginning of each term, particularly those parents who did not have a tuition loan scheme, as one estate provided. Due to higher fees, "More children are failing to continue in school."

In terms of nursery school, parents generally agreed that now, more children are going to nursery school, and some are going for a longer time than before (two to three years). One parent speculated that the cost of education was encouraging parents to do more family planning: "We can only afford to educate two to three children, and should not have more children than we can educate."

## Family Size

Family size was an area of contradictory information from the parents. Mothers spoke about how families had grown, how children were more healthy, how fewer children died, and so on. Yet other parents spoke of the increase in use of family planning methods and the desire of many to have fewer children. The reality appeared now to have caught up with the intent, however, as many mothers mentioned the large families on the estate, many of which had single-parent mothers. In summary, "In the past, women didn't plan families, while in recent years, more family planning and fewer children now—though this has taken quite a while."

## Social Structures and Services

Only a few activities that could be viewed as providing social support or services were mentioned by parents. These included sports and other recreational opportunities, often described as "mainly for men." A women's choir had begun on one estate. Few self-help groups were mentioned, although several mothers stated, "We wish we had a women's self-help group here!" The canteen appeared to be fulfilling a social function—particularly those canteens that provided for adult literacy with newspapers, television news, and sports, and *barazas* (meetings with a local chief or manager), or parent meetings. As one father put it, "There's been some recreational improvement, but much more is needed."

As previously discussed, several of the wives of tea factory workers and supervisors described themselves as somewhat idle and anxious to obtain training and employment. In one case, the diet of the children was enhanced through the efforts of the estate director general's wife, who had provided enriched porridge (with milk) and fruit for preschool children, regular health screening, followed up by taking children to a clinic, and a hot lunch program, serving children from toddlers to students in Standard 8. When our research team visited this estate, however, she was out of the country, and some of these activities had not been maintained in her absence.

## Child-rearing Practices

As briefly discussed in an earlier section, many mothers expressed the concern that they could not provide the time and attention they knew their youngest children required. As one mother stated, "It is a fortunate mama who can find a neighbor at home in the morning, or a relative to help care for her young children!" Several aspects of children's development appeared to have improved, however, including the provision of free medical care on the estate. "Now, children are fairly well looked after here—especially on the side of health."

Parents also expressed interest in better services for under threes in the preschools, or in other settings on the estate developed specifically to meet the needs of the younger children. They also expressed the desire to have more time during the day to breast-feed, to take their children to the clinic, and to meet other needs for their children's care.

## Relevance of Preschool Education for Culture Maintenance

In the setting of the plantation, the question of the relevance of preschool education for culture maintenance presented several interesting "challenges." First, there was great ethnic and cultural diversity among the workers in the estates. Many languages were spoken, with Kiswahili being the lingua franca of the plantation. This meant, in part, that there was not one local culture or mother tongue to "protect" and perpetuate. If anything, preschool and primary education served a sort of assimilationist function, with teachers commenting, "We're one big culture here, and we use Kiswahili for most teaching." This is discussed in more depth in the section summarizing teachers' interviews on the estates.

Second, the provision of child care appeared to be the overriding goal, in fact, a necessity. These were settings in which long hours of labor provided by many women were needed, and offering some level of child care was considered plain and

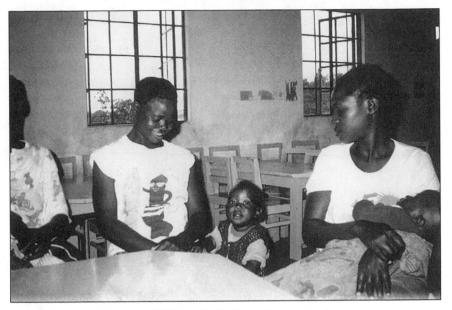

Fig. 5.2    Kericho Mothers and Children in Tea Plantation Preschool

simply "good business." This became even more clear as we interviewed managers.

Thus for parents, if not for all teachers, the question of the cultural relevance of preschool education was a purely academic one. The real questions were, "Is my child safe and cared for while I am working in the tea fields?" and "Are my child's basic needs being met?"

This question was not easily answered by the teachers interviewed. In part, their responses showed that "traditional" parents and child-rearing activities were not visible in the multiethnic setting of the plantation. Rather than a question of cultural relevance, then, the matter of formal preschool became a question of economic necessity—the provision of day care for children of workers was necessary, given the large numbers of mothers employed as tea pluckers.

Teachers' comments reflected this need to provide safe custodial care for large numbers of children. As one teacher stated, "The only mode of care available for these children is our preschool—this is the only way an adult is available to care for, love, and provide safety for these young children!" Preschool teachers or child-minders also saw their role as providing stimulation through play, songs, and storytelling, some of which reflected the cultures of the children in care.

Some preschool programs also met other physical needs of children, including providing a feeding program. An example of this was found in an estate, mentioned previously, which provided both morning porridge (which was often enriched with milk and accompanied by fresh fruit upon occasion) and a hot lunch before children returned home in the afternoon. Since the porridge (*uji*) was prepared in a traditional manner, using local ingredients where possible, this could be viewed as a culturally relevant supplement/weaning food for the youngest children.

When asked whether parents ever raised the issue of the relevance of the preschool curriculum and program to their culture, family, or children, all teachers indicated that they had not.

## Activities Supporting Home Culture

Teachers were then asked about any activities that they provided in the preschool to support children's home culture. The most frequent example was songs in different mother tongues, followed in frequency by role play (of activities done in children's families and communities) and poems. Other activities mentioned by at least one teacher included language development (e.g., teaching words) and providing a home corner. Again, this was not seen as a critical function of the preschool, which functioned primarily as a child care or custodial setting.

# CONTRIBUTIONS OF TRADITIONAL PRACTICES TO EFFECTIVE CHILD-REARING

A related question concerned teachers' perceptions of the contributions of traditional care to effective child-rearing. In the context of the plantations, the only example teachers shared was the frequent use of older children to stay home to baby-sit younger siblings. Such care by older siblings has long been a tradition of the ethnic groups from which the workers come. The difference in the current context may be that the age of a sibling, rather than the gender, tended to be critical in the specific roles children played in the care of their younger brothers and sisters.

Children also tend to be left alone to supervise younger siblings for longer periods of time than they might have traditionally. For example, rather than caring for a baby while the mother cooked or gathered firewood, older siblings would divide up these tasks among themselves, as their mother was gone for at least 8 to 10 (and up to 12) hours each day.

# FAMILY AND COMMUNITY INVOLVEMENT IN EARLY CHILDHOOD CARE AND EDUCATION

This group of parents is perhaps the least available, in many respects, for active parental involvement in their children's preschools and even in their care. Their long hours, including working on Saturday (typically until 2 or 3 P.M.), leave only late afternoon Saturday and Sunday for food shopping, gathering firewood, cleaning, working in the kitchen garden, and going to church or to other religious observations.

Thus scheduling parent meetings, parent-teacher conferences, or toy-making workshops, or involving parents in cooking for the feeding program and so on are challenging at best. Yet parents expressed interest in their children's preschool, and they raised strong concerns about recent problems (e.g., the termination of a feeding program, the lowering of teachers' salaries, and the lack of a playground and materials for older preschool children). Parents also tried to attend meetings called by the preschool teachers or management. As one mother put it, "When a meeting is called, we come!"

The most frequently mentioned contribution of parents to their children's care and education was the provision of materials. For example, one father stated, "We buy some materials, such as books, and send to school with our children." In terms of recycled materials for resource making, the factories or tea companies appeared to provide most (e.g., cardboard, old tires, paper, etc.). Mothers described making toys, rattles, and dolls for their young children, as did older siblings for under threes. It should be pointed out, however, that in two of the estates sampled, parents reported that they were not involved in collecting materials or making toys.

At one estate, the women's choir makes baby clothes and sells them to other mothers. The choir has 30 members and makes many warm clothes—a direct contribution both to their own financial welfare (self-help, income-generating scheme) and the warmer, better clothing of the youngest children on their estate.

In terms of involvement of parents in the governance structures of preschools, only one estate had a parent membership-based preschool committee. Two members of that committee were interviewed and reported that elections for new members were overdue and that many issues needed to be addressed (e.g., feeding program, teachers' salaries, degree of cost-share by parents which was currently higher than most neighboring estates with fewer services for children, lack of a playground, and lack of napping facilities and special training for teachers in working with under threes).

Turning to fund-raising, parents generally stated that the funding of the preschool/day care was management's or the company's major responsibility. In some cases, however, they reported that they had responded to fund-raising appeals for a project to improve their child's preschool.

Finally, all of the mothers interviewed took their children to the clinic for regular visits, even if that meant missing some picking time and so on. They also said that when there were health education talks, "We go on time to hear the lectures."

Similar to the parents interviewed, teachers confirmed that it was the company or management of the estate that was most directly responsible for the preschool program. They reported holding meetings to discuss preschool issues, although usually only once a year. One estate had a preschool committee to oversee its activities (as discussed in the parent section). Fees varied from 10/= Kshs. (Kenya shillings, approximately US $0.20) per month per family (no matter how many children were enrolled) to 100/= per month (which was being lowered to 25/= due to parent demand, resulting in the loss of the feeding program).

Teachers had not held toy-making or other workshops and only occasionally asked children to bring in materials from home. They reported that most of the materials they received (e.g., cardboard and tires) were provided by the company. Teachers expressed a desire to further mobilize parents, but they again commented on parents' long working hours.

When asked what the most effective ways were of getting parents to participate, they said writing letters (sent home with children) or going directly to homes and informing parents of meetings, problems affecting their children, or other needs. They also said that when management supported attendance at such parent meetings, attendance was usually good.

## Siblings' Contributions to Child Care

When asked to describe a typical day's activities, before and after school, primary children named a variety of duties in the home. The largest number of these pertained to household chores (e.g., washing, sweeping, cooking, washing utensils, etc.). Second in frequency to chores, children mentioned caring for (e.g., washing, feeding, comforting, and toilet training) and playing with their younger siblings. Older children also made toys, including balls and shakers, for their younger brothers and sisters.

Another role which older children filled, as previously discussed, was taking their youngest siblings to either a neighbor or a nursery school on the estate. Children also told stories and taught songs to their younger siblings; in fact, many children demonstrated by singing and telling folk tales during the interview. At least two children, including the boy quoted earlier, prepared food both for younger children and often for the rest of the family.

Other roles of older siblings included providing health care for younger ones. They could tell when the younger ones were sick (using signs such as a high temperature, sleeping too much, appearing tired, not playing, increased crying, loss of appetite, etc.), and they also described the actions they took when their younger sibling(s) were sick. These included telling a parent or neighbor so that the child could be taken to the dispensary or hospital (if the child had a high fever) and using traditional medicine or other medicines available in the house.

Older children also reported providing various types of "training" and guidance for their younger siblings, including training for independence (e.g., how to eat, wash themselves, use the latrine, dress themselves, etc.) and moral training (e.g., how to behave). Older children also described how they comforted their younger siblings, such as singing lullabies and songs (again, some lullabies were sung during the interview), giving the child something to play with or write with, and feeding the baby.

Thus children were involved in virtually all aspects of caring for their younger siblings, and they filled a critical gap created by the long working hours of their parents and the limited facilities for the care of under threes on most of the estates visited.

## TYPICAL CHILD CARE ARRANGEMENTS FOR CHILDREN UNDER THREE AND RELATED CONCERNS

Several of the parent interview questions were directly related to the issue of child care for under threes. The first was a series of questions about the parents' youngest child's early health and developmental history. In response to the first question "Where are your youngest children during the day?" parents on three estates said that they were in the preschool, often with older siblings taking them there and then caring for them in the mid-to-late afternoon. The role of sibling care was captured well by this mother's quote: "The Standard 4 child prepares lunch for the Standard 1 boy, and the Standard 1 child takes care of the nursery school child." One of the interesting insights from the estate parent interviews was that age, not gender, appeared to be the basis for assigning child care responsibilities to older siblings. Thus if the next older child was male, he might be responsible for the baby during the day, including taking her to preschool with him and taking care of her until the mother's return from the field.

Mothers also reported that there were "few neighbors home during the day and no grandmothers to help care for the children." At-home mothers, or homemakers married to tea factory workers or estate supervisors, were only interviewed on one estate. In response to the same question, regarding where their youngest children were during the day, they said, "At home; otherwise, for mothers who are working there is free child care." As discussed earlier, this setting showed the most commitment to the care of under threes of any of the estates visited; *uji* (often enriched with milk) was prepared each morning, and two child minders were employed. There were limited manipulatives, facilities for napping and toileting, but the attempt to meet their needs was evident.

In terms of where children's births had taken place, first births tended to take place in a hospital and subsequent births at home. Others had given birth to all of their children at home, assisted by Traditional Birth Attendants (TBAs) or relatives, particularly mothers and mothers-in-law.

All mothers breast-fed, typically for between one and a half to two years. Predictably, those women who worked as tea pickers typically introduced weaning/supplement foods earlier than those at home with their children. The average time for tea pickers at which weaning foods were introduced was between three and four months, and for other mothers interviewed in the estates, between five and six months. One mother reported that her milk was not enough to satisfy her baby and that she had supplemented it with cow's milk and porridge as early as two weeks.

Mothers reported using the following weaning foods/supplements: *uji*, cow's milk, bananas, rice, mashed potatoes and mashed beans, and some "tinned foods." In terms of toileting, most described putting some paper down, then throwing it in the latrine. All parents interviewed in the Kericho estates reported taking their children to the clinic for their full course of immunizations and for growth monitoring and promotion (GMP). The major health problems, as already discussed, were malaria, colds and upper respiratory illnesses, and undernutrition (underfeeding) of children.

When parents were asked "What activities do you provide to make your youngest children happy?" the most common response of mothers was "feeding them—nursing them!" The second most frequent response was "sing lullabies," to which some of the parents added "also rocking and walking with them." The third most frequent response was "make or buy playthings and give to them" (including making balls, bean bags and dolls and also buying small toys for their babies). Parents also commented that, "Older children often make toys for younger ones."

In terms of what parents liked most about being a mother or father, the most typical response was the assistance that children can provide, when they were sick, older, and so on. This was expressed as follows. "When you're sick, children give the best assistance, and when you're old, children can really help!" Other specific examples of assistance from children included, "They can build a house for you, and even help with clothes."

The second most frequent response (which had been the most frequent in most other districts sampled) was: "The children—having children." There were several variations to this, including the "cultural necessity" of having children. For example, one mother said, "If you have no child, you have no respect!" A father put it this way. "When you are a father, you have respect as a leader in society." Parents' identities also were closely linked to their children; several mentioned that what they liked most about being a mother, for example, was being called "Mama" (e.g., "Mother of Beatrice"). Next in frequency was the fact that they would be lonely without children. One mother said, "It's sad in life not to be a parent. You are lonely!"

Such pride in being a parent also was evidenced by the following quotes. "It's good to be a parent—I was brought up well by my parents, and I'm proud to bring up my children!" and "Leadership comes from a family—it starts there . . . and when a child is well brought up, they bring pride and joy!"

The most frequent responses to "What's hardest about being a parent?" had to do with parents' failure to meet the basic needs of their children (e.g., failing to properly feed and clothe them). "When you have more children and fail to clothe them, you aren't recognized as a parent." Most of these difficulties were due to lack of funds to properly support their family: "Problems with money are the hardest we face!" Another parent, who was a casual laborer, stated, "We lack land and sometimes lack employment, which means that with the high cost of living, we have great difficulties providing for our children!"

Mothers tended to feel that being mothers was the easy part, but providing for children was the hardest. As one put it, "Giving birth (motherhood) is no problem—it's providing the facilities to care for them that's hard." Two of the mothers made reference to losing a child as the hardest thing they had faced in being parents. "Being without a child—losing one, that's the hardest!"

Four of the teachers' interview questions related to this research question. Again, their responses closely mirrored parents' and siblings' responses. The two most common child care arrangements were sibling care and the use of the preschool as a day care facility, at least until mid-afternoon. Teachers stated that older siblings served as "maids" for younger ones, and that more of these child caregivers were girls, who were thought to provide better care than boys.

Many children were also brought to the preschool for care, typically carried on the back of older siblings. As one teacher put it, "Children from six months come to preschool strapped on the back of an older sibling, but parents do not pay. They play but don't pay!" One teacher of a "baby class" stated, "I have under threes and I enjoy working with them and would like to continue catering for them, and try to keep them happy and busy." Thus teachers accepted that younger siblings would come with older ones to preschool, and they attempted, given their limited facilities and other resources, to meet their needs.

When asked whether parents of under threes ever came to them for advice on child-rearing or to discuss specific problems, most said that they did not (which was true in most settings sampled in the larger study). If anything, they called on the parents when a child had problems and initiated the discussion. "Only at admission time do parents come and give us more information on their children." Probing the question of why parents rarely seek child development advice or information from preschool teachers, the teachers responded, "Parents prefer to go for advice from the clinic." The marginalized role of the preschool teachers on the estates as being "child minders," and not typically trained teachers, perhaps also contributed to parents' preference for medical personnel. The only setting where parents appeared comfortable coming directly to teachers also had the largest number of trained teachers, materials, and programs for young children, which may have contributed to a more "professional atmosphere."

## Children's Perceptions of Preschool

All of the children interviewed had attended preschool, several of them on the estate where they currently resided. When asked what they remembered about preschool, they recalled learning to write letters and numbers, learning songs, playing, modeling, and the feeding program.

When asked to compare preschool and primary school, children responded that in preschool there was a feeding program (with porridge and/or milk) that they missed having in primary school. They also said that learning was easier in preschool and had become much harder in primary school. Finally, they stated that they were not beaten or mistreated in nursery school, whereas beatings were now more common.

All of the children interviewed thought that all children should go to nursery school. When asked what the best place was for under threes to be cared for (in the estate), most responded "the nursery."

## Parental Aspirations for Children

> Their future will be harder!
> —Father in tea plantation

Turning to parental aspirations for their children, the most frequent hope was "to learn—to get a good education and later, a good job!" These two—education and employment—were frequently stated as parents' primary goals for their children's future. Some parents gave more specific examples of what a "good job" might be, for example, "to work in an office," "to be a pilot," and even "to be president someday!" Other employment goals for children named by tea pickers included teacher, nurse, saleswoman, doctor, army officer, guard, engineer, officer with the Ministry of Agriculture, and several business or office careers. None expressed the desire that their children work in the tea estates, as they were doing.

Other parental aspirations (in order of frequency) for children included:

to stay well;

be respectful of others;

to be safe;

to stay with his or her family, happily;

to be able to assist others;

to be saved (in a religious sense); and

to come to the United States.

Finally, when asked how their children's lives would be different from theirs, the majority of parents responded that their children's lives would be even harder than their own. For example, one father said, "Although we're complaining of high prices, during our children's time, they'll be even higher! The cost of education will be even higher then." A mother stated, "Their future will be harder—the cost of living will be even higher!" Another mother added, "The price of food will be higher, due to land shortages, etc.," and another stated, "Education will have gone up, so that even educated people may miss jobs." One added that even firewood would become scarce in the future: "Firewood will be scarce and the population density high."

When asked whether good early childhood care and education would help their children have a better future, all parents agreed that it could. When asked why, they did not have detailed reasons. The most common response was that preschool would prepare children to better themselves in later schooling and thus make their children more employable in the future.

In summary, parents hoped for a brighter future for their children, primarily through better education. They also felt that the cost of living would continue to escalate, making life difficult for their children. One mother stated, "I want their lives to be different! The country's changing, and things are much different than before."

## Children's Aspirations for Career and Family

Near the end of the interview, children were asked what they wanted to be doing in the future, as well as what they thought their younger brother and/or sister would be doing. Five children wanted to be a teacher, and others wanted to be a mechanic, a nurse, a doctor, a manager, a secretary, a driver, a clerk, a pilot, and a tailor. Three children wanted both their brother and sister to be teachers, and three children wanted their brothers to be doctors. Two children wanted their sisters to be managers, and two wanted their sisters to be secretaries. Others wanted their sisters to be a nurse, a pilot, and a tailor. Finally, other children wanted their brothers to be a mechanic, a driver, a clerk, and a tailor.

Finally, we asked children how many children they would like to have in the future, if they had their own families. Three children wanted to have two girls and two boys (four children) and boys tended to want bigger families than did girls.

## WORKING WITH UNDER THREES: LIKES AND DISLIKES

When asked what they liked most about working with under threes, teachers gave the following responses:

"Telling them stories";

"The way they are very active";

"They are easy to work with, as they obey and hardly complain";

"They keep me very busy as I have to change activities frequently to keep them attentive and interested";

They are free to talk to"; and "They like to play—with water and sand particularly."

These responses showed teachers' developmental sensitivity to many of the needs of under threes.

Centers were usually lacking in napping and toileting facilities, as well as in feeding programs—important in the care of the youngest children. One "baby class" had very limited manipulatives (a few sticks and bottle caps), and others had large benches and desks that were inappropriate for the youngest children to use. Some teachers also expressed concerns about older siblings bringing under threes to preschool. Children as old as 8 to 12 were occasionally still attending preschool, which sometimes created problems. Management reportedly required parents to send children to primary school and not to continue to use the low-cost nursery schools when children were "too old," but these policies were not consistently enforced.

When asked about the problems of working with under threes, teachers most frequently replied "class control." As one teacher stated, "Unless you keep them active, they can be difficult to control, as they have low attention spans." Related to this were some teachers' complaints that "these children haven't learned manners or proper behavior." Other complaints included communication (e.g., children could not yet talk and make their needs known) and frequent crying. They also expressed concerns about toileting.

## Resources Needed for Under Threes

Finally, when preschool teachers were asked which resources they needed to better cater to the under threes, they named the following:

plenty of learning and play materials, for both indoor and outdoor use;

a larger room and a safe play space;

a feeding program (in the settings that did not have one);

bedding and blankets for sleeping;

an enclosed/fenced compound for the children's protection when playing outside.

When asked other questions concerning the design of a "model" program for under threes, teachers gave a number of more specific responses. Again, the most frequent response concerned learning and play materials. Other needs included "a teacher who is interesting and happy," and "a teacher who has the interests of the children at heart and provides good care." The safety and location of the compound also were raised by several teachers. Some felt that the preschool, particularly by the year or two before primary school, should be on the grounds of the estate's primary school, sharing a playground, more permanent building, and other resources. Other teachers felt that the needs of under threes were best met at or near health centers, with more direct involvement of the nurse and/or nutritionist.

All teachers felt that a feeding program was critical, and that napping facilities were badly needed. For example, they named "a warm room," "a resting room for sleep," and "warm clothing and blankets" as being necessary for under threes. They also mentioned "a place for changing nappies" (diapers) and access to clean water as being important.

Some of the teachers felt that the needs of under threes were best met at home, *if* the mothers were there. They felt that the most important priority was care being provided in an "environment that caters for them." In the absence of mothers in the home and the inability of families to afford maids or baby-sitters, all teachers felt that the preschool offered the only alternative. They also mentioned some of the benefits of early participation in group care, including "learning to socialize with other children" and "close attention and supervision—under threes need child minders for their care."

## INTERSECTORAL COLLABORATIONS FOR CHILDREN AND FAMILIES?

This series of questions corresponded to the research question that examined the nature and effectiveness of community-based intersectoral (inter-agency/ministry) collaborations serving children and families. We also asked parents how these collaborative efforts could be strengthened. Four of the parent interview questions related, indirectly if not directly, to this research question. In Kericho, as in Kiambu, the question was in many ways less relevant to parents and communities due to the number of services provided by the company or estate. In other words, plantations were not settings where government agencies or NGOs were greatly involved. The exceptions to this were the Ministry of Agriculture, the Ministry of Education (particularly through the DICECE), and the Ministry of Health. These were not typically services that parents on the estates were familiar with, except for the Ministry of Health, in the event that they took children to a government clinic or a hospital rather than use the dispensary/clinic on the grounds of the estate.

Again, teachers on the estates indicated that management provided all facilities (e.g., buildings, teacher salaries, a feeding program, where it existed, most of the materials, etc.). As one teacher stated, "Parents are hardly involved, due to lack of time." They also indicated that no NGOs were working on the estates, and that there were, in fact, few outside agencies of any sort working with them.

Exceptions to this were the Ministry of Education, primarily through the DICECE and through a NACECE/Aga Khan Foundation project, which teachers viewed as "more interviews" or as mainly a research undertaking. Teachers also mentioned that they worked with the nurses from the clinics on the estate, who were not Ministry of Health personnel but employees of the company.

When probed about any other types of collaboration they could think of, they named the Kericho County Council and parents. Parental involvement, as previously described, consisted of attending meetings, serving on a committee, and paying a small monthly fee. They appeared to welcome the idea of more collaborators and outside support. The local DICECE collaborators ended each interview with some consultation and support time, discussing training, ideas for parent workshops, and issues to be raised with their preschool committee (when there was one) and/or with management.

## Summary

As anticipated, the plantation preschools faced a number of challenges, as did parents working on the tea estates of the Kericho District. With the exception of one tea estate, no plantation-based preschools in our sample provided snacks or a hot meal, although some had in the past. Many under threes attended the preschools/child care centers, which had been designed for children three to five. Babies and toddlers typically were taken to preschool with an older sibling, which had the effect of delaying some children's entry to primary school until their younger siblings could go to preschool on their own. Few arrangements were made for nursing mothers, and maternity leaves were only provided to "permanent" workers.

In the food and housing areas, a number of problems were identified. Although the estates provided free housing for tea pickers and other workers, this typically consisted of small one- or two-room houses that the families we interviewed had outgrown over time. Cooking took place outside, and finding sufficient places for everyone to sleep and stay warm on cold evenings was often a challenge. Few estates made garden plots available to workers, forcing them to buy all of their food, which was considered a hardship for many families, who commented on the rapid growth in prices of food in Kenya and on their difficulty in feeding their children a well-balanced diet. Parents were hopeful that some of the managers would reinstate feeding programs for children at the preschool, as they often left for work very early, and children tended to carry cold lunches—often *ugali* from the evening before—to school. They felt that a hot lunch should be provided.

In terms of health care, all estates visited provided at least first aid and primary health care services. Mothers typically went into the town of Kericho to a hospital to deliver babies, but some gave birth at home. As will be seen in the Kiambu narratives, mothers hesitated to take time off from tea plucking to take children to the clinic, as they needed to pick a minimum amount of tea in order to be paid.

Several of the preschool teachers we interviewed talked about the problem of unsupervised children—of all ages—on the estates. Preschool typically was provided only during the morning and early afternoon, while parents did not return home from the fields until much later in the day. Although attendance at primary school was "required" by management on all of the estates we visited, truancy was frequent, and a number of children picked tea instead of going to school, as the family urgently needed the money. Another striking impression of most of the estate preschools was the large number of children. In one case, there were over 120 children, with only three teachers. The children ranged in age from six months to eight years. In such circumstances, it was nearly impossible for the teachers to provide even minimal custodial care. Children were often tired, hungry, cold, and dirty. Teachers were committed to meeting children's basic needs and were frustrated at the lack of resources with which to work.

One program in Kericho stands out as a more "optimal" setting, particularly when compared to other estates we visited. In this case, the manager's wife had taken a particular interest in the mothers and children. A feeding program served children from toddlers through primary school, and class sizes were smaller than those just described. A number of self-help and enrichment programs had also been developed for mothers (e.g., crafts making, a choir, and a self-help group that assisted with income-generation activities for its members). Although these activities were encouraged, it also was reported that relatively few women participated in them, as they were too busy working and were too tired. This setting had a special program for the under threes, which emphasized stimulation, nutrition, and care. Again, the numbers were large, and children had only one caregiver/cook, but at least their needs were being catered to far more than in other estates in the district.

On the estates, it was clear that employers (especially managers) were in a position to make the lives of their workers better and provide needed services for workers' children. The local DICECE collaborators were obviously maintaining positive relationships with most managers and felt that, with work, over time more services would be provided—particularly for the youngest children and nursing mothers. Much remained to be done, but the DICECE trainers had taken a consulting/advocacy role and appeared committed to doing all they could to improve the lives of children on the tea estates of the Kericho District.

# Chapter 6

## Kiambu Coffee and Tea Estates:
## It Takes a Weighing Station and
## Supportive Manager to Raise a Child

It is the major aim of the company to cut down expenses and make huge profits—it is the children who lose!

—Father on a tea plantation

## SETTING

The Kiambu District is one of the five districts in Central Province. It is located at the southern part of the province and has a total area of 2,451 square kilometers. The Kiambu District adjoins the Nairobi Province (on the north and west) and also adjoins the northern part of the Kajiado District and includes the towns of Limuru, Kiambu, and Thika. Some parts of this district could be described as peri-urban.

Kiambu is the fourth largest district in Central Province. The estimated population in 1993 was 1,076,000, and it is projected to increase to 1,189,000 by 1996 (Oucho, 1993). In terms of further demographic breakdowns for the district's population, 47.6% of the population of the district was in the 0 to 14 year age cohort, and 3.2% of the total population was above 59 years of age in 1993. The Kiambu District is quite densely populated, although the population is fairly evenly distributed. The Embu District Development Plan (Embu DDP, 1994–96, p.19) notes that there has been "considerable migration of people from other parts of the country to major towns

141

Fig. 6.1    Naptime at Child Care Center in Kiambu Coffee Plantation

in Kiambu District." Local collaborators often discussed both the rising cost of land in the district and the subdivision of family farms to such a small parcel that only kitchen gardens were feasible.

Kiambu has a range of agricultural potential, with both coffee and tea production in both smaller farms and larger corporate estates in the highlands. Wide variations in altitude, rainfall, and temperatures between the highland and lowland areas contribute to this diversity. The district is an agricultural zone favoring growth of cash crops such as tea, coffee, pyrethrum, and various produce. Maize, sisal, cotton, sorghum, millet, cassava, tobacco, sunflowers, onions, and tomatoes are grown in the low fertility areas, with ranching practices in the even more marginal areas.

Thus food crop farming and livestock production are practiced. The Kiambu District is also rich in forests, and building stone is mined in each of its seven divisions, so it is considered to have high economic potential, although unemployment has risen there, contributing to the urban migration to neighboring Nairobi.

In terms of ethnicity, the district is predominantly Kikuyu, but with labor migration to the many tea and coffee plantations, it is quite ethnically and linguistically diverse. The town of Kiambu is the district headquarters and location of the DICECE. Kiambu was selected primarily for its plantation sample, which included both tea and coffee estates, as well as some smaller farms, and for its short distance from Nairobi (less than one hour to most parts of the district).

In contrast to several of the other districts included in our study, Kiambu does not have many voluntary agencies carrying out development projects. Plan International has been the major development NGO in this district, operating mainly in the Limuru and Thika divisions (as well as in the neighboring Embu District). The *Harambee* movement has helped start most of the educational, health, and water facilities. Some women have organized into semipermanent *Harambee* movements, in which needs are identified and resources are pooled to fulfill them. This led, for example, to the formation of Women Bus Unions, which buy and operate buses, with other groups buying and developing rental houses.

Turning to the distribution of labor, most of the employees are working in coffee and tea estates. Coffee plantations employ approximately 50% of the district's labor force and tea estates employ around 20%. It was estimated (Embu District Development Plan [DDP], 1994–96) that by 1996, 46,000 people would be employed on coffee farms and 16,500 on tea estates. Dairy and mixed farming employ approximately 17,000 people, while the major industries of the district employ 23,000 people. The most recent development plan notes that the majority of workers in coffee and tea plantations are temporary employees who are paid on a piece rate. This report also noted that there is significant discrimination against women, who tend to be employed in the textile and food processing industries. The report also notes that, "Child labor is prevalent in the district, especially in the agricultural sector" (DDP, 1994–96, p. 52). This was noted during our field work as well.

Finally, turning to educational services, preschools increased in the the Kiambu District from 445 in 1989 to 574 in 1993, while primary schools increased from 322 in 1989 to 346 in 1993. Enrollment in primary schools reached 218,415 in 1993, while secondary school enrollment rose from 38,284 in 1989 to 40,619 in 1993 (DDP, 1994–96, p. 58).

## KIAMBU SAMPLE

Three tea and coffee estates were sampled, representing different geographic regions of the Kiambu District. Two of these plantations had previous contact with DICECE staff and had at least one DICECE or CICECE trained teacher; however, for the third estate visited, this was the first contact with the NACECE/DICECE. At this estate we had difficulty gaining access to parents, particularly casual laborers, and we only interviewed two parents. All interviews were held at the estate preschools. Typically, interviews with teachers were held the first day, and interviews with a group of parents were held on the following day.

A total of 22 parents and grandparents were interviewed, including 15 mothers, 4 fathers, and 3 grandmothers. The ages of first-born children ranged from 5 to 25 years, with a mean age of 13.5. The ages of last-born children ranged from 1 to 5 years, with a mean age of 2.9. It was also striking that several of the mothers interviewed on coffee estates had lost children, including one mother who had lost two and another who said, "My only living child is six years, the others died."

When asked about their roles in the community or on the estate, two fathers were members of a school committee, and one said, "I was a member of the pre-school committee until it was dismantled." One father was a member of the Welfare Committee for an estate, and one was involved in youth committee leadership. In terms of self-described work roles, five were tea pluckers, three were homemakers or housewives, three were coffee pickers and pruners, two were overseers or supervisors, three were preschool teachers or child minders (not interviewed with teachers), one was a security guard, one was a nurse/nutritionist, and one was a cleaner. Their time on the present estate ranged from three months to 25 years, with nine living there nine years or less, and the remainder living there from 14 to 25 years. The length of time many families stayed in the same estate was striking and offered a contrast to Kericho, although in both districts some parents we interviewed had worked at their present estates for over 20 years.

Turning to the preschool teachers, eight female teachers were interviewed. The estates sampled employed between two and six teachers, with an average of four, including two to three women called "baby-sitters" or "child minders." One estate had two separate preschools, one of which served as an evening social hall; the other two estates had one preschool. Only one of the preschools had a feeding program. Two of the schools charged no tuition to parents. Teachers interviewed ranged in age from 25 to 41 years, with a mean age of 31.2.

In terms of their formal education, four teachers had completed Form 4, one had completed Form 2, and three had completed Standard 7. Five of the teachers were untrained, two were in (DICECE) training now, and one was trained. One teacher was doing a private "college" ECE course. Years of teaching experience ranged from three to twenty, with five teachers having between three and six years of experience, and three having from 10 to 20 years of experience. Even the teacher with 20 years of experience, however, had the job title and pay scale of "caretaker," not "teacher."

Six teachers had only taught in their current preschool, and two had taught in another preschool, not on a plantation. All eight teachers reported that the estate or company paid their salary, and six reported no other income sources. Two teachers reported that they also were involved in a small business. Five of the teachers were single, and three were married, although all but one teacher had at least one child. First-born children ranged in age from five to 22 years, with a mean age of 13.5, and last-born children ranged from three to 10 years, with a mean age of six. One teacher gave birth within a week of our interview.

Turning to the primary children interviewed, 10 children, five girls and five boys, were interviewed at their schools, which were near the estates sampled. Children ranged in age from seven to 13 years, and they were drawn from Standard 2 (N = 5) and Standard 3 (N = 5). Five of the children ranged in age from seven to nine years, and five ranged in age from 10 to 13 years. Ages of their youngest siblings ranged from two to seven years, with seven children having a sibling between the ages of two and three.

## PROBLEMS AND CHALLENGES FACING FAMILIES

### Portrait: Single Father on Tea Plantation

*My wife is dead, so I play the role of both mother and father. In the morning I prepare food and help children get ready for preschool and school. Children come home for lunch, and my 12-year-old son cares for the 5-year-old after I leave early in the morning for work. Then he walks with the younger one to preschool and goes on to the primary school. It is hard, but we work together—what else can we do?*

Interviews with preschool teachers correlated strongly with parent interviews, particularly on the topic of problems facing families on the tea and coffee plantations visited in the Kiambu District. Many of the problems described by parents and teachers related to economic hardships and crowded living conditions. The most frequently mentioned problems were illnesses, including instances, according to teachers, when children were sick and parents did not realize it. Diseases included kwashiorkor, scabies, measles, worms, and respiratory infections. Families also lacked money to buy sufficient food and clothing for children and, as several participants in the study put it, "The company hasn't done much—except the free preschool."

Crowded living conditions also were mentioned frequently—especially by parents. The lack of good shelter was particularly a problem for large families, in which three generations might share one room, or families with over six children who lived in one or two rooms. Working hours in the field were too long to permit additional income-generating activities or the cultivation of even small kitchen gardens to raise vegetables, and access to land for such cultivation was extremely difficult. Many teachers felt that children were not growing as they should, not only physically but in a "lack of morals, manners, and respect of elders." This often was attributed by both teachers and parents to the unavoidable neglect of children's needs with the long hours worked by parents, often single mothers, with no time to check on children during the day. Thus most young children were left in the care of older siblings or were carried, if still nursing, to the field on the mother's back. Lack of "time" was often named as a problem facing families, as parents typically left by 6 A.M. and did not return until 5 or 6 P.M., being paid by the number of kilos picked.

Children lacked warm clothing and frequently suffered from exposure in the cold tea and coffee growing areas that we visited. Hygiene also was listed as a problem, as public water taps were sometimes broken, and water needed to be carried from the river, often far away from workers' homes. The differences in working conditions (including maternity leave and access to medical care and preschool) between causal and permanent laborers also were dramatic, with casual laborers having an extremely precarious life.

## Ways Problems Affected Children

From the preschool teachers' perspective these and other problems affected children in many ways, including "poor or variable attendance at preschool" and primary school and "children not growing as they should—often lacking food." As one teacher put it, "When children's stomachs are empty, they cannot learn." Another described children as "so hungry that they try to take another child's lunch." Preschool teachers and child minders also reported that "near the end of the month, children are more hungry." This was related to the fact that parents were paid monthly, at the beginning of each month. Yet, according to some teachers, "On pay day, many parents are drinking (home brew), and they may neglect or abuse their children."

Other problems included personal hygiene. "Parents have no time to wash young children, and by Thursday or Friday, they're really dirty." Parents "also have a hard time providing children with enough warm clothing," so children are more vulnerable to illness.

# Changes in the Past 10 to 15 Years

The following sections summarize the ways in which parents described changes affecting their family, across different social and economic domains or aspects of daily life.

## Food

As in other settings, the major change observed by parents was the increasing cost of food and the loss of the means to grow their own food. Four parents commented that, "The diet is poorer, due to the high cost of food." One mother stated,

"We purchase all the food now. In rural areas, we used to grow most of the food." None of the estates we visited appeared to provide even permanent workers with any land near their houses on which to plant a kitchen garden, although some parents on a coffee estate said that they still had relatives in "the reserve," not far from the plantation, and that they were attempting to grow some maize or vegetables there.

In terms of the diet of young children in the Kiambu estates we visited, only one (a coffee plantation) provided a feeding program, which consisted of serving a morning snack of beans and maize that was cooked in a kitchen adjoining the preschool. The others no longer provided any food to the nursery school. One parent commented, "The preschool used to provide food, and we were deducted from our salaries to purchase it. This has stopped due to the high cost of food." (When we met with estate managers, we strongly recommended that the feeding programs be reestablished.) Mothers named milk, *paw paw* (papaya), *uji*, bananas, potatoes, and greens as the most frequent weaning foods.

## Housing

As in the estates where we collected data in the Kericho District, the housing that was provided to permanent workers (or, in one case, rented by workers) on the estates was very small and crowded, especially for growing families with young children. Parents' comments regarding housing included, "We live in one single room," and "We even live in one room with our parents!" (in reference to a rare case of grandparents living together with grown children on a plantation). Casual laborers who were not "permanent" employees of the estates (even though many had worked on the same estate for multiple years) rented their housing and commented, "Rents are now very high!" They also described the cost of living as "very expensive— our salaries are no longer adequate to meet the needs of our families." During other parts of the interview, the theme of crowded housing was frequently mentioned— whether in the context of breaking old taboos about grandparents, parents, and grandchildren sleeping in the same room, or in terms of the lack of space and privacy needed for raising healthy children.

## Health

The nature of work on plantations (low-paying, long hours of physical labor, with pay based on the quantity picked, often requiring a minimum weight to be picked in order to be paid for that day's work), combined with the colder, mountainous environments where tea and coffee grow well, appeared to have negative effects on both child and maternal health. Most larger plantations did, however, have their own dispensaries or clinics. A nurse/nutritionist we interviewed on a tea plantation, which was very ill equipped with few medicines or medical supplies, stated, "There are many children with malnutrition, measles, and colds due to both lack of proper feeding and exposure to cold." As parents on a coffee plantation told us, "Even when children are sick, mothers have to go to work, since no work means no pay." They went on to describe in more detail how difficult it is to even take children to the clinic, as they may not be able to make the daily minimum "debits" required to be paid. In some cases, other mothers attempt to pick extra tea so that the mother taking a sick child to the clinic will not be penalized.

The quality of health services provided on the grounds of the tea and coffee plantations in Kiambu varied greatly. One clinic was extremely well equipped, as the health officer put it, "much better than most Ministry of Health clinics and even some hospitals in the area," including refrigeration for medicines such as immunization serums and a good supply of medicines and first aid supplies. Another one, previously mentioned, had very few medicines or supplies that would be needed in a work-related emergency. Perhaps the most encouraging health-related finding in the three large estates sampled in Kiambu was that parents reported that "all children" were immunized.

Yet, as many parents observed, "The company does not give adequate care to sick children," and "there are not enough drugs and often no transport in an emergency—or for a mother in labor." As one father put it, "The major aim is to cut down expenses and make huge profits—it is children who lose!" The lack of clean water for drinking also was named as a health concern on some of the plantations. "We now collect water from the river, as the pipes to the (communal) tap have broken."

The lack of maternity leave for casual laborers—sometimes the majority of employees on a particular estate—was raised many times by parents and teachers as a health and child-rearing concern. "Mothers return to work shortly after the birth of their children, as they will lose pay and perhaps their jobs if they do not. This is a serious problem for mothers who have had Caesarean sections or other difficulties with the delivery!"

## Education

As in other settings, parents commented that, "Education is very expensive!" In these estates, only preschool education, which served as partial day care, was provided on the plantation's grounds. Children attended primary school in neighboring rural or peri-urban schools where the rising cost of education was often a problem for tea and coffee pickers and other casual laborers. The cost of uniforms, many books, and fees were mentioned by parents as barriers to educating all of their children, although they expressed a desire to do so. Preschool teachers and some managers stated that, similar to in the Kericho District, children were not discouraged from tea or coffee picking and were also often needed to care for younger siblings while the mother was in the field. Thus in the areas of both health and education, plantation life presented a number of complex and embedded challenges to families trying to do the "right thing" for their children.

In terms of preschool education, a major concern was the lack of feeding programs in most plantations. As previously discussed, some estates that had previously offered snack or lunch programs for children had stopped doing so due to the rising cost of food in Kenya. Thus children were carrying cold lunches and, as several preschool teachers observed, "The little food children bring goes bad by lunch time." Another teacher agreed, "It is not good for children—they need hot food." This was a particular concern during the rainy seasons and winter, when the tea and coffee growing regions were "baridi sana"—very cold.

## Social Structures: Loss of Traditions

Grandparents, parents, and children all sleep in one room. This was taboo in the old days, but here we have no alternative!

—Mother on coffee estate

The major change in social structures related to the family that was discussed by Kiambu participants in the study was the increase in single mothers. "There are many single mothers, which was not the case before." Another change was that, "The families do not own any land here—they are all squatters." Among the many social pressures that this worsening economic situation had created was one related to the housing shortage. Parents interviewed expressed their concerns about the loss of traditions, given the hardship of life on the plantations. As quoted above, one mother lamented, "Grandparents, parents, and children all sleep in one room. This was a taboo in the old days, but here we have no alternative!"

When asked about any self-help groups, particularly women's groups, a typical response was, "There are groups, but hardly any time is available to organize activities due to pressure to work!" When we asked where single mothers and other parents obtained advice on child-rearing or received any sort of support, the response was, "Issues are discussed when weighing the tea." The use of the weighing station as a source of support turned out to have multiple meanings in the context of the care of under threes. When we first drove past such a weighing station, the local collaborators pointed out the number of under threes (most appeared to be 18 months to three years of age) who were sitting or playing next to the piles of tea leaves. The only visible adult with them was the overseer who weighed the tea and kept records of how much each worker picked. When we inquired about this— during interviews with parents and the preschool teachers on the estate—we were told that these children were the ones who were "too young to be enrolled in nursery school" and "too big to be carried with the mother while she picks tea, which she puts on her back, and it is too damp and cold to set the little ones on the ground where she is picking." Thus the weighing stations at this plantation in any case had become a communal, informal child care setting, with the overseer or clerk providing minimal adult supervision, along with a few older siblings who were apparently attending neither nursery school or primary school. This also was a setting in which mothers nursed babies while their tea leaves were being weighed. We asked managers about nursing mothers, and they told us that there were no special breaks for this and that this was done "on their own time."

## Child-rearing and Family Size

When I joined here I was alone, but now I have six children and I am a single mother.

—Mother on coffee plantation

As discussed above, a major change in child-rearing was the increase in the number of single families, particularly on the tea and coffee estates (in both the Kiambu and Kericho Districts). As one mother observed, "Most families here have 6-7 children and most are single mothers." Others argued that, "Gradually, families have accepted family planning, hence parents now have fewer children." The economic and housing pressures on families have led many to have fewer children, another perspective on changes in family size.

In response to our questions about maternity leave, we were told that a fairly standard guideline for plantations was that, "Mothers who are permanent workers get two months' maternity leave." When asked about casual laborers, who sometimes outnumber "permanent" employees, we were informed that, "Casual laborers have no maternity leave. They resume work as soon as they can after delivery." We continued to ask why single mothers lack traditional social supports (e.g., a grandmother or extended family members). A mother replied, "Some mothers take their babies to work—carrying them on their backs." Others agreed with this, saying, "Most of the mothers carry their babies to work so that they can continue breastfeeding them. This means no time is wasted."

The other setting, aside from the weighing station, in which babies and other under threes were cared for—or at least taken to—was the nursery school. Older preschool children were frequently observed, in both the Kiambu and Kericho Districts, carrying younger siblings to nursery school on their backs. They often would remain in the nursery school for much of the morning. Alternatively, the younger ones would wander about the already crowded preschool classroom, looking for something to eat or to play with, or for someone to give them attention and care.

## Problems Facing Under Threes and Their Families

There is no time to play with or care for the children. The day is very busy, going from 6 A.M. until 5 P.M., and even when I come home, there is no time for the children—so many chores must be done!

—Mother on tea plantation

As already discussed, the issues of neglect and inappropriate care arrangements were high among the problems facing the youngest children on the tea and coffee estates. From parents' perspectives, the greatest concerns about meeting the needs of their youngest children revolved around the high cost of food and the related problems of malnutrition and hunger and the problem of small, "very crowded houses or rooms." "Most families of four, five, or six people share one room—how can children have enough space to grow and be healthy?" The other concern most frequently mentioned by parents was the "high cost of living." As one father put it, "Our small salaries are not enough to meet the basic needs of our families." He and other workers lamented over the "lack of farms, no matter how small, to grow some foodstuffs such as vegetables for families' needs. If some small land were available, this would help to supplement our small family incomes!"

Another concern related to the care of under threes was the lack of "child care support for mothers on plantations." As previously discussed, there was typically no formal care arrangement available for children considered too young to be enrolled in the preschool. The only plantation in the study that had a "baby class" was a large tea estate in the Kericho District, in which the (British) general manager's wife had shown a special interest and established a feeding program, infant class, and other sources of family support. In Kiambu, in contrast, there was a "lack of adequate services for children, who often spend many hours each day at the preschool." When we visited one coffee estate, for example, we counted nearly 50 children, most of them under three, trying to sleep on a cold, cement floor with minimal blankets and no mattresses or napping mats. Many were sick, and it was obvious that communicable diseases would easily spread among the children. In adjoining rooms, the older children (ages three to six) were "napping" while sitting at large desks. (These conditions were brought to the attention of the manager, and mattresses were donated to the program following data collection on the estate.)

Another concern raised by both parents and preschool teachers related to the lack of "parental education for teenage mothers." With a rising birthrate among young single mothers, many were concerned that the care of young children would become even more neglectful or even harmful. Several parents also commented on the "indiscipline among older children—particularly teenagers—they hardly obey their parents." Parents felt that this breakdown in traditional respect for elders was directly related to the lack of supervision and guidance on the plantations, with parents gone many hours of the day and children dropping out of school when parents could not pay their fees or did not discourage them from picking tea or coffee to contribute to the family's income. Indeed, the issue of child labor was a "serious problem. Children have to work to supplement the meager incomes of their parents." The theme of a lack of time to care for one's children was a pervasive and a passionate one among the families interviewed in the Kiambu District. "There is no time for mothers to look after their children here. Mothers have a very long working day, starting at 6 A.M. and going until 5 or 6 P.M. Little time is left for child care!" This also was related to the poor nutrition or diet of the family—not only did they lack land to grow even a kitchen garden and lack money to buy food, they also lacked time to prepare proper meals, thus children frequently ate cold food. This was perceived as contributing to children's greater vulnerability to childhood illnesses and malnutrition. Yet, when children got sick, "Mothers do no take care of their sick children because absence from work means no pay, which mothers cannot afford!" This vicious cycle of poverty and unintended neglect was clearly a source of deep concern and regret among the Kiambu District families participating in the study.

## Ways Families Are Coping

When asked how families were coping with these pressures and problems, the coping mechanisms echoed the problems. For example, parents told us that, "Some mothers, in order to make sure they breast-feed their babies, strap them on their backs and feed them on breaks from picking." They also expressed concern about this practice, as pesticides and other chemicals were used—particularly on the coffee plantations—and it was cold and damp in the fields. Yet, it was given as an example of many mothers' determination not to practice early weaning and to provide better attention to their youngest children. Another nutrition-related coping strategy was to send food to the preschool with the children. "Where there is no feeding program, parents give children food to carry. Unfortunately, some of the food given is overnight leftovers which go bad by lunch time the next day." Parents expressed a strong desire to organize a feeding program in the nursery school, but they could not afford to do so without the assistance of the estate management. They also expressed fear of raising the issue, lest they might lose their job. This need to be grateful for employment and to be subservient, while not surprising in a plantation context, was disturbing and clearly undermined the dignity and self-worth of parents in many cases.

Another ironic coping strategy was the use of older children to supplement the family's income. As already discussed, children were not encouraged to stay in school, but they were often encouraged to pick coffee. Although the parents realized that this was a temporary coping mechanism and that children would likely be better off with further education, they often expressed having little choice—or little control—over their older children's behavior. Perhaps the best coping strategy parents employed was their conversations together—some of which took place at the weighing station, as mothers nursed their babies. Preschool teachers also were caring women who, even after school ended in early afternoon, were observed to have many young children following them home and saw their jobs as extending beyond their (under)paid work day.

Teachers added their observations to the list of ways in which families in the plantations were coping. These included borrowing money for school fees, although this often led to families "borrowing until they cannot repay their debts." Other parents visit the headmaster if the child does not want to go to school, or if they cannot afford the fees or other related costs. Occasionally this has a positive outcome, or an extension for fee payment is granted, but this was described as "rare." In terms of the frequently expressed desire of families to be able to grow some food, some plantations were "providing small plots for kitchen gardens." Food also was "loaned" to families, but only to permanent pickers and not casual laborers, who needed it even more.

In terms of the lack of family or adult recreation and support services, two of the tea plantations visited had small canteens, and in one setting the larger preschool (of two on the plantation) was used by men in the evening to play darts, but "there's nothing for the women."

## Parental and Community Contributions to Early Education and Care

Parents are quite ready to provide the little they can provide!
                                        —Preschool teacher on tea estate

The most frequently mentioned "good thing the community has done for young children" was "taking their children to preschool." Some teachers told us that "parents pass through the preschool to see what the child does—they have little time, but they do care!" Other parents reported that they were "involved in the stimulation of their children by making toys and playing with them—especially on the weekends." Others said that they worked hard to provide food for their children and took their children to the health center when they were sick and for immunizations. Families had less time for growth monitoring and promotion (GMP) activities, but some parents reported that they took their youngest children for weighing.

In terms of any direct parental contributions to preschools, one preschool teacher summed it up, "Parents hardly contribute because they have literally no time left out of their busy schedule and long working day!" Teachers felt that the greatest contributions plantation parents made to their young children were feeding them, clothing them, and sending them to preschool.

Teacher interviews raised similar points to those made above. Teachers stated that there was "very little" parental involvement, due to parents' long work days. They reported that, "Parents want a feeding program, but either can't or won't pay for it." A major difference between community-based preschools (in Kenya) and plantation preschools was that, "Everything goes through the management—they run things, and there is no school committee," or other structure to involve parents in decisions affecting the preschool. Yet at least one teacher felt that, "With managers' help, we can hold parent meetings—if they start after 3 P.M., parents don't miss money." One estate we visited had a preschool committee with five members, including management, one teacher, and two parents.

Other teachers felt that, even given their full work schedules and lack of time, "Parents can assist with materials-making by giving things to children to carry to school." Another agreed, "We ask parents to come in with songs, instruments, stories, and anything else they are willing to share with the children." As one optimistic teacher stated, "Parents are quite ready to provide the little they can provide!"

## Typical Child Care Arrangements for Children under Three

Typically, children under three were cared for in the home, according to several of the parents we interviewed. "Parents provide for the needs of their children at home—they feed them and wash them before going to work." Older siblings often care for younger children while the parent(s) are working. "They play with them, make them toys, wash them and feed them." As already discussed, they also bring younger siblings with them to preschool. For this reason, in both Kiambu and Kericho plantation preschools, there was a wide age range of children, including babies on the backs of older siblings and "preschool" children ages six or seven and even older. In other words, children (particularly girls) are sometimes held back from primary school in order to care for their baby brother or sister. Four teachers commended that, "Girls are still kept home, including girls who carry the baby to the field with the mother." Very few families could afford an *ayah* or a child minder, or, as a preschool teacher observed, "Only the wives of managers or supervisors could afford an *ayah*."

As previously described, "Some mothers take their babies strapped on their backs into the fields so that they can feed them between working hours." In many cases, "The child follows the mother wherever she goes." Parents and teachers agreed that, "Most of the under threes, after weaning, are taken to preschools. Finally, "A few—very few—parents can afford to employ a maid (*ayah*) to look after the baby." This was more true of middle managers and professional staff on the plantations and was not observed or reported among the tea and coffee pickers.

In response to the question of where the best place for the care of under threes might be, the consensus was, "Home with their mothers or with a relative is best— here, however, this is not possible, as the mothers are very busy working and cannot afford a maid." Thus parents felt that the preschool was the next best place to being cared for at home, even though it was not really intended for the care of such young children. As one mother put it, "In the preschool is best, as the teacher has more time to play with them and see to their needs." Preschool was clearly viewed as providing more custodial than educational services to children.

Teacher interviews offered a somewhat different view of where most under threes were cared for, with many teachers stating that, "There are many under threes in the preschool—and even some babies." "Mothers who might usually carry small children with them to the fields bring them to the preschool when the coffee plants are being sprayed with chemicals, and some come with older siblings—if they are not left at the weighing station." Sometimes mothers of infants were reassigned to other tasks, such as pruning, when spraying was being done so children were not exposed to the chemicals. One preschool teacher was critical of parents taking infants into the fields, saying, "Most parents are not enlightened—they take small babies into the coffee fields, which can be dangerous, including exposure to chemicals, possible injuries, cold and rain!"

With many casual laborers who did not have the two-month maternity leave, mothers often "brought babies to the preschool and leave food and ask the teachers to change the nappies and feed the baby." Several teachers expressed concern that, "Parents want to bring the younger ones, but there are no facilities and the preschool is cold and ill equipped for meeting their needs."

When we asked teachers about factors related to preschool attendance, they stated that the fact that preschool was "free" or "low cost" (10/Kshs. per month) made income less a factor in the estates than in communities where fees tended to be higher. In some estates, preschool "attendance is required—and enforced" to varying degrees. Thus preschool or child care services were typically provided and even required on the estates, whether or not they were equipped to meet the needs of the large numbers of young children who attended them. In response to the general question, "Who is caring for under threes here?" one teacher stated, "We are caring for them—teachers and child minders" (who served as classroom assistants in several plantation preschools visited). Another teacher in a tea plantation added, "Yes, we are caring for them, and also the clerks at the weighing stations!"

## JOYS AND CHALLENGES OF BEING A PARENT

I ask God to add to my days to see my children educated and taking care of their own children!

—Mother in tea estate

As in other settings and districts, the greatest joy and benefit of having children was "to *be a parent*. This is both self and socially fulfilling!" "My greatest satisfaction is to be able to provide for my children and budget for my family," one mother said. Another mother stated that she liked "the feeling that my children will look after me in my old age."

In terms of what was hardest about being a parent, much of this chapter reflects the complex and challenging lives of child-rearing in a plantation context. In response to this question, parents simply stated "bringing up children" and "providing for my children."

### Parental Aspirations for Children

When asked about future aspirations for their children, the most frequent response from parents in the Kiambu District was, "I would like my child to be well educated and learn well." This was followed by, "I would like my child to be well fed." Other responses included the desire for children to be self-reliant and to obtain better employment some day. "I would like my children to be able to provide for themselves and bring up their families well," and "I want my children to get good jobs—to be clerks, doctors, or secretaries." Other responses included, "I want my children to be God fearing." Some mothers spoke of the present and said, "I would like to be able to provide a good house for my children," and "I would like to be able to be at home and be with my young children." Finally, one mother summed it up, saying, "I ask God to add to my days to see my children educated and taking care of their own children!"

## Relevance of Preschool to Families' Traditions

Similar to the Kericho District, both teachers and parents commented that "traditional lifestyles are not so obvious on estates," and that many different cultures or ethnic groups were represented among the workers. Thus some teachers felt that preschool was used primarily for custodial care by busy working parents who did not care much about culture maintenance. Others felt that preschool was relevant and consciously attempted to respect and honor the home cultures of their children. When we asked whether parents discussed this issue, most teachers said "No," and the two teachers who said "Yes," told us, "Parents commend us." One teacher stated that, "Preschool is relevant to all cultures," and another told us, "When I teach a song in a particular language, it can help children better understand that culture."

When we asked whether there was ever an "issue made" about Kikuyu teachers working with Kamba or Kisii children, teachers stated, "There are very few problems—I use Kiswahili when teaching, and only occasionally teach a song in another language." Teachers stated that they were aware of children's home cultures and mother tongues and tried to speak some of the children's languages at times, but that they taught mostly in Kiswahili and that this did not seem to be causing any problems with families—or children.

## Activities Used to Support Children's Home Culture

As in other settings, the most frequently mentioned ways in which teachers tried to support children's home culture were through "role plays of home activities" and teaching "traditional songs and dances." Storytelling and riddles also were used by teachers. Returning to the theme of languages used in the classroom, one teacher stated, "Children learn Kikuyu after about one month, including Kisii and Luo children who learn to speak Kikuyu." In this case, the teacher did not tend to use Kiswahili and added, "We don't make special adaptations for different ethnic groups—we're one tribe here!"

# GOALS FOR CHILD CARE OF UNDER THREES

When asked about what their goals would be for a child care program for under threes, the most frequent response of preschool teachers was "food—we should look for a parent or elderly mama to cook and wash dishes and have a feeding program." Other goals would be to have many materials for children to play with, to have a playground with facilities and equipment, and to have "an enclosed, warm place." Teachers also felt that "the compound should be limited to them—not have older children in the same place." Other priorities for a program serving under threes included bedding and napping facilities, toilets (small potties), and "a change of clothes for when clothes get wet or soiled." As one teacher summarized, "Food, sleep and playing—all are needed by the young ones!"

## Best Place for Under Threes

When teachers were asked where the needs of under threes were best met, they all stated that the preschool was the best place in the estates. "You ask parents to provide, but at home they can't always provide." "As a teacher, I think I understand them better—parents are only with them about two hours a day, then they sleep!" Other comments included, "Nursing mothers just take their babies and leave them at a weighing bin with the clerk—a day care center is better!" Teachers also felt that, "Under threes need a place of their own—not with so many older children!" As discussed in the last section, teachers felt that a special program serving under threes was needed and that "a special child care center would be the best place for them!"

Other needs of under threes included growth monitoring and immunization, which was typically done at the clinic or dispensary. Children also needed warmer clothing and access to clean water. One teacher added that, "What is needed is better training and pay for teachers and a chance to visit other preschools!"

In terms of teachers' vision for a "model program" for under threes, the most frequently mentioned needs were "facilities, including classrooms, toilets, and small furniture," "plenty of learning, teaching, and play materials," and "napping mats or mattresses to protect children from the cold floor." Teachers agreed with parents that "a feeding program" was needed "at least two times every day, including a morning snack and a hot lunch" prepared on site. Teachers also emphasized the need for better recreational facilities, such as a safer, better-equipped playground and a van that could transport children on field trips and to the clinic. They also emphasized the importance of a health program, including immunizations, and weighing equipment for babies and regular checkups, and they felt that mothers should be given time off for these important activities with their children. Finally, teachers felt that uniforms, or at least "proper, warm clothing," were needed.

## CHILDREN'S INTERVIEWS

## Portrait: 13-Year-Old Girl on Coffee Estate

*I wake up at 5 A.M., make the fire, bathe, then prepare tea; I take the younger ones (ages three and seven) to wash, and breakfast (warming the previous evening's food) is shared among us by our mother. I leave for school at 6 A.M., going quite a distance, and by the lunch hour the younger child was in nursery and this child carries a tin to school. After leaving school, I wash utensils, make a fire, sweep the house, and warm washing water. The nursery school child gets home at 1 P.M.; we collect firewood in the coffee estates, and mother prepares supper. While mother cooks, I do my homework. Then my mother tells me to prepare my books for the following day. My father and mother tell us stories in the evening, and then we go to bed early, very tired!*

## Children's Involvement in Sibling Care

As evident from the parents' and teachers' interviews and from our observations on the plantations, sibling care was a vital, if vulnerable, link to child survival and the mother's (parents') ability to work to support the family. During the day, older preschool children and primary-age children were often seen carrying younger siblings on their backs or playing with them in the (workers housing) compound or near the preschool. As in other settings, children were not only involved in child care but assisted their families with many domestic chores, which are detailed in this section. It should be noted that the only child who was not involved in the primary care of a younger sibling was a boy whose family employed an *ayah* (child minder and maid). This was rare among plantation families, and in this case, the father worked in a salaried or "middle management" level on an estate.

Among the child care related tasks that primary school children and older siblings of under threes described were "washing the baby," "looking after the baby," "warming the baby's food," helping the baby with toileting, playing with younger siblings, and "teaching the younger child" things they had learned in preschool or primary school. Older siblings also washed the younger children's clothes and carried the baby with them wherever they went. When we asked what sorts of things children did with their younger siblings to keep them happy, these included giving them utensils (e.g., a spoon) to play with, "making balls, dolls, and ropes," "drawing pictures for the baby," and "playing games" with them. Others said that they "modeled toys" for the little one or "just played with the baby."

## Caring for Sick Children

When asked how they could tell when a child was sick, the most frequent response was, "They have a high temperature," or "They are hot." The second most frequent response was, "They are tired," or "They are sleeping too much." Other ways they knew a younger sibling was ill included, "Coughing indicates chest problems," "They are not playing," "They are dull and bored," and "The child has pains and is unhappy."

In terms of their response when a child got sick, five children reported that they "tell the mother and get some medicine." Other children reported that they "gave medicine such as cough syrup, painkillers, and malaria tablets" to younger siblings when they were sick or that they "give them food." Children also responded to sick children by carrying them and comforting them and "trying to play with him." In terms of how parents responded when children got sick, older siblings said that their parent(s) would "take the child to the hospital after trying home treatments," and others stated that "first they try medicine we have at home."

When asked how they comforted a crying baby, children's responses included "singing lullabies" (five children), "giving the children food," "carrying the baby," "rocking the baby," and "playing with him."

## Children's Preschool Memories

All of the children in the Kiambu sample had attended nursery school. Five children had attended for two years, three had attended for three years, and one had attended for four years. Children had memories that contrasted to children's preschool memories from other settings in the study. The most frequent memories were medical and "nutritional"—"Doctor checked and injected me," "A child fainted and was taken to the hospital," and "We were given food." Two children recalled that they were "sent home for lack of fees," and three children remembered "hearing A, B, C, D" and "being told to write."

When asked to compare their memories of preschool to their current experiences in primary school, children said, "Primary students are more clever and know many things," "Children in primary school are bigger and able to write," and, "In primary, there is more learning." Several also stated that in "preschool we got food—here we do not."

All children interviewed thought that "nursery school" was the best place for children under three because, "There is no one to care for them at home," and "The child will be better looked after in the preschool." Children agreed that it is good to go to nursery school because "The child becomes clever," "Young ones should be in school to learn," and "There is no one at home to care for them so they must go!"

## Managers' Interviews

In each estate visited, we had both an entry and an exit interview with the general manager. We also interviewed other central staff, including the health officer or nurse. Interviews began with a discussion of how things had changed over the past 10 to 15 years, with a focus on workers' lives. We also inquired about the number of employees, services offered, and whether they were involved in any intersectoral collaborations. These interviews are summarized in this section.

## Types of Change

In terms of food, managers agreed with workers about the lack of kitchen garden space. As a coffee manager put it, "Kitchen garden spaces have not been provided for workers to grow vegetables. No maize can be grown in some areas, as it can ruin the soil for coffee." In contrast, the manager of another coffee estate told us, "There has been a lot of change—salaries have increased, and we're now providing small plots for workers to grow vegetables and have established nursery schools in all our estates." A nurse in one tea estate felt that, although malnutrition among children was a persistent problem, "People have started eating different foods over time, as available and affordable. Before, families fed mainly on mashed foods— bananas, potatoes, maize, and beans, but now they are frying many more foods."

When asked about feeding programs, one tea estate manager responded, "The company finds it hard to find the money to meet such basic needs for children as a feeding program. We pay the preschool teachers' salaries and also the baby-sitter's salary, we provide facilities and some materials to the preschools, so that leaves the rest—including food—to the mama, who's frequently unable to provide." In fact, only one estate in Kiambu had a feeding program for its preschool programs, and only one in Kericho had a feeding program for children from infancy through primary school. That program had been run by the manager's wife for eight years at the time of our interview, but it was being discontinued due to cost.

In terms of housing, one manager stated, "Every worker should have a house, but they don't." We inquired about the number of employees. "We have 700 permanent workers and at least 500 casuals are here most of the year, working in both the coffee estate and the flower company" (on the same large estate). In other words, casual laborers had none of the family benefits such as housing and child care, however insufficient, which the permanent workers had.

Turning to education, particularly preschool and primary, the estate that appeared to have the greatest commitment to preschool education had sent one teacher for DICECE training and was preparing to send a second teacher for training the following year. This manager was interviewed with a clinical supervisor with a government (Ministry of Health) clinic in the reserve just outside of the estate. He described the ways in which management was attempting to provide for preschool education and to support primary attendance. "There is only one preschool, but we have also hired a baby-sitter. So, there are three teachers (mostly for three to five year olds) and one baby-sitter. They all operate out of the same preschool." We observed that the older children were served in the relatively small preschool, leaving the under threes and their baby-sitter outside, where it was cold and often rainy. We discussed this with the manager, who agreed to look into putting up a second building for the younger children.

Turning to primary education, the same manager stated, "We encourage school attendance very much—especially for children to complete primary. We even give parents soft loans or ask headmasters about allowing parents to pay with install-ments." When asked about attendance rates, he continued, "It's a rule here for all children to go to school, and approximately 80%, I'd say, go . . . but some refuse to go—and the big ones may help parents with coffee picking. The problem is that once they've tasted money, they refuse school!" This theme was echoed at other estates in both the Kiambu and Kericho Districts. The manager of another coffee estate observed that, "There are two primary schools near here, and the primary schools are like any normal government school—not maintained and not so good." When we inquired about whether parents could afford the school fees and other expenses, he responded, "The building funds, etc., are a problem for many, but we require parents to send children to primary school. We even sack parents whose children don't attend school."

In terms of health services, the best-equipped dispensary visited in perhaps the entire study was found on a coffee and flower plantation in the Kiambu District. The manager stated, "We also provide transport when needed to take permanent workers to the hospital." Again, this service (like maternity leave) was not extended to casual laborers. Yet many health problems were described in our interviews, particularly with the nurse-nutritionist at a tea estate. "We've had some child deaths here recently—in fact, several children were left in homes without food for several days. Some parents are irresponsible!" Previously this nurse had visited homes and had checked on children's care, but she was "very busy now with clinic office hours" and reported that she rarely had time to visit the preschool to check on the children's health and growth.

## Problems Facing Families with Young Children: Managers' Views

Without preschool it would be disastrous—the children would not survive!
—Nurse on Kiambu tea estate

The consensus of managers and health personnel was that malnutrition was the greatest problem facing families on the estates. "The lack of *uji* and milk is a problem—many children are underfed, and some (mothers) could even stay home a bit longer in the morning and prepare a better breakfast." Although one estate did have a provision of a small number of kitchen gardens, the others did not. As one manager stated, regarding kitchen gardens on the estate, "We had been doing that, but no longer, since the estate is now very full of tea—even the former owners believed that we should plant every possible bit of land in tea!" Another manager commented on the spending priorities of workers. "They are paid twice per month, and often a bit of this goes for drinking, but more could go for healthy food."

A discussion with both a nurse and a general manager on one estate included the following observation by the nurse-nutritionist. "We have a big problem, from the first month of the mother's pregnancy until when the child is five . . . that mother may not be able to feed her family or even maintain her own nutrition for nursing. Let's say a mama is making 66 shillings per day, or 1,500 Kenya shillings per month, then this is not adequate for a large number of children!" The manager added, "Parents are on the job by 6 or 7 A.M., and a mama's time is limited, so we allow baby-sitters to pick up children from their homes and escort them to the two preschools on the estate. By the time they are in preschool, children have not taken breakfast, and some don't even bring a lunch!" The health officer at another estate told us that nutrition was "a very big issue—most workers don't have farms, and only a few grow vegetables in a small garden here . . . so we advise parents according to the income of the family. For example, in a rural setting, you might recommend eggs and milk more than here."

One health officer felt that the "biggest education problem here is kids dropping out from school at (coffee) picking time!" He clarified that, "Children supplement the family income, so parents may be encouraging children to pick."

Managers and health professionals at all estates emphasized the importance of family planning and the problem of workers having "more children than they can feed and house" in all too many cases. As one manager put it, "Family size is the greatest problem, including extended family and lack of funds . . . there are still taboos." The nurse observed, "Mamas are not well educated in family planning, or are not successful in their attempts to use it . . . only about 50% of our mothers practice family planning, I would say." At another estate, the manager said, "Mothers get help from the clinic, including expanded family planning services, including films promoting family planning. They can also get help with breast-feeding." The health officer at the clinic on this estate reinforced the emphasis on family planning, stating that, "The economy dictates the need for family planning!"

A summary of services provided at this estate clinic from the health officer there included "family planning services, preventive health for mothers and children (e.g., immunization, growth monitoring, and nutrition advice), and a drug dispensary." He continued, "We give both curative and preventive medical services, and these services are free to permanent employees here and in the other estates . . . that is, we treat workers from two estates here." When we asked about any health services for casual laborers, the health officer stated, "They are only treated when they become sick while on duty or have an injury . . . then they are transferred to the government hospital." Children of casual laborers were not treated. "We cannot treat the whole family when these workers are here one week and gone the next."

The common illnesses treated were malaria, diarrhea, and upper respiratory/chest infections, and all children who came in with coughs were dewormed. Clinic hours were from 6:30 A.M. until 4 P.M., "so that workers have an hour before and after work to visit the clinic if they do not want to miss working hours."

In terms of other "good things the estate is doing for families," two managers mentioned that workers "paid nothing for water" (which was there unless electricity for the pump was turned off, which it was during our visit). Nursery school, as previously discussed, was either free or inexpensive (i.e., 10 Kenya shillings per month in the program, which included both porridge and lunch at school). One manager noted that nursery school services "started a long time ago . . . they were here long before I came." The health officer on the same estate observed that, "If parents don't take their children to preschool they would have to hire an *ayah*, so almost all go . . . and most children go on to primary school, as it is required by the management, although picking and making money can cause some children to leave school at the peak time." Another estate provided "two nursery schools, in different locations" to better serve the 400 to 500 permanent employees.

Perhaps the best thing estates were doing for at least their permanent workers was providing health services, including free clinics and medicine, immunization, child and maternal health promotion, and (in one case, at least in the past) a visiting nurse. Two of the nursery schools were free to families, and housing—although limited in size and typically quite crowded—was free to permanent workers. When we asked what the consequences would be of poor or nonexistent preschool services in the estates, the nurse responded, "It would be disastrous! Unexplainable! The children could not survive!"

Several managers we interviewed spoke about the low school attendance rates of primary schoolchildren and the problems caused by either "idle youth making trouble for younger ones" on the estate or damaging property while their parents were picking coffee or tea. A paternalistic attitude was frequently noted in the interviews with managers, including one who, when asked about the "best place for children under three," stated, "If it's my wife—at home, with her," but for workers, "The preschool is where they must be looked after."

## INTERSECTORAL COLLABORATION

When we asked teachers whether their preschool was working with any other agencies, all but two teachers said, "No—just the company," and the two who responded "yes" added, "but very little!" As discussed earlier, the company running the estate was in charge of the preschool, clinic, and any other services for the employees. One teacher told us, "There is a preschool committee with five members, including two elders, two mothers, and someone from management." Other teachers stated that the only outside agency with whom they had contact was "the Ministry of Health," and four teachers mentioned their work with the Kiambu DICECE "sometimes."

Only two of the teachers we interviewed had undergone DICECE training, and others complained that they were "not visited by the zonal preschool supervisors." Access to the estates was sometimes challenging, as our research team experienced directly on two occasions in the Kiambu District.

## Focus Group Interview with Professionals

In addition to the interviews with estate managers and their health officers and nurses, we conducted a two-hour focus group discussion with six professionals involved with education and health services. Their responses corroborated the parents' and preschool teachers' perceptions of how life had changed and the greatest problems that were facing families, such as workers' salaries being too low to properly support families (on the estates) and the associated malnutrition and illness among children. Parents were seen as trying hard, but basically they were unavailable to their children for many hours of the day, leaving older siblings in charge of young children—sometimes leading to neglect. Primary schoolchildren were viewed as typically "going to school without breakfast and being very tired." Families were large, and parents often had trouble meeting the cost of educating all of their children, with high dropout rates seen among children of tea and coffee pickers. As one person put it, "Children are refusing to go to school when they can earn money from coffee picking." The lack of land for kitchen gardens was again raised as a contributing factor to the lack of a balanced diet among many families working on the estates.

In terms of other health concerns, medical professionals reported that they were seeing an increase in cases of asthma and other respiratory diseases. They attributed this to increasing pollution and to chemicals used to spray the fields—particularly in the coffee estates. Agreeing with early interview data from health officers, focus group participants observed that there were fewer home visits made by nurses or primary health workers now and that clinics were extremely busy and often underequipped. The shortage, and increasing cost, of drugs also was mentioned as a problem in the Kiambu District. Concerns also were raised about malaria, pneumonia, scabies, and other diseases.

## Good Things the Community [Estate] Is Doing

When professionals were asked to describe the good things the community was doing for families with young children, the most frequently mentioned was "nursery school." Other ways in which the community, including estate management, was contributing included "a welfare committee in which workers have a representative to raise issues to management," "a nurse who visits homes," and "hiring of child minders to assist the nursery school teachers" (in at least one tea estate). Several of the other things mentioned had to do with the "benefits package," so to speak, for workers, which included "free housing" (if small), "free firewood during the cold season," and "drugs at the estate clinic." One person observed that, "New mothers are placed near the nursery" when they go back to work, and another stated that, "Transport is provided for sick people who need to go to hospital." At least one estate had supported the training of its preschool teachers through the DICECE course, and others were considering it. Only one was explicitly refusing training for its preschool teacher.

## Suggestions for Supporting Families in Poverty in the Kiambu District

Particularly given the World Bank's Early Education and Development Initiative in Kenya, we discussed ways in which there could be a distribution of resources to assist families in greatest need. The focus group made several suggestions, including, "Materials and in-kind things are better than funds—funds can be misused more easily," and "Funds should be used for the improvement of facilities for children and health facilities." Other suggestions included "training for staff and parents," "hiring more child minders and preschool teachers" to work with the large numbers of children needing care," and "using funds to pay tuition, other school fees, and to buy books."

The focus group was divided on whether there should be any direct payment made to families through a bursary or a child development trust fund. Some argued, "There should be no direct payments made to families," and others argued, "Some funds should be given directly to poor families." A compromise was that, "Communities should cost share," using in-kind as well as financial cost-sharing mechanisms. In terms of a mechanism for the equitable distribution of funds, which might become available to benefit families, group members agreed that, "Local committees, including representatives of the recipients, should oversee the management of the funds." Various checks and balances were discussed, and the emphasis was on local communities deciding how to best use any funds or other forms of assistance that might be made available.

## SUMMARY

Similar to Kericho, families living and working on plantations were faced with many challenges and exploitations. Although housing was provided, it was typically too small to accommodate the number of children many families had. A lack of child care, particularly in the afternoons when the preschool day ended, was another pervasive problem. Only one estate we visited provided a lunch for children at the preschool, and the same facility had other problems related to a lack of facilities for the youngest children, particularly for napping. Seeing over 75 young children trying to sleep on cold concrete was one example. The same plantation refused to allow their veteran, yet "untrained," preschool teacher to participate in the DICECE short course or other training for preschool teachers in the district. She, like other teachers we interviewed, felt isolated and powerless to make significant changes that might benefit children on this estate.

The nature of the work on tea and coffee plantations is such that mothers are discouraged, if not outright prevented, from seeking needed health services for themselves and their children. As discussed in this chapter, babies were left at weighing stations, where mothers attempted to nurse them while tea was being weighed. If a mother needed to go into "the reserve" for a clinic appointment, she could lose a day's wages unless other women helped pick for her. Siblings only slightly older than the under threes were often charged with caring for baby brothers and sisters and were left with little food and other resources. Caring teachers did what they could, often working informally in the afternoon and overseeing the children in the houses near the preschool.

Some of the conditions on both the Kericho and Kiambu estates were reminiscent of the plantations in the United States, which depended on the labor of enslaved Africans and, later, on sharecroppers. As an estate manager in another district had stated to the visiting researcher in 1994, "We provide for preschool, but discourage attendance in primary school, as children will be less likely to want to earn their living with their hands and we need their labor." Although the managers we interviewed appeared to support education and be aware of, if not always sensitive to, many of the difficulties facing families with young children on their estates, many told us that child labor was a reality that they could do little to change.

Some of the more positive services for families included a well-equipped clinic on a large coffee estate, which had a much better supply of medications, immunization serums, and maintained facilities than Ministry of Health clinics in the district. Yet the many services of this clinic were only available to "permanent" workers, so the majority of workers did not "qualify" for the health services offered by their employer.

In the Kiambu District, even more than in Kericho, the DICECE staff faced the challenge of being able to enter some of the plantations. When free technical assistance and support and affordable training for preschool teachers are refused by management, how can DICECE staff and other child advocates, NGOs, and so on have an impact on the conditions facing the youngest inhabitants of the plantations and their families? Other managers were far more open to DICECE support and had sent at least one teacher for training. They also were open to attempting to provide better services specifically for children under age three, but they expressed concerns about being able to "afford" what they knew they should provide. We left Kiambu with many unanswered questions. A plantation may provide housing, access to water, and sometimes wood for heating and cooking. It also may provide a preschool or child care program, but it remains a difficult setting in which to raise children, particularly children under age three.

# Part IV

Rural/Agricultural Contexts:
Embu and Machakos

# Rural/Agricultural Contexts:
# Embu and Machakos

Forty-six percent of rural Kenyans live in absolute poverty.
—President Daniel arap Moi, October 1994

Kenya is primarily a rural, subsistence agricultural nation. As previous chapters have detailed, there is great variability in productivity or agricultural potential across the provinces, districts, and communities, and often within districts. Thus when selecting two districts to represent the range of "rural/agricultural" contexts in Kenya, we considered a number of settings and factors and decided on two neighboring districts that offered great contrasts within their boundaries. Both districts represent a wide range of geographical and agricultural potential, from high rainfall and rich soils to low potential (dry, semi-arid, and eroded soils). The Embu and Machakos Districts are still mainly dependent on agriculture but are increasingly dependent on a cash economy as well. Land tenure patterns are changing, with land increasingly demarcated into family holdings and nuclear families replacing extended families or clans, thus they represent rural communities in transition and are considered excellent contexts for studying the impacts of social and economic change on child-rearing and early education practices.

We also took into consideration the capacity for collaborative research and built upon successful projects in the past that had directly involved DICECE staff in data collection. Additionally, the visiting researcher had visited several preschools in both Embu and Machakos during her first trip to Kenya in 1992 and had maintained contacts since that time (particularly with the Embu DICECE and two preschools in the town of Runyenjes in that district).

Both of these districts are known within the NACECE and DICECE network as highly successful in community mobilization and support of preschool teachers. Sampled

169

communities represented, in general, mobilized communities, in which parents and community leaders took an active part in decision making regarding development projects and were involved with schools and preschools. Both districts also have benefitted from the strong role of local churches in support of both the democratization process and early education. Embu was, by this time, becoming known for its cooking demonstrations, in which traditional and locally available foods are used to prepare nutritional weaning foods. It also was encouraging to learn about the formation of teacher "panels" or support groups at the sublocation level, in which teachers engaged in projects that included lesson planning, income generation, and mutual support on personal issues. The Machakos DICECE was known for its close collaboration with the Ministry of Health in training preschool teachers (particularly in Wamunyu) in primary health promotion. Activities such as monthly growth monitoring were taking place in both Embu and Machakos, and preschool teachers in Wamunyu were teaching parents how to use oral rehydration solution and to practice better environmental hygiene. Thus entry into these districts was already underway, and the research skills of local collaborators were well known to the national collaborators.

The following two chapters present a synthesis of the findings from these districts and also offer insights into the critical role played by the DICECE staff in supporting the care and well-being of young children. In both districts, however, preschool was rarely serving children under four years of age. It was, in most locations we visited, considered most appropriate for children during the year before they entered primary school. Thus our lengthy discussions about the needs of children under three served both to heighten awareness of this underserved population and to clarify current practices regarding the child-rearing of rural children in these representative settings.

During the period of data collection (1994–1995), both districts were divided, creating four new ones (Embu, Mbeere, Machakos, and Makueni). The locations we sampled remained in either the Embu District or the Machakos District, however, which did not directly affect our study.

*Chapter 7*

# Embu District: It Takes Traditions and Intergenerational Support to Raise a Child

Unemployment is almost complete—some don't own land, look for casual labor, squat on relatives' land, and are living a hand-to-mouth life most of the time.

—Mother in Embu

## SETTING

At the time of this study, the Embu District occupied an area of 2,714 square kilometers and was the smallest of the six districts of Eastern Province. It borders the Kirinyaga District and Mt. Kenya to the west, Kitui to the east, Meru to the north, and Machakos to the south. The District is divided into five divisions: Runyenjes, Siakago, Manyatta, Central, and Gachoka. Runyenjes, a fertile, agriculturally productive division, has the highest population density and is the second smallest division (with the Central division being the smallest). Much of the land area of the district is available for agriculture and livestock, with most land considered of medium potential, marginal, or range land. The Embu District slopes toward east and southeast, from Mt. Kenya and is characterized by highlands and lowlands. Elevation varies from 515 meters above sea level at the River Tana Basin in the east to over 4,570 meters on the top of Mt. Kenya in the northwest (Embu District Development Plan, 1994-96). The southern part of the district is covered by the Mwea Plains. The district is also served by six major rivers, which form part its boundaries.

171

Fig. 7.1     Embu Primary School Boys Dancing During Cooking Demonstration

Agricultural potential and production are directly influenced by the contrasting geographic characteristics described above. Variations in altitude, rainfall, and temperature between the highlands and lowlands give rise to varying soil types and different population patterns. The upper highlands and most of the northeastern parts of the lower highland areas are cool, wet, and steep, and forestry is the main land use. In the lower highlands of the Runyenjes and Manyatta divisions (where much of the data was collected), coffee and tea are grown. In the low lying areas of Gachoka and Siakago, cash crops such as cotton and tobacco are grown. Other food crops such as maize and millet are grown, and livestock is raised. In the high potential zone of the district, which includes the Manyatta and Runyenjes divisions, the land is steep and there are many problems with soil erosion.

Turning to demographics, the projected population of the Embu District was 416,634 by 1994 and 442,694 by 1996 (the end of the district development planning period). Its population continues to expand at a high growth rate, particularly in high potential areas such as Runyenjes, which (like parts of the Kiambu District) is becoming quite populated with land prices rising and land parcels shrinking in size. The subdivision of family farm land over time also has contributed to the large number of small *shamba*s (or farms) and the more frequent occurrence of sharecropping or hiring out land and labor to other land-owning families in the area. The age group distribution shows that children under 15 years old were more than half of the district's population in 1993. Those over age 60 account for only 5.2%, and the "economically active" population that provides most of the district's labor (ages 15 to 59) accounts for about 44.3% of the total population. The implication drawn in the District Development Plan (1994–96, p. 13) is that, "The labor force has to support a very large proportion of the total population. Thus, about 55.7% of the population is supported by 44.3% of the labor force."

Urban and market centers obviously play a critical role in the development of the district. Embu and Runyenjes are the only centers within the Embu District considered towns. Embu is a municipality (with an elected mayor) and Runyenjes has a town council. The population for the town of Embu was 18,200 in 1989 (last census), while Runyenjes' population was 2,000 that year. Thus the majority of the district population lives in either rural areas or in small market centers, making Embu an optimal district in which to sample rural families involved in agricultural production.

Embu is a district with a rich history and a scenic location, on the eastern slopes of Mt. Kenya (or Kirinyaga, meaning ostrich in Kiembu). Its land ranges from highly productive maize, beans, and even rice schemes and tea production—both large scale and smaller farms—to more marginal, drought-ridden land in the northeastern parts of the district.

The visiting researcher had come to Embu and had visited a number of preschools during her first trip to Kenya in 1992. Close ties with this district have been maintained since that time, including establishing U.S.-Kenya partner preschools and donating a small motorcycle to the Embu DICECE. This DICECE enjoys a positive reputation nationally and is particularly known for its encouragement of the use of traditional weaning foods through cooking demonstrations, appropriate technology (e.g., "fireless cookers," described later in this chapter), and preschool teacher panels, which serve as a source of social and emotional support, professional development, and income-generating activities for teachers at the sublocation level.

Mrs. Gladys Mugo, programme officer of the Embu DICECE, is widely respected both in the Embu District and among NACECE/DICECE colleagues as a child and family advocate, educational leader (former Headmistress of a well known girls school in Embu), and an innovator. Among her recent innovations is the establishment of what would be called in the United States a "child life specialist" program, in which teachers/tutors are hired to work with children who are chronically ill and hospitalized for long periods of time. She also works with a program for former street children and their mothers (sponsored by the Catholic Church), and she has empowered a team of DICECE trainers and officers that does extensive outreach and community mobilization activities benefitting children. We underscore Mrs. Mugo's many accomplishments in part because of her key role in the conceptualization of the study and in support of the visiting researcher in a number of different ways. Thus both Embu and Machakos were selected, in part, due to their successful mobilization of communities for early childhood care and education and their willingness to participate as full, collaborative partners in this research.

## Description of the Embu Sample

Five locations, representing five contrasting zones, were sampled, which included agriculturally productive, medium productive, marginal, and urban settings within the Embu District. Many of the interviews were conducted individually or with two to three parents. One exception was a large group interview with a women's self-help group, including both younger mothers and grandmothers.

A total of 36 parents and grandparents were interviewed, including 18 mothers, 7 fathers, 10 grandmothers, and 1 grandfather. The ages of first-born children (of parents interviewed) ranged from 4 to 24 years, with a mean age of 14 years. Last-born children ranged from 10 months to 6.5 years, with a mean age of 3.8 years.

When asked about roles in their community, 28 were members of self-help groups, 8 assisted in church activities, 5 were members of school committees, and 3 were officers, 3 were active in grassroots political work, 2 were officers or committee members in their church, and 1 was a "religious leader." Other community roles represented by the community leaders included a member of the Community Welfare Projects Committee, a member of the board of Christian Community Services, and an elected zonal counsellor.

In terms of work roles, 23 mothers and fathers were farmers, two were involved in small business, one father farmed and also did casual labor, one father owned a matatu (mini van used for public transport), one father was a cook for a preschool, one mother was in adult education, and another was a primary teacher, and one father had a professional leadership role in a church. The length of time in their community ranged from 18 years to their entire life, with 29 participants reporting that they had lived in their present location throughout their lifetime, and six reporting that they had lived there for 18 to 20 years.

Turning to formal education, two had completed Teachers College, three had completed Form 4, two had completed Standard 7, one had completed Standard 5, one had completed Standard 3, and one had completed Standard 2. It should be noted that we did not collect this information individually for the women's group members interviewed as a group.

Seven female preschool teachers were interviewed in the Embu District. The average number of teachers at rural preschools was two, although some had only one, and two preschools were preparing to hire a second teacher. In terms of formal education, two teachers had completed Form 4, two had completed Form 2, one had completed Standard 8, and two had completed Standard 7 (KPE). The range of years of teaching in their current position was from two to 25 years, with one teacher in her current position for two years, three teachers in their positions for eight to nine years, two for 15 years, and one for 25 years. All seven teachers had only taught at their current preschool.

Six teachers were DICECE trained, and one was currently in DICECE training. One teacher had completed a short course (two months). Teachers ranged in age from 26 to 47 years, with a mean age of 33.4 years. Four were married, and three were single, including two single mothers. The ages of teacher's children ranged from 6 to 28 years, with a mean age of 13.8 years. Last-born children ranged in age from 2. to 15 years, with a mean age of 7.3 years. Six teachers reported that parents paid their salaries, and one was paid by an NGO-Compassion International. When asked about other income sources, three said that they had none, three were involved in small-scale farming, and one was in small business, selling rice in the market.

Eight primary children were interviewed, including four girls and four boys. All children were in Standard 4, and their ages ranged from 8 to 10 years, with six children nine years of age. All had younger siblings, most with at least one sibling under age three. Children were sampled from a private, middle-class primary school in the town of Embu and from a public rural primary school to provide a contrasting sample.

## Portrait: Father and Small Farmer/Casual Laborer in Runyenjes

*We are up early, with the mother preparing tea and my four-year-old son getting ready for pre-school. I think it is very important for the child to feel like he "owns" something, so my son has a goat and takes care of him in the morning and the evening. We take breakfast, and I do different activities, including bean-sorting. I get casual income, for example, from the coffee factory, and the mother is at home when our child comes home—on his own—from nursery school, or sometimes I may bring him home. After lunch my son is home with his mother and after I come home we take supper. By 8:30 or 9:00 p.m., it's bedtime. In terms of my child's future, it is hard to plan very far ahead when you do not even know what next week will bring! We live from day to day and month to month, trying to be good parents and raise a responsible son.*

The Embu District provided one of the widest arrays of settings and people. Settings ranged from agriculturally productive, more densely populated Runyenjes to the tea fields and casual labor settings on the slopes of Mt. Kenya to the more drought-vulnerable, less fertile parts of the district, such as Ishiara and Machang'a. Similarly, the parents, grandparents, and even children interviewed represented contrasts in lifestyle, income, and to a degree, priorities. Common themes across the district included a reliance on agriculture, and to a lesser extent animals, a bustling small enterprise or market economy, patterns of growth and change in the more fertile areas, whose problems of rapid growth paralleled more urbanized areas, and hard-working parents trying their best to provide for their children as the cost of living continued to rise.

One of the more illuminating group interviews was conducted one evening (in part, by flashlight), as we joined a rural women's self-help group in its weekly meeting on the chairlady's *shamba*. Here we had the opportunity to talk with three generations of mothers—similar to the opportunity afforded to us in parts of Narok—

and "listen in" on their issues, challenges, and reflections on changes and their effects on child-rearing.

## Portrait: A 9-Year-Old Boy in Embu

*I woke up, washed my face, brushed my teeth, took tea, and came to school. Then, after school, I washed my clothes, washed the house, and cooked food—my mother is in the hospital in Embu, so I cooked bananas, potatoes, and carrots. I teach my little brother ABCs, and we sing and play.*

In Embu, we sampled two primary schools from contrasting settings—one a private, privileged school in the town of Embu and the other a rural, public school near Runyenjes. (This was similar to the sampling of children done in the town of Kisumu—refer to that section for further comparisons.) For example, children from more privileged (and more "urbanized") families did not perform as many of the household tasks and had far fewer child care responsibilities for younger siblings; as they often stated, "The maid does that." They also tended to be taken to school and other places in a private, family car, had two-earner professional families, and were very competitive about their schoolwork. In fact, at the beginning of the children's interview, when they are asked to draw "things they like and members of their family," one boy at the private school in Embu asked, "Are we supposed to make as many pictures as we can? Should we fill this paper?" This sort of question indicated a great desire to please adult "teachers," and it also indicated a sense of competition. Also, for these more privileged children, recreation tended to involve electronic media—watching television or videos, listening to cassettes, or going out to an amusement arcade or a movie. Children interviewed were primarily asked to describe roles they played in the household, particularly as they pertained to child care and other activities with siblings who were under three.

## MAJOR PROBLEMS FACING FAMILIES WITH YOUNG CHILDREN IN EMBU

Life is very demanding—it is just living hand-to-mouth. . . . We are supporting the (education) system rather than benefitting from the system and there's no going back!

—Father

The most common parental response to this question was "the lack of resources to meet basic needs." The effects of the rising cost of living and of raising a family were a common theme in all of the Embu District interviews, as in other sampled districts. Lack of school fees and lack of employment were listed second in frequency. Other parents mentioned the "lack of land to grow food, which can result in some people being reduced to squatting on land to try to feed their families." One father put it this way. "Unemployment is almost complete . . . some don't own land, look for casual labor, squat on relatives' land, and are living a hand-to-mouth life most of the time."

Other themes were related directly to the cost of living and included "the high cost of building materials," "the high cost of land rents," and "the rising cost of food for a balanced diet." The issue of even food being a costly item for families was in contrast to the agriculturally productive appearance of many of the rural routes taken in the course of the study. Drought also was mentioned as a problem in parts of the Embu District.

As one father stated, "We have a lack of resources to sustain our needs—like my child in Standard 7 who is very clever, he's in the top 5 of his class, but we have problems with money, and I wonder, how can I send him to high school?" In fact, this father was attempting to supplement the family income by fishing and by working as a cook in a preschool. Serving as the cook also meant that his younger child's preschool fees were greatly reduced. He added, "Life is quite difficult, and although some forms of help are there, they don't go far enough . . . how can we send the children on for a better future when the present is like this?"

Access to cash to purchase needed goods and services was a pervasive theme among parents in the Embu District. As one father stated, "It's a challenge to be able to purchase food. Families need money, and when they are not employed, they must sell animals or some produce . . . so a drought means having fewer animals and less food—and that means less money!" Another parent stated, "Life is very demanding—just living hand-to-mouth and having to pay so much more for education, which was free before, is very hard!"

## Good Things the Community Is Doing

Turning to a more positive perspective on family life in the Embu District, when asked what good things their community was doing for young children and their families, the most frequent answer was, "We've put up a preschool on a *Harambee* basis." Parents showed pride that their communities were "aware of the needs of children and have tried to provide for them."

Many of the other "good things" listed by parents involved their direct contributions of materials and labor to the preschool. These included planting trees in the nursery school compound, participating in material development (e.g., toy making) for both preschool and home use by children, and assisting with a feeding program. Parents expressed pride in their children's achievements and stated that they were "actively involved in our children's education, including sports, examinations, etc." Finally, in Ishiara, we were told of someone who had "put up a private nursery school which caters for under threes." This program was a home-based child care model, which was quite new to the area. Pride, willingness to work hard and to do their part, and support of education, beginning with nursery school, were evident.

## Social and Economic Changes and Their Perceived Impacts on Child-rearing

This section summarizes questions and responses related to the research question that asked about both changes related to child-rearing and the impacts of these changes on the nature and patterns of participation in early childhood programs (both formal and informal). Parents' responses to this question paralleled in many ways their answers to the question regarding the problems families face. The most frequent general change cited was the "high cost of living, making it difficult to provide basic needs for our families." Again, the lack of land or the growing scarcity of land was mentioned as a negative change, which meant that, "We have no place to grow food to feed our children." Once more, several domains of change are summarized in the following sections.

### Food

As previously discussed, the most frequent response to how things have changed regarding food was that now, "Food is often not enough due to lack of adequate land for cultivation." Weather changes and droughts also were considered a change directly affecting food, as were rising land rental costs. Some parents felt that they now are "more conscious of providing children with a balanced diet."

In terms of under threes, parents described changes in weaning foods. Several felt that there was more variety now (e.g., milk, porridge, fruit, peas, bean, bananas, etc.), whereas others felt that mothers today did not have time—or did not take time—to prepare the more nutritious traditional weaning foods and had resorted to using more tinned foods, tea, and other less nutritious foods. (This and other issues related to breast-feeding are discussed further in a later section.)

### Housing

In terms of housing, parents described similar patterns of change as parents in other districts had discussed. Building materials have changed from traditional thatch huts to corrugated iron sheets, and there is increased use of "modern" housing materials, including wood and stone. Houses also were described as "bigger and more spacious," although it was also pointed out that few people could afford such houses.

As one parent stated, "As children grow, they want to live in a different area, but that challenges their resources and expectations of housing materials (e.g., grass thatching). Before, when it rained, you had to fix the (thatch) roof often, but now, there are newer and better ways of building a roof—with metal." Another parent added, "The materials are better now, but it's difficult to find or afford building materials now."

## Health

The consensus of parents in the Embu District appeared to be that generally children enjoyed better health than they had 15 years ago, and that this was due in part to the availability of more health facilities. Parents stated that most children today were immunized and treated for common diseases, although there were still persistent problems (e.g., colds, worms, fever, malaria, etc.). In terms of childbirth, parents indicated that many more children were not being born in the hospital, and that antenatal care had improved.

The health problem that appeared to be increasing was malnutrition. Some parents felt that underfeeding and malnutrition had increased in the past 10 years, due largely to the economic hardships already discussed. As one mother put it, "People are weaker now due to the lack of adequate nutrition." Some areas experienced seasonal hunger, particularly in the tea-growing and drought-prone areas. Fewer families owned *shamba*s, and many worked as casual laborers, or they rented small plots on which to grow food for their families.

In terms of environmental hygiene, some parents mentioned that, "More places now have latrines," and "Most people here have latrines now."

## Education

In general, parents in Embu felt that the community's commitment to education had steadily grown, yet it was not much harder to afford to educate your children. One mother also raised the issue of changing attitudes related to gender and education. "A very big change in education is that people here didn't believe in education for women . . . and now, more girls are in school and boys are not just taking care of animals. All this change has happened in the past 10 years!"

Although education was frequently described as less affordable, ways in which children could get reduced tuition also were described. One mother said, "We're getting more serious about education, and even some children are coming for free, if the parents are too poor to pay the fees." Yet the hardship of schooling a family was argued strongly by this father. "Before, there was a common fund (to help with school fees, etc.), but now there are expenses for so many school-related things. We are supporting the system rather than benefitting from the system, and there's no going back!"

## Family Size

Parents agreed, overall, that family sizes were smaller than 15 years ago. "More families are using family planning—because they cannot afford as many children." Another parent referred to the many negative changes we had been discussing and said, "All these factors have brought about awareness of family size—only an ignorant person would miss family planning!"

## Social Structures and Services

The most frequently mentioned change in social structure was the growth in the number of economically supporting self-help groups. As one parent stated, "There are so many more groups now . . . for example, some have a revolving fund, with members taking turns getting the collective funds, and this has united mothers and has given them money for uniforms and other school costs." Another parent added, "A similar approach has been used to meet funeral expenses and to help families when they lose a provider."

Still another parent said, "So many organizations have come up in the past 10 years—especially women's groups, and also some men's groups, including ones for buying and developing plots." One father commented that the women's groups were more successful than the men's and said, "We need guidance on this—on how to be more effective. Women are more united on this than men!"

The need for recreational places also was noted. "We don't have a recreation center, we need one, but until land is allocated for one, we are using a school field." The need for such facilities was tied to parents' concerns about more children taking to the streets or getting into trouble. Several parents also discussed a breakdown in both children's respect of elders and in the availability for elders, particularly grandparents, to advise and counsel youth.

## Child-rearing Practices

Now there are more working mothers and fewer supports for child care.
—Mother in Embu

Several parents felt that there was better care provided to under threes than previously, due in part to increased parental education about health care and nutrition. As one father put it, "Under threes are better taken care of now—we know the importance of healthy practices, versus buying tinned baby foods, etc., and children are generally taken better care of . . . more young children are now going to preschool, and there are better lives for our children now."

Not all parents shared this father's optimism. Others felt that the growing number of single and working mothers had eroded the care children had previously received. As one mother stated, "Earlier on, mothers were not employed and cared for their children knowing what they needed. Now, there are more working mothers and fewer supports for child care." The cost and lack of dependable care of maids or *ayahs* also was raised in the context of the rising number of women who were working because of economic necessity.

In terms of breast-feeding and weaning practices, there was contradictory evidence from different locations sampled and people interviewed. Some older mothers felt strongly that younger mothers were engaging in premature weaning—as early as four to eight weeks. Younger mothers, in fact, described the "inability to provide

Fig. 7.2 Cooking Demonstration of Traditional Weaning Foods

enough milk" for their children, thus causing them to introduce weaning foods earlier than commonly recommended. This may have been due in part to the young mother's own diet. As one grandmother said, "If young mothers were drinking enriched *uji* and not just tea, they would have plenty of milk for their babies!"

One of the mothers interviewed also was an adult educator who worked with other mothers a great deal. She stated, "Some mothers stop nursing after even one month, and then there can be a problem with the baby having diarrhea. In such cases the mother says, 'I don't have enough milk . . . I'm working hard and my diet isn't good enough. I just don't have enough to keep the baby well.' " Bottle feeding appeared to be effectively discouraged, with some clinics taking bottles away from mothers and explaining why.

Another change in child-rearing that was noted—especially by the grandmothers interviewed—was the lack of time grandparents now had with their grandchildren. "Before, the grandmother would counsel the granddaughter on many things, and now the child is in school for many hours a day and often doesn't live near the grandmother any longer." The combination of a lack of time and traditional counseling was lamented over by several of the parents interviewed. It also was pointed out that, "Grandmothers are younger now and have little time for grandchildren, as they are busy working." Similarly, it was asserted that many mothers are younger now and more likely to be single and raising children on their own.

## Family and Community Involvement in Early Childhood Programs and Care

As discussed earlier, parents in Embu prided themselves on their level of involvement in and support of their children's education—beginning with preschool. The two most frequently mentioned types of parent involvement in preschools were: (1) supporting feeding programs, through money, contributing foodstuff, and providing labor, and (2) helping to make learning and play materials. One mother described parents' involvement in the feeding program this way. "We give some sorghum and maize or donate money—we prefer to buy and provide a 2 kilo tin, and that is mandatory. The problem with children carrying food is that it's cold— a hot lunch is much better."

Other parents described helping construct a playground. "We helped build the playground (swings), although mostly it's a carpenter or mason who constructs things now, versus the earlier days when parents might literally have built the preschool." Additional ways parents were involved included: assisting children with their homework (primary); participating in growth-monitoring activities; visiting preschools to inquire about their child's progress; and participating in parental education workshops in which issues related to child growth and development were discussed (e.g., weaning foods cooking demonstration).

## Typical Arrangements for Care of Under Threes

The most typical child care arrangement for under threes appeared to be home care provided by the mother, followed in frequency by home care with a child minder, sibling, or grandmother. Other child care arrangements included preschool care and the assistance of fathers in child care.

It was frequently observed, as we traveled about in the Embu District, that many mothers took their youngest children with them wherever they went—to the *shamba*, which may be some distance if it is rented land, to the market, to gather water, and to look for firewood or other fuel. The baby is on the mother's back across these various settings, as has been the tradition.

Turning to parents' goals and concerns for child care, several parents felt that the best place for under threes was preschool, so that "They can learn to socialize," or "They can have their needs by someone who understands children." However, to this was added "The preschool must have trained child minders or teachers."

Several other parents argued that the best place for under threes was at home— particularly if the child could be with his or her mother. Fathers were "needed to be fully involved in the care of their children," and "Parents must work together to assist one another in the care of their children."

## JOYS AND CHALLENGES OF BEING A PARENT

The biggest joy is just that child. Even if you have money, but have no child, the child is a bigger blessing!

—Mother in women's self-help group

Turning again to parents, when asked what they liked most about being a parent, once again the most frequent response was "the feeling of being called a mother" or a father. As one father put it, "Being a parent gives you hope—the child is the best 'riches' and is my strength!" A mother said, "Being a parent gives meaning to life," and another mother said, "Having a child makes one feel fulfilled." The other side of parenthood, childlessness, was again mentioned. "Childlessness is there—and it serves as a reminder of our blessing—of having children." This sentiment was amplified in the following quote from a mother. "The biggest joy is just that child. Even if you have money, but have no child, the child is a bigger blessing!"

The mutual caretaking of children by parents and later of parents by children was also mentioned as a benefit of parenthood. "Knowing that there will be someone to help me in my old age" was how one parent described it. Finally, a father described the enjoyable aspects of fatherhood as "Seeing that my child is happy, learns, and does things that he wants—and is good,"

When asked what was hardest about being a parent, the theme of being unable to provide for all of one's children's needs was again apparent. As one young mother put it, "It only turns out sour if the basic needs are not met or attended to!" One father equated unmet needs to an unhappy family. "Being a parent of an unhappy family is difficult! There is no way to keep control." Another father added, "One of the hardest things is when I don't have the resources, for example, buying things or getting a better house, or even clothing my family—that is hard!"

Another concern for parents was their children's behavior. "It's hardest to be a parent when your children become undisciplined, such as using drugs." Finally, parents here, as in all other locations sampled, found it hard when their children were sick.

## Parental Aspirations for Children

Three aspirations were mentioned most frequently in response to "What are your hopes and dreams for your children's future?" These included: (1) that children "will do well in education"; (2) that children "will grow up to be self-reliant and independent"; and (3) that children will be gainfully employed. Others included the wish for children to be hard working and for children to have a better life than the parents. Parents also named two specific jobs to which they would like their children to aspire—teacher and lawyer.

# SIBLINGS' INVOLVEMENT IN CHILD CARE

The most frequent responses to how involved children were with their younger siblings, in order of frequency, were: (1) "playing with the younger one"; (2) "making toys for the younger one"; and (3) "teaching the younger ones what I learn in school, such as ABCs and numbers." These were followed in frequency by telling stories and talking to the little one (which included teaching words in English, Kiswahili, and Kiembu). Finally, some children, particularly older sisters, stated that they fed and bathed the baby, sang to the baby, and "taught younger ones good manners, including what to do and what not to do when there were visitors."

In terms of participation in household chores, there were marked contrasts between the middle-class children in the town of Embu and the rural children. For example, rural children reported that they carried out various household chores, including sweeping, washing, cooking, child care, animal care, garden work, and fetching water and firewood. Urban children reported that such things, where relevant, were generally done by the "maid or my mother."

In terms of how children comforted younger siblings when they cried, responses included the following: (1) feed them something (e.g., "Give them a sweet," "Give them some fruit," or "Give a ripe banana"); (2) carry him or her on their backs; (3) take him or her for a walk; and (4) draw pictures for the younger one.

When asked how they could tell if a younger sibling was sick, the most common responses were that the child was hot or had a fever, and that the baby cried a lot or "looked unhappy." In terms of what children did when a younger sibling was sick, the most common response was "comfort her," followed by "Tell the grandmother or mother," and "tell him I shall buy him sweets" (if he stops crying). When parents were informed that a younger sibling was sick, they "take the baby to the dispensary or hospital," or they "buy medicine and give it to the baby."

## Children's Preschool Memories

Turning to children's memories of their own preschool experiences, all children interviewed in both rural and urban settings had attended at least one year of preschool. What children most frequently remembered was "playing with materials and toys" and on playground equipment, including swings, slides, and ropes. Other memories included learning letters and numbers, listening to and telling stories, and singing. When asked about the differences between preschool and primary school, children's responses included, "We learn many things in primary," "What we learn in primary is more difficult," and "In primary, we learn to speak Kiswahili properly."

In terms of older siblings' opinions about the best setting for the care of children under three, slightly more children thought that preschool was the best place. Reasons included: "Preschool is good, as one learn letters, numbers, and to read and write," and "Children are prepared for primary school learning." Two children felt that home was the best place, stating, "Home is the best place for under threes, as they can eat, play, and be taught by family members." This view was expressed by rural children. Urban children tended to think that an academic preschool setting was best for young children.

## Children's Future Aspirations

Finally, turning to children's career and family aspirations, girls living in town wanted to work in a supermarket and be an artist, and rural girls wanted to be a doctor and a driver. Boys in town wanted to be a pilot and a doctor, and rural boys wanted to be a pilot and an army officer. In terms of siblings, children wanted their sisters to be nurses and businesswomen and wanted their brothers to be policemen, teachers, doctors, and pilots. In family size, similar to other settings, boys wanted to have more children (two to four) and girls wanted to have one or two (with a preference for daughters).

## INTERSECTORAL COLLABORATIONS FOR CHILDREN AND FAMILIES

In response to questions about which sponsors, NGOs, or other groups parents knew about that were working in their communities, only one NGO, Plan International, was mentioned for its work in building schools and other education buildings (e.g., TAC, or Teacher Advisory Centers). Two churches, the ACK (Anglican Church of Kenya) and the Catholic Church were mentioned in teaching religious education to children.

In government ministries involved with early childhood care and education, both the Ministry of Health and Ministry of Education (particularly the Embu

DICECE) were named. Clinics were primarily credited with treating the sick and giving immunizations to children.

## Teachers' Perspectives on Family Change and Child Care

### Problems Facing Families

Similar to parents' responses, teachers raised a number of challenges and problems facing families that affected children as they observed them in the preschool context. Seasonal hunger was a major problem identified by teachers. This was particularly acute in the tea-growing areas, where "Some tenant workers with families are squatting on land or may rent a small place and often the mother and children are underfed." Another teacher added, "We see evidence of this hunger when we serve morning snacks and children show other signs of hunger and undernutrition." At another preschool in the tea-growing areas we visited, a teacher stated that, "The families are normally very large, and parents cannot afford to feed and educate their children adequately. Many boys leave school and get employment as animal herders and some parents do not send their daughters to school." As in other settings, the root cause of most problems listed by teachers was economic, or poverty. As another teacher put it, "The biggest problems are caused by finances—especially when parents cannot get money for fees, clothing, and food."

As further evidence that children were undernourished, one teacher stated that her preschool children often said that they had not taken breakfast before coming to school or supper the night before. As one teacher told us, "You see a child crying and ask why, and they may say, 'I took nothing in the morning—mama left early to pick,' or tell you that the older children woke up and finished everything—'They drank my cup!' " Effects of hunger included children "being sleepy and appearing dull." Other children were described as "coming to school dirty . . . and it is too hard for these children to cope!"

Other problems facing families included difficulty in affording sufficient, warm clothing or school uniforms for children. Teachers felt that, "Poor clothing makes children get frequent colds and other illnesses." Among teachers' other concerns was the increase in single-parent families. As one teacher put it, "Sometimes children from single-parent families have problems; for example, they may be staying with their father or grandparent if their mother is gone and may not get the best care." Another teacher added, "For children staying with grandparents, some may come with jiggers and we remove them." Another teacher told us, "Children are often falling sick . . . we send them home, but there's no money for medicine. This adds to absenteeism and disrupts the child's learning." Another form of absenteeism was children dropping out of school. "Many children who do not attend school run away from home later and end up as street children in the towns."

# Ways Families Were Coping—
# and Preschools Were Helping

In terms of the ways in which families were coping and the preschool was trying to help, teachers stated that, "Parents with low incomes work for those who can afford to pay them," and "Mothers normally carry their under threes with them wherever they go." Some preschools were making special arrangements for families who had trouble paying the fees or buying the uniform, including allowing parents to pay fees in small installments (e.g., 10 Kshs./month) or providing some "scholarships." "The preschool assists the parents with large families by educating their children free." Another preschool allowed parents to purchase the uniform over time. "They can first buy the shirt or pants and send their children while they are waiting to buy more of the uniform. We no longer make them wait to send."

Teachers felt that when children came to preschool, they were happier and also were better prepared for primary school. "Sometimes children come to school stressed and unhappy . . . when they play with materials, especially the fixed outdoor equipment, they get happy. Many do not eat breakfast at home, so the mid-morning snack makes them happier and makes their health improve." Some children "stayed around the preschool in the afternoon" rather than went home. One teacher felt that when they "call the parent to discuss the problems, there is an improvement." For example, "Some parents were sleeping when the children left for school, and our discussions may create a change. We've had good progress—in both feeding and clothing" (after talking with parents).

Turning to ways in which parents were involved in the preschool, this varied greatly depending on the setting and lifestyle of the parents, with the least reported parent involvement in the tea-picking areas and the most involvement in rural areas where children came from nearby *shamba*s (farms). A teacher who had been successful in communicating with and involving parents reflected, "When parents know the teacher is interested in their children—and when we plan together, listen, and—first and foremost—give parents a chance to express their feelings and find ways to give feedback without being too harsh, then parents want to be more involved." She continued with this example, "You have to know how to discuss problems—for example, you don't say 'You have dirty children,' but you say, 'Now my dears, some of the children have been coming to school a bit dirty, and I'm wondering what we should do about this?' "

In several preschools, teachers reported that, "Parents are involved in collecting and making materials." These materials were in evidence in many of the preschool classrooms we visited. For preschools with feeding programs (and more did than in most of the other districts sampled), "Parents bring the maize and millet," and "They employ a cook." Parents also brought younger children for growth monitoring, although only "twice per term," and "Parent meetings are called to discuss problems." For example, "We discussed the need for better playground equipment, and we got the materials from parents and made swings." Parents had been involved in making most of the playgrounds we saw, and they "also buy learning aides" and "bring money to buy food" for feeding programs.

Parents also were involved with the school committee in several preschools and primary schools and came to meetings when called by the head teacher. "Parents fund school development, such as the construction of buildings," and they have "participated in cooking demonstrations and changed the way they feed their families," using more locally available ingredients and traditional, high-nutrition weaning foods. In terms of issues raised by parents, some parents seemed concerned about school readiness. As teachers stated, "Parents emphasize the importance of children learning to read and write," and "The importance of good discipline for children is another frequent concern."

## Factors Related to Preschool Enrollment

In terms of factors related to preschool enrollment, the major reason for sending children was seen as school readiness or increasing the likelihood of success in primary school (Standard 1). "Children are sent to preschool to gain entry to primary school." Another teacher felt that, "Children are also sent to socialize, as well as to learn reading and writing." Some parents became concerned when they did not feel that academics were being stressed sufficiently in the preschool, as reflected in this quote: "Parents do not want to see children playing or hear them singing often. They want them to learn reading and writing!" "The importance of good discipline" was another frequent concern. Most children attended preschool only the year before they entered primary school, hence the academic emphasis of so many parents. As one teacher summed it up, "The value of education is known by some parents, and they tend to send their children to preschool."

The other major factor, especially when younger children were sent (threes and young four-year-olds), was child care. "Some parents send their children to get them away from home and leave the mothers free to go about their business," was the perspective of one teacher. The need for child care was particularly great in areas where families did not own land and tended to work as casual laborers, tea pickers, or on rented land, which was often far from where they lived, making it more difficult for them to bring their children with them to the fields.

## Relevance of Preschool Education

Most teachers felt that preschool was relevant to "traditional" families, and that a number of activities were consistent with, or supported, children's home culture. As one teacher put it, "Preschool is relevant to our traditions, because the curriculum includes our traditions." The most frequent activities listed that were "used to support children's home cultures" included role-plays, learning corners, dramatization, storytelling, discussing pictures, and learning poems. Instruction began in the mother tongue, with Kiswahili and English being introduced throughout the year before primary school. Other teachers listed "indoor free choice activities, role-plays, the home corner, riddles, and news telling" as ways in which the curriculum "takes care of home culture."

## Typical and Optimal Care Arrangements for Under Threes

According to preschool teachers, most children under age three were cared for at home—by their mothers, an *ayah* (when reliable or available), or a relative—typically the grandmother. Many mothers working on *shamba*s took their youngest child(ren) with them to the fields, although this created problems for both mothers and children, and there was a clear need for better care arrangements for under threes. When asked whether they ever worked with under threes at the preschool where they taught, most had not. Two had worked with two- and three-year-olds in Sunday school, and others had cared for their own or relatives' young children, but they had not formally taught them in preschool. One teacher described the "joy riders" who came with older siblings to nursery school but were never enrolled in the preschool. Only one teacher argued that under threes should not be in the preschool, but should be cared for at home. When asked why, she stated "because they've not reached the right age to come to school." Another teacher said that her preschool had "admitted under threes, but I find it difficult without a second teacher! With under threes, we need to be able to give them more time and attention."

Some teachers felt strongly that, "The needs of under threes would be best met in the preschool, because mothers are busy and the care of house maids is often neglectful of children." Four of the teachers interviewed felt that mothers were not as involved or concerned with their children's care as in the past, making preschool services more necessary. "In tea-picking areas, some children follow parents or older siblings to work or school . . . before mothers were more responsible and alert to children's needs, including a plan for them to get a hot lunch or *uji* during the morning, but that is rare now!" Other teachers described a home visitor or a "roving teacher" model, which had apparently been tried earlier in the Embu District, but felt that preschool was a more viable option. "A central place would work—versus a 'roving teacher' or home visitors programme . . . especially since parents are not home during the day, but are busy picking tea or in the *shamba*."

When questioned about what they liked about working with under threes and what they would need to provide an appropriate preschool program for younger children, responses were similar to other settings. One teacher described her recent experiences with three-year-olds saying, "I like it—especially when they are given suitable materials, they are quite active!" Another teacher who had worked with under threes at her church stated, "I liked the response of the young children—especially in singing simple choruses." When asked what would be hard about it, responses included, "They would get hungry and they would cry. They would not know how to use the toilets. I wouldn't like looking after them, it would be difficult."

In terms of program requirements for under threes, teachers stated, "We need to work with a smaller number to meet their needs, and they don't like sharing, so we need more materials," and "The safety of materials is important—and they should be durable—they could be rough on materials!" Again, feeding programs were named as being very important for preschools serving under threes, as was the importance of play, as expressed by another teacher. "The program would mostly cover a lot of play to build physical growth and for socialization and enjoyment." Other recommendations for programs for under threes included "Oral work, including storytelling, poems, and discussions, should be used to improve their language," and "Visits to see people working in factories, markets, shops, and other places in the community should be part of the program." The importance of an appropriate and a sufficient number of materials was again emphasized, as well as a large enough space, a playground, toileting facilities, and enough caregivers to assist teachers in meeting under threes' basic needs.

In terms of what would be the necessary next steps in expanding preschool programs in the Embu District or local communities to better meet the needs of under threes, teachers stated, "NGOs are not here, and there are no feeding programs outside that provide *uji* to children—some support for a feeding program is needed." This was in an area where many families were struggling to feed their families, and teachers felt that outside resources would be needed for a feeding program to be successful. Health concerns also were raised. "Government clinics and growth monitoring are available at the village level, and that is good. Drugs can be the problem." This teacher felt that children were often sick and that local dispensaries lacked medicines, or that parents could not afford to buy needed drugs from the chemist (*duka wa dawa*). In summary, two teachers said that they would like to work with under threes: "We'd like to prepare for a baby class for three-year-olds!"

## Summary

Much of the data from the Embu District can be viewed as providing a case study in community mobilization for children. As stated earlier, both Embu and Machakos have had strong leadership among their DICECE staff, who have built upon local communities' commitment to children's well-being and education. From cooking demonstrations of traditional weaning foods to materials-making workshops to primary health promotion activities, the Embu DICECE worked closely with most of the preschools we visited and had mobilized teachers, parents, and other community resource persons (e.g., nutritionists and health care workers) on various projects. The encouragement of rural preschool teachers' formation of "teacher panels" also was an example of the commitment and creativity frequently evident in this district. In other words, the training of preschool teachers was just one of the many roles provided by the DICECE.

In most Embu settings we visited, preschool was viewed by parents and community members as serving primarily a school-readiness function. An exception to this was found in the tea-growing areas on the slopes of Mt. Kenya, where preschools served more of a custodial child care function, as they had in the Kericho and Kiambu Districts. While preschool teachers in Embu expressed their willingness to work with younger children, they observed that with the current scarcity of preschool classrooms and teachers and the high demand for preschool learning for pre-unit, or four- and five-year-old children, it was not surprising that the infrastructure for serving younger children in preschool was lacking. Younger siblings of preschool attendees were served in other ways, however, including growth monitoring and other primary health projects. The weaning foods demonstration obviously was aimed at younger children, as were other activities engaged in by the Embu DICECE trainers.

The acceptance of preschool education in Embu was widespread, as evidenced by the frequency of community-funded or Harambee preschools, typically attached to primary schools and occasionally in churches or more private settings. Runyenjes was one of the richest farming areas of the district and, as such, had a very dense, if rural, population. Farm land was scarce, and land tenure issues were similar to those found in other settings, with subdivision of land through inheritance creating very small parcels of land for many young families. Other families rented land or work as hired labor for land-owning neighbors.

The child-rearing finding that came as the greatest surprise to both the visiting researcher and the local collaborators was indicative of early weaning in a number of young mothers. This appeared to be correlated with the land tenure problems just described, as such mothers might walk long distances to work in rented plots and found this to be incompatible with nursing their youngest children, since they traditionally would have nursed for many more months. Grandmothers we interviewed in a women's self-help group lamented over the use of expensive tinned foods and formula, and they felt strongly that valuable child-rearing traditions were being lost.

Another observation we made was the strong involvement of fathers in the lives and early education of their children and grandchildren. Serving on parent committees, volunteering their services, donating milk, or even fund-raising to purchase a cow for a preschool were all common in both the Embu and Machakos Districts. The home-school-community partnership for children was in ample evidence in each of the diverse, contrasting settings in which we collected data.

# Chapter 8

## Machakos District:
## It Takes Preschool Teachers As
## Health Workers to Raise a Child

Children are your wealth—without children, you are not a proper man—something
is missing.

—Father and farmer in Wamunyu

## MACHAKOS DISTRICT DESCRIPTION

At the time of this study, the Machakos District was comprised of a narrow
strip of landmass 125 kilometers wide in the north and 20 kilometers wide in the
south, sloping in a northwest to southeast direction. It had a total area of 14,254
square kilometers and bordered several other districts. Its district headquarters, the
town of Machakos, is 60 kilometers southeast of Nairobi. The Kajiado District lies
to the west, Nairobi and Kiambu to the northwest, Kitui to the east, Murang'a and
Embu to the northeast, and a new district, Makueni, to the south. One of 10
districts in the Eastern Province, it lies within a plateau between the Eastern Rift
Valley and the Nyika plateau. The district consists mainly of a large plateau, and
its elevation ranges from 1,700 meters in the western slopes to about 700 meters
above sea level in the south.

The topography of the district has impacted on its development. Coffee is the
major cash crop and is grown in the hills. Other crops such as tomatoes are grown
under irrigation. The lower plains receive the least rainfall, but they are suitable for

Fig. 8.1    Preschool Teacher in Machakos District Demonstrating Oral Rehydration Therapy to Parents

ranching. Sand is one of the most important resources in the district, and it is used for construction within and outside the district. Machakos is the main supplier of sand to Nairobi. Where terracing has not been practiced, soil erosion is a serious problem, and the district development plans in recent years have emphasized soil conservation activities. Similar to Embu and Kiambu, high population density in some areas has resulted in the fragmentation or subdivision of land holdings into uneconomical sizes. This has contributed to migration into the less populated parts of the district in search of land.

Machakos has six divisions, and there are four local authorities in the district. The primary locations sampled in our study were Wamunyu and Masii. In terms of population, the current population is 572,259. Before the division of the district, its population was over 1 million people. The growth rate between 1969 and 1979 was 3.9%, but decreased to 3.09% in 1989, in part "as a result of vigorous family planning campaigns supported by rising income levels" (Machakos District Development Plan, 1994-96, p. 9). Other demographics relevant to this study include the fact that in the 20 to 54 age group, the number of males is less than the number females by a large margin. This is attributed (Machakos DDP, 1994-96) to males migrating to other areas outside of the district in search of employment. The percentage of children from birth to age 14 was 52% in 1979, and current estimates are similar. The percentage of people over age 59 was 4%. Another relevant statistic from the Machakos District is that the number of school-going-age girls is slightly higher than the boys. This has been attributed to the higher proportion of females in the under-14 age group.

In the Machakos District, women participate in development activities, but their participation remains limited by traditions, household demands, and limited resources, which are most evident in the towns. A study in 1986 found that women's labor force participation was 59% compared to 81% by males in urban centers. Women continue to dominate all levels of rural labor, however, and women contributed most of the labor required for food production. Similar to Embu, the majority of people live in the rural areas. The history of the district, as outlined in a calendar of local events in the district's socio-cultural profile, lists a number of major famines, dating back to 1840. This pattern continued into the late twentieth century, with many concerns expressed about food security, seasonal hunger, and drought—particularly in certain locations of the district.

The largest ethnic group in Machakos is Kamba, who are the indigenous group of the area. At the time of the 1979 census, the Kamba accounted for 97% of the district's population. Other ethnic groups in the district include the Kikuyu (who account for approximately 50% of nonKambas), Embu, Meru, Tharaka, Kisii, Luhya, Kuria, Mijikenda, Luo, Kalenjin, Masai, Boran, Gabbra, Basuba, and non-African Kenyans. These latter groups account for less than 2% of the district's population.

## MACHAKOS SAMPLE

Four locations in the Machakos District were sampled, on the road to and surrounding Wamunyu, and included Masii. Interviews were held at area primary schools and preschools. A total of nine parents were interviewed, including six mothers and three fathers. Their first-born children ranged in age from 4 to 24 years, with a mean age of 15.1 years. Last-born children ranged from 2 to 7 years, with a mean age of 4.5 years.

In terms of parents' roles in the community, three fathers were church elders or leaders, three fathers were officers in village self-help groups, and three mothers were members of self-help groups. Two parents were choir members, and one was a choirmaster, one was a member of the school committee, and one was a youth group leader. One father was a member of both the local and sub-location development committees, and two parents said that they helped other parents and did informal counseling.

Turning to work, three parents interviewed were primary school teachers, two were involved in small businesses (e.g., selling porridge, vegetables, and newspapers), three were farmers, including two housewives who were farming, one ran a small hotel, and another was an assistant headmaster of a primary school.

In terms of formal education, four parents interviewed had completed primary teacher (college) training, three had completed their O Levels (Form 4), one father was trained in the ministry, and four parents completed Standard 7. Seven of the parents interviewed had lived their entire life in the same community. One had lived there for 16 years, one for 10 years, and one for one year.

Nine preschool teachers were interviewed. Most preschools employed two teachers, although as in the Embu District, some employed only one. All preschool teachers taught in rural preschools. In terms of formal education, three teachers had completed their O Levels (Form 4), two had completed Form 2, two had completed Standard 7, and two had completed their KCP (primary certificate).

Years of experience in their present teaching position ranged from two to 20. Two teachers had taught for two to three years, five teachers had taught from nine to 12 years, and two teachers had taught from 18 to 20 years. Seven teachers had only taught at their present school, and two had taught for five years at another rural preschool.

In terms of ECCE training, one teacher was DICECE trained, one was currently completing DICECE training, and one had taken the DICECE short course. Six teachers had completed the County Council short course, offered at the zonal level nearby. Three of the preschool teachers in the sample were trained by the Ministry of Health as community health workers, which included training in growth monitoring and promotion. Teachers ranged in age from 24 to 49 years, with a mean age of 35.3 years. Seven teachers were married, and two were single. Teachers' first-born children ranged in age from 7 months to 25 years, with a mean age of 14.1 years. Last-born children ranged from 1.5 to 12 years, with a mean age of 5.7 years.

Seven teachers reported that parents paid their salaries, and two (both head teachers) were paid by the Machakos County Council. When asked about other sources of income, six teachers reported involvement in a shamba or small-scale farming, one kept cattle, one did some farming and operated a small kiosk, and one had no other sources of income.

Eight primary children were interviewed, ranging in age from 10 to 12 years. They were from several classes, including four from Standard 4, two from Standard 5, one from Standard 6, and one from Standard 8. All had at least one sibling under age three.

## Portrait: Mother and Primary Teacher in Wamunyu

*Some days I leave for work at 4:45 A.M., and other days I leave the house at 8 A.M., depending on the duty roster at school. I do not reach the house until 6:30 P.M. most days. My three-year-old daughter is awake until 8:30, and then goes to bed. In the little time I have with her, we play and I teach her how to write, county things, and such. She stays with an ayah, but I am not always satisfied with her care.*

# Problems Facing Families with Young Children in Machakos

These days, I only spend Sundays with my youngest son—I am far away on weekdays working, so for one or two hours on Sunday, I help with repairing the bicycle, etc.

—Father in Machakos

Most of the problems facing families related to health and dietary concerns affected by both poverty and drought conditions, combined with a higher cost of living overall. Because Machakos is an agricultural district which, like the Embu District, is varied in productivity and growing conditions, a family's well-being was directly affected by drought. Some parents interviewed related the recent drought to their inability to pay for school fees and to provide their children with a proper, balanced diet. Specific health problems affecting children included ringworm and skin rashes, malaria, and respiratory illnesses. Parents were concerned that, "Children carry cold food to school and sometimes the diet is not balanced—only porridge." As in other districts, there were few feeding programs in preschools, although there were often health promotion activities (e.g., growth monitoring of under threes and instruction in mixing oral rehydration salts), discussed in further detail in the section on health.

Second in frequency to health and nutrition concerns were child care concerns, including finding enough time to give proper care and attention to young children. As one young mother stated, "My greatest problem is the lack of time to be with my baby with my work." Others stated that, "Housemaids are a problem—they are hard to find and often don't give proper care of the baby—not the way you would!" Another mother put it this way, " When you can find a maid or *ayah*, they are not able to feed or keep children clean." Several parents named the "lack of child care for working parents" as a major problem facing families in their communities of the Machakos District.

## How Are Families Coping?

Parents described ways in which they kept going and did their best to provide for their families. The Machakos District has, for example, over 900 registered women's self-help groups. Although not all of the registered groups are still functioning or meeting regularly, they provide one source of support and income generation for families in the area. Parents also responded to this question with descriptions of ways in which they were supporting the preschool and primary school—often in ways that did not cost much money, if any. "We try to buy items needed by the school—uniforms, clothes and books, but these are very expensive, so we pass along books from one child to the next. This has become a problem, however, when the curriculum has been changing so quickly." This comment was related to the changing of the national education system to an 8-4-4 system, with several more subjects required in primary school, necessitating more and different text books than used in the past.

## GOOD THINGS THE COMMUNITY IS DOING FOR CHILDREN AND FAMILIES

Again, self-help groups were mentioned. "In self-help groups, people encourage each other and learn from each other—for example, learning about planting of fruit trees and vegetables that can benefit children with better diet." Another example of the benefits of self-help groups was that, "Young women are trying to educate others on health care, including importance of boiling water, personal hygiene, and use of energy saving *jikos* (cookers)." *Harambee*s also were mentioned as another way to receive help in collecting funds to pay fees, make access roads, plan trees, build dams, and construct terraces for farming. A truly holistic view was taken by the parents we interviewed, in that they saw community development, whether agricultural or economic, as directly related to child development issues. Finally, some parents commented on the community's role in building preschools and primary schools, "thought they are not usually furnishing them."

## EFFECTS OF PROBLEMS ON CHILDREN: CHANGES IN THE PAST 15 YEARS

A consensus of the many parents we interviewed in the Machakos District was that, "Life is harder now, and more expensive." As in other chapters, the following sections summarize parents' experiences with particular types of change.

### Food

As one mother summed up, "Food is expensive and available on a seasonal basis." As discussed under problems facing families, "The area is suffering from drought," and it is very dependent on their harvests. Another parent commented that, "There are more food varieties than before, but they are often costly." In terms of specific dietary changes, mothers stated that, "We are now eating more rice, greens, and vegetables than in the past." Similar to Embu, more families were eating "tin foods," although these were not affordable by most rural families interviewed. "Packaged foods are high, and meat has gone up . . . I do have a *shamba,* but food is only available at certain times."

The discussion of food often led to a discussion of changes in farming and food production in the location. "In terms of farming, there are reduced herds and greater cultivation. There are also new breeds of cattle. In farming, we now use plows and tractors, and we're now using fertilizer . . . before we used manure, and now we're using chemicals."

## Housing

Responses related to changes in housing included, "Housing is a problem, and rents are high." This also related to a phenomenon that was observed in the Embu District (and elsewhere in Kenya), namely, that families who had previously owned land or a home were unable to provide land to all of their children. Thus many younger families were working on other people's land and were renting their homes. Some parents commented on changes in homes and other buildings. "Buildings have improved, but they are more expensive to put up—we've gone from thatch to metal, timber and glass." Others stated that, "Building a home now requires expensive materials, and it costs too much to build a big home—not like before, and ten years back there were even better buildings, but now they are too expensive."

## Health

As in other districts, health costs had risen and more private fee-for-service clinics were available, if not affordable. Several parents commented that there was "a problem getting enough medicines, so we have to buy from the chemist, which is very expensive." Other parents commented, "Private clinics charge much money! We need a hospital with medicines, as there is much malaria and people are dying—there's no medicine now (at the chemist), and what they have is too costly!" As one mother put it, "I was trained by the District Nutrition and Health Officer on primary health care and was taught the symptoms of disease and family planning techniques, but I still have no medicine!" These strong feelings were echoed by parents who were concerned that, although preschool teachers were now trained in primary health promotion, they "don't have needed supplies—like ORS (Oral Rehydration Salts) packets," and "First aid is useless if you don't have the needed supplies!"

In terms of environmental hygiene, "There are now latrines and better sanitation. Before we did not boil milk, used no nappies (diapers), only leaves, and now that we're doing these things, children are generally healthier." Another health-related issue was access to water and a greater awareness of risks from unsafe drinking water. "Before we used fresh water, and now we have catchment tanks and know about boiling water and using boreholes . . . there are less water-borne illnesses as a result."

In summary, most parents interviewed in Machakos thought that their children were healthy, but that food shortages remained a problem.

## Family Size

A fairly frequent response to questions regarding changes in family size was, "They are growing—oh yes! Now there are many more children and families before (in this location)." Improved child survival, emphasized by community health workers and reinforced by preschool teachers, was likely at least partially responsible for the greater survival rates of young children. As one mother put it, "I have five children—I might have had three." Several people also commented on the increase in young, often single, mothers in their communities. "People are getting more children when they are young—you can see a single mother with four or five children!" Others, however, felt that family sizes were decreasing with more family planning, and that the cost of raising and educating children was increasing. One interesting theory on a perceived rising birthrate in Machakos was, "Before, people (husbands and wives) didn't have much time to meet, but now, if a man and his wife are around more and they're hungry and cold, they make more babies!"

## Education

Education may remain for rich people only, who plan for the children of poor families to be working in their homes as servants. How can families raise Kshs. 4,000/ with no income? It's like a kind of slavery!

—Father in Wamunyu

The primary way in which education had changed, from the perspective of the parents interviewed, was that it was "much higher in cost now." For example, "Before it was 200/Kshs. for high school and only 15 to 20/Kshs. for primary—and now it is too high!" Another parent continued, "Even in government schools you can't pay less than 4,500/Kshs. in fees only, and then you have to buy uniforms, supplies, books, and pay other fees for examinations and building funds. In national schools it's over 10,000/Kshs. and you must have a minimum of 8,000/Kshs. for one child to be enrolled!" When asked about a community bursary, one father responded, "You must know about it first, and it isn't easy to get funds there . . . before the Chief managed it, now it is centralized and left for secondary, not primary." Several mothers agreed strongly with this statement and dismissed the bursary as something not available for them and never used for younger students.

## Child-rearing Practices

Half is the parent and half is the teacher, and we must work together.

—Mother

Most women in the communities sampled go to the hospital to give birth, however, "Some do not get there in time!" All children appeared to be immunized, and parents said that this was in part due to the fact that immunization was "a free service." Breast-feeding was still widely practiced, although, "A few mothers do early weaning, and this is largely based on their income." Similar to some of the early weaning practices identified in the Embu district, typically by mothers who needed to work long hours as casual laborers on farms, early weaning was described. Growth monitoring was widely practiced, and many mothers seemed proud that they had monitored their children's growth for "the full five years!"

In terms of weaning foods and practices, most mothers stated that they breast-fed their children for "about two years." Some children, however, were "weaned as early as four to six months, or earlier," particularly if they had a young, working mother. Weaning foods included uji, beans, soup, *ugali*, avocados, potatoes, bananas, and fruit juices. In terms of toileting, "A child is shown where to toilet, then it is disposed of in the latrine."

Turning to other aspects raising of young children, one parent stated, "If someone's poor, they can't raise children as well . . . even when milk is needed, you may not have a cow." A father stated, "Nowadays, we leave children to the teacher—you may sit with your children briefly at night, but there is no time for advising children, and the increase in crime, smoking, and drugs [is] a result of no respect of elders." Agreeing, another father said, "There is a lack of good role models—a teacher may be smoking but saying, 'Don't smoke!'" Other parents felt that children received greater attention and advice in the past. "A few years ago, it was better—there have been many changes, and now education is academic and some preschool programs are costly. There's little time with parent and child, and recreational facilities are beyond the financial means of most families. Thus, problems are brought to the teacher, and children may already be spoiled by age four or five." A mother added, "Parents should start advising their children—half is the parent and half is the teacher, and we must work together!" Many mothers agreed that, "Guidance and counseling is needed for parents to do a better job of child-rearing."

## Social Structures and Services

One change that several parents noted was the lack of respect for elders and, as one father stated, "In the past, there was better training of parents." Others, however, felt that mothers now "know better how to feed and clothe young children." The impact of community health promotion was again evident, as captured in the following quote. "Parents are concerned about the health of children, and they try to practice growth monitoring, use of ORT, and other things they've been taught."

Another issue related to changing social structures was class. As one father put it, "There is a gap across class, and it's much bigger now!" With the subdivision of land, urbanization, and the gradual shift of wealth from agriculture to various businesses, several parents felt that the "rich are getting richer and the rural poor

Fig. 8.2    Preschool Children Walking Home in Wamunyu

are worse off." This even applied to becoming members of many self-help groups. "It is hard for people without income to become members." For example, as one mother stated, "Women's groups used to be viewed positively and were doing well. They were viewed as a vehicle for development in general, but now they have become exploited by the administration." Another mother continued, "By the time objectives are set, the administration can bring in different criteria, or even cancel a project." A father added, "The community is not free—we are being forced to do things in different ways!" Although many parents were critical of this sort of "politization" of traditional self-help groups and community project, they did "see a need for more self-help through groups" in the future—particularly if such groups could be free from outside interference, including local and district officials.

## RELEVANCE OF PRESCHOOL TO "TRADITIONAL" FAMILIES

Half is the parent and half is the teacher, and we must work together.
—Mother in Wamunyu

Parents should be taught, through community meetings, versus only having *Harambee* fundraising functions with parents.
—Father in Wamunyu

## Parent and Community Contributions to Early Childhood Care and Education

Parents, grandparents, and community leaders interviewed in the Machakos District listed a number of ways in which families contributed directly to preschools and related services. As in other districts, these included planning and organizing feeding programs (where they existed), donating funds, building supplies, and labor for the preschool and fund-raising for ongoing expenses of the school, and making toys and other learning materials. Parents also stated that paying fees and "taking children to school" were contributions, as was their work with children in "teaching them to write their letters in the sand." Finally, parents felt that "providing protection and safety, including practicing improved hygiene" were direct contributions to children's care and well-being.

## CARE OF CHILDREN UNDER THREE

When parents were asked where they had gotten most of their information on child development, an interesting response was that they "learned it when we were children ourselves, from games and from experience caring for other children." Other, more frequent responses were "from our mother" and "from teachers." Three mothers said that they learned about caring for young children from the clinic, and three others said that they learned "from books—especially home science."

In terms of their typical child care arrangements, most under threes in the sampled areas were cared for at home by the mother, if available, older siblings, or a child-minder (where the family was economically better off). Representative of many working mothers, one stated, "Most mothers have time with the baby or under three in the evenings and on Sunday—Sunday is usually the day they spend with the child." Another mother responded, "Mine are funny—they don't want to miss me, they want to play with me—and on Saturday or Sunday is the only time we can!" One preschool teacher with a young child at home added, "My young daughter wants me to stay with her—she wants to go to the *shamba* and see what I'm doing there . . . she asks questions and wants to help. After school, she is busy looking in my basket, asking me why I'm late, and in the morning she pleads, 'Let me do with you!' But the grandmother stays with her while I work on the *shamba* or at school."

Some of the mothers interviewed were literally with their youngest children all day. "Me, I am always with them. For example, when washing utensils, she (a young child) touches the water, later she imitates sweeping, and then goes to the *shamba* with me." Other mothers and fathers described letting young children participate in chores with them.

All of the children in the sample were immunized, although preschool teachers reported that when they inspected for or asked about immunizations, they were still finding children who were not. The majority of children were born in the hospital and were taken regularly to the clinic or dispensary for growth monitoring and immunizations. As previously discussed, however, treating illnesses had become more costly, which was a problem for many families we talked to.

When parents were asked what they did to make their youngest children happy, responses included buying them toys and providing play materials, such as paper, balls, swings, mud, clay, toy cars, and models.

## Best Place for Under Threes

The consensus of the Machakos parents interviewed was that "Mother is best!" but preschool also was acceptable, particularly as children got older. As one mother put it, "Home is best, but a child can go to preschool if the mother is not there, and the teacher knows how to care for these very young children." Reasons given for the home being best included, "Home is best because the child can be free and can get frequent feedings," "Young children tend to be shy at school," and "Preschool is far away, and children can be tired and sleepy." Some parents had concerns about preschool teachers' lack of preparation to work with under threes. "Some teachers are ignorant of their needs and actually ignore the youngest children and only teach the older children," was one concern the mothers expressed. "Under threes may be a bother to the teacher and will not get good care." Others discussed adaptations in the current preschool that would have to be made. "Limiting class size would be necessary if under threes were admitted." Another parent stated, "Facilities for under threes are needed and also smaller groups."

## Joys of Being a Parent

As in other settings, one of the greatest joys parents expressed was that of being identified as a parent and for the child to continue their name and heritage: "When the child takes your name—the continuity of the name." As the father quoted at the beginning of this chapter stated, "Children are your wealth. Without children, you are not a proper man—something is missing!"

Another father agreed, saying, "Sometimes, when you look at your children, you feel more manly—and you like them very much." Others expressed pride at being able to provide for children, "Being able to provide for the child with food, care, and school makes me happy." While fathers expressed pride over having children, mothers tended to express joy at being with their children and doing shared activities and household work. "Keeping busy with my children makes me happy" was how one mother put it. In contrast to other settings, parents in Machakos did not emphasize the role of children doing work for them, taking care of them in old age, running errands, or minding other children. They appeared to take great joy in the experience of being a parent and of doing things together with the child(ren).

## Challenges of Being a Parent

In terms of what Machakos parents found difficult about being a parent, one parent summed up several of the responses, saying, "The hardest thing about being a parent is that you are challenged—if you don't meet their needs, they may feel like they don't have a parent!" Indeed, parents' greatest concerns were about "not being able to get food, school fees, and clothing for children during times of drought." One mother said, "You strain to get all that they need." Mothers also felt that it was becoming more challenging to raise children: "The hardest part is bringing them up!" Fathers, in contrast, said the hardest part was "educating them—particularly given the rising costs." As one father put it, "There are many obstacles in the way!"

## Parental Aspirations for Children

As in other districts in the study, one of the most frequently expressed aspirations for children's futures was that "they have self-reliance and be self-sufficient." Equally important to parents in Machakos was "that they have a better life and are more happy and self-satisfied than we are." Parents also hoped that children would "be able to fight and overcome problems," "to get married and have their own families," and "complete schooling and get jobs." Several parents anticipated that their children would be able to help them in the future, and some parents said that they hoped their children would always have "good behavior."

When asked how life would be different for their children, the most frequent response was, "Things will be more expensive and harder!" Others described the changing face of land tenure and agricultural patterns in Machakos. "Life will be different. There will be no looking after cattle—land will not be available." Others commented, "It will be harder to get jobs!"

When asked how early childhood education might help prepare their children for the future, parents felt strongly that it would have positive outcomes in terms of doing well in school in the future and, therefore, in finding employment. "Early identification of talents and skills can help train them for particular jobs" was the perspective of two fathers. "Children with handicaps can get proper intervention." This was one of the few times that the issue of children with disabilities or special needs was raised by parents (a residential program for children with mental challenges and physical differences was based in Wamunyu, a sampled location). Other ways in which preschool could help children included, "They will get a good foundation for education," "They will be more reliable," and "Children will take better care of their children the way they were taken care of." This latter comment was in reference to the education preschool children received about the importance of growth monitoring, how to mix ORT solution, and other primary health information they learned at school.

## Preschool Teachers' Perspectives

When preschool teachers in the Machakos District were asked about the major problems or challenges facing the community, they corroborated what parents had told us—the cost of living was high, and parents often had difficulty meeting their children's needs. More specific problems listed by teachers were that, "School fees are very high," "Many families lack adequate food, hence they cannot provide a balanced diet," and "There is a lack of medicine in the dispensaries." They also commented on the long distances many families had to travel to the health centers, giving this as a reason for the preschool's involvement in primary health promotion activities. One teacher summed it up, saying, "In a word, the greatest problem facing our families is poverty." One teacher commented on the "lack of commitment by young parents to the care and welfare of their children." The most frequent response, however, was "having to provide all the facilities and services in school, and people do not have enough money."

## How Parents Are Coping

Again, similar to the information gathered from interviews with parents, teachers felt that self-help groups helped a lot in obtaining money for school fees, and they stated that, "Parents organize *Harambees* to assist those that are in need for school fees, hospital bills, or other expenses." Self-help groups were seen as "initiating income-generating projects to meet basic needs." Others commented on the ways in which parents had helped the preschool and, thereby, their children. "Some parents contributed money to construct a water tank," or "Some parents buy water for use in the preschools." One teacher, who had earlier expressed concern about young parents' neglect of children's needs, stated, "Where young mothers abandon their children, grandparents take over the care of their children."

## Effects of Problems on Young Children

The effects of hunger were among the most frequently mentioned problems affecting children in preschool. "When children are hungry, they can easily get sick and lack attention in school." Teachers also commented that, "The lack of proper diets results in malnutrition and stunted growth." As in other districts, children were sent home when they did not have school fees, and "when sent home, they miss learning." An interesting aspect of being "chased away" when their parents had not paid fees was that, "Children learn to cheat to be allowed back . . . many say the parents were not at home." Another preschool teacher observed, "Children are emotionally disturbed when they are chased away from school. Some do not go home; they'd hide and wait to go home with the others, because they do not want people to know they were chased away from school."

Other observations related to the impacts of poverty on young children. "Poverty and dirty environments may result in sickness in children." One teacher commented, "When parents cannot afford to buy uniforms or soap to clean clothes, their children come to school without a uniform or dirty. This makes them feel bad, and they are emotionally affected."

## ACTIVITIES USED TO SUPPORT HOME CULTURE

Teachers and families in the Machakos sample shared the Kikamba language and culture. Specific ways in which teachers tried to reinforce the home and the children's culture included role-playing of home activities and responsibilities, storytelling, traditional dances, and constructions (where children construct houses, toys, etc., similar to what they would do at home). Other examples included "home corners in the preschool where children can role-play, learn about home and local environment, and make constructions."

In terms of the ways in which preschool contributed to or complemented traditional systems of child care, teachers stated that, "Activities provided in preschool offer stimulation to children, as they would get at home." Another response was, "Children in preschools are taught to respect their elders, as was the case in the old days." Finally, "Children are told stories and oral history in preschool, as they were told in the old days."

## PARENT AND COMMUNITY CONTRIBUTIONS TO PRESCHOOL

The most frequently mentioned contributions of parents to the preschool (as stated by preschool teachers) were that, "Parents contribute materials and develop learning and play materials," and "Parents attend meetings, and some parents serve on the school committee." Other contributions included, "Parents put up the preschool buildings and maintain and clean the compound," "Parents do *Harambees* for putting up the preschool," and "Parents contribute money to buy books and supplies." One teacher mentioned that parents provided the feeding program, and another said that parents hired the cook. Several teachers stated that parents come to the preschool to inquire about their child's progress and also to bring younger children to participate in growth monitoring and primary health activities at the preschool. Finally, a teacher stated that, "Parents come in to tell riddles and stories."

When probed about the most effective ways of mobilizing parents, teachers agreed that the headmaster should call parents for meetings. "If the headmaster calls for parents, all will come." When asked about the common concerns raised by parents, three themes were identified: "cleanliness of the school," "progress of their child," and "health of their child." With the exception of ways in which children were "chased away" from preschool when their parents had not paid their fees, the many types of partnership between home and school in the Machakos District were evident and were encouraging examples of the "village raising the child."

## Child Care Arrangements for Under Threes

Supporting the parents' perspectives, preschool teachers observed that, "Most under threes are at home with their parents, with the child carried wherever the mother goes, or left with a grandmother" (in which case, the child was carried wherever she went), "or maid." Preschool teachers also noted that, "Many parents lack *ayahs* (maid/child minders), so they would prefer to send their 2–3-year-olds to preschool for custodial care." Other teachers stated that, "A few under threes come to preschool with their older siblings."

Teachers raised several concerns about caring for under threes in the preschool setting. These included, "They are shy and fearful," "They are not toilet trained," "They spoil materials," "They need a lot of attention and materials," and "They cry a lot!"

## Teachers' Goals and Concerns in Providing Care for Under Threes

In a district that is known for primary health promotion and GMP (growth monitoring and promotion) activities, it was not surprising that 11 teachers stated that children needed "proper health care," including "medicines, immunization, GMP, clean clothes and bodies, and clean and safe environments." The second most frequent concern related to a more appropriate environment and materials to meet children's specific needs. "They need their own and suitable facilities, including toilets, warm classrooms, and a safe environment," and "They need plenty of learning and play materials." Other similar responses included, "They need a warm room to sleep" and "a proper diet—especially fruits." Teachers felt strongly that feeding programs should be a requirement of preschools serving children under three. They also commented that under threes "need water to be washed when they have soiled themselves, and for drinking."

Some preschool teachers focused on the educational needs of both parent and under threes. "Parents of under threes need to be made aware of their needs." They also felt that children needed "character training, including being taught how to share materials and facilities and to take turns." In summary, teachers did not feel that it would be impossible to serve under threes in preschool settings if those facilities were adapted and improved to meet the specific needs of younger children.

# INTERSECTORAL COLLABORATION WITH PRESCHOOLS

When asked for examples of intersectoral collaboration with preschools where they taught, the teachers most frequent response was, "The Ministry of Health," which provided scales and charts for growth monitoring and family planning services and worked to involve rural preschools in these activities. Second in frequency were the County Council, which "assists in putting up preschools and paying teachers' salaries," and the Ministry of Education, which, though the DICECE and DEO (District Education Officer), "give advice, materials, and training to preschools and teachers." Two NGOs (Christian Children's Fund and World Vision) were mentioned for "helping some families with school fees," "building latrines and water tanks for self-help groups," and other forms of support. An orphan's home also was identified as assisting with some of the children, and "the Catholic Church assists to build homes and provide water tanks" in some of the communities sampled. The church also "sponsors some of the children by buying them school uniforms."

# CHILDREN'S INVOLVEMENT IN SIBLING CARE

## Portrait: 11-Year-Old Boy in Machakos

*I get up early, wash my face, drink some tea, and put on my uniform, put books in my bag and go to school at 6 A.M. After school I fetch water, collect firewood, wash utensils, then we sometimes go to church, where we sing, pray, and then come home and eat. My brother is four years old and my sister is not yet three. I wash them and play with them when I am at home.*

Children in the Machakos District were extensively involved in the care of their younger siblings. Older children did the following to help in their care (in order of the frequency with which children named each activity or role): "washing and keeping younger ones clean" (including combing or shaving hair, bathing child, and cutting nails); "making toys and other play materials for younger ones" (mentioned 15 times during children's interviews); "teaching the younger ones what we have learned in school—including writing and reading and songs"; "teaching them to talk [in a] new language such as Kiswahili and English;" and "feeding them." They also listed an array of more general household chores that they were expected to carry out, including washing, sweeping, fetching water and firewood, and cooking. Working on the farm and caring for animals also were named, more frequently by boys, while domestic work appeared to be shared between boys and girls, with girls having greater child care responsibilities. All of the children interviewed said that they played with their younger brothers or sisters, including hide-and-seek and "pretending" games.

## Childhood Illness

When children were asked how they could tell if the younger ones were sick, responses included, "They cry a lot," "They refuse to eat," "They are sleepy," "They look unhappy," and "They feel hot—they have a high temperature." In terms of what they did when younger ones were sick, most said that they "ask for help from neighbors if my parents are not around." Other responses were, "I wait for my mother and inform her the baby is sick," and "If I know where my mother is, I run and inform her." Children reported that parents would then take the sick child to hospital or clinic or would buy medicine for the baby.

When asked how they comfort a younger brother or sister, the most frequent response was, "Give the baby some food," followed by "Sing them a lullaby," "Carry her on my back," and "Give him toys or things to play with." These were very similar to responses from older siblings in other districts and demonstrate the sensitivity to ways of caring for under threes, which many primary school children (ages eight to 12) have acquired since an early age.

## CHILDREN'S MEMORIES OF NURSERY SCHOOL

All of the primary school children we interviewed had attended preschool, and most remembered it well. Their memories included "playing many games," "modeling using clay," and "going swimming." As in other settings, children contrasted the discipline techniques and "caring" of the preschool teacher to more recent primary school teachers. As one child recalled about nursery school, "Teachers were friendly, we carried their bags, teased them, joked with them, and played with them—in primary, this does not happen!" Or, as one boy put it, "When we came late, we were not beaten!"

Other contrasts between preschool and primary school that children made were, "Teachers in primary school are serious—we do not play with them," "In preschool, we did not learn English, as we are learning in primary," and "In preschool, we were told stories and sung to much more." Other contrasts dealt with the daily routine; "in preschool we were provided with a snack at 10 A.M.—in primary we do not have a snack," and "We went home at 1 P.M. in nursery school, but primary school is much longer!"

## SUMMARY

Positive changes over time, particularly in terms of child health, were noted by several parents in the Machakos sample, yet the memories of drought, the lack of farm land for future generations, and the higher cost of living were all concerns raised by parents. Similar to Embu, the vital role played by the DICECE team was evident in the many preschools and communities we visited. Again, most preschools were build on a *Harambee* basis and were attached to rural primary schools. Parents, both fathers and mothers, were active on school committees and enthusiastically took part in our interviews. In several cases there were more fathers than mothers who volunteered to be part of our study. Several of the preschool teachers we interviewed had been trained as community health workers and collaborated well with local health clinics and health officers.

As in the Embu District, preschools in the rural Machakos District were primary attended by children the year before they were enrolled in primary school, thus functioning in many ways as kindergarten does in the United States and other settings. We did visit several preschools where children under four were enrolled or joined their older siblings in coming to school. This appeared to be related to both the policies and capacity of the preschool and the distance children had to walk to get from home to school.

A number of parents expressed deep frustrations over their inability to provide all they felt they should for their children's well-being. The added fees under recent structural adjustment policies and loss of free government services were felt deeply by many families and teachers interviewed. Many were engaged in both farming and work as laborers or in other income-generating schemes or informal sector employment. In Machakos, as in Embu and other rural districts, the number of women's self-help groups was very high—some government reports estimated that over 900 women's groups were registered and functional. Such community-based mutual support strategies were further evidence of rural Kenyans continuing to function as a village committed to raising its children to the best of its ability—even given the recent droughts and worsening economic conditions.

# Part V

Urban/High Population Density:
Nairobi and Kisumu

# Urban/High Population Density: Nairobi and Kisumu

We urbanize, but with no direction!

—Father in Nairobi

A nation is considered "overurbanized" when it lacks the capacity to support its urban population. Walton and Ragin (1990) found that overurbanization is one of the primary causes of (Third World) protest against austerity measures, noting, "The urban poor and the working class are affected by a combination of subsidy cuts, real wage reductions, and price increases stemming from devaluations and the elimination of public services" (p. 877). As Bradshaw, Noonan, Gash, and Sershen (1993) state, "Externally imposed structural adjustment may be a key determinant of the growing overurbanization in many poor countries." The World Bank estimates that, "By 2010, most of the world's people will live in cities, and more than two-thirds of those urban dwellers will live in developing countries. In two more decades, developing countries will host 2.6 billion people and have more than two and a half times the size of urban populations as developed countries" (1992, p. 5).

Wallman (1996) cautions that, as in other less developed parts of the world, the rate of change in the urban proportion of the population in African cities is "not exceptionally high. In the third quarter of this century it grew from 16.7 to 28 percent," which is comparable to more developed nations. What is unprecedented, however, is the growth rate of urban populations, particularly in major African cities (p. 9). For example, in the 1980s, the urban population in East Africa grew at an average rate of over 7% annually, leading the continent in urban population growth (United Nations, 1989). Still, Africa remains one of the least urbanized regions of the world (Wallman, 1996). In terms of a demographic profile of East African city dwellers, the combination of young adults, high fertility, and a life expectancy averaging 50 years, "The population consists largely of families and households with numerous children and high dependency rates" (p. 9).

As Jamal and Weeks (1988) observe, "African cities are in particular crisis. The real wages of urban workers have fallen sharply, the earlier relative security of formal work is largely gone, and the rural-urban gap has narrowed markedly if not altogether vanished." This has resulted in acute problems in providing and maintaining urban services (Stren & White, 1989), and has also contributed to family problems that require complex survival strategies. Many have turned to the informal economy or microenterprise, including many salaried workers whose formal income does not come close to covering family expenses. Mettelin (1987) asserts that between one-quarter and one-half of the working population of major African cities are involved in the informal sector. In Dar es Salaam, Malimyamkono and Bagachwa (1990) found that, "Virtually every family has one or more—often all—of its members engaged in the informal economy" in some capacity.

Earlier in the century, males outnumbered females in urban areas, and women remained in the rural home. This pattern has changed, however, with females in the majority of cities such as Nairobi, particularly in some of the slum areas (e.g., the Mathare Valley). With a rapid increase in single-parent, urban families and with more mothers (single and married) in the workforce, the need for better child care arrangements is dramatic. Thus we selected two of Kenya's largest cities for inclusion in the study and sought to sample a cross section of family situations.

The urban settings sampled in our study were selected for both their contrasts and their similarities, and for the many ways in which they were representative of Kenyan cities and municipalities. The population of Nairobi is estimated at 3.5 million, with 70% living in sprawling urban slums. Nairobi is a province in itself, and Kisumu is a municipality within the Kisumu District. The demographics of these two cities also offer rich contrasts, with Kisumu predominantly Luo (over 85%), with other Western Kenyan ethnic groups represented, including Luhya (6%), Kisii (1%), and Asian (less than 1%). The dominant ethnic groups in Nairobi include Kikuyu (32%), Luo (18%), and Luhya (16.4%), as well as other groups that have migrated into the capital (e.g., Kisii, Kelinjin, Maasai, and Somali). Asians, both citizens of Kenya and non-citizens, comprise just over 1.5 percent of Nairobi's population, and ex-patriots, mainly from Europe and the United States, comprise just over 0.5%. Both cities have sizable Asian populations as well as a number of ex-patriots. Nairobi has a particularly large ex-patriot population due to the number of NGOIC, U.N. agencies, including East African regional offices, missionaries, and those involved in businesses such as tourism.

Both Nairobi and Kisumu reflect the rapid urbanization discussed earlier, including a growing number of single-parent, female-headed households. The growth rate of the urban population of Kenya is estimated at between 4.8% and 5.5% (Government of Kenya and UNICEF, 1998). Street children and young mothers with infants and toddlers living and working on the street were an increasingly common site in both cities, and living conditions in many of the urban neighborhoods were harsh. Our sampling strategy, however, was to try to talk to families and children from different class backgrounds, not only sample slum areas. The Kisumu interviews achieved this to a greater degree than the Nairobi ones, with a cross section of income groups and various ethnic and religious backgrounds sampled. This may reflect the diverse nature of the populations with whom the Kisumu DICECE and their colleagues work. It likely also reflects the research and sampling expertise of the Kisumu local collaborators who have been involved in a number of previous studies. The Kisumu sample included Ishmael Muslim families, as well as Luos, the majority ethnic group of this region of Kenya.

One of the unique aspects of the Kisumu interviews was the large number of participants in each focus group discussion, as can be seen in the description of the sample. It was not unusual for there to be 15 to 20 parents or preschool teachers in a group interview. The number of participants interviewed in Nairobi was smaller and tended to come primarily from densely populated slum areas in different parts of the city. We also conducted four different focus group interviews with community leaders and professionals working with children and families in Kisumu, including headmasters and headmistresses of both public and Islamic primary schools, school inspectors and TAC (Teacher Assistance Centre) tutors, and social workers, community development assistants, and a nutritionist from the Kisumu Department of Social Services. Both urban contexts offer striking similarities in the problems facing families, as well as contrasts in the different community responses to these issues.

# Chapter 9

## Nairobi: It Takes Money and Partners to Raise a Child

I have stayed in this slum since 1982 and sell charcoal. My parents died when I was young, and I never went to school. I have five children and am a single mother. On a typical day I am just trying to get enough money for food and caring for my youngest children. I get some help from my children and often take them with me when I am selling charcoal. Before, people here were all living in cartons, then in 1984 they all burned. We only got a dispensary recently, and there is only one pay toilet for many families. My children and I are often hungry.

— Single mother in Mukuru, Nairobi

## SETTING

Nairobi is the capital city and the smallest province in Kenya. According to the 1989 population census, there were 1,324,570 inhabitants. In 1993, it was estimated that Nairobi had a population of 2.5 million, and by 1999, it was estimated at 3.5 million. Urban migration of people from rural areas looking for employment has contributed to this rapid growth rate and has resulted in a strain on housing, health, education, water, sanitation, communication, and electricity. The sprawling slums, estimated to house 70% of the population, have obvious negative impacts on

Fig. 9.1    Preschool Teacher in Nairobi Slum

the social lives, living standards, and general maintenance of cleanliness in the city. Like many urban slums, the infrastructure to support the rapidly growing population is often virtually nonexistent. The majority of people in the slums live below the poverty line, and approximately 20% of the families are headed by females. Life in the slums has adverse effects on young children. Most of the mothers are away from home many hours a day, working in small businesses such as hawking or selling homemade brew, charcoal, and secondhand clothing. Many children end up on the street, in part because their families cannot afford school fees and related expenses.

Nairobi has approximately 398 health facilities, which include hospitals, health centers, and dispensaries. Kenyatta Hospital, the largest public referral and teaching hospital in the country, is in Nairobi. In recent years, physicians have been on strike for better wages, but these labor actions had ended by the time the research began. The Nairobi City Council also runs a large number of health centers and dispensaries. However, due to increasing demands and cost-share stipulations of structural adjustment policies, these facilities are extremely strained. Unfortunately, these facilities do not begin to adequately serve slum dwellers. The NGOs have greatly assisted the slum population by establishing health facilities that charge minimal or no fees for treatment. The majority of the well-equipped health facilities are private. Their charges, however, are very high and are only affordable by those in the upper-income brackets of the city.

Regarding to nutrition and health, the nutritional status of children living in the slums is low and the incidence of malnutrition is high. This is due primarily to poverty, poor personal and environmental hygiene, lack of adequate water and sanitation, congestion, poor housing, and lack of health facilities. Diarrheal diseases, respiratory infections, intestinal worms, and skin diseases are common in these areas. The health status of Nairobi's growing number of street children also is quite poor, with HIV/AIDS infection rates growing and risks of injury, burns, and infections very high. Drug usage among street children also is pervasive, particularly glue sniffing and the use of *mirrah* (marijuana).

## NAIROBI SAMPLE

Five locations were sampled within one division of Nairobi, which encompassed several large slum areas, including sections of the Industrial Zone (Lunga Lunga and Mukuru), Kariobangi South, Civil Servants, and Kawangwari. A total of 19 parents and grandparents were interviewed, including 14 mothers, 3 fathers, 1 grandmother, and 1 grandfather. Parents' first-born children ranged in age from 1 to 27 years, with a mean age of 9.3 years. Last-borns children ranged in age from 3 weeks to 10 years, with a mean age of 2.8 years.

When asked about their roles in the community, five parents reported "providing support to other parents," three worked with or were members of self-help groups, three were involved in youth projects (e.g., through the YMCA, with drug awareness, etc.), and 12 helped with church activities (e.g., choir, special events, doing home-based fellowships, mothers' union leadership, etc.). Note that several parents were involved in more than one of these activities, and some of the single mothers in slums were not involved in any. Two of the men we interviewed ran preschools and child care centers, in part as a community service as well as a small business. One child care center was part of a slum-based self-help project. The other was a private, home-based neighborhood service responding to the urgent need for child care, particularly for children under three. The man who ran it was a minister who lived and worked at home and clearly considered this home-based child care center part of his urban ministry. The latter had a much more conducive environment for under threes, with better ventilation, more light, materials, and some concern about the training of his teachers.

In terms of work, as self-described, three mothers were involved in small business (e.g., selling used clothing, vegetables, or charcoal), two fathers were involved in tailoring and small enterprise business, two mothers were primary school teachers, and one was a social worker. Two fathers were school or preschool administrators, one father was a minister and family counselor, two mothers were office workers, two mothers were housewives or homemakers, one mother was a child minder in an under threes' self-help nursery, and four mothers were unemployed.

When asked about length of time in their present community or location, the range was six months to their entire life, with three living there from six months to two years, five from three to five years, two from 8 to 10 years, four from 12 to 14 years, two from 15 to 20 years, and three their entire lives. Turning to formal education, two had completed Teachers College (P-1), one had completed Form 6 (A Levels), two had completed Form 4 (O Levels), five were Form 4 leavers, and one had completed Form 4 (B-1). One parent had completed Form 2, one Standard 8, and three Standard 7. One mother reported that she had no formal schooling, as she had been orphaned as a youth and was now a single mother of five children and a charcoal seller.

Eleven female preschool teachers were interviewed in Nairobi. The average number of teachers at Nairobi preschools in the sample was three, which included a head teacher. Two of the teachers in the Nairobi sample were unpaid and were volunteer teaching while undergoing training, to gain experience, and they hoped to be employed in the near future.

In terms of formal education, nine teachers had completed Form 4 (O Levels), and two had completed Standard 8. One teacher also was trained as a Friends (Quaker) pastor. Teachers' years of experience in their present position ranged from one to seven years, with five teachers in their position from one to two years, four from three to five years, and two for seven years. Five had only taught at their present school, and others' previous experience ranged from one to five years.

Turning to ECCE training, four were CICECE (City Centre for Early Childhood Education, Nairobi) trained, and one had completed DICECE training in Narok before moving to Nairobi from Nakuru. Two teachers had completed a six-month Homecraft course, one had taken a Nakuru County Council short course, one had completed a two-month Catholic Workshop, and another had Montessori training. Note that some of the teachers interviewed had taken more than one training course. Two of the teachers were untrained.

Preschool teachers' ages ranged from 24 to 32 years, with a mean age of 27 years. Four teachers were married, and seven were single. Four teachers had children, with first-born children ranging in age from 4 to 10 years, with a mean age of 7 years. Last-borns children ranged from 20 to 30 months, with a mean age of two years.

Five teachers reported that the management of the preschool paid their salaries (from parent fees), two were paid by the YWCA branch, one was paid by the warden of a Friends Centre, and one was paid directly by parents in a cooperative. As previously mentioned, two teachers were unpaid. When asked about other income sources, four mentioned their husbands, and seven said "none." In fact, two teachers commented, "We have no time for income-generating activities—we're too busy with teaching!" One woman said that she sold bananas (in addition to income from teaching and her husband). The salary issue was particularly acute for a single, unpaid teacher who worked with a baby class at a YWCA and was anxious to receive further training.

Due to time constraints, only four primary children were interviewed. They were all Standard 4 students in Kawangwari and had younger siblings, with at least one under age three. They were interviewed during Phase II, in the same location as a community leader focus group.

## PROBLEMS FACING FAMILIES WITH YOUNG CHILDREN IN NAIROBI

### Portrait: A Young, Single Mother

*I stay in another slum near here, and have lived there since 1987. Before that, I lived in a village where Sister first built a school. I went to school there through Standard 7, and was selling* sukima *(kale greens), then I got my first child . . . now I have two children, age 3 and 6, and one is very sickly. There are 10 people in my family, I'm unmarried, and my mother is not working. I completed catering training, which was a 2 year technical program, but I am still unemployed. I last ate two days ago . . . whatever I can find goes to my children, which is why I was here to see Sister and try to get some assistance.*

Once again, most of the problems cited by parents were related to the high cost of living and their limited resources to meet family needs. Similar to the estate samples, parents also expressed concerns about their (and other parents) lack of time to spend with their young children, and the negative changes that similar to those reported in other settings. Many parents also expressed their frustration with being responsible for trying to support both children and an extended family, common to several of the parent interviews conducted in slum areas. As in Kisumu, there were marked class contrasts between parents interviewed in Nairobi.

These circumstances were affecting many children (e.g., the rise in the number of street children as education went beyond the financial reach of more and more families). The cost of living was the problem mentioned most frequently and included lack of money, ways to make a family budget stretch, and providing basics such as soap, fruit, clothes, and shelter. As one mother put it, "It's hard to get any of these things for our children, as they are too expensive!" Closely related to this was the problem of providing a balanced, healthy diet for children (e.g., the lack of meat and milk). One mother said, "We can only afford fruit once a week," and several mentioned their desire to have a kitchen garden and to grow more vegetables for their family—although they lacked land.

Teachers interviewed strongly agreed that lack of money to meet family needs was the major problem facing families. Funds for fees, uniforms, food, proper clothing, rent, and other needs were seen as the major manifestations of the high cost of living and growing unemployment. "Low income is the biggest problem," was how several teachers summarized family problems. They also saw links between poverty and child abuse. "Sometimes parents can't do what they want or need to do . . . and child abuse issues are there with some—they may take out their frustrations on children, or just neglect them."

The next most frequently mentioned parental concern was providing for all of the children's needs, particularly as a single parent. Mothers described in detail what it was like to be the breadwinner, either for much of their adult lives or more recently, as in the case of two recently separated or divorced mothers. School fees were particularly difficult for all lower-income parents to provide. Similar to the other districts sampled, parents complained that fees for school, texts, uniforms, and other related expenses were very high. Again, teachers interviewed also empathized with single mothers, who "have many problems, including financial, and may keep a child at home a long time when they can't afford to pay for care and education—even when the child was alone. They also commented that daughters of working poor families were now becoming single mothers, creating further burdens for their families.

Two other problems were related directly to child-rearing and care. First, many parents lamented over the lack of open spaces for children to play, as well as over the lack of equipment. They saw their neighborhoods becoming more crowded, dangerous, and even "bushy" or unkempt, with trash piled high and fewer open spaces for children to play. Related to this was the lack of affordable child care for working parents and the many problems associated with finding, affording, and keeping good maids or *ayah*s. Others had found child care but still had concerns about aspects of the program, particularly of nutrition and napping facilities. As one mother put it, "After children have learned in the morning, the day care lacks facilities for them to nap—there are no blankets, mattresses, or even mats for children to sleep on."

One concern that was unique to urban parents had to do with poor city services, including the lack of trash removal, water, road repairs, and better security and protection against violent crime, which was clearly on the increase in many Nairobi estates and slums. This concern about the diminishing urban infrastructure and lack of services carried over into the area of health, with parents complaining that clinics lacked medicines, which forced them to go to more expensive private clinics. Several recalled earlier times when visiting nurses and plentiful free medicines had been available at government hospitals. Again, this was evidence of the impact of austerity measures associated with structural adjustment policies.

In the health area, several diseases were mentioned, particularly respiratory illness, which was described as brought on by dust, smoke, and urban pollution, made worse in slum areas where people did not typically have kitchens and cooked outside. A health problem for babies in one slum was the loss of hair, which can be a sign of HIV/AIDS. Dysentery also was a problem, made worse by crowded conditions, few latrines, and a general lack of environmental hygiene. Malnutrition and hunger also were mentioned as health problems facing both children and parents. The mother quoted earlier, in fact, was visibly hungry, thin, and tired during the interview.

## Effects on Children's Development

Similar to the other districts sampled, teachers reported a number of ways in which the above problems affected children's general development, as well as behavior in the preschool classroom. The most frequently mentioned issues were associated with poor nutrition and its direct effect on children. "Children cannot learn on an empty stomach!" Hunger and loss of sleep were both seen as affecting children. "Sometimes children are tired and have trouble learning."

Other problems were described in terms of emotional or psychological suffering. "I saw a case last year that even when you said her name she'd cry— then it got better, with some gentle attention." This teacher interpreted the child's behavior as the effects of neglect. Fighting and sulking also were seen as effects of home problems on children's behavior at preschool. As one teacher stated, "One child said he saw his father beating his mother, and these stories are quite many!" Several stories of domestic violence and child abuse were shared by teachers, including children being locked out of a house overnight or a mother and children being chased away from their own house, and so on. Other times, teachers observed that, "A child may ask to go home when they're worried about what is going on there."

Another interesting "side effect" of pressuring children to do academic work at increasingly younger ages was seen as making children "tired, confused, and stressed when they are pressured to learn too much too early." Teachers saw the 8-4-4 system and the pressures associated with the competitive Standard 1 interview in many of the "better" primary schools as creating additional pressures on already vulnerable children.

## How Are Families Coping?

Basically, the parents interviewed were trying hard to provide for their families. "We strain ourselves—we really budget for food, rent, clothing, and school fees!" Another parent stated, "We take part-time jobs, divide lunch in two and share what food we do have, work hard, and stretch what we have!" In terms of the health problems and lack of medicines in the public or government clinics, parents reported that they had "resorted to using private clinics." This meant a sacrifice in some other area of the family budget in order to afford medical treatment for a sick child. Some mothers were in self-help groups, but many said that they worked very long hours and had little time to participate in any outside activities.

Teachers made several observations concerning poor families' coping strategies. As one teacher put it, "Surely they're struggling—we see secondhand uniforms and people seeking small loans." *Barazas* and parent meetings also were seen as a way in which schools and communities were helping parents cope. Several teachers stated that, "Parents prefer to bring under threes to nursery school, where a teacher can concentrate on the child and her needs, rather than leaving their children with house girls or *ayahs*." They also saw feeding programs in preschools, where they existed, as helping families cope by providing porridge and milk. Teachers described how they tried to be sensitive to different kinds of families and avoided discussions of fathers, for example, as many children did not have a father in their lives.

Middle-class parents clearly had the most resources for coping, and their problems tended to be related to time—finding sufficient time to spend with their youngest children and provide guidance and counsel to their older ones. One father described how his family had sacrificed financially so that his wife could stay home with their young children. He tried to be an involved father as well, but he had little time with his children except on Sundays.

## Good Things the Community Is Doing

Some parents expressed surprisingly strong feelings in response to the question, "What good things is the community doing for families and young children?" One mother said, "Nothing! They're not doing any good things for me or my family—they're not doing much for anyone." Others were more positive and cited the work of churches, particularly a local Catholic mission, which provided free or low-cost education to over 3,500 children, many of whom would otherwise have been on the street.

One father expressed delight over and appreciation of his children's child care center, which was run by a former private school headmaster who had decided to serve his own neighbors with home-based child care, including a special program for under threes. He said, "Sometimes mothers are working at night, and they even bring their young children here—they really have no other place to go . . . and families come here for assistance, and they do what they can." The retired headmaster/child care center owner also provided informal family counseling and appeared to offer a "safe house" for struggling parents.

Some parents felt that their communities had done far more for children and families in the past. "Years ago there were more child welfare and parent mobilization activities, including home outreach, but now you never see them!" Several parents missed home visitors, including visiting nurses, as reflected in this quote: "Health workers stay in their clinics now, there are probably fewer of them. Home visiting would be a good idea to bring back!"

## SOCIAL AND ECONOMIC CHANGES IN THE PAST 15 YEARS

As in other districts, many of the answers were related to the high cost of raising a family. Parents said, "We can't afford as much now—it's much harder to provide proper nutrition to a family." Another said, "We used to have a lot and it was cheap—now we have a little, and it's expensive!"

## Food

Although food had clearly gotten more expensive, its availability had apparently improved. "Before there were fewer people selling vegetables, maize, etc., and now there are many more kiosks, and the food is there—it's expensive, but it's there!" In reference to the rising cost of food, another parent said, "Even five years ago, foodstuffs were cheap; for example, some things which cost 50 cents are now 5–10 shillings . . . we can't even cater for a full family in food these days!" Another said, "Before we had access to food, it was there and not so expensive."

## Housing

The consensus of all of the parents and teachers interviewed was that rents were much higher now, and as a family grew, they needed to rent another room and so on, causing a further increase in rent. Other parents complained about how estates had become "dirty, crowded, and bushy" in recent years, with no safe places for children to play outside.

One interesting discussion about changes in housing recurred in three interviews in one slum location—first with parents, then teachers, and finally with local community leaders, including elders. This had to do with how, when the village was started, most people had been building from cartons and plastic, and homes were vulnerable to bad weather, fire, bulldozing over by the City Council. A new chief came in the early 1980s and said, "I cannot be the Chief of cartons—there are no shops or schools, and I stand as the Chief who will change that!" One of the nursery schools visited was started in the same year (1982), as many community improvements were undertaken, roads were made, and more people began to build with corrugated metal, cement, and other more permanent materials.

In terms of the cost of rents to family budgets, one mother said, "Our income bracket is low, and our biggest expense each month is renting our place. It's very crowded, and there's only limited movement for children, but we do have a place to stay." Others described how many families have to rent out one of their rooms in order to get more money, which contributes to the crowded conditions.

## Cost of Living

A consensus of parents interviewed was that, "Income has stayed the same, but the cost of living has really gone up!" Another variation on this theme was that, "The quality of life is even worse, but the cost of living is more." In this context,

Nairobi parents tended to mention the lack of services, poor or nonexistent roads, drainage problems, lack of trash removal schemes, and lack of water. One father estimated that there had been a "50–70% increase in the cost of living in the past 10 years."

One corollary of the rising cost of living mentioned by several parents was the increase in family planning, with more "small families" now (i.e., with three to four children). Also mentioned in this context was the higher rate of unemployment, again contributing to parents' inability to support a large family.

## Health

Again, upper respiratory illnesses, including pneumonia, were raised as increasing health problems in the past several years, and they were seen as being caused by pollution, dust, overcrowding, and poor hygiene. There also were more cases of diarrhea and skin diseases than parents remembered from 10 to 15 years ago. Some parents attributed these problems to the lack of clean water. As one mother stated, "The water's not like before—it's not clean, and it's also much more scarce. We must buy it by the jerry can, as we cannot use the tap." Some parents saw a slight improvement in hygiene over the same time period, although they commented that, "The lack of access to water and toilet facilities remains a big problem." One of the preschool sites visited, in fact, was part of a self-help project that had as one income-generating project a pay toilet (2/= Kshs. per use, plus toilet paper). In another slum area, one mother commented, "There are now just a few more latrines being built in other locations, and we've waited, but never saw toilets nearby where we live."

As discussed earlier, the loss of free City Commission Clinics and visiting nurses was seen as contributing to the increase in health problems, as well as to the inability of many families to pay the higher health care costs associated with private care. Some city clinics were seen as "being out of medicine most of the time" and only giving immunizations and having maternal and child health clinics. There had been some improvement, however, in the distance parents had to travel for medical care in the past. "Before there was no dispensary here, and we had to go into town; now, there's one nearby" (run by the Catholic Mission). Another parent acknowledged that "AMREF and Sisters of Mercy have been the main groups helping with the sick. Now, there's free immunization at a local clinic." Parents also commented that there was a need for greater awareness of AIDS and how to prevent it, and of family planning.

Finally, several parents interviewed discussed how health facilities at times appeared to serving fewer people. "There are fewer beds available in the hospital, and local clinics even run out of growth-monitoring cards for our children!" Parents were in agreement, however, that, "People don't get some of the diseases now that used to kill them!" This referred particularly to the effectiveness of immunizing children.

## Education

Parents from all five of the areas sampled agreed that, "You need to educate a child—but this is now so expensive!" Parents reported that it cost more each year to educate their children. Also, in Nairobi, some parents felt strongly that their children needed to be in a good school, not just "any school." As one father stated, "Emotionally, as a parent, you are not settled when your child is in a lesser school." Parents also stated that class sizes had gotten bigger, and now often had 60-80 children in classes. In two of the slum areas, parents said that there were now more primary schools, which was good, but that these neighborhoods still needed a secondary school.

An example of a positive change came from Mukuru, in which, as one mother put it, "Education has changed for the better here, thanks to the Catholic Mission and Sister!" Fees are very low (100/= Kshs. per term), and food is included! Uniforms were not only not required in this school, but they were actively discouraged, because they "are too expensive" and "are often stolen." Another mother saw this as not so positive, saying, "With more children and more school costs, the burden is often on the mother to pay!"

Another remark that was representative of many parents interviewed was, "Many families have not been able to send their children to school, for example, if you have four older children, all in school, some children may not be eating or dressing properly because of the money paid for school." Other parents spoke of having to decide which children to educate, as they could not afford to educate all of them.

## Family Size

As alluded to earlier, many more families were seen as "only able to afford to have two or three children, due to the high cost of living." Another interesting change in the demographics of some slum areas, particularly those in the industrial area of Nairobi, was that earlier mostly men were looking for work as casual laborers and so on, and now there are many more women, children, and families. As one mother put it, "There are now 30 times the number of women in Lunga Lunga as 10 years ago!"

Some parents saw family planning services as being more necessary now. "There are some family planning services now, but many more are needed!" was how another mother framed it. Parents agreed that children are very expensive to have, and some, but not all, were having fewer children. One parent related family planning to housing, saying, "The highest rent most families can afford is two rooms . . . still, there are more children there, and our areas are now overpopulated!" Urban migration was seen as a problem, with many people competing for a few jobs and some employed persons running away to the slums to escape the high rents in the more established housing estates in Nairobi and its suburbs.

## Social Structures and Services

As one father put it, "Life years ago was so different—there were so many organizations helping children—and now, these services are not there!" He felt that activism today focuses more on AIDS and family planning and less on children. Other parents stated that the main ways people socialized were in churches and household fellowships, as there were few if any social halls in their communities.

One more positive trend had to do with the increase in self-help groups. As one parent stated, "Now, people are more organized than before—for example, we didn't used to know about self-help groups, especially about bookkeeping and record-keeping, and now more people do." Churches also have started self-help groups. Another encouraging comment was, "People are always caring for themselves—trying to do their own things," and also helping each other, particularly in the context of the self-help movement.

## Child-rearing Practices

A remark that spoke for many of the parents interviewed was, "We parents have no time for raising children! Children are brought up by maids, which we cannot afford, although we are all working." Several parents felt that young children are left on their own at an earlier age now and that "this is not healthy or safe."

Another change some parents noted was that parents were now more "free" with their children, meaning that they were more honest, straightforward, and not as "shy." Some discussed the fact that perhaps children used to fear their parents more than now. They also raised issues that parents in several other districts had raised, regarding the loss of intergenerational interaction, especially between grandparents and grandchildren. As one mother said, "In the older days, there were more interactions between the old and the young—now, there's more peer or youth culture. The traditional belief was that some things should not be told to children, and girls were taught by their grandmothers and boys by their grandfathers." Now, with more mobile, nuclear families, children were seen as being less accessible to their grandparents. Another parent added, "At least we now have more schools to help in raising our children."

# Relevance of Preschool Education

The overwhelming response by teachers to this question, which was framed in terms of "families maintaining traditional ways," was, "Very few people maintain traditional cultures in the city," or "That doesn't happen in this community." When we further probed this issue, teachers discussed their attempts of teaching to respect cultural differences and traditions. For example, one teacher said, "We try to plan activities related to home culture and traditions and want to make preschool relevant to children's home cultures."

Other teachers felt that preschool education was least relevant to Maasai families and raised assumptions about gender roles, "Some Maasai parents may feel that formal education is for boys, but not for girls, as boys will stay in the family and girls will marry, so it may still be viewed as a waste of money to educate girls."

Most teachers felt that preschools in Nairobi were most relevant for child care purposes for working mothers and for primary school preparation. They reported attempts to provide a number of activities to reinforce children's home culture. These included, in order of frequency, environmental education, for example, posters of traditional Kikuyu dress and role-plays of aspects of family life, mother tongue stories and poems (mainly in Kikuyu and KiKamba), traditional songs, dances, and movement to music, and inviting parents into the nursery school to teach about their culture. In addition, teachers felt that teaching practical daily living skills such as toileting, hand washing, and self-help skills reinforced the instruction they were receiving at home, expected by parents.

## EFFECTIVENESS OF TRADITIONAL CHILD-REARING PRACTICES AND SYSTEMS OF SUPPORT

The majority of teachers interviewed felt that traditional practices and child-rearing systems were effective, although threatened by rapid social and economic change. One example was food, including the tradition of using local versus white flour, making *uji* (traditional millet and sorghum porridge), and eating locally grown vegetables. Traditional weaning foods, which tended to be high in protein and vitamins, were considered better than some of the "modern" alternatives that urban mothers had tried. Two teachers also mentioned the importance of teaching children how to use and clean traditional cooking utensils, which would be "useful to children's future lives."

Regarding child-rearing beliefs, one teacher said, "You can answer many questions from our traditional, child-rearing beliefs." Several preschool teachers found it useful to combine their knowledge of traditional (primarily Kikuyu and KiKamba) child-rearing practices with their training in ECCE in order to better meet the needs of children. Another teacher stated, "When you meet the basic needs of a child, they can grow in all areas!"

Teachers also discussed the changes in Kenya, from traditional extended families to nuclear families. "Now, we are missing the grandmothers and great-grandmothers, although there are some still here." Another agreed, saying, "Overall, there is little contact with grandmothers now, and they are so helpful in child-rearing!" In summary, teachers and parents agreed that traditional child-rearing practices were beneficial, but that they were fast disappearing, particularly in urban areas.

The preschool was seen as one setting for maintaining such traditions and for teaching children about their culture, especially when family elders were no longer available to young children.

## FAMILY AND COMMUNITY INVOLVEMENT IN EARLY EDUCATION AND CARE

From the perspective of parents, providing good child care to their own children was seen as an important form of "involvement." This included breast-feeding, completing immunizations, and taking children for regular clinic visits for growth monitoring and promotion. One father proudly talked about teaching babies how to smile—and later to talk. Another related area that many parents commented on was time—taking the time to play with children, to make toys and learning materials for children, and to volunteer in their children's nursery schools or day care centers. Such materials included rattles, shakers, balls, dolls, and cars, and they were made by both parents and older siblings. Mostly these were described as made for home use, but parents also expressed their willingness to make materials for their child's preschool, if asked to do so.

Two fathers interviewed, in fact, felt that parents should be "required to volunteer time and other resources" (e.g., labor, materials, and funds) to the preschool. One father suggested that, "Parents could provide books, stationery, gravel, and even toilet paper!"

Most teachers agreed that all parents should be involved in the preschool program, with the exception of a few teachers who had not pursued parental involvement beyond a minimal once a year parent day and the collection of fees. (These teachers said at the end of the interview that they intended to actively involve parents in the future, based on our discussion of this issue.) In fact, the question originally asked, "How do you involve parents?" which was based on our first few Nairobi teacher interviews, had to be changed to, "Do you involve parents? If so, how?"

The most frequently mentioned methods of parental involvement were parent meetings and conferences. One program, serving more middle-class families, had brought in a counselor to discuss single parenting, and another concerned involving parents more in decision making at the center. The same program offered a monthly open house, where on one Friday a month parents were invited to drop in and discuss issues with the teachers and administrator. When asked what sorts of issues these more privileged parents raised, teachers agreed that most were academic concerns, with parents asking, "Is he reading yet?" and other readiness questions. The topics that lower income parents discussed was child health and how to obtain assistance in sending older children to school. Preschools serving lower income families concentrated their parent education on nutrition and health advice.

The second most frequently mentioned way in which parents were involved was with service on the school or preschool committee. When probed about the gender makeup of such committees, head teachers tended to say, "We have representatives from every section—our committee is mixed by gender, age, etc., and several fathers are active on the school committee." The degree of policy setting done by such parent-run committees varied, with some acting more in an advisory capacity, helping the head teacher collect fees or set fee rates.

Several teachers interviewed stated that parents donated materials. Again, this appeared to vary greatly by the income or class background of the families served. For example, in the more middle-class settings, parents donated magazines, calendars, and many recycled materials, whereas, in lower income settings, teachers said, "No, parents rarely bring in materials—they are very busy and either can't get the time off to come or do not have anything to give as they are so poor." Still another form of parental support of ECCE programs consisted of paying for the feeding program. Once more, this varied across the class background of settings and families served. One preschool in a high poverty area also was also a project site for a NACECE/ CICECE under three initiative, and it had sponsored a toy-making workshop with the assistance of its CICECE representative. This was the only parent workshop they had held, however.

## Typical Child Care Arrangements for Children Under Three and Related Concerns

A patchwork of child care arrangements was used by most parents in the Nairobi sample, as described by teachers, older siblings of under threes, and parents themselves. Most working mothers described rising very early and possibly even preparing the next day's food the night before. Often the youngest children in a family, if funds allow, are left with an *ayah*, whereas the older children (ages three to five) are taken to a preschool. In the afternoon, preschool and lower primary children return home, where they are in the care of a child minder, whether an *ayah*, a neighbor, an older sibling(s), or another relative.

Parents raised particularly strong concerns about the care of their under threes. Concerns about *ayahs* included their high turnover rates and lack of knowledge about child development. Some parents felt that children were neglected during the day by the house help and would be better served in a nursery school or day care center if the appropriate facilities were available. Teachers saw preschools as lacking the funds and facilities to better serve under threes, and raised several related concerns, such as the lack of provision of food, the lack of toileting and napping facilities, and the lack of sufficient staff to meet the needs of younger children.

In terms of older siblings, all children in the Nairobi sample helped care for their younger siblings. Among the ways in which they helped were staying with the little one after school and either feeding the baby or finding the mother when the baby cried. Others said that they taught various preschool skills to their younger brothers and sisters, including language, counting, songs, and stories. Most children also reported making toys for their younger siblings, such as dolls, rattles made from bottle tops, and homemade balls, and they also gave little ones pots and pans to play with.

Similar to the children interviewed in other districts, Nairobi children could tell whether a younger child was sick by their high temperature, by crying, and by sleeping "too much." When a younger sibling was sick, children called a neighbor, took the child to the closest clinic or even to the hospital, and told the mother, who gave the child medicine, or if the situation was more serious, they took the child to the hospital.

All children interviewed in Nairobi (Kawangwari) had gone to preschool, and most remembered a feeding program. In fact, children had very specific memories of foods they had eaten in preschool (e.g., rice, green grams, porridge, and *ugali*). They felt that all young children should go to preschool, and they remembered drawing, making ropes and other toys, and learning new skills. When asked to compare nursery and primary school, one child responded, "In nursery we ate—here, no!" Another appeared to speak for many children, when he said, "Here we are learning very difficult things!"

## Parents' Perceptions of Parenting and Goals for Care

When asked what they liked most about being a parent, Nairobi mothers and fathers echoed the sentiments of other participants in the study. The overwhelming response was simply "being a mother" or "being someone's father." This also was expressed as "giving birth," or the experience of motherhood. As one mother put it, "To bring up a child well and have someone to struggle for and take care of—it's hard work, but good work!" A father stated, "Children are a gift from God, and prestige in the community comes from being a father!"

In terms of what parents found hardest, the most frequent response was the inability to provide for one's family, as stated by one father. "When you have not, and want to provide—but cannot." A mother said, "It's hardest when you cannot afford to fulfill your duties as a mother—both in terms of affording money and time!" Providing food, clothing, and education also were considered among the hardest aspects of being a parent.

Parents' goals for their youngest children's care were safety, being with children of the same age, being provided with age-appropriate activities and materials, and learning skills needed for later life and education. Over half of the parents interviewed felt that preschool or another organized small group care setting was the best place for children under three, so children could "start learning more," and because

"Housegirls don't teach!" And other parents felt that children in group care were less spoiled. Other parents felt that home was the best place, particularly if a grandmother or the child's mother was available to care for the youngest children. Several parents realized that the ideal of familial care was not a realistic one, and said, "If care is not available at home, then the best place is in a preschool or day care, especially if children are taught similar things as they would learn at home and are given good care."

## EFFECTIVENESS OF INTERSECTORAL COLLABORATIONS FOR CHILDREN AND FAMILIES

The focus groups in Nairobi had the most to say in terms of intersectoral collaboration. Parents and teachers typically mentioned a couple of groups that had either provided services to their community or school in the past or possibly were still involved, but generally they were not aware either of those groups or agencies working together. Both parents and focus group participants felt that different groups working together in communities needed to better coordinate their activities, and that more such initiatives should be undertaken in their communities.

In terms of resources needed and strategies for community oversight of new ECCE initiatives, home-based and parent cooperative models of under-three care were considered viable for the Nairobi locations sampled. Sustainability and motivation with any new initiative was stressed, and a *baraza* (public meeting with the area chief) was recommended for mobilizing local communities.

When asked how to ensure that funds reached the poorest families, it was pointed out that teachers and parents typically know those who are most in need and that a committee made up of "trusted hands" should be elected to both plan and provide funding for services. Direct payment to families was dismissed as ineffective; rather, subsidizing services to make them more affordable was recommended. Other recommendations were that, "Local leaders should be involved," and "Good records should be kept." One person stated, "Transparency and accountability is required for this to work." The endowment model was favored and should "cater to the entire family." Parents were seen as needing seminars and support—basically, a "family enhancement model" was recommended, which respected parents and built on their strengths.

## SUMMARY

As in the other areas we visited, a number of dramatic changes were described by urban parents, preschool teachers, and community leaders. The high and growing cost of living, the lack of sufficient and affordable housing, the high cost of educating one's children, and increasing child health problems associated in part with the loss of free government services were all concerns that were frequently raised. A difference in the urban samples, particularly among the Nairobi families (and slum dwellers), was that there were fewer options available in the urban setting. In other words, a cash economy without the means to grow even a kitchen garden or keep an animal for milk, combined with the lack of extended family child care support, meant that mothers—often single mothers living in great poverty—were forced to work long hours, often in the informal market sector. Child care options in such cases were extremely limited—especially for children under three.

The role of community agencies, such as church-funded schools, community health agencies, and local self-help projects, was critical and could mean the difference between families being able to raise their children and families losing their children to the street. A powerful example of this was the Mukuru Primary School, which (at different sites) provided primary education for nearly 10,000 children, many of whom would be on the street without the safety net that this school provided through its tuition-free classes, its policy of no required uniforms, its lunch program, and its health and social services. This program, like others serving families in the Nairobi slums, was stretched to its limit and relied on many volunteers and the Catholic Church for funding. Another example, discussed in some detail in the chapter, was the self-help group that was attempting to provide full-day child care for working mothers; although the facilities were far from optimal, they represented a start and provided some hope for single mothers overwhelmed by the demands of urban life and lacking the resources to support their families.

As elsewhere in our study, the greatest need for care was for children under three whose parents, often single mothers, worked long hours and could not afford or find reliable *ayahs* or in-home child-minders. This was slowly being addressed both by nursery schools, which were adding "baby classes" for two-year-olds, and by some child care programs, which offered full-day custodial care. One of the most positive examples of creative care for under threes in Nairobi that we observed was the home-based child care center started by a minister and his family in their home. It had grown to include two smaller buildings on their compound as well as several rooms in their modest home, and it had begun to provide evening and overnight care for parents who were forced to work night shifts. It was clear from the brief visits we made to this home-based child care setting that the pastor/proprietor also did extensive family counseling with young couples and single parents who were struggling in the face of poverty and difficult circumstances to care for their families.

To spend time in the sprawling slums of Nairobi, often nestled close to the large estates of wealthy Kenyans and ex-patriots, was to experience and witness the "stark geographies of exclusion," described by Sibley (1995). Lack of water, or paying increasing fees for the use of one tap shared by dozens of households, lack of access to land to grow vegetables, crowding, dangers from crime, violence, and other environmental risk factors, and lack of affordable health care and child care programs were pervasive. Yet the dedication of those who were providing services for young children and their families and the impact of an array of self-help and privately funded community agencies were moving to witness. These were islands of high energy—teeming with children who were, when not too tired from chronic hunger or frequent illness, eager to learn and happy to be in preschool or child care settings. The not-so-lucky children, particularly boys who were coming of age (10 to 14 years old) in homes that simply could not meet their needs, and without the financial ability to attend school, lived and worked in growing numbers on the streets of Nairobi and its more affluent suburbs. Thus a window for creating a "thirdspace" (Soja, 1996) of "unimagined possibility" existed for children growing up in urban poverty. Such possibilities were realized when a combination of allies and partners—community, self-help groups, donor-sponsored agencies, local leaders, and concerned parents—pulled together for the future of the urban village, its children.

# Chapter 10

# Kisumu Municipality:
# It Takes *Ayahs* and Preschools
# to Raise a Child

The village is not being allowed to co-raise its children.

—Community leader

## DESCRIPTION OF SETTING

Kisumu is one of the seven districts in the Nyanza Province in western Kenya. It is located on the eastern shore of Lake Victoria and is part of a large lowland. The Kisumu District covers a total area of 2,660 square kilometers, of which 567 are under water. It is the second largest district in the Nyanza Province. The Kisumu Municipality was the setting of the data collection. Agricultural areas surrounding the Kisumu Municipality feature maize, rice, cotton, sugarcane, and sorghum, and fish is another popular food there. The district's population has continued to grow, with an estimated annual growth rate of 3.35%. Infant mortality rates (IMR) have been decreasing, due to increased primary health promotion and improved prenatal and postnatal care and the use of clinics, as well as better access to health services and clean water. The IMR decreased from 123 (deaths per every 1,000 live births by age 12) in 1987 to 92 at the time of data collection. The district reduced its rate from 92/1,000 to 70/1,000 (the same rate as the Embu District) by 1996. The major causes of infant mortality include malaria, acute respiratory infection, diarrheal diseases, poor

239

Fig. 10.1    Kisumu Parents During Interview

maternal health and diet, poor environmental sanitation, and vaccine-preventable diseases (Kisumu District Development Plan, 1994–96, p. 79).

The population at the time of data collection in the Kisumu Municipality was 131,323, with high population density and often crowded living conditions. While public sector employment has been steadily decreasing in this district, the informal business sector (Kisumu DDP, 1994–96) is thriving, with businesses such as posho mills, knitting and tailoring shops, carpentry and furniture stores, barbering and hair "saloons," small repair shops, *jua kali* (open air) welding and scrap metal shops, auto repair shops, and vegetable dealers (p. 77). A UNICEF survey on feeding practices found that most mothers breast-feed for a minimum of 16 months. The proportion of mothers breast-feeding for less than six months is less than 10%, and most mothers surveyed introduced food supplements at less than six months. AIDS/ HIV has been an increasing problem in Western Kenya and in this district, with only one government hospital in the town of Kisumu.

Similar to Nairobi, Nakuru, and Mombasa, the number of street children in the Kisumu Municipality were growing at the time of the study, with the number of children's homes increasing from six in 1989 to 16 (including those receiving final approval) by 1995. Many of these children came from other districts in Western Kenya. The Kisumu District Development Plan (1994–96) states, "The District also has a multi-racial population which tends to be generous to children's homes, street children, and street beggars; a gesture that is highly appreciated by the district administration and which must be encouraged if the ever rising number of street children is to be taken care of and contained at an affordable level." (p. 82).

Finally, turning to the status of women and girls in the Kisumu District, the participation rate of girls in preschools is higher than boys, with girls comprising 51% of preschool enrollments. At primary school, girls account for 48%, compared to boys at 52%. Girls still drop out of school at higher rates than boys, estimated in 1994 to be 60% for girls and 25% for boys. Reasons for high dropout rates include early marriages, poverty, and lack of interest (Kisumu DDP, 1994–96, p. 89). The female literacy rate in the Kisumu District is 28%, and the male rate is 31%. The low levels of female literacy have had adverse effects on child survival and on the status of women. An average household in the district has five members, with an increasing number of female-headed households. Similar to other parts of Kenya (and the world), female-headed households are generally associated with a high incidence of poverty. A number of husbands leave Kisumu to seek employment in Kericho, Nairobi, or Mombasa. Women's contribution to household income is only 20%, and they have low participation rates in wage labor; their lack of access to household income has detrimental effects on child survival, as the mother is expected to maintain the family in terms of food, health care, and clothing.

## Kisumu Sample

Four locations in Kisumu Municipality were sampled, representing four contrasting zones, including one location in which parents and teachers from two zones were interviewed. The sampled Municipal Council Zones were: Eastern (including Manyatta), Western, Central, and Southeastern. These areas included contrasting lifestyles and both urban (including middle-class and low-income families) and peri-urban settings (e.g., Western Zone). The number of participants in group interviews during Phase I tended to be large, frequently with 12 or more respondents, thus making it challenging to record individual data at times.

A total of 69 parents and grandparents were interviewed in Kisumu, including 59 mothers, 5 fathers, 4 grandmothers, and 1 grandfather. Ages of parents' first-born children ranged from 2 to 24 years, with a mean age of 7.5 years, and ages of last-born children ranged from 8 days to 5 years, with a mean age of 2.3 years.

In terms of work, 21 mothers were homemakers, 7 parents were in small businesses, 15 were teachers (10 preschool, 2 primary, 1 secondary, and 2 supervisors), 3 mothers were office workers, 3 fathers were farmers, 1 mother was a social worker, 1 was a tailor, and 1 mother was a hotel manager.

A total of 40 preschool teachers were interviewed, including 39 women and only one man, who was a preschool owner/manager and part-time teacher. Teachers were interviewed in groups ranging from 5 to 20 participants. The average number of teachers at urban preschools was three to four, and peri-urban preschools appeared to have an average of two teachers. (Note: Individual data is incomplete for one large group from the Southern Zone and complete for the other zones.)

In terms of teachers' formal education, one (an ex-patriot) had her bachelor of arts degree in education, one had her PAG, five had completed Form 4, and one had completed her EACE (East African Certificate of Education). Five teachers had completed their Kenya Certificate of Education (KCE), four had completed their Kenya Primary Education (KPE), and four had completed their Certificate of Primary Education (CPE). Preschool teachers' years of experience in their present position ranged from three to 25 years. Ten teachers had only taught in their present preschool, five had taught in two others, four in three others, and five in five different preschools.

Turning to ECCE training, 18 teachers were trained, and only one was untrained. Two teachers were currently enrolled in additional training. Most had completed DICECE training, one (male) teacher had done a short course at the Kenya National Museum, and another teacher had undergone Montessori training in Nairobi. Teachers' ages ranged from 24 to 45 years, with a mean age of 33.2 years. In terms of marital status, 19 teachers were married, and two were unmarried.

Regarding salary and employment issues, eight teachers' salaries were paid by parents, five were paid by a school or a school committee, four were paid by the Kisumu Municipal Council, two were paid by churches, one was paid by the Aga Khan Education Services (AKES), one was paid by the Sikh community, and one was paid by the Kisumu Municipality. Although most teachers were married, 16 reported no income sources other than their teaching pay.

Finally, three focus groups of community leaders and professionals were conducted in Kisumu, which included two Teachers Advisory Centre (TAC) tutors, three headmasters and two headmistresses of primary schools, a zonal school inspector, and four staff with the Social Services Department in the Kisumu Municipality. The staff included welfare officers, case workers, and community development assistants (CDAs). Community leader interviews were conducted during the first phase of the project, and focus groups with education leaders took place in April 1995 during Phase II.

The themes of the many Kisumu interviews are discussed in the following sections.

## Major Problems Faced by Families with Young Children in Kisumu

By far the most frequent response to this question, from both preschool teachers and parents, was "financial," with school fees considered high compared to families' income. As one preschool teacher described it, "Parents get a loan for the first payment and cannot continue to pay." The rising cost of living and many financial difficulties faced by most families were considered the greatest problem.

The second most frequently mentioned problem concerned sickness, with children often contracting illnesses such as malaria, typhoid, measles, colds, diarrhea, and so on. A related concern was nutrition—both families' inability to provide a sufficient diet for young children and the tendency (from the perspective of preschool teachers) of some families to allow children to select their (snack) foods, for example, those carried to the preschool (and many of these were not high in nutrition).

Health and nutrition concerns were followed (in frequency) by changes in the family, including the death of a parent, a divorce, and a marriage or remarriage of a parent. Still another pervasive problem facing families was that of maids (*ayahs*) and of finding good child care in general, especially for the youngest children.

The next most frequent response was related to "unsafe environments," including hygiene concerns such as sewage and trash located where young children played. The issue of clean water, or even access to sufficient water was also mentioned as a problem for families with young children. This was particularly true in the more crowded, urban slum areas of Kisumu.

## How Problems Affected Children at Preschool

Preschool teachers answered this question in a number of different ways. The most common responses related to the emotional responses of children, including, "They are very sad," "They are shy," and "They isolate themselves from other children." Teachers also described a lack of concentration and said that problems at home made children "dull." Other concerns were poor hygiene or lack of access to water, which children described as "dirty."

Undernutrition and poor diets, as described briefly in the last section, also were seen as problematic. Some children were described as "no longer bringing in lunch or a snack" and as "hungry—some do not take breakfast before they come, or did not have enough to eat the evening before." Teachers also discussed the 1993 famine in the Kisumu area and said, "When children came, they just slept—they didn't even play." Others said that hunger and other negative conditions at home "made children act cruel to each other." One teacher said, "Children look sickly and lack energy."

## Good Things the Community Is Doing for Children

The most frequent response to the question of what good things the local community was doing for children was "nursery schools." Specific comments included, "There are many more preschools now," and "Nursery schools are good—but expensive—especially if you have two or three children." Parents felt that nursery school prepared children for Standard 1 and primary school and, in fact, that "children are handicapped without it!" Several parents commented on the many ways in which parents helped with early education, including building classrooms, buying desks, and contributing to *Harambee*s and so on. Others felt that education in general had improved (e.g., "Basic education here is very good!").

Two parents felt that family planning and "proper birth spacing" made life better for children in their community. Others felt that churches were doing good things for children, such as "sponsoring children for school" and running a "workshop for street children."

Two parents felt that the community was doing little, if anything, for its children. One responded "Nothing!" when asked what the community was doing, and another said, "No—there isn't (anything good)!" This view was not shared by several other parents interviewed, most of whom felt that the Kisumu community, or their local community, was making children a priority, even under challenging circumstances. As one mother summed it up, the best thing the community was doing was at the family level, by "making children a priority—whatever is in the house we try to give to the youngest child."

## Parental Involvement

When asked about specific forms of parental involvement in preschool programs or with young children, two parents commented, "At home, we work with children in books, making drawings, etc." Four parents mentioned that they sent in whatever materials the preschool teacher asked for, although materials-making workshops and growth-monitoring or other health-related activities for parents and younger children were infrequent in Kisumu preschools. Parents seemed willing to share materials, stating, "When we send materials to the preschool, we know they're put to good use, and at home the older children make things for the younger ones."

Three parents commented on preparing foods for children to carry for lunch in their tins; such lunches might include bread, juice, *uji*, *mandazi* (sweet fried dough), maize, beans, potatoes, or tea. Two parents said that they had collected money from other parents for a feeding program at the preschool. As one stated, "If young ones are fed, they can learn!"

When asked whether they had visited their child's preschool after enrolling their child, only five parents out of 64 had done so. They also stated that there were "very few parent meetings," but that "parents were called in to discuss their child's progress." Four parents commented that they were "more often called to school for *Harambee*s and *baraza*s" than to discuss the individual progress of their child(ren) in the nursery school.

Others parents lamented over the loss of Luo traditions, for example, "Before, songs carried the messages, but now there is no time for some of those traditions!" As in Nairobi, others felt that urban life had displaced many of the ethnic traditions.

# SOCIAL AND ECONOMIC CHANGES
# RELATED TO CHILD-REARING

As in Nairobi and other settings, the most frequent general responses of parents to the question of changes affecting their families related to the rising cost of food, housing, and education.

## Food

When I go to the market, I go only to admire, not to buy!

—Mother in Manyatta

This statement from a frustrated mother was echoed by many others in the Kisumu sample. Six parents listed the price as food as the most dramatic change in the past 10 to 15 years. Other comments included, "We don't cook because we cannot afford to," and "The differences in the cost of food are great—14 years ago there was a lot of food and you could buy easily—now, there's food, but it is too expensive." Other mothers named foods that they no longer eat, or rarely purchase, such as fruit, maize, milk, eggs, and sugar.

One father described how he made less money now than when he sold cows. "I've been in the cow business for 10 years; before cows sold at over 1,000 Kshs/ (Kenya shillings), and now they sell for 10,000, but before we got at least 200–300 Kshs/ in profit, and now it is only 100!" Other parents interviewed agreed that they now made less profit selling animals than they had in the past, yet meat was unaffordable for their family.

## Housing

When we moved to a place we could afford, it was
so small that the furniture didn't fit!

—Father in Kisumu

Housing was clearly a challenge for parents in Kisumu—seven parents commented on how high rents had become, and others talked about needing to move into more affordable accommodations and feeling crowded, as their families had grown. They remarked, "When my children are all there, it's so squeezed!" and "Now there are large families in small houses—many one-room (10 by 10) houses have three to four children." As quoted above, one mother said, "When we moved to a place we could afford, it was so small that the furniture didn't fit!" Others agreed that sufficient space for the healthy raising of children was a major problem facing families in the Kisumu Municipality, as it had been in Nairobi.

Three parents commented that there was "very little land for constructing houses," thus the need for small houses. Several parents also said that, "Because of land scarcity there is over-use of the land, which is becoming exhausted." Two parents remarked about the problems of accessing water in urban areas where they were living. "In self-contained units, water is a big problem." Others said that Municipal Council houses were "not maintained" and "did not even have water and electricity. A final comment on housing was that there were better houses now, "More permanent, like Nairobi, but more expensive."

## Cost of Living

Income is low—demand is high—you can't meet
basic needs with this low income!

—Father in Kisumu

The sentiment and experience captured in the above quote was shared by the majority of parents interviewed in the different locations of Kisumu. In particular, "Clothing and education are really high," and "Education is not free, and parents must buy everything." When parents complained about the cost of clothing they also were referring to the cost of the school uniform. As in every other district we sampled, the cost of living was embedded in many of the parents' responses, as it is in the other sections of this chapter. A difference in the Kisumu sample could be found, however, in the class stratification it represented. Parents, including Asian and ex-patriot families, in two of the preschools we visited could be described as middle class or wealthy by local standards. Their primary concerns with preschool included readiness for the Standard 1 interview and gaining access to Kisumu's better primary schools. These parents valued trained teachers, well-equipped centers, and in some cases "developmentally appropriate curriculum." More choices in preschools were available to these parents, including programs offering international (and American) religious and Montessori curricula. It should be noted that the Montessori school was located in a more working-class/low-income area, with the directress receiving her training in Nairobi, dedicated to serving families with greater financial need. Parents from lower income backgrounds echoed those we interviewed in Nairobi. They were concerned with obtaining safe, affordable, full day care, and they expressed concerns about the *ayahs* they had employed to look after their youngest children. Parents of every income level expressed interest in both family-based child care and the extension of preschool programs to children under three.

# Education

Books, uniforms, building fund, admission fees are all required,
and if you don't have them, children are sent home!

—Mother in Kisumu

School fees and other related education costs were most frequently mentioned by parents in terms of changes regarding education. They recalled when education was more affordable, and they were concerned about the "new" education system (8-4-4), which required more subjects and, therefore, more textbooks. "Materials are very expensive—especially textbooks are high." Other comments on the 8-4-4 system included, "School is very demanding now! Changes due to 8-4-4 and pushing children up are a big change." As another parent stated, "Children must now start early, and there are more pressures on children, including enrolling children earlier in preschool than the parent might choose." Others from more middle-class backgrounds commented on parental peer pressure to work with children and encourage them to learn earlier, with the result that, "There is limited time for family leisure activities." As another parent put it, "Education is improved, but parents must spend much time teaching their children, or taking them for tuition" (tutoring). Two parents commented that feeding programs were needed in the schools, particularly in preschool settings.

# Health

Children die! We have no money to take them to
to the doctor or hospital; there are more deaths these days.

—Mother in Kisumu

This powerful quote was echoed by six parents who expressed regret over the loss of previous medical and primary health care in recent years. Four other parents stated that health care had become more expensive over the years and that families now must "buy their own medicine." As in other settings, parents described previous health care that had been more affordable. Similar to the comment that houses were better now, but less affordable, three parents said that there were more hospitals now, although, "Many are private and very expensive!"

On the positive side, two mothers said that traditional birth attendants (TBAs) did assist, as did the much-acclaimed Bamako Initiative, which "provides some drugs and credit facilities" to families. The Bamako Initiative is a primary health promotion model that was designed in Mali and has been replicated throughout Africa and other developing countries. Other parents discussed the higher immunization rates, including an Aga Khan Hospital plan in which, for 300/Kshs, children received all of their immunizations, from birth to age five at the hospital. Yet, said one mother, "At public hospital, you even have to pay for the syringe!"

Another issue raised by parents concerned the growth rates of children, including birth weights. Two parents said that "more children are underweight" and "undernourished from birth to five years." They related this pattern to the fact that food was less affordable, and families had a harder time meeting the nutritional as well as general health needs of their children.

## CHANGING SOCIAL STRUCTURES/CHILD-REARING

### Portrait: Mother of 2-Month-Old in Western Zone (Peri-urban) Kisumu

*I get up between 6 and 7 A.M., fetch water from the stream nearly 2 kilometers away, clean the house, and, while the baby sleeps, light the fire. By now the baby is usually awake and older siblings look after the baby. I boil water for bathing, prepare tea or uji, take breakfast, breast-feed the child, then do the laundry while the child is sleeping. After that I prepare lunch and rest briefly, if there is time, then I fetch firewood and go to the market to buy food, or send someone. I prepare food for supper, finding someone to watch the baby as I cook. After we eat supper I nurse the baby and then we retire.*

The first response of parents to the question of how social structures affecting child-rearing had changed was that there was "less extended family and more nuclear, with just a few people willing to help" (with the children). As one parent stated, "The issue of traditional child-rearing is no longer there—you are alone and raising children." One mother said, "It's not affordable to provide play materials at home," and another added, "And there's no time to make things with so much work."

The most positive responses to this question were related to the growing number of support groups, particularly women's groups. These included, for example, the Mothers Union, in which each member contributes 120 Kenya shillings a month, and any member can borrow from the group in emergencies, but as one mother put it, "It's still a man's world!" Yet five mothers discussed the benefits of membership in women's groups, stating that, "Women's groups are coming up, with the aim of pooling funds and providing loans." When we asked about other roles played by the women's groups, responses included, "assisting with funerals, including buying clothes, coffins and food, but not assisting with school fees." Another woman added that, "In sickness, we can borrow from the group."

### Summary of Changes and Challenges Faced by Families

The major problem or challenge raised by Kisumu parents was the rising cost and the added demands of education. As one parent put it, "Even with education, girls get pregnant and little employment is available." Especially in the slums, finding the money to do the right things for children was considered a major problem and a change from the past. Second in frequency was housing, with the issues of lack of land, lack of affordable housing, and crowded living conditions mentioned by many parents. As one father summed up, "In terms of health, food, and housing, we are generally worse off than 8–12 years ago."

## Child Care Arrangements for Children Under Three

In general, under threes are at home, with either the mother or a maid.
—Preschool teacher in Kisumu

Clearly, the most frequent child care arrangement for Kisumu families with children under age three was the use of house help or *ayahs* (child-minders), especially for children under age two. Twelve parents interviewed stated that they employed *ayahs* to care for children, among other duties, while they worked, or to assist them in the home. Nursery schools tended to enroll children, as in other parts of Kenya, at age three, but at least two private (and relatively elite) nursery schools in this municipality had baby or toddler classes and accepted children at age two. Five mothers, most of whom could be described as lower middle class or middle class, stated that, "Mothers care for the youngest children themselves." These mothers, who included Asian and European women, were not employed at the time and stayed home to care for their children. Most of these at-home mothers, however, also had house help (*ayahs*).

When asked whether the extended family played a role in child care, parents agreed that they were no longer available. As one mother stated, "Extended families are few these days, and older siblings are going to school and not available to care for younger children." This response echoed other urban and peri-urban settings in the study, and it reflects a general trend documented in this and other recent research. In summary, the majority of under threes represented by the large number of parents from four contrasting settings of Kisumu felt that under threes were cared for in the home and that the care was not often provided with the level of support it had enjoyed in the past. Parents shared many concerns about the lack of reliability and underqualification of young child minders, and they felt strongly that more group care settings (e.g., nursery schools or family child care homes) should be made available for the care of under threes whose mothers were working. Their views on this topic are discussed further in the following section.

## Best Place for Under Threes?

The consensus of all of the parents participating in group interviews in the Kisumu Municipality was that the nursery school was the best place for under threes, if it was appropriately equipped, and if teachers were prepared to meet the needs of these younger children. When asked why, parents responded, "Children are best when under the care of teachers, where they can play with other children," and "Even maids are not there—children are left alone at home and want to play and need care, but no caregiver or even siblings are there." Others seemed to feel that maternal care was optimal but no longer realistic. "Even for under threes, preschool is the best place because their mothers are busy and at school they'll have more opportunities for socialization with age-mates, access to play facilities, etc."

## What Teachers Liked about Under Threes

Many of the preschool teachers interviewed in Kisumu appeared to enjoy working with under threes and to have some experience with it. Several teachers felt that children ages three and under "got things quicker," were "more cooperative and friendly," and "were more attached to the teacher—they watch the teacher." Another said, "The young ones know who loves them!" and others agreed that, "You must love them, or they won't learn—you must form an attachment!" One teacher commented that she "enjoyed the voices of the young ones and how they are learning to talk."

In terms of what was needed in caring for children under three, one teacher said, "You must love them as a teacher—and as a mother!" Others felt that children should be grouped by age, and that it was important to provide toys, napping facilities, good nutrition (including a snack and lunch program), and a clean, safe environment. Some teachers also felt that transportation should be provided, both to needed services (e.g., to clinic) and to preschool. They also thought that health services such as visiting nurses (who previously existed, but not any longer) should be "brought back." They also suggested that small furniture and an adequate building with good ventilation were important. Teachers agreed, as stated earlier, that under threes needed "teachers who have commitment and love." Finally, they felt a playground with age-appropriate equipment was important.

When asked to design a "model" program for under threes, Kisumu preschool teachers listed many of the same things above, including (in order of frequency): good, loving, caring personnel (both teachers and child minders) who are "well trained and well paid," "water and toileting facilities, including washing facilities for nappies," a "full-day program, with sufficient nutrition program, as mothers work all day," and "space to play." These suggestions were followed in frequency by "fresh air," "a good staff, including a cook, watchman, and part-time nurse," "plenty of toys and learning materials," "health and nutrition programs, including growth monitoring," and "transportation—a mini van to pick up and drop off children who live farther away." Several teachers agreed that a model program "should always be in touch with the parents" and try to involve them in many ways. Finally, the need for napping facilities was mentioned as a priority, including mattresses and blankets and washing facilities for bedding. The overall environment of a model under-three group care setting was described as "a decorated, welcoming environment."

## Relevance of Preschool to "Traditional" Families

The preschool teachers and parents interviewed agreed that preschool had become a virtual necessity, because "Other sources of support are not there now," and "Fewer traditions are being maintained." In terms of cultural maintenance, one teacher stated, "Preschool has some relevance to traditions, but this is not always apparent." The most frequent examples of the ways in which formal preschool programs supported cultural traditions included role-plays, traditional songs, dances, costumes and drumming, and other performances occasionally put on by students for parents and community members. Another teacher said, "We try to build on children's home culture and reinforce it, where possible, at school." Another way in which preschool was seen as supporting home culture was through the continuation of traditional gender roles, with, for example, "girls playing at cooking and boys minding animals."

An interesting comment from teachers in an Asian-owned, culturally diverse private preschool in Kisumu related to parents "preferences for teachers . . . they may prefer a Luo to a Luhya, or an Asian to an African teacher, particularly if the teacher can use the child's mother tongue." Other teachers felt that parents, particularly in middle-class families, were anxious for their children to learn English in order to perform well in primary school and beyond.

## Benefits of Being a Parent

Seeing one coming up and seeing yourself in that child—that's the best thing!

—Father in Kisumu

In response to what they liked most about being a mother or a father, five responses related to companionship, including, "Children are a companion," "They are someone to talk to," and "When you are with children, you are not alone." A variation on this was that children provide valuable services to the parents and family (e.g., "somebody to send on errands," or "someone to help you as they grow older").

Similar to the parents in all of the districts and settings sampled in this study, Kisumu parents felt that they were respected and were addressed as "Mama" or "Baba." One mother said, "People interact with you and your child and know you through your children." They expressed the value of having responsibility for someone else and the genuine satisfaction in bringing up children and taking on the commitment of child-rearing.

Finally, parents expressed the feeling that having children was a way to maintian their language and culture. As one mother put it, "You know that your language is left, even after you are gone," or as one father said, "They keep up your lineage!"

Yet another variation on this was, "Seeing one coming up, and seeing yourself in that child—that's the best thing!" This theme of culture and family maintenance was one that was implicit in many of the earlier parent interviews but was seldom stated as explicitly as it was by the Kisumu parents interviewed.

## Challenges of Being a Parent

The most frequent response to the question, "What is hardest about being a parent?" (stated by nine different parents in three focus groups) was, "Providing the care!" or "Total care is hard." The responsibility of being a parent, especially given all of the changes and challenges discussed, was generally considered the hardest aspect of parenting. One mother said, "The hardest thing is knowing all the things you should provide—material things and time and love." Others felt that the hardest things were feeding children and taking them to school. Many parents expressed concern about their ability to provide sufficiently for their children's future.

Another problem expressed by parents was a lack of support. "If you don't have support (in raising your children), you lament and cry a lot!" one mother said. Support was framed in both material and emotional terms. As one father stated, "Until they're married—it's much work and expense!"

## Parental Aspirations for Children's Future

In response to questions concerning their aspirations for their child(ren)'s future, the most frequent response was, "We want our children to be better off than we are—we have problems!" This was expressed in various ways by six parents. Other responses were framed in more positive terms, including, "We want our children to come back and assist," or "We hope that our children will find work and be able to assist themselves in the future." Yet another variation on this theme was, "I want my children to get a good education and to help in the future."

On an even more basic level, three parents stated that they wanted their children to be "well fed and healthy" in the future and to "be able to bring up their own children well." Parents returned to the topic of the importance of a good education several times, including the importance of "being well educated in order to become successful and have a good job."

## How Will Your Children's Life Be Different From Yours?

Responses fell into basically two broad categories, which could be viewed as negative or positive predictions for the future. The majority of parents interviewed felt that their children would be better prepared or better educated than they had been, and that preschool and early education would help "prepare them for a better life." Responses included, "If you give the child a wrong beginning, then bad things can happen later . . . early childhood care and education should be done well for a good start in life!" They also saw nursery school as a place where children in challenging situations (e.g., domestic violence, poverty, etc.) could have some respite and be cared for in a "place of love" or from "the other side." Not only was the need for school readiness expressed, but children's social development was emphasized by several of the parents, who felt strongly that early childhood education would provide their children with a better future than they had experienced.

On the negative side, responses included, "If the economy keeps up the way it's been going, things might be even worse for them!" and "If things continue to change in bad ways, our children may go even further into the slums than we have." One father stated, "By the year 2000, things will probably be worse—less land, fewer resources, and higher prices!" Even these parents were quick to state, however, that, "We hope their lives will be better than ours, but we are not sure of that."

## Community Leaders' Perspectives

A cross section of community leaders was interviewed, including four head teachers (of both public and Islamic primary schools), two TAC (Teachers Advisory Centre) tutors, a zonal inspector of schools, and four social workers and health professionals working in the Department of Social Services for the Kisumu Municipality. Interviews took place during both phases of the research project, and the local collaborators conducted the Phase II (April 1995) focus group interviews with education leaders. As in other districts, the focus group discussions reflected many of the same themes of the interviews with parents and preschool teachers—particularly the topic of the dynamics of social and economic change and the ways in which these had affected child-rearing. Themes of family change are discussed in the following sections, followed by community leaders' views on the care of under threes and the future needs of their community, concerning children and families.

### Health

The issue of class or income was the backdrop for focus group discussions of health and access to health care, with both positive and negative changes described. As in other settings, cost sharing was viewed as making health care "no longer affordable for the majority who are poor." Professionals felt that there were still "too many preventable deaths," and that although the overall number of facilities had increased, "they were not fairly distributed" among families. Those interviewed generally agreed that, "Services for young children, birth to age three, had greatly improved, thus reducing mortality and morbidity." Factors associated with these health improvements included "exposure to Maternal and Child Health" programs and the fact that "immunization had been stepped up."

The headmistress of a Muslim preschool and primary school stated that, "Apart from a lack of medicine at the moment, there's been an improvement . . . 10 years back there was only one hospital—the municipal one, and now there are many more, including the Provincial General Hospital. More licensing of private clinics and hospitals has been done, too." She, as well as others interviewed, cited the World Health Organization (WHO) and UNICEF's "Health for All" campaign, which had "speeded up the process of improved health," and reported that infant mortality rates had decreased. "Which is why," she added, "there are larger numbers of children in school." The AIDS crisis has also grown in the past 10 to 15 years, which has led to a rapid increase in orphans due to parents who have died from HIV/AIDS.

The social welfare officers and social workers at the Department of Social Services described their roles and those of CDAs (Community Development Assistants), the latter of whom work with community health volunteers as part of the Bamako Initiative. When asked for a description of this primary health initiative, we were told that, "Community mobilization is done by the CDAs, who explain the initiative and organize people according to plan—representation is very important!" Elections are then organized by the Village Health Committee (VHC), which nominates the Community Health Workers (CHWs), who undergo intensive two-week training (10 days spent on drug administration and five days spent on community health work). Over 50 CHWs are typically trained in a village or a community of about 4,000 people. Preventive measures are emphasized, as are prenatal and postnatal care and environmental and personal hygiene. Other activities of community health workers include control of minor diseases and curative measures, including use of "10 essential drugs" and the use of oral rehydration solution and anti-malarial drugs. It should be noted that Kisumu is a high malaria zone located at sea level, with high humidity and many mosquitoes.

Social services professionals agreed that the cost of medicine and health care in general had increased greatly in recent years in Kenya and in the Kisumu District. "Medical care is very expensive . . . it is the Bamako Initiative that makes it more accessible." Another colleague commenting on the rising cost of medical care put it this way: "You merely say 'Good morning, Doctor' and it can cost you 400 bob (Kshs/)!" The Bamako Initiative also was described as a "vehicle carrying many passengers," as it was reaching a growing number of households in the municipality and in peri-urban Kisumu. In terms of the total population that they hoped to serve, "The population is over half a million in Kisumu town and if we include peri-urban areas, it is well over 1 million." Some home visits were done by social workers and community health workers, but it was "mostly the Ministry of Education which makes home visits."

## Housing

In terms of changes in housing in the Kisumu Municipality, a headmaster stated that, "Urbanization has created congestion and strain to the existing structures."

Another education professional stated that, "Tremendous changes have taken place both in terms of the demand for housing as well as acquisition of modern houses." Several people commented on the need for privacy, with families moving away from the "old communal living" with more "fencing of compounds and building of walls" than in the past. The sizes of home, especially in the suburbs and slum areas, "compel families to squeeze into a 10' by 10' house where children end up very uncomfortably when it comes to bedtime." This, in turn, was seen as "affecting the growth and development of children." In contrast, "The elite have more spacious houses for the few children they have." Due to the parents' involvement with work, children are often "left alone with the *ayah*, where they have too much freedom," which can impact on children "negatively as they grow up." The issue of parents having too little time with their children was raised in several of the Kisumu focus groups, as it had been by parents and teachers. In fact, some community leaders observed that, "The role of the parents in shaping the child is very minimal."

A number of other ways in which crowded housing, or even more isolated and high security privileged housing, could negatively affect young children's development were discussed by the focus groups. Life in the more traditional rural areas in which children had "a lot of accessibility to each other and to supervision" and in which "children interact with each other" was seen by several professionals as preferable to the "more secure urban lifestyle" in which people living in nuclear families were seen as "living like an island and not exposing children to reality and to their surroundings." Another comment related to children growing up in crowded, often one-room homes was that when visitors came, they had no place to sleep, and they did not do their homework.

One interesting observation regarding housing in Manyatta, Kisumu's largest slum, was that, "Those who buy land from outside end up with mansions in the midst of the slums." Thus, "You find families from two different worlds in the same environment." At least one education professional felt that the negative influence "from the slum children who may have very little moral control" was problematic for their more middle-class friends.

Another change that was noted was that, "People are becoming increasingly aware of their environmental sanitation—the need for latrines, clean and safe water, drainage, and clean compounds." Yet crowded housing conditions appeared to be the norm for many families in the Kisumu Municipality. As a social worker observed, "The housing shortage is the most serious problem in Kisumu. The housing problem cuts across the levels of income . . . before, houses could be vacant one month, now they're not vacant for even one hour!" Community leaders and professionals agreed that rents were high, and although the municipal units were more reasonable, they were harder to obtain. A CDA observed that, "Now one house can have four families living in it! Crowding, little privacy, serious indiscipline of children—and these factors cause truancy, school dropouts, and other problems."

## Food and Nutrition

Lately, feeding in most families has changed from bad to worse.
                              —Mother in periurban Kisumu

The theme of the rising cost of food was again pervasive in the focus group interviews. "Food has become so expensive! Before, it was very cheap! For example, before it was 11 Kshs/ for a kilo of meat, and now, it is 90–100 . . . sugar was two Kshs/ and now it's 40 . . . milk was 70 cents and now it costs 14 Kshs/." "Families are unable to provide what is required, but will only give what their pockets can allow," was how one participant put it. "This inadequacy ends up having serious effects on the growth and development of the children." Although this problem was seen as affecting poor children in the most dramatic ways, families who could afford *ayahs* also were seen as potentially affected by poor nutrition. As one person stated, "In some instances, the food may be provided but the person who will handle the food—the maid—cannot prepare it well or be sure whether the child was properly fed. Comparatively, children of poor families are fed on what they can afford." One headmistress summarized the changes in food by stating, "Food security, in comparison to the early years, has gone down! This is especially true in the rural areas, and farming is now costly—for example, for tractor hire with larger scale farming."

In discussing the rising cost of feeding Kisumu families, another focus group member stated, "It is prevalent in this community that in a family of say 10, only one or two persons may be the sole breadwinner. One meal a day is a common situation. Good feeding is nearly impossible as the socioeconomic status of the majority of families does not allow it!" Aside from the general rise in the cost of living and the limited purchasing power of many families, changing lifestyles also were blamed for poor nutrition. Here, as in Embu and other districts, it was observed that, "Lifestyle has made some families neglect commonly available foods which could be affordable." Other focus group participants argued that, "There is a need to give nutritional talks to the community to go for cheap and easily available local foods which could be affordable." Specific examples of high protein, locally available foods included *omena* (small fish from Lake Victoria).

A nutritionist interviewed at the Department of Social Services felt that there was a growing awareness of family nutrition. She observed that, "Ten years back, many people were not aware of a balanced diet—they didn't know about kitchen gardens or the three food groups, but now they know. Now even young mothers are learning to make enriched *uji*." A social worker added that, "Food is very expensive, so we try to teach mothers about using locally available foods and kitchen gardens. We do cooking demonstrations and in extreme cases of malnutrition, children are referred to the Health Department." CDAs also facilitate parent meetings. Even with these positive measures, however, a TAC tutor summarized the changing food and nutrition situation by saying, "The growing lack of adequate and balanced feeding will continue having a negative impact on both the growth and intellectual development of the children. Underfeeding is now a very common phenomenon in most families."

## Child-rearing and Education

Most parents are strangers in their own homes.
The village is not being allowed to co-raise its children.

—Father in Kisumu

In terms of changes in child-rearing practices, focus group members generally agreed that care responsibilities for young children had shifted from grandmothers and older siblings to maids or *ayahs*—often with negative results. As one focus group participant put it, "Rearing practices have changed greatly since the care in the hands of the elderly is no longer possible." The person quoted above stated that, "Most parents are strangers in their own homes, leaving the care (of young children) in the hands of the inexperienced maids." Others agreed, saying, "If a maid is not well treated, she is likely also to mistreat the child or children she cares for," and "When employing an *ayah* (maid/child-minder) it is better to have someone with experience." Another concern was raised regarding problems when "leaving older siblings as the sole caregiver."

Turning to changes in preschool and formal education, a headmistress observed that, "We had no pre-primary at the beginning and now there are many!" Other professionals agreed, saying, "By this time, we have reasonable educational facilities—beginning with nursery schools. Many of these were put up by both the municipality and private community groups." Older members of one focus group recalled a time when, "Very few children could go to any school." Some focus group participants argued that, "Schools are still not adequate in number, and it is very costly to send children," and "More schools are needed with the increasing population of children here." Turning to the cost of education, another person stated, "We may talk of free education, but the demand for school funds, desks, building fund, books, uniforms, activity fees, etc. is really high! In the late 1970s, sending one primary child to school could cost 400/Kshs. per year—now you can spend that in a day!"

An interesting correlation between the introduction of the national 8-4-4 curriculum 10 years earlier was made between teachers' time to be involved in community development activities and other issues, including the pressure on children with the increased number of academic subjects. "This curriculum is still an experiment. . . . It's been 10 years now and the community says, 'It's a heavy curriculum!' Children go to bed without eating due to fatigue . . . they face long days and start at an early age of five or six years." Another colleague added, "The teachers are also overwhelmed by it! Teachers are no longer active in the community development work, which they used to be very active in . . . now, no longer, since 8-4-4 has pressurized them, like it has the children!" In another focus group, a school inspector felt that, "The attitude of current educators is fairly disturbing—there is little commitment." He blamed this on the lack of support from parents and community and the need for better facilities. He also felt that the 8-4-4 curriculum was part of the problem. "The curriculum is quite wide to encompass additional concepts and skills but hard to fully implement." In terms of cost of education, "Cost sharing has made life difficult for parents. This inability also contributes to learners dropping out because their families cannot pay for recommended textbooks, alongside the other issues."

Finally, some focus group participants felt that children were exposed to many more aspects of technology and the "wider world" beyond their community than in the past. As one headmaster put it, "Today's child is more exposed and has access to the surrounding technology . . . they come into contact with vehicles, televisions, radios, etc., and this exposure facilitate's a child's learning or intellectual development." In contrast, this educator felt that, "Rural children are fairly disadvantaged" in terms of preparation for modern life, "Although it is completely improved compared to the past." Concerns about the popular media were raised in this discussion. "Parents have no control over what is broadcast or screened. This will promote acquisition of some ideas borrowed from the programs. Such imitation erodes the upbringing of children and can result in indiscipline."

Finally, the shift from a collective or a community child-rearing ethic to a more individualistic, nuclear family approach was discussed—particularly by social services staff. As a social worker observed, "Another child-rearing change is that the village is not being allowed to co-raise its children—and this must be taken care of in disciplining children!" This appeared to be a significant concern across focus groups, with another colleague adding, "Due to social changes in so many ways, it's brought so many problems of the community—society has grown apart . . . I now have no say over even my brother's child. A communal discipline was there—but the 'we' feeling is gone, and now it is an 'I' feeling!" The comment about a brother's children is particularly interesting, given the Duluo culture and the critical role of the uncle in children's upbringing, traditionally including wife inheritance (i.e., when a man's brother died and he took in his brother's wife as a second or an additional wife).

## Community Services

It is increasingly difficult to join hands on community services now.

—Social worker in Kisumu

Social services professionals agreed that, "Earlier, 4-K, Girl Guides, Boy Scouts, and other groups were there and very active, but now children are less involved in their community. For example, school children don't even have direct contact with community elders anymore." Again, the need for parents to work and the cost to their children of their diminished involvement in the home was viewed as one source of this problem. "When a parent takes three-fourths of their time out of the home, this really affects the children. By 1985, we saw many children dying in the hospital because of poor care! For example, they were left with *ayahs* offering poor feeding. Long ago, grannies were there and they really assisted with child care and child-rearing." The lack of respect for adults was another issue raised in the focus groups. "Before, children respected adults much more . . . now families have difficulty disciplining their children." Several people interviewed commented on the growing number of street or "compound" children in Kisumu. Many came from families that could not afford to educate them and where the parent(s) was gone from the home for long hours each day trying to support the family.

The person quoted at the beginning of this section added that, "People say they are willing to work on community issues, but they have little time . . . they have vegetables to sell or need to earn a living." Educators in other focus groups agreed that Kisumu still had far to go with community mobilization for families with young children. "Things are not quite improved. Most of the under threes are cared for by the maids who may not be experienced or properly trained as caregivers." Across the focus groups, participants agreed that child care centers would help address this need. "The need to have day care centres is paramount, as only in these centres can the children get the care and stimulation needed." A headmistress said, "Since parents have very little time with their children due to other socioeconomic problems, they are not well placed to have better understanding of their own children." Thus the need for better supports, including education, for parents of young children was seen as integrated with the need for the community to provide more quality child care.

## GOOD THINGS THE COMMUNITY IS DOING

Particularly among social service professionals and community development assistants, the first response to the question of what good things the community was doing for children and families? was "The Bamako Initiative!" "In both rural and urban areas, some older mamas (grandmothers) are taking care of children—and that's good." Social workers felt that the Bamako Initiative had begun to increase health awareness and access to basic medications and had prevented many problems.

The headmistress of an Islamic primary school told us that, "Muslims have done a good thing—they look into families who cannot afford the fees and help them come." She also described an orphanage where children could stay and then attend her school. In terms of intersectoral collaboration or funding partners, she said, "Muslim Services gets help from Saudi Arabia, which sponsors some of these programs." She felt that "more mobilization for sending children—especially girls—to school" was needed in the Islamic community.

In general, education professionals felt that, "The community is becoming more aware on their role for the care of under threes." They mentioned as examples the "establishment of women and income-generating groups which will go a long way to improving the lives of the children and the family standards of living." As in many other communities in Kenya, the Kisumu community had "started nursery schools to cater for the young children," and these were serving increasing numbers of children. There were contrasting views, however, on the effectiveness of these early childhood initiatives. As one person stated, "The community has yet to do a lot for young children and their families. Though nursery schools have come up, many lack the required facilities, and not all families can afford to pay the fees."

One problem that was not unique to Kisumu but was particularly pronounced there was due to the AIDS epidemic. Social services staff commented that, "Orphan care is organized within specific, often religious, communities, versus the community at large . . . and gets funds from particular groups." There was an increasing problem of children under age three being orphaned, and one of the largest orphanages there, the Mama Ngina (widow of former President Jomo Kenyatta) Home, was having great difficulty in keeping up with the growing need. Social workers commented that "AIDS death of young parents and the grandparents' inability or unwillingness to cater to the children's needs" was a serious problem. They told us that, "Some grandparents are even running away!" As one social worker put it, "These children are missing all their cultural and traditional roots, as well as missing their parents!" While these issues were raised as complex problems facing young children in the Kisumu Municipality and district, they were also used as examples of intersectoral collaboration and the involvement of literally dozens of NGOs and church and civic groups.

## Summary

Similar to other districts, parents, teachers, and community leaders in the Kisumu Municipality frequently discussed the impacts of the rising cost of living (or "rising cost of everything," as one parent stated), coupled with the rising demands of education under the relatively new 8-4-4 national curriculum. The twin issues of needed child care for working parents, including single parents, and school readiness created a number of tensions in both child-rearing and in the search for affordable, appropriate early childhood care and education. Middle-class families had more options, but similar pressures; they expressed concerns about not being able to find reliable *ayahs*, about pressures on their children to perform well on the entrance interview for primary school (all interviews happeneded the same day, thus adding to the pressure), and about their frustration over not having more time to spend with their children. Some middle-class families had an at-home mother, but many parents were involved in wage labor or informal economic sector activities and could not bring their youngest children with them, as they might have in a more rural setting. Lower income parents expressed concerns about rising school and preschool fees, and they wanted feeding programs to be included in their children's preschool offerings.

Parents across all ethnic groups and income levels expressed concerns about options for children under three. Only two high tuition/elite nursery schools had baby classes or served under threes, and these were part-time nursery school arrangements, not full day care. Thus a heavy reliance on in-home care, typically provided by *ayahs* or mothers, was noted. Once again, an absence of traditional extended family care was lamented over. Another theme, particularly among those living in the more crowded slum areas of the Kisumu Municipality, was a lack of sufficient housing. Similar to the plantation housing issues described in earlier chapters, family size grew but affordable homes did not—crowding, lack of access to clean water, proper hygiene and sewerage, and related childhood illnesses were of great concern to parents.

In terms of community mobilization for children and families, both the Kisumu DICECE (District Centre for Early Childhood Education) and MuCECE (Municipal Centre for Early Childhood Education) worked closely with other social services and health governmental offices and NGOs. The rising number of AIDS orphans, the need to renew access to primary health care through grassroots efforts modeled after the Bamako Initiative, and other child health promotion strategies were encouraged by a collaboration between preschools and community agencies. A number of service organizations serve areas of need in Kisumu, including the programs for street children described at the beginning of the chapter, yet most people expressed concern about the widening gap between the need and the means to overcome problems affecting more and more children and families in their community. It was clear from the dozens of parents, teachers, children, and community leaders we talked with in the Kisumu Municipality that the urban village was still trying hard to raise its children but, like elsewhere in Kenya, it was struggling hard to do so and not always succeeding.

# Part VI

Conclusions, Recommendations, and Reflections

# Chapter 11

## Making Meaning:
## Does the Village Still Raise the Child?

African families face serious crises today. They are under economic, demographic and political pressures of all kinds; yet, families are not mere hapless victims of global change. They are proactive, resilient agents and creators of change.
—Thomas Weisner, Candice Bradley, and Philip Kilbride,
*African Families and the Crisis of Social Change*

## INTRODUCTION

A number of themes emerged from the interview data, which were presented in some detail through the voices of participants in the previous chapters. Taken as a whole, they can point to a number of visions for the future of early childhood care and education in Kenya, capturing the spirit of the quote above. The notion that child care should be shared by all in the community was implicit in many of our interviews and discussions with DICECE collaborators. Yet the erosion of this collective responsibility for children's well-being was evident and could readily be interpreted in social, economic, demographic, cultural, and policy terms. This chapter reviews the major findings of the study, including both similar and contrasting findings from different locations sampled, and it draws broad conclusions, engaging again the increasingly complicated question, "Does the village still raise the child?" We situate the findings within multiple and connected theoretical frameworks, drawing from cultural geography, particularly the concept of "thirdspace" (Soja, 1996) and postcolonial theory, also utilizing "African feminism" (Mikell, 1997) in our analysis. We also make both programmatic and policy recommendations, and in the Epilogue we conclude by raising further methodological and ethical issues for consideration in doing cross-cultural collaborative research.

It should be noted that this study was not an early education efficacy or access study. We collected primarily anecdotal, self-reported data related to the impact of children's participation in early childhood care and education programs and the impact of macro-level changes (e.g., economic, social, and policy related) on families' experiences of child-rearing, with a focus on children under three. Across the contrasting settings, stakeholders' reports on the impacts of early childhood care and education were generally positive, particularly where nutrition (e.g., feeding programs), growth monitoring, and other health promotion activities were involved. Both parents and teachers and community leaders and primary schoolchildren, felt strongly that at least one year of preschool was important, if not necessary, for children's success in school and their general well-being in childhood. The following sections summarize and further contextualize the interview themes between and across settings, emphasizing once again the impact of rapid social and economic change on families and young children. Summaries are followed by a discussion of policy and programmatic implications of our findings in the context of postcolonial theory.

## Socioeconomic Changes and Associated Problems Affecting Families

Our biggest problem is . . . the higher cost of everything!

—Mother in Narok

Responses to questions about social and structural changes affecting child-rearing and concerning the major problems facing families were typically quite similar, often overlapping, with a discussion of changes leading directly into a list of social and economic problems.

The most common theme in this regard was the overarching issue of increasing poverty and an array of related economic problems. First among these, in terms of the frequency with which different financial problems were mentioned, was the cost of living; second was the rapidly rising cost of educating children in Kenya. The cost of living had several dimensions, including the loss of purchasing power for basic necessities for families or, as one mother in Narok put it, "the higher cost of everything." As the Kenyan press frequently laments, the gap between the day-to-day realities of the majority of citizens living in poverty (wananchi) and the distanced and donor-dependent economic policies of its government is widening. The following sections summarize and further analyze specific aspects of change affecting families in contrasting settings and circumstances.

## Food and Nutrition

The first necessity was food. Parents and others interviewed stated that it had become much harder to feed a family due to the rising cost of food. In fact, parents often said that they now better understand the importance of a balanced diet, but they find it harder to provide what they know they "should." The role of both the preschool and the primary school in providing at least a supplementary diet for children also was raised, with many parents lamenting over the loss, or sporadic functioning, of the school milk program and the cancellation of a number of pre-school feeding programs in recent years. The latter were typically canceled due to the cost to parents (i.e., on plantations) and to the loss of donor support, for example, when the funding had been "drought related" and the drought ended and/or the project was terminated. In other words, the whims of donors, plantation management, and changing environmental and material conditions also were factors relevant to children's nutritional status. This also raised questions regarding how to ensure food security in especially dry (arid and semi-arid) regions, as well as in densely populated areas where environmental degradation had left little arable land or access to land. We also noted changes in diet, which included changes from extended breast-feeding to earlier weaning practices, as well as from traditional, locally available weaning foods to greater use of tinned foods and infant formula. The costs, both economic and health related, were often quite high and were raised as a concern by a number of teachers and parents, particularly grandmothers.

The issue of food was closely tied to a lack of access to sufficient land for a garden, a decreasing number of animals, and a lack of money to purchase food in the market. More families were renting land than in the past, making growing food for a family more costly, and urban families rarely had even a tiny kitchen garden, thus being completely dependent upon purchasing food. For communities that had formerly owned land communally (e.g., Masai and Samburu), the demarcation and subdivision of land, with more individual and single-family ownership, had also affected many families' ability to provide sufficient food for their families. Such parents also talked about having fewer animals than in earlier times and also about having a much smaller profit margin when an animal was sold.

## Housing Constraints and Safety

Another aspect of the high cost of living was housing. Rents had become much higher, and as families grew their living conditions were more crowded which created a number of problems, ranging from discipline difficulties to the rise in the number of street children (as older out-of-school boys, for example, were often not discouraged from leaving their mothers' homes). Some of the most crowded housing conditions encountered were on the plantations, where, although "free" to permanent workers, large families often occupied one or two small rooms. Similar to workers' housing built during colonial times in Nairobi for single males and now housing large, extended families, housing on plantatations was crowded to the point of some parents reporting that there was virtually no place to sleep. Participants raised concerns about the impact of such living conditions on the morals and values of their children. The related issue of workers' rights, including a right to housing, was raised in several of the interviews.

An additional problem associated with housing was that many urban and peri-urban estates, and some rural areas, had become more dangerous, with higher crime in many locations. Nearly daily accounts of armed gangs invading residences in both rural and urban areas appeared in the newspapers. The visiting researcher's home was burglarized, and another colleague experienced an armed robbery during the 1999 follow-up visit. Some families reported leaving their homes and literally living "in the bush," due to fear of gangs and violent robbery. There also were fewer open spaces, playgrounds, and other recreational settings for children—particularly in urban areas. Those interviewed in rural areas also described more squatters, some of whom were living on relatives' land and others just starting a small *shamba* on another's property. Some of these squatters were reported to be a source of "compound kids," the rural equivalent to "street kids" in urban areas. Such children were idle during the day, going home to get food and occasionally doing casual labor, and they were seen by several people interviewed as a "bad influence" on other age-mates.

Access to housing also was a growing problem in urban areas, with rapid expansion of slums, estates growing through the addition of illegal extensions to existing housing units, and crowding frequently mentioned by the parents interviewed in both Nairobi and Kisumu. Such uncontrolled growth frequently meant that few services were available (e.g., water, sewerage or latrines, trash removal or rubbish burning pits, etc.), making environmental hygiene a major problem. This in turn led to outbreaks of disease, including dysentery, which was particularly problematic in one of the Nairobi slums sampled in the study. One of Nairobi's largest slums, Kibera, had grown to over 2 million people, with no paved roads and little infrastructure, by 1999, and other areas we visited had similar challenges. A letter to the editor of the *Daily Nation* (June 13, 1999) puts some of the housing difficulties in historical persective. "Given the temporary nature of residence in the city, the social infrastructure for the African labourers in the city was extremely limited. This was the least developed aspect of city life because Nairobi was supposed to be a settler city built for the needs of the while highlands and in conformity with the predilections of the European settler elite." The author goes on to observe that, "Housing turned out to be the most serious omission in colonial times."

Even when people were able to arrange temporary or semipermanent housing in such slum settings, the possibility of entire neighborhoods being bulldozed by the City Council, Kenya Railways (which owned some of the land where communities have sprung up), and so on, was a serious problem. Although one community was no longer using cartons (cardboard and plastic) as housing materials, with the associated risk of fire, the same community was still being threatened by the bulldozing squads that could render hundreds of people homeless in one night. In terms of housing, health, and other environmental issues, slumdwellers in urban Kenya continue to have a precarious existence at best.

Many of these issues point to the failure of the government of Kenya to plan and provide basic infrastructure for housing and environmental hygiene. The need for greater public awareness of hygiene and sanitation was noted by several of the community leaders and parents we interviewed. The lack of sufficent and affordable transportation was another factor in the problem of urbanization and dislocation. For example, lack of transportation was a major factor in the development of slums near the industrial areas, where people could walk to work. Several slum dwellers described their lack of access to water, including the high fees charged by those who had access (legally or illegally) to water taps. Again, the role of urban planning, community development strategies, and infrastructure is critical to addressing these complex, housing-related issues.

Another set of problems frequently named in most of the settings sampled had to do with issues of family change. These included the growing number of single parents, usually mothers, raising children and living under great stress and financial hardship, and the associated rise in divorce and separation. Regarding the latter, some participants in rural areas also stated that the informal systems previously used to prevent divorce (e.g., members of a women's self-help group going to talk to a woman who was not getting along with her husband, etc.) were rapidly disappearing. Land tenure patterns and urbanization also contributed to this phenomenon, with landless rural families migrating to towns and cities, or fathers leaving rural families to look for work. As stated in the first chapter, one-third of Kenyan children are being raised by a female head of household.

## Changing Family Patterns—Young, Single Mothers

In some areas, study participants reported that women were becoming mothers at a younger age. The assertion is reflected in data from other studies, with larger samples, which show the average age of mothers is lower than 10 to 15 years ago (Adams & Mburugu, 1994). Thus grandparents also were described as "younger and busier meeting their own financial needs" and less likely to be available for some of their traditional caregiving roles. Another aspect of the isolation of children from their grandparents had to do with the loss of counseling and "preparation for life" role that grandparents, particularly grandmothers, had played in previous generations. In other words, the passing down of traditional stores, metaphors, and advice for living was now cut short by time, distance, and rapid social and economic change.

## IMPLICATIONS FOR EARLY CHILDHOOD POLICY AND PROGRAM PLANNING

According to the World Bank's Early Childhood Development (ECD) Mission to Kenya (1995), "The effectiveness and sustainability of ECCE programs and activities is likely to be greatly increased if such programs are designed, monitored, and supported by the community itself—including building on past initiatives" (e.g., the fact that 75% of preschools are community initiated and supported). Although a detailed national needs assessment, carried out at the grassroots level, was beyond the scope of our study, the data summarized in this volume may contribute to the ongoing planning process for a strengthened early childhood care and education infrastructure—particularly for children under age three, where no national or local infrastructure currently exists. Given the limitations of the sample, and the inherent dangers of overgeneralization, we recommend unique local applications of nationally viable models for the care of Kenya's youngest children and the support of their families. In other words, unique local solutions must be found, and a local infrastructure for finding these solutions must not be bypassed (e.g., local and district development committees, local opinion shapers and leaders, and DICECE and zonal education staff—particularly preschool supervisors, Ministry of Health local staff, existing elected parent groups, including school committees, and local NGO staff, where there are existing NGO or church-sponsored projects affecting children and families). More focused studies on specific communities also are recommended.

The following sections address questions that are relevant to program planning for expanded ECCE services in Kenya, and they are intended to both summarize our conclusions and raise issues of interest to readers concerned with child and family social and educational policy. We also advocate family-centered, culturally relevant, and integrated or comprehensive strategies for the enhancement of early childhood development in Kenya. We believe that policies are critical if we are to make a real difference in the lives of young children and their families. Policies should "facilitate the shifting of resources to structures and programmes for children and families" (Kabiru, Njenga, & Mutua, 1998, p. 8).

## Communities' Traditional Perceptions of ECCE

It should be noted that the broadest definition of early childhood development, education, and care services was employed in this study. In other words, ECCE was not narrowly defined as a center-based, formally organized group care or preschool arrangement. Rather, it included traditional familial and extrafamilial care of children, from conception through age six. It also attempted to view the needs of the developing child in multiple contexts—health, nutrition, socio-emotional, cognitive, spiritual, and in the "nested contexts" (Lubeck, 1987) of family, community, and culture.

As anticipated, the Samburu and Narok samples reflected the most "traditional" perceptions and practices of child-rearing and early childhood caregiving and education. Grandmothers were largely responsible for the care of small groups of children under three (and often older), assisting younger mothers who were physically better able to gather firewood, carry water, go to market, and perform other domestic chores, including *shamba* work. This division of labor appeared to be well understood and accepted, with more recent additions of "formal" preschool programs with younger, hired teachers considered quite acceptable for the older (i.e., ages four to five years) children. Other more recent inputs to the traditional child-rearing system included better preventive health care (e.g., taking children to the clinic for immunizations and growth monitoring), improved access to water, and better personal and environmental hygiene practices. These latter inputs varied greatly, however, with few latrines being dug, for example, even in semipermanent housing settings where families had lived for eight to 10 years. As previously discussed, this was likely due in part to cultural taboos. In other settings, mothers' care was considered optimal for the youngest children, as supplemented where possible by grandmothers' and older siblings' (particularly sisters') care. Yet many families in "traditional," pastoralist settings advocated formal preschool for children as young as three; we fine problematic the role of formal early education and care, particularly where family child care arrangements were still plentiful.

Other community perceptions of ECCE included an emphasis on health and nutrition, particularly in the area of feeding programs. Nutrition and preventive or primary health measures often were mentioned by parents and teachers as critical components of ECCE. Some of the preschool teachers interviewed were trained by the local Ministry of Health as primary health workers, providing growth monitoring and parent education functions in their local communities, through their preschools. The researcher also had the opportunity to observe both growth monitoring and cooking demonstrations of traditional weaning foods in the Embu District (Runyenjes location) and "health talks" by preschool teachers on oral rehydration therapy in the Machakos District (Wamunyu location). For a more detailed analysis of the relative effectiveness of such preschool-based primary health initiatives, see Gakuru and Koech's (1995) contextualized case study of under threes in the Machakos District, and preliminary project reports of a teen mother's training and support initiative in the same district (Kabiru & Njenga, 1997, 1999).

In the related area of nutrition, many of the mothers and grandmothers interviewed discussed their perceptions of weaning practices, both traditional and contemporary. Bottle feeding was clearly not an option in many of the areas we visited (with baby bottles literally confiscated by local health workers in clinics and dispensaries), although early weaning and supplements were a factor in both the Embu and Machakos Districts. Other communities reported that a strength of traditional child-rearing was the length of time, at least two years and sometimes three, for breast-feeding children (e.g., in the Masai and Samburu cultures). It was particularly difficult for mothers working on the tea and coffee plantations to properly breast-feed their children. They had only very short breaks, while the tea leaves they had picked were being weighed, and had no lunch hour and often worked extremely long hours. As discussed elsewhere, women were more likely to be casual laborers and, as such, they often did not qualify for health services or maternity leave. Similarly, urban mothers tended to be away from their babies for long periods of time, making early weaning more likely than in more traditional, rural settings.

Another perception of ECCE in general concerned its role in cultural transmission and maintenance. Caregivers were seen as passing on values, language, stories, and traditions of the culture. This was most disrupted in both the plantation and urban settings, where groups of children in care came from several cultural/ethnic backgrounds, with a different vernacular spoken in the home, and often they had a teacher or a caregiver from a different ethnic background.

Where more traditional care persisted (e.g., in the Samburu and Masai areas), grandmothers still told stories in the evening, sang traditional lullabies, and were responsible for many forms of cultural transmission. With more single-parent mothers raising families in poverty, necessitating the mother's absence for long periods of time to work or look for food, firewood, and so on, the cultural maintenance function of child care often was lost, at least to a degree. Many of the parents interviewed lamented over such losses, and they also described children as "hurried" and "busy," especially as they went into primary school with its many subjects and time demands, particularly under the still "new" 8-4-4 national curriculum.

Another aspect of group care, particularly noted in the more "traditional" communities, was the importance of the age set. ECCE was viewed, in such contexts, as providing opportunities for socialization and preparation for other rites involving the age set. This also was mediated by gender, with boys and girls being prepared for quite different future experiences and expectations. Closely related to this preparation for life was the role of discipline and guidance in ECCE. Although lamented over as being lost with nuclear families and more "private" attitudes regarding child-rearing (versus the "community raising the child"), the role of discipline and training in good manners and culturally acceptable behavior was no small part of parents' expectations of ECCE.

Other, more custodial functions of child care also were named as roles filled by preschool with some frequency. ECCE was seen as keeping children safe, while parents or other caregivers performed essential work. It also was seen as providing protection to children from various dangers (e.g., from wild animals, fire, drowning, or exposure). In fact, for under threes, the custodial functions of child care appeared to take precedence over aspects of ECCE such as early stimulation, verbal interaction, and the opportunity to play and use manipulative materials.

Finally, a rapidly growing expectation of preschool (particularly for the "pre-unit" or 4 to 5 year old children) was the preparation for primary school and beyond. The "readiness" function of preschool was unquestioned by most parents interviewed—across all settings. The place where the least emphasis was placed on readiness for Standard 1 was the plantation sample, where the custodial day care function of preschools was predominant. Even in the most traditional samples, however, preschool was assumed by a cross section of participants to be a prerequisite for primary school. In other words, preschool has been rapidly institutionalized as the downward extension of a public school education, and it was in fact at least unofficially a requirement for admission (through the Standard 1 "interview" or screening process) to primary school in many communities we visited.

## BENEFITS OF ECCE TO CHILD, FAMILY, AND COMMUNITY

Closely related to community perspectives on ECCE are the expectations and perceived benefits of early childhood development and care. Expectations and perceived benefits varied across settings, and these will be discussed separately for each of the types of settings sampled.

### Roles of Preschool in Plantations

In coffee and tea estates, the expectation for preschool was clear—working mothers had urgent child care needs, and children needing care throughout the day (as mothers did not even have lunch hours at home) also were viewed as requiring feeding programs. These programs more closely resembled full day care facilities than most of the nursery schools visited in the study, including at least minimal provision for napping and custodial care of under threes. Teachers in such settings were called "childminders" or "baby-sitters," and parents expected safe custodial care, which ideally included shelter, minimal activities, a snack and lunch (often cold lunches carried in tins), and supervision by one or two child-minders. Both parents and managers lamented over the large numbers of children with few teachers or caregivers, but this care was viewed as minimal and necessary, thus a custodial model was pervasive in plantation or estate settings.

Therefore, ECCE programs on plantations were viewed as an economic necessity of a female-dominated labor pool (e.g., coffee and tea pickers), which provided an alternative to conditions of neglect, namely, leaving children alone. Families still relied on older siblings, however, given the longer working hours than the hours of operation of the nursery schools or day care centers. Benefits of preschool for "preunit" children also included school preparation, but this was mentioned less than in other settings. The benefits of preschool in the estates were viewed by parents and even older siblings as the provision of custodial care, the guidance of non-familial caregivers, and, to a lesser degree, the stimulation of young children. It remained unclear where the majority of infant care (under ones) took place. In some tea estates, infants were left at weighing stations with one or more older siblings and with an overseer informally watching over the group of babies. In some of the coffee estates, babies were taken into the fields by their mothers to be breast-fed and comforted when possible. Both of these arrangements were particularly problematic during the rainy season and when the fields were sprayed with chemical pesticides and fertilizers.

As previously discussed, issues related to workers' rights were pervasive in our interviews. We questioned the role of management in the provision of better facilities and family supports. We also wondered whether workers' unions might be sensitized to raise this issue and bring more effective pressure to bear on the plantation management. Finally, we wondered about policy issues related to laborers' rights. An advocacy agenda regarding employees, both permanent and casual, on agricultural estates in Kenya was evident.

## Roles of Preschool in Rural, Agricultural Areas

In rural areas, a number of "transition issues" were apparent. For example, many parents commented on the change over time from traditional caregiving (i.e., mother, grandmother, and often older siblings) to group care and nursery schools. As previously discussed, there had been rapid growth and much community support of nursery schools, which were typically viewed as "only" for the older preschool-age children (e.g., four to six years) and not for the under threes. Exceptions to this included the casual laborers and women who traveled to rented land to work on small *shambas* and needed full-day child care. We saw such mothers walking to their rented land with infants on their backs, but they did not bring older children with them. Feeding programs were also viewed as an important component of many nursery school programs, and preparation for school also was considered important—beyond custodial expectations.

It was interesting, particularly in the rural Embu District, to note that children were not typically sent to nursery school until they were at least four years old. This was explained by parents as mainly sending children the year before primary school as preparation for Standard 1 and the admission interview, and it was explained by teachers in terms of a lack of space, sufficient teachers, and facilities for younger children. The same teachers often commented that, "A family cannot miss sending a four- or five-year-old child to nursery school," although they typically waited until the year before primary school to send most children.

Finally, the rural districts sampled provided some of the richest examples of community- based innovations centered in the local preschool. These included integrated health programs, cooking demonstrations, teacher panels (for mutual support, curriculum development, and income generation), and parent involvement in toy and learning materials-making workshops. Such examples demonstrated the high potential for community mobilization when rural preschools, communities, and DICECE trainers worked closely together. They also represented a vision for the future that parents held for their youngest children, as evidenced by their willingness to donate time, money, labor, ideas, and ongoing participation in programs to benefit their children.

## Roles of Early Care and Education in Traditional, Pastoral Settings

In the traditional, pastoralist areas, as already discussed, traditional family care was still considered best for young children—particularly for under threes. More of the youngest children, however, were seen as participating in organized preschool settings (both in open air and in classrooms). Such children were still under the care of their older siblings, typically their older sisters, who carried them on their backs to the preschool or play group setting. In the Samburu and Narok Districts, the availability of caregivers was not yet a critical issue, although several of the parents and professionals interviewed predicted that this issue would become more important in the coming years, with the gradual transition from communal extended family to individual nuclear family and child-rearing patterns.

Interest in training for home-based caregivers (e.g., grandmothers) and organized under-three play groups was high, as these reflected the traditional way of caring for children. Enhancing existing systems of child care with the addition of feeding programs, primary health promotion, and child development training caregivers was recognized as being beneficial to under threes, particularly given the hard economic times and the need to better meet young children's needs. In program planning in traditional settings, it will be important to recognize the importance of both formal and informal learning, and to recognize the importance of maintaining traditional practices. ECCE is supported and generally well understood among the Samburu and Masai people, but care must be taken to ensure that their traditions are respected and not contradicted by more formalized ECCE programs. Given the fact that a number of the parents interviewed in these areas felt that children under three should be cared for in preschool settings, we wondered how the traditional child care system could be better integrated into the formal early childhood care and education programs available. We noted that a form of family-based child care, with one mother or grandmother caring for several under threes, was a continuing practice in both the Narok and Samburu Districts. This appeared to be meeting community needs and complementing other, more formalized preschool programs.

## Roles of Preschool and Child Care in Urban Settings

Turning to urban settings in the study, families from contrasting class backgrounds must be addressed separately, as they offer distinct contrasts in perceived benefits of ECCE. In slums, or "urban informal settlement" settings, there were a number of parallels to plantation samples. Many mothers interviewed were single parents, attempting to support their families through casual labor or in small market or microenterprise activities. Similar to mothers on the plantations, they were away from home for many hours each day, and they faced many economic hardships. Often unable to pay for school fees, mothers in slums left older siblings to watch younger ones, and they also occasionally left young children alone and unattended. Such families also were more likely to have one or more children on the streets (Kilbride & Njeru, 1995; Swadener and Mutua, in press).

Thus the perceived benefits of nursery school included custodial day care, enhanced nutrition, where feeding programs were available, and, as children approached primary school entrance age, preparation for Standard 1. Of the models of ECCE programs operating in slums, self-help cooperative child care centers, home-based programs that might even include evening drop-in care and family counseling, and church- or NGO-sponsored programs were seen as providing a viable alternative to taking young children into the workplace, or—worse—leaving them locked in a room or unattended in a slum area while the mother worked.

For middle- and upper-class families, preschool was important from an early age (e.g., privileged parents in Kisumu wanted their children to enroll in the "best" nursery schools by age two in order to be well prepared and positioned for the primary entry interviews at the best schools, which all took place on the same day and which put great pressure on both children and parents). Such middle-class families, in the towns of Kisumu, Nairobi, and Embu, typically had either an at-home mother (homemaker) and/or a maid (*ayah*) making nursery school a half-day enrichment and readiness experience, not a needed caregiving or day care setting. It should be noted that some two-career families were interviewed, and they appeared to view a quality nursery school program with a trained teacher as being much more beneficial to their children than leaving the children with an untrained *ayah* for the entire day. Such parents saw early reading, writing, and other school-related skills as critical. These social, class-mediated expectations of early education mirror the research in a number of national contexts and raise issues of equity in a number of areas.

## Maintenance of Child Care and Early Education: Community Contributions

Traditional child care, where it still exists, is more sustainable in several respects, as it requires the least new inputs for maintenance. In any setting, community contributions are the most sustainable. Such contributions, as previously described in more detail, include parents' and the community's contributions of labor, materials, advice, active involvement on school committees, *Harambee* organizing and financial contributions, and help in organizing and supporting feeding programs. Concerns about community sponsorship, as previously discussed, include the uneven funding base of reliance on parent fees and the low pay or even intermittent pay of preschool teachers who are often "untrained."

A "children's trust" or other source of small-scale loans to be used for the enhancement of existing ECCE services, or the creation of new ones, was recommended by our research team as a viable model for many communities. Such loans or seed money could be used to pay teachers a better or more consistent salary, to support more teachers in undergoing training (both short course and full residential training), and for the initiation or maintenance of feeding programs and expanded services for under threes. When family and community contributions are severely limited due to economic hardship, a loan fund or purchase of services scheme could go a long way in ensuring that ECCE programs are sustained under current conditions of socioeconomic transition. One such proposal, which has yet to be piloted in Kenya, was to establish a community trust fund, providing seed money and making small loans to enhance access to early childhood education and child development services in high poverty communities.

We also felt that DICECE trainers and zonal preschool inspectors would continue to play a critical role in sustaining ECCE services to communities, both rural and urban. Providing inexpensive transportation (e.g., motorcycles or small vehicles) to DICECE units would seem to be a wise investment of limited resources, as DICECE staff are community mobilizers who can do much to ensure program success and continuity if they can reach communities and teachers, including those in more isolated areas of their districts.

Active involvement of parents also is of critical importance to the sustainability and success of any ECCE program. As many parents affirmed in our interviews, parent meetings must go beyond merely an annual, often third-term, parent day and include an ongoing program of parental and community involvement. Such activities can include toy- and materials-making workshops, cooking and primary health demonstrations, preschool work days, growth monitoring for under fives, and involvement on a preschool committee. Several of these activities (e.g., cooking demonstrations, toymaking, and growth monitoring) also are likely to benefit under threes who are not yet enrolled in a formal preschool program, and they can serve as a base for outreach and parent education. Such low cost programs can reach those who cannot afford institutionalzed services, including preschool education.

## FAMILY AND COMMUNITY CONTRIBUTIONS TO ECCE IN THE FUTURE

Our study provided an array of evidence that future enhancements of ECCE in Kenya should build upon traditional parent and community involvement and support and should not impose new models on communities that are already successful at mobilization for ECCE. This is not to say that no new approaches are needed—

in fact, in order to serve children under three, new models (e.g., family-based child care and toddler or "baby" classes in preschools) will be needed. Rather, it will be critical to obtain the opinions of a cross section of community members and continue to carry out "client studies" in order to plan projects and approaches that are most likely to be supported and sustained by local communities and parents.

It is equally important not to assume that the same service design and delivery model(s) will work in all communities. By working closely with DICECE and other local professionals and community leaders, the most appropriate model for distinct types of settings and communities can likely be found. For example, in some semi-arid settings where livestock are still relatively plentiful, a "Kajiado model" might be considered. This project, as supported by the Arid and Semi-arid Lands (ASAL) project (funded by a Netherlands-based NGO), entails a number of ECCE programs with community matching funds coming from the sale of cattle by elders.

We would also recommend that community-based initiatives actively encouraged by several DICECE at present be promoted, including the establishment of teacher panels (at the zonal and even sub-zonal levels) and self-help groups, whose activities include income-generating schemes and personal and professional support. A related model that has been tried with some success in Siaya and is now being replicated in other districts, including Nairobi, is the formation of "Child Care Consultative Groups." Such groups provide input from a variety of opinion shapers, community leaders, and service providers, and they can be instrumental in encouraging intersectoral collaboration to support families from pregnancy through the preschool years.

Additionally, our study provided evidence that parents should continue to become encouraged to be actively involved in as many aspects of ECCE as possible, including materials making, assisting in feeding programs, digging latrines, making or purchasing appropriate furniture and playground equipment, and hiring teachers. Many communities still require education on what is needed for appropriate ECCE, particularly pertaining to children under three. Similarly, kitchen gardens and feeding programs in all preschools can provide an important source of nutrition for young children.

In terms of the oversight of successful programs and the application of external programs and resources to ECCE, the consensus in both the community leader and professional groups was that locally elected committees would be the best way to ensure that the funds or other assistance were effectively used and to oversee their application over time. Building on existing management structures (e.g., school committees) and encouraging a more active role for the community in planning and providing for ECCE services were emphasized in the interviews. Finally, providing training, technical assistance, and other forms of support to local leadership bodies, with regular follow-up at the zonal or district level (from DICECE and Inspectorate, as well as Ministry of Health, where appropriate) was seen as critical to the successful application of additional resources for ECCE. Human resource development and support was seen as key to the early childhood care and education initiative.

## CONSTRAINTS TO ECCE IN KENYA: PAST AND PRESENT

Constraints, as described by participants in the study, most often related to the lack of funds required to provide necessary program components (e.g., feeding programs, learning materials, age-appropriate furniture and other facilities, and teachers' salaries). Local preschool committees also were seen as being in need of training in management. The stakeholders we interviewed emphasized that the following questions be addressed:

1. Is money banked?

2. Are accurate financial records kept?

3. How are teachers recruited, supported, and evaluated?

4. Are teachers regularly and fairly paid?

These areas related to poor management and organizational weaknesses, including financial mismanagement and lack of skills in record-keeping, management, and service planning. Each of these areas, in turn, should be addressed in future ECCE initiatives.

Other constraints to a number of ECCE programs include lack of access to clean water and related environmental and individual hygiene problems, particularly in semi-arid and slum settings. This problem is likely best attacked through intersectoral collaboration of education, health, water, and other local authorities, and certainly through parents. Finally, another current constraint to ECCE services is the lack of feeding programs in many preschools and other community-based settings. As stated earlier, ideally such programs should provide between 25 to 30% of children's daily nutritional requirements, with a higher percentage required in plantations settings, as well as in urban slum areas. Other problems include distances to services and taboos (e.g., going to government hospitals) that prevent access to health care resources.

In terms of how these constraints are traditionally and currently relieved or avoided, particularly by the family and the community, feeding programs can utilize locally available, nutritional food, as well as the labor of parents. As described several times by parents and professionals during interviews, the sustainability of such programs can be enhanced when food is collected by parents and stored in a centralized area, to be shared with the preschool (e.g., the Embu model). Also, the contribution of small amounts of cooking oil, firewood or charcoal, water, and labor (e.g., taking turns cooking) can all contribute to the sustainability of feeding programs, particularly in rural or peri-urban areas, where foodstuff is available.

Community mobilization has been, and will continue to be, critical to countering the above constraints to ECCE programs. For example, *Harambees* (local self-help fundraisers) and *barrazas* (public meetings or forums, usually led by the local chief and possibly by a primary school head teacher) were often cited by teachers, parents, and others interviewed as helpful ways of coping with problems and improving services to children. Parent and community education or "family enhancement" strategies also are viable models, and several local community leaders and opinion shapers (e.g., the chief, school head teachers, DICECE trainers, local authorities, Ministry of Health and Ministry of Social Services staff) are critical to the success of such efforts. Particularly helpful are trained village health workers and other home visitors (e.g., social workers).

## Consequences of ECCE Constraint or Failure

I can't imagine how things would run without it [the preschool]!

—Manager of coffee estate in Kiambu

This question was addressed in terms of both current problems where few services, particularly for children under three, existed and hypothetical problems that a lack of services could present (discussed in this manner in focus group discussions mainly). One of the strongest, most frequent responses to the question of the consequences of a lack of currently available ECCE services was, "Children would be malnourished, neglected, and more would die!" This was particularly in reference to the importance of feeding programs and nutrition education for parents, programs of care and early education for preschool age children, and immunization and other preventive health measures, now quite widely available. The stakes for the first five years of life were seen by everyone interviewed as quite high, with health and nutrition inputs being of greatest importance. Other respondents said that, "Disease and illness would be much worse" without primary health care measures now available to families, and "We would lose more children to preventable disease," again referring to the importance of the expanded immunization program in Kenya.

In plantation samples and some urban, low-income settings, child care also was seen as a critical means of preventing the neglect of children and other dangers of being either left alone or with untrained caregivers, often only a few years older (e.g., siblings). One manager of a coffee estate in the Kiambu District shook his head and said that a lack of at least some child care for workers was "unthinkable. We've had child care here for many years before I started in this job, and I cannot imagine how things could run without it!"

In rural, traditional, and many urban settings, parents and others interviewed spoke of the importance of preschool as a preparation for success in primary school, and far less about stimulation through play, language development, and other aspects of ECCE needed for optimal child development. The view of nursery school education as preparation for further schooling was quite pervasive, and the lack of preschool education was addressed as "a great problem for children entering Standard 1 without it—all children today need at least one year of nursery school before entering primary school." This nearly universal acceptance, by parents, of preschool education also was a comment on the perceived consequences of its absence. The consequences of the lack of both nursery school and primary school education (due to parents' inability to pay fees and other expenses), according to many parents, were the rapidly increasing number of street and compound children—the out-of-school youth whom many people interviewed felt would not be on the street or idle in the rural areas if they had gone to at least nursery school and lower primary school. We feel that these issues make a case for holistic early childhood development services that involve the training or retraining of teachers and increasing parents' awareness of broader issues of "preparation for life."

## IMPLICATIONS FOR POLICY AND PROGRAM PLANNING

We want a world where basic needs become rights and where all forms of violence are eliminated. . . . In such a world women's reproductive role will be redefined: Child care must be shared by men, women, and society as a whole.
            —Development Alternatives with Women for a New Era (DAWN)

One basic and foundational recommendation based on our study was that a very inclusive definition of early childhood care and education (ECCE) or early childhood development (ECD) be employed by all bodies involved in the related policy and program planning process. Such a definition should encompass not only preschool and other "institutional" or formally organized settings but should include traditional child-rearing, small, home-based child care centers (which will likely grow in number in the coming years to address the urgent need for care for under threes), and "family enhancement" and education activities, which include strengthening families' ability to raise healthy, well-prepared children. Future policies should emphasize family centered programming, which takes into account the stated needs and goals of parents and local communities. Such local goals are expected to vary widely, in terms of contrasting local resources, lifestyles, and challenges. The emphasis on family-centered program planning, however, we feel should clarify the fact that ECCE services include providing child-rearing support and resources to families as well as resources for the expansion of formal early childhood education programs.

A specific aspect of family-centered programming that was mentioned as something parents had appreciated in the past but was no longer widely available was the home visitor model. Whether village health workers or social workers, such visitors were described as providing support and advice for healthy child-rearing, access to free or low-cost medicine and diagnostic services, and improved personal and environmental hygiene. A related model that was strongly supported by the professionals interviewed (i.e., social work staff in Kisumu) was the Bamako Initiative. This community health approach involves the short-term intensive training of community health workers who are provided with 10 essential drugs and trained in primary health practices and community mobilization. They provide a form of mobile clinic and often home-based health care services, as well as low-cost medicine. This model has been successful in several African settings, and it is being replicated in a number of Kenyan communities. Funding for the accelerated implementation of the Bamako Initiative is encouraged, particularly where the training of village health workers emphasizes the care and development of young children and the empowerment of their parents. The expansion of mobile clinics also is strongly recommended in order to address the long distances many parents must travel to take children to clinics.

A related policy and programmatic issue in family enhancement is the need for services that support young mothers, particularly single mothers. Older, experienced mothers, health workers, adult educators, and other community members could be encouraged to form informal support systems for young mothers. Women's self-help groups also can provide both social and emotional support and income-generating schemes that both indirectly contribute to enhanced child-rearing.

Second, although the Ministry of Education, largely through the NACECE/DICECE system and the Inspectorate, should remain the lead agency for ECCE policy and program implementation, greater intersectoral collaboration across governmental ministries, local authorities, NGOs, and religious organizations or sponsors should be emphasized in order to meet the complex needs of both children and families in Kenya. Models of community empowerment, income generation, and local program planning, along with donors and relevant local government officials, should be encouraged. Such local providers of technical assistance to parent and community groups should benefit from increased means of transportation for outreach to the locations and sublocations of greatest need.

Other specific policy recommendations include the establishment of a "Children's Trust" or other type of small loan-making scheme. Such a trust could provide seed money for income-generating projects, expanded care models, more equitable teacher salaries, and facilities and materials needed for ECCE programs. In locations where care for children under three is an urgent need, funds from the Children's Trust should be targeted primarily to establishing or enhancing services for the youngest children in a particular setting or community. We would not, however, want the Children's Trust model to become an additional bureaucratic barrier to the activities of NGOs and local initiatives on behalf of children and families.

Smaller, home-based child care facilities should be strongly considered as a viable model for care of the youngest children requiring extrafamilial care. Support and education for the home-based caregivers or teachers should be emphasized in the planning of such services. Teacher panels or other support systems should also be encouraged to prevent isolation and to provide professional and personal development opportunities for home-based caregivers/teachers. Additionally, parent cooperative models should be actively explored. Such informal programs would involve mothers (and fathers) taking turns caring for a small group of children, freeing other mothers to work in a variety of settings (e.g., in their *shambas,* in the market, in paid labor, etc.). Work schedules and requirements should be explored to allow women more flexible hours in order to provide for participation in such shared child care schemes, as well as to nurse their youngest children. The plight of mothers working on plantations as casual laborers must clearly be addressed as well.

As services are created or enhanced, it is further recommended that sliding fee schemes be implemented in order to make ECCE services more accessible to the poorest families. Local determination of the criteria for reduced fees will be critical to the success of such an initiative, which should not be seen merely as an expanded local "preschool bursary" fund. Some of these recommendations seem unrealistic, however, given the evidence of decreasing community support of preschool programs, including the cutbacks in County Council support of preschool teachers' salaries during the late 1990s.

Where possible, feeding programs should be required and subsidized, as they can often make the critical difference in child survival and optimal development. Supplementing the nutritional role of preschool programs with expanded nutrition information for parents also is recommended. Cooking demonstrations, using affordable, locally available and high nutrition weaning foods, as described in chapter 7, were a viable model of collaboration between DICECE staff and local nutritionists. Again, these demonstrations tended to reinforce the traditional weaning practices and discourage the use of expensive, less nutritious "tinned" baby foods.

In terms of policy implications for Kenya's youngest children, maternity leave policies need reexamination. The two-month (unpaid) maternity leave for mothers in permanent employment should likely be lengthened, paternity leave policies explored, and better health and leave benefits considered for women working in the informal or casual labor sector.

Policies that recognize what it means to be a child, and the fundamental rights of children, as endorsed at the World Summit for Children and found in the U.N. and Convention for the Rights of the Child, continue to be warranted. Passage of the Kenya Children's Bill in 1995 was a positive step in this direction, although many would argue that, like other "unfunded mandates," it is far from a full implementation. One question that recurred during the process of carrying out the research was, "Are parents and policy makers aware of the need of a child to be a child?" This was particularly problematic when children were observed working long hours in plantation settings, caring for younger children, and even working hard in nursery schools that emphasized academic preparation and performance in Standard 1 interviews.

Finally, economic supports to empower communities to meet minimum basic standards for children are recommended. Examples of projects that could be undertaken at the community level include:

1. a community book fund, to help families purchase required school books

2. better use of school buildings for community meetings, workshops, and child health services

3. formation of self-help groups and other forms of family enhancement

4. establishment of home-based child care to serve under threes

Additionally, two other priority areas to help ensure the success of any ECCE initiative in Kenya are training and transportation. As Adams' (1995) national study underscores, the need for expanded training of preschool teachers, parent education, and training of local preschool committee members in management and leadership areas is critical. Training in primary health promotion also should be expanded, with both preschool teachers and parents benefitting from such efforts. The area of transportation is a critical one for DICECE staff in particular. Because much of their job description involves community outreach, supervision of pre-school teachers, and mobilization activities, the provision of at least minimal trans-portation support should be a high priority in future planning for ECCE.

The above recommendations should be pursued in the context of the promises made to children at the U.N.-sponsored World Summit for Children in 1990. The basic rights of Kenyan children to health, education, nutrition, and protection from abuse and overwork must become a stronger advocacy agenda in Kenya. Again, the passage of the Children's Bill was a positive sign that the Kenyan Parliament is recognizing the children's crisis and beginning to respond.

## CONCLUSIONS AND CONTRADICTIONS

We now return to the question posed in the title of this book, "Does the village still raise the child?" Out findings were, as could be expected in many contexts experiencing rapid social, economic, and cultural change, mixed and at times con-tradictory. Parents and extended family members expressed strong commitment to the collective well-being of children and to doing all they could to enhance their own children's life chances and future opportunities. Many parents interviewed, particularly on plantations, in some rural locations, and in urban settings, ex-pressed deep concern about the loss of many of the traditions related to child-rearing. Even in the more persistently traditional or pastoralist communities, Masai and Samburu participants expressed concern that their ways of life and child-rearing were threatened by a number of factors, including land tenure issues such as land privatization and subdivision, loss of grazing corridors and livestock, and the growth of the nuclear family. The loss of the traditional support and cultural maintenance roles of grandmothers in particular was fre-quently raised as an issue of concern.

The enriched social support network that children in East Africa have traditionally experienced (Kilbride & Kilbride, 1990) is indeed threatened. Increasing instances of child abuse and neglect, the growing number of children living and working on the street, and the loss of intergenerational support systems for child-rearing and cultural maintenance are disturbing phenomena. Yet we would agree with the Kilbrides and others who have studied changing child-rearing in Kenya, that the solutions to the problems addressed in this study must be based on a "locally derived child-centered Africanity" (Kilbride & Kilbride, 1990, p. 248). Such approaches respect the diversity of ideas, and these approaches offered by communities vary dramatically yet share the commitment to continue to pull together in the original spirit of *Harambee* to raise the child and build the future of the nation.

## TOWARD A POSTCOLONIAL "THIRDSPACE" FOR CHILDREN AND FAMILIES IN KENYA

As we have reflected on the study reported in this book, we are continuing to situate our findings within various theoretical frameworks, and we have found it useful to draw from cultural geography's conceptualization of space, including the notion of "thirdspace" (Soja, 1996), as well as the trialectics of spatiality and othering, as described by philosopher Henri Lefebre (1991). As discussed in the Introduction and in chapter 2, our study sought to break (in at least some small way) with persistent colonial traditions of cross-cultural research and anthropology. We have attempted to do what cultural geographer David Sibley does in challenging his colleagues to, "Go out into the world . . . not on an imperialist and colonialist mission, but in order to experience the life-worlds of other people" (1995, p. 185). This movement away from "othering" to listening in the spirit of collaboration, while not denying difference, was a constant challenge in our study. Moving beyond an essentializing set of binary categories (e.g., "insider" versus "outsider"; "traditional" versus "modernizing"; "rural" versus "urban") to a more inclusive, less tidy analysis was another challenge in our attempt to understand some of the complex subtleties of changing child-rearing at the grassroots level. Yet we were working within available spaces of representation, restricted further by time limitations and the material requirements of the funders of the study.

Thus from the more distanced view of analysis and reanalysis of data, through conversations by e-mail and fax, and through returning to various sites of the study, more spaces for possibility in understanding and meaning making have become available. We have all experienced the tensions between the practical sorts of recommendations made in this concluding chapter and in the "vision work" that also is needed in the face of economic injustice experienced as everyday life by many Kenyan families. We would want our collaborative project to convey the

Fig. 11.1    Visiting Researcher with Members of Oloototo Women's Group,
Narok District

spaces of possibility that were echoed time and time again in the stories and
aspirations of parents, grandparents, and children themselves. We also would
agree with the quote that began this chapter, that Kenyan families are "not mere
hapless victims of global change. They are proactive, resilient agents and creators
of change." Families and communities require support, partnership, empowerment, and our careful listening to better create narratives, programs, and spaces
of possibility for members of the "African village" to nurture their greatest wealth—
their children and grandchildren.

# Epilogue: Methodological Reflections

Much of qualitative research has reproduced, if contradiction-filled, a colonizing discourse of the "Other."

— Michelle Fine, *Working the Hyphens*

A critical aspect of this study was its emphasis on collaboration and its attempts at "decolonization." We would argue that such cross-cultural research must be based on mutually defined goals and the stated needs of indigenous people, and must actively seek to improve the conditions of people—in this case, children and their primary caregivers in Kenya. Throughout the process of completing this research, we noted the challenges as well as successes in collaborating across discipline, culture, nationality, and language differences. Another unique aspect of the study was the inclusion of a multigenerational sample. Children, parents, and grandparents were surveyed, including some group interviews that included at least three generations of women.

Given the limitations of a single visiting researcher on a tight time line and an underfunded research budget, extremely busy collaborators in national leadership positions, and the various cultural and linguistic differences bridged in this collaborative endeavor, we were delighted with the process and outcomes of the study. One of the most difficult aspects of authentic collaboration can be a sense of "losing control." For those of us with certain amounts of power and privilege, learning to listen, slow down, be patient, or move faster and keep up when needed, and otherwise adjust our personal preferences, habits, and cultural assumptions to the patterns and wishes of our collaborators proved a challenge. Being open and responsive to feedback from multiple perspectives, as well as being willing to give feedback when asked, and sharing both the work and credit of writing, editing, and disseminating the research findings all move us closer to authentically collaborative ethnographic projects. Such projects may be of benefit not only to the researchers and the scholarly "field," but to those with whom we would co-construct our studies and cultural learning.

These were some of the issues we confronted as a Kenyan-American collabora-tive team, in our effort to combine a contextualized, cultural analysis with narratives that challenge the false dichotomy of "fantasized gulf between the West and its Other" (Tsing, 1993, p. 13) and essentialized depictions of Kenyan child-rearing. We do, however, share Rosaldo's (1989) concern that self-positioning or intertextual narratives of researcher and researched have limitations, even as they are increasingly utilized in order to provide an authentic or a representative "voice" of socially excluded or marginalized persons. As Tsing (1993) puts it, drawing from Rosaldo's earlier work, "It would be easy and unfortunate to deintellectualize this literature as the recording of the essential experiences of Others. . . . Instead, the goal is to open new possibilities for thinking and writing: anyone can participate," (p. 14). We also would agree with Cameron McCarthy (1998, p. xi) that, "[W]e are living in a time of an extraordinary ethnicization of culture." That is, the distinctions between and among the various ethnic groups interviewed in the study also pro-vided for challenging cross-cultural encounters both in terms of the "foreigner" or visiting researcher and at times for the Kenyan collaborators.

Whether anyone could participate in this study remains an open question—gatekeepers to participation in the project included the local DICECE collaborators, the head teachers (headmasters), who typically provided the interview venue and often helped recruit parents and teachers, and occasionally a school inspector. The DICECE collaborators in some districts (e.g., Narok, Kericho, and Kiambu) were all male, although nine of the 21 local collaborators were female, including two programme officers, as were several of the head teachers and other local educational leaders who assisted in the study. Yet participants volunteered and came from a great variety of backgrounds and affinity groups, as can be seen in the description of the sample.

We tried to include in our study the "out-of-the-way places" about which Tsing (1993) so powerfully writes. Our participants included provisionally settled and semi-nomadic families—particularly among the Samburu and Maasai. In other ways, one could argue that life on plantations also was a "provisional settlement" and a precarious existence for families. There were a number of ways in which our study navigated physical and cultural spaces that call to mind the work of cultural geog-raphy theorists, particularly Soja (1996) and Sibley (1995) in their analysis of power, geographies of exclusion, and creation of a "thirdspace" of possibility for children. In particular, we listened for discourses and observed actions that transcended pre-vailing binary opposites of sufficiency/poverty, traditional/modern, and powerful/powerless, and we tried to engage in the complexity and contradictions within contemporary Kenyan family life. Spaces of possibility, or of transcendence, were not readily available narratives for many participants in this study, but they were clearly being created by local change agents engaged in child advocacy, whether they were parents, preschool teachers, local research collaborators, or leaders or self-help groups. Their visions for the future of children in their community were not limited by material conditions of poverty but appeared to be informed by a deep belief in the transcendence of human possibilities and resilience.

Since we were interested in better understanding the complex dynamics of how—and indeed whether—the village raised its youngest children, we often interviewed parents who shared affinity groups, including the same preschool, the same employer (especially in plantation samples), the same sublocation, the same clan or extended family, or the same neighborhood. If we were slightly overrepresented in male collaborators, we were underrepresented in male teachers and fathers—although this should come as no surprise to readers. Fewer fathers or grandfathers volunteered to take part in the study, and fewer than 1% of preschool teachers in Kenya are male.

Did we interrogate class and gender-related power differences between researchers and participants? Indirectly we did, particularly in discussions between the visiting researcher and female colleagues/collaborators; directly, we seldom examined these dynamics. At the end of a day "in the field," our conversations typically turned to family and work issues or other experiences of the researchers, often in response to "chords which had been struck" by the conversations with other parents during the course of the day. These discussions proved particularly helpful to the "outsider" of the group, as they often better illuminated or contextualized the concerns raised by parents and teachers during our more "formal" interviews. Another opportunity to discuss the content of the interviews came when local collaborators corrected the transcripts and occasionally added their reactions and interpretations.

## KENYAN COLLABORATORS' REFLECTIONS

As we were completing work on the book together in Nairobi in 1999, Margaret Kabiru and Anne Njenga reflected on their participation in the study and the collaborative process. Their narrative follows.

> This study was a learning experience for us and good training in listening to people, allowing them to express their deep concerns, dreams, and hopes for their children. As researchers, what we had to do was develop the interview questions that would serve as a catalyst for people to talk about their innermost feelings and perceptions. We also felt encouraged by the fact that a number of community members participating in the study proposed solutions that they could start working on at a grassroots level. People did not feel desperate and fully dependent on outside agents to come and solve all their child care problems. Through the interview discussions with local collaborators and the visiting researcher, participants saw some of the problems as challenges to

organize themselves, create community-based structures, and utilize the resources they already had.

Overall, we thought the research went on well, although we were dealing with varied cultures, languages, and geographical situations. The participation of DICECE officers from different districts was crucial to the success of the research. They understood the local culture and spoke the languages. In many cases, they were personally known to the communities in which they were conducting the interviews, and were trusted by the participants. The commitment of our U.S. collaborator was a big motivating factor in that she visited all the sites, was part of all the interviews, listened to the translations, transcribed all the interviews, and analyzed the data. This is something we admired, and we now try as much as possible to be fully involved in the process of data collection. We believe that Beth's participation was the greatest influence on the enthusiasm of the local collaborators and the quality of the outcome.

We also think that the long acquaintance of the collaborators and the elaborate discussions held during the preparatory period, during fieldwork and at the time of data analysis, were important to the success of the study. Since the collaborators each brought different professional training, including anthropology, psychology, and education, and had different cultural and linguistic backgrounds, it was necessary to have these discussions in order to ensure that the strengths, viewpoints, and expertise from all three of the collaborators were maximized. The discussions also helped us to understand one another and engage in more meaningful research. Even more consultations would be required with the communities to ensure that the local people contributed to identifying critical research questions that focused on issues important to their lives.

Since the methods we used were participatory and the participants and local collaborators reviewed important issues to local communities, such research should be followed with supporting intervention and empowerment. The communities can, as they indicated, cope with some of the needed changes to benefit children. In many cases, NGOs and government efforts may need to intervene to respond to the families' many suggestions for improving the lives or their families and their ability to provide for their youngest children. NGOs can assist by mobilizing additional funds, and the government provides the supporting environment, plus legal and regulatory mechanisms. The researchers can also provide follow-up expertise through training, consultation, and advocacy. Since the conclusion of this project, we have become more involved, as consultants and community-based researchers, in just this sort of work. We are no longer in Ministry of Education leadership positions and are now able to spend more time in the field—planning programs for teenage mothers and working on other grassroots initiatives focused on young children and their families.

# Appendix A
## List of Local Collaborators

*Embu District*
Mrs. Gladys Mugo, Programme Officer
Mr. S.A. Nyaga
Mr. J.J. Karunyu
Embu DICECE

*Kericho District*

Mr. Philip Cheruiyot
Mr. Ezekiel Mutai
Kericho DICECE

*Kiambu District*

Mr. Njuguna Wangunya, Programme Officer
Mr. Joseph Gitua
Kiambu DICECE

*Kisumu Municipality*

Mr. Hesbon Ogalo, Programme Officer
Kisumu DICECE
Mrs. Susan Ouko, Programme Officer
Kisumu MUCECE
Mr. Eliud Onyango Owino, School Inspector
Kisumu Municipality

*Machakos District*

Mr. Nelson Mulinge
Mrs. Jane Mutingau
Machakos DICECE

*Nairobi (CICECE)*

Mrs. Mary Ngugi, Acting Program Officer
Mrs. Lois Wanoike
Mrs. Bernadette Nzoi
CICECE

*Narok District*

Mr. David ole Sadera, Programme Officer
Mr. Paul Kishoyian
Mr. Santau Kamwaro
Narok DICECE

*Samburu District*

Mrs. Beatrice Waraba, Programme Officer
Mr. George Lenaseiyan
Mr. Peter ole Kashira
Samburu DICECE

# Appendix B
# Research Questions

The research questions had at their matrix issues identified at two Kenyan-U.S. early childhood collaborative seminars (in 1992 and 1994), as well as a review of Kenyan reports and other relevant literature. The research questions were modified several times, in close consultation with the NACECE (national) collaborators, including faxed feedback to the visiting researcher when the proposal was being developed. The research questions guided the design of the study and the process of data collection and analysis. They are later used, in chapters 3 through 10, to organize and interpret the findings.

The following questions guided the overall study and were systematically employed in both the analysis and discussion of the data and findings:

1. What are the major challenges/problems facing Kenyan families today, and what are the impacts of recent social and economic change on families, particularly on child-rearing practices?

   1a. How are families coping with these problems?

   1b. What are the effects of these problems on children's development and behavior in preschool and other contexts?

   1c. What are some of the good things the community has done/is doing for children and families?

2. How do families and community leaders describe changes in areas (or aspects of life) directly related to child-rearing, and what are the impacts of these changes on the nature and patterns of participation in early childhood programs, both formal and informal?

More specifically, what kinds of changes have been noted in the areas of: food, housing, cost of living, health, clothing, education, family size, social structures, services, and child-rearing practices?

3. What is the relevance of preschool education for families maintaining more traditional lifestyles (e.g., in pastoralist and rural communities)? What is the relevance in settings where mothers are more likely to be in paid labor (e.g., urban, peri-urban, and plantation settings)?

4. How do specific traditional practices and systems of support contribute to effective childrearing, and how can these be maintained in program planning?

5. How are parents, older siblings, and community members involved in early childhood programs and care (e.g., preschool, child health and nutrition, and under-three child care), and how could their involvement be strengthened?

6. What are typical child care arrangements for children under three, and what are family and community concerns about, and goals for, their care?

6a. What are family and community concerns and goals for child care?

6b. What are parental perceptions of ECCE, parenting, and aspirations for children, including children's own aspirations?

7. What types of intersectoral collaboration are working at the community level for children and families?

7a. How effective are such collaborations?

7b. How could they be strengthened or enhanced?

# Appendix C

# Research Methodology and
# Description of Procedures

## INTERVIEW AND FOCUS GROUP PROCEDURES

Interview questions were derived directly from the research questions in a collaborative process involving both the national collaborators and a majority of local collaborators. It was decided to use a semi-structured interview approach in the study and also to use focus groups to clarify issues raised in the Phase 1 interviews, as well as to elicit further data on intersectoral collaboration and community mobilization. In semi-structured interviews, we asked participants (across different groups) many of the same questions, but changed the order, wording, and sometimes the content of questions to fit each setting and situation, a common practice in qualitative research. We felt that we would get richer data and encourage personal narrative responses using a semi-structured and open-ended interview approach than using a structured orally administered survey, with closed-ended items. Aspects of the interview protocol, of course, were similar to a more close-ended survey—particularly the demographic information collected at the beginning of the discussion with participants.

Given the social, family, and group orientation of the cultures we were interviewing, we felt that small group interviews would be a good way to capture how each "village" or sublocation tended to raise its children. Local collaborators were encouraged to probe and seek further information and examples, as culturally appropriate, and the visiting researcher often sought additional information during the interview. Thus the interview protocols or questions served as a framework for eliciting the narratives of participants in the study.

The most "structured" or consistent interview across settings was the children's interview, as we were typically taking primary students out of their classes and wanted the interview to be as brief and nonstressful as possible. We continued to refine the wording so that a clear and an understandable series of questions was used. Children were typically interviewed in groups of four, with two boys and two girls. Interviews began by giving the children paper and crayons or markers and asking them to draw their family and some of their "favorite things." At the conclusion of the interview, children were given their drawing and a "*ziwadi kidogo*" (small thank-you gift for their participation), which included crayons or markers, a pencil and sharpener, stickers, a Kiswahili children's book, and some paper). Preschool teachers interviewed were given a packet of supplies and two or three children's books, and parents of under threes were given plastic blocks or snapping beads and a children's picture book (written in Kiswahili).

Glesne and Peshkin (1992) and many others advocate the use of semi-structured interview procedures, stating that, "Qualitative inquiry is evolutionary, with a problem statement, a design, interview questions and interpretations developing and changing along the way" (p. 6). Among the types of questions used in the interviews were "grand tour" questions (Fetterman, 1989, p. 51) and more specific questions. Survey or grand tour questions are "designed to elicit a broad picture of the participant's world and experience," and can be used to "focus and direct the investigation" (p. 51). Examples of grand tour questions used in this study included, "How has life changed in the past 10 to 15 years?" and "How have things changed regarding food . . . shelter . . . education . . . child-rearing, etc.?"

Specific questions focus on an area of "some significance" to both the researcher(s) and the participants. These questions tend to be used more frequently as the study progresses and tend to be adapted, as necessary, for each participant, and aim at eliciting information or stories that are specific to that participant's or family's experience and context (Fetterman, 1989). In our study, these questions tended to be follow-up questions or probes that were used to elicit specific examples or to pursue a topic of relevance to the local collaborators' work with preschools and families. For example, if growth monitoring was being practiced and promoted in a preschool, local collaborators were interested in how often growth monitoring was conducted, how many mothers brought babies, and what their observations about child health might be in that sublocation. We also probed during focus group interviews about the ways in which future early childhood development activities could be more successful and locally relevant.

## Data Analysis Approaches:
## A Recursive, Interpretive Process

Given the recursive nature of qualitative research, the analysis and identification of emergent themes is a constant process and not one that only takes place at the conclusion of the study. Given the diverse nature of the sample, both constant comparative and interpretive data analysis procedures were employed throughout the study, culminating in a shared data analysis process conducted by the three principal investigators (and co-authors). Constant comparative analysis utilizes an analytic inductive process of "scanning the data for categories of phenomena and for relationships among such categories, developing working typologies and hypotheses based upon an examination of initial cases, then modifying and refining them on the basis of subsequent cases (Goetz & LeCompte, 1984, pp. 179-180). According to Goetz and LeCompte, this method should "focus on identifying categories and on generating statements of relationships" (p. 182). Given the nature of the parent interviews, in particular, narrative analysis also was utilized in order to "uncover the common plots or themes in the data. [Such analysis is] carried out using hermeneutic techniques for noting underlying patterns across examples of stories" (Polkinghorne, 1988, p. 177).

Perhaps the data analysis approach that best describes the process followed by our research team is the interpretive one, which attempts to understand the personal worlds of people and "how they create and share meanings in their lives" (Rubin & Rubin, 1995, p. 35). They further note that, "Interpretive researchers try to elicit interviewees' views of their worlds, their work, and the events they have experienced or observed" (p. 35). This quote reflected our team's concern with trying to capture and accurately reflect the worldviews and meaning making of family life held by the participants in the study.

## Research Protocols/Instrumentation

Research protocols/interview questions (see Appendix B) were developed initially by the visiting researcher, based on the research questions, as well as on the partial replication of earlier studies done in Kenya on child-rearing, community involvement in ECCE, and the care of children under three. Interview questions were then revised by the national NACECE collaborators, along with the visiting researcher (in early September 1994).

Research protocols were further refined by the 17 DICECE, MUCECE (Municipal Centre for Early Childhood Education in Kisumu), and CICECE (City Centre for Early Childhood Education in Nairobi) collaborators, and two NACECE collaborators, who were participants during an orientation session held at NACECE in early November 1994. Much of the meeting was spent in small groups reviewing and revising the various interview protocols. Revisions included the addition of items considered locally relevant to the issues addressed in the study as well as the removal of any items that may have been culturally inappropriate (e.g., asking mothers how many children they had).

## Piloting of Instruments

Following the November orientation, each of the interview protocols (i.e., for parents, teachers, children, and community leaders) was piloted by at least two DICECEs during December 1994 and early January 1995. Pilot data and feedback on the proposed instruments and process were sent to the visiting researcher during January 1995. Feedback from the piloting exercise was then incorporated into the "final" version of the interview protocols, which were used in carrying out Phase 1 of the study in the eight participating districts.

## Language Translation and Vernacular Interpretation

The majority of interviews with parents, children, and some leaders and teachers was conducted in the mother tongue. When interviews utilized the mother tongue (a total of 10 local languages were used in the study) or Kiswahili, local DICECE collaborators provided translation, with one colleague facilitating the interview, the second colleague translating, and the principal investigator taking thorough notes in English upon translation. In cases where interviews were primarily in English, they were tape-recorded and transcribed from both the recording and from the interview notes/written transcript.

The local researchers proved very helpful when it came to data analysis and interpretation. Much of the description in the field data was a direct translation into English from the mother tongue (in fact, from 11 different languages in the larger study). To the visiting researcher, such a description could easily have been misinterpreted, misunderstood, or made no sense at all. The local researchers served as "culture brokers" or translators, they culture of the communities in the study.

Later, after transcripts had been typed, both local and national collaborators also were consulted on the meanings given to certain words and metaphors in mother tongue vernacular. For example, when asked what they liked most about being a parent, many mothers answered, "giving birth." It was later clarified that this meant the experience and recognition of being a mother, not the act of giving birth. Cultural metaphors (e.g., "the boy who broke the goat's leg" used in reference to a young man who had gotten a girl pregnant) and references to traditional stories and characters also needed further explanation in order to ascribe accurate meaning to the transcripts—particularly the interviews with grandmothers and elders.

The visiting researcher was directly involved in all aspects of these data collection activities, and all field and interview notes were transcribed in a timely manner (within a week to 10 days). A constant comparative method was applied, even while data was still being collected and a data coding system, based on the research questions, was developed collaboratively by the three principal collaborators. This scheme was used in conducting a thematic content analysis of all of the typed transcripts. This was done over a two-week period, part of which was in a "retreat" setting to minimize interruptions and to maximize opportunities to discuss emergent themes from the data with the national collaborators.

## Validation Procedures

Typed transcripts of all interviews were mailed promptly to the DICECE collaborators in each location for (1) an assessment of their accuracy and validity and clarification of information where questions arose during transcription, and (2) for an initial interpretation and identification of relevant themes. These themes, when identified, were often incorporated into the second research visit to that district, during the focus group discussions, and in any additional individual and small group interviews that were conducted. During Phase 2, emergent themes also were discussed with the full DICECE staff in some cases, often at both the beginning (as a briefing) and the end (as a debriefing) of the final visit to that district.

## Sample

The study was carried out in eight districts (listed in chapter 2), sampled to be representative of contrasting environments, socioeconomic backgrounds, lifestyles (including contrasting family/work participation patterns), resources, and approaches to ECCE. Purposive sampling was employed. Sites were chosen after consultation with the NACECE collaborators and were intended to complement ongoing NACECE research and programmatic projects in some areas (e.g., Samburu, Kericho, and Narok) and sample new communities in other areas (e.g., Kiambu, Kisumu, and Embu).

In each of the districts or municipalities sampled, a cross section of communities representing further contrasts in lifestyle, available resources, income, and other factors was selected by the local DICECE collaborators, based on criteria discussed at the orientation session. In most districts local samples included four to five distinct settings, locations, or communities. In urban areas, for example, all samples included slums and some peri-urban growth areas, as well as one or more working-class and middle-class settings. In rural areas, both high, medium, and marginally productive areas were sampled. In pastoralist communities, both traditional, semi-permanent, and more permanent mixed herding and cultivation areas were sampled. The attempt also was made, in recruiting the sample, to interview both trained and untrained teachers and to include some sites that were new to the DICECE staff.

## Sampling Procedure

After the participating districts were identified and the orientation was complete, local collaborators, generally two DICECE trainers, set about identifying the local sample. Consistent with purposive sampling, their guidelines were to select areas that offered contrasts, as discussed above, yet were not so far apart that travel time would become problematic (i.e., we wanted to have more time for interviewing and spend less time traveling to distant locations in the district).

Once such sublocations were identified, the local collaborators visited key sites and individuals (e.g., head teachers, TAC tutors or zonal preschool supervisors, and chiefs) to seek permission to conduct the study in their community. Head teachers and sometimes preschool teachers were instrumental in identifying participants for the study. DICECE trainers tended to select the preschools and teachers to be interviewed, although the majority of teachers interviewed in most districts were not DICECE trained. Responding to the request to interview parents, a number of head teachers recruited one or two members of the school committee to be part of the interview. As previously discussed, gender balance also was sought, where possible (e.g., our request was to interview both fathers and mothers and a smaller number of grandparents, if available).

## Participants in the Study

More detailed descriptive statistics of the sample from each district are included at the beginning of each chapter reporting district findings. By the end of Phase 1 (March 10, 1995), 384 participants (parents, teachers, children, grandparents, and some local leaders) had been interviewed. By the end of Phase 2 (May 19, 1995), 78 local leaders and professionals had participated in focus group interviews, brining the final number of participants in the study to 462. The breakdown of family member participants included 160 mothers and 32 fathers (or under threes), 25 grandmothers, 6 grandfathers, and 60 older siblings of children under three (30 boys and 30 girls, ages 8 to 12 years). Community members and ECCE professionals included 101 preschool teachers (100 female and 1 male), 36 community leaders (e.g., religious leaders, women's self-help group officers, local government and community leaders), and 42 other professionals working with families (e.g., social workers, community health professionals, head teachers/headmasters of primary schools, NGO program staff, and community volunteers).

Many of the teachers were interviewed individually, particularly in rural areas where only one teachers was employed and there were greater distances between preschools. Group interviews with teachers usually consisted of two to three teachers, but went as high as 20 in one district, becoming more of a focus group context. Parent interviews often included at least four or five parents, and at times also reached as high as 20. Where appropriate, individual data was collected (e.g., background, personal family information, education, role in the community, experiences with children, including child care arrangements, and individual aspirations for young children's future). Even in group interviews, every attempt was made to code interview notes so that individual responses were not "lost" in the discussion notes. At other times, group responses were recorded—particularly when the group reached consensus. Others times, particularly when there were differences of opinion (e.g., on the question "What is the best settings or environment for the care of children under three?"), individual opinions were recorded.

In Phase 2, which consisted of focus group interviews with community leaders and professionals, as described above, DICECE collaborators were requested to recruit between six to eight per group, with a maximum of 10 for optimal group dynamics and the opportunity to hear from everyone in the group. Many of the focus groups became larger, however, and in some cases busy people came and went during the interview, as they were called away. Avoiding market and meeting days (typically Monday for meetings of town councils and other local authorities) was considered when scheduling leader focus groups. It also should be noted that no interviews were scheduled for the last three weeks of April, when DICECE staff were heavily involved in residential teacher training activities with preschool teachers.

Due to transportation constraints, the visiting researcher was required to cancel or reschedule Phase 2 focus group visits in four districts. Two of these districts (Kisumu and Machakos) proceeded with previously scheduled focus groups and sent all participant background sheets and group interview notes to the researcher. These notes were transcribed and mailed back to the districts, along with all other Phase 2 notes.

Thus the Samburu and Kericho Districts are missing complete Phase 2 data. Since the principal investigator had participated in three community leader meetings in the Samburu District (Maralal and Baragoi) during October 1994, these notes and the related report were used to complete the "picture" for the Samburu District. Similarly, the Kericho District (DICECE) has been participating in an Aga Khan supported NACECE Under Three study and project, and related documents, including preliminary reports on this project, were used to complete the data for Kericho.

## OBSERVATION

Observations were informal and typically consisted of half-day observations in representative preschool and other child care settings in that location. Staying in small, local hotels and visiting the homes of local collaborators and their friends also provided opportunities to get a sense of the community through participant observation. Finally, the visiting researcher always attempted to make note of how children under age three were being cared for—and by whom. These observations were discussed with local collaborators and included in the field notes for later thematic analysis.

While in the Kericho District, the visiting researcher stayed on a tea plantation for one week and entered the culture of one of the research sites in more depth than elsewhere. Making multiple visits to other settings (e.g., a total of five visits to

Oloototo in the Narok District) and spending time in a cross section of homes also helped the researcher get a feel for daily life and for the ways in which young children were cared for in non-school settings.

## Triangulation and Trustworthiness Issues

Triangulation, or the use of multiple sources of data to corroborate findings and identify disconfirming cases, is widely accepted as a way of determining the "trustworthiness" of qualitative data. Fetterman (1989) writes that triangulation "is basic in ethnographic research . . . [and] is at the heart of ethnographic validity, testing one source against another to strip away alternative explanations and prove a hypothesis." We might disagree that hypotheses, or grounded inferences drawn from recurring themes in qualitative data, can ever be proven, but we do agree that triangulation is a basic requirement for qualitative inquiries. Goetz and LeCompte (1984) state that triangulation of participant information is an integral part of qualitative analysis, and that, "Guidance for this procedure comes from asking questions of participants as well as checking alternative groupings and orderings of specific events" (p. 172).

In our study, triangulation included interviewing different groups of stakeholders in early childhood education and care, as described earlier in the chapter. We compared the perspectives of parents, grandparents, teachers, children, and community leaders on a variety of issues related to the research questions guiding the study. Since local collaborators were also DICECE staff, their multiple roles at the district level included keeping a variety of preschool-related statistics and conducting needs assessments in local communities. Thus when teachers discussed a particular concern, enrollment pattern, or problem facing families, local collaborators could validate it or compare it to previous data they had collected. Since a large part of the DICECE role is in staff training (intensive in-service training of preschool teachers during the three-month-long school holidays) and follow-up technical assistance, they were quite aware of the issues facing families and teachers in their districts. Yet it was interesting to note that, in part due to the open-ended nature of the interview questions and the encouragement of stories, local collaborators sometimes expressed surprise or were impressed about the new information or issues that our discussions with parents and others revealed. As previously mentioned, local and national Kenyan collaborators also triangulated or clarified assumptions that the visiting researcher made concerning the interview responses and observations. This constant "cultural member checking" was considered critical to the validity of the study.

Another use of triangulation in the study was comparison of our emergent findings to previous research conducted by Kenyans (primarily through the Ministry of Education and NACECE) and various NGOs working with children and families in the districts sampled in our study. The fact that the two national collaborators on the study were also involved in, or at least aware of, other relevant internal studies of similar topics (e.g., care of under threes, child care conditions on plantations, and community mobilization) made such reports more accessible to the visiting researcher. In other words, preliminary reports or even raw data from other concurrent studies were made available and comparisons between emergent findings were possible. A thorough literature review also was undertaken by the visiting researcher, both before going to Kenya and upon her arrival. Thus a broad literature on child-rearing and early education in Kenya was accessed and used in the interpretation and analysis of narratives, field notes, and other data collected in this study.

Finally, the use of multiple data techniques was employed. Interview data could, therefore, be triangulated with repeated interviews in the settings sampled. Similarly, discussions with DICECE collaborators sometimes led to the addition of a question in the semi-structured interviews, which served to clarify an issue and further triangulate the findings. As previously discussed, all interview transcripts were typed and mailed to local collaborators, for both corrections and interpretation. Editing of the transcripts was detailed, with a number of corrections and clarifications typically made on each transcript returned to the visiting researcher. The response rate for this process was 100%, further strengthening the validity or trustworthiness of the findings.

## Challenges and Limitations

Major limitations, or parameters, of the study, not surprisingly, included time and money. The funding of the Fulbright research project was limited and the principal investigator was responsible for collecting all of the data, particularly during Phase 1. Use of research assistants could have increased the sample size, as well as the number of individual interviews carried out. This was not seen as a major limitation, however, as 462 participants had been part of small group interviews by the completion of data collection.

The initial support for the study, a 10-month Fulbright African Regional research grant, for example, included only $3,000 for research expenses. Only near the end of the study did the team secure further funding to compensate both NACECE and DICECE collaborators, as well as reimburse a number of expenses absorbed by the visiting researcher (e.g., all of the expenses associated with fieldwork, including petrol, compensation of drivers, food and accommodations for members of the research team, etc.). This, combined with a small number of available NACECE vehicles, meant that return travel to some districts was restricted. Again, collaboration played a key role, with local colleagues collecting focus group and other data when the visiting researcher could not obtain transportation to return to some of the more distant districts during the final phase of the project.

During Phase 2 of the study, a lack of NACECE drivers and high usage of the limited vehicles necessitated the cancellation of three of the researcher's return trips (i.e., to the Kisumu, Kericho, and Samburu Districts) and the shortening of another (Machakos). In two of these settings, Kisumu and Machakos, the local collaborators proceeded with already scheduled community focus groups. They were provided with the materials to be used, and they promptly mailed their interview notes, sign-in sheets, and any other data to the principal investigator. Thus data was complete for all participating districts except Kericho and Samburu. It was felt, however, that Samburu and Narok provided quite similar information, as did Kericho and Kiambu, so this was not considered a major limitation.

In terms of the national sample, two parts of Kenya that were beyond the scope of the study were the Coastal Province and Northeastern Province. Since these areas represent the highest percentage of Islamic families in Kenya, this can be viewed as a major limitation. The researcher had visited the Coastal Province (e.g., Kwale, Kilifi, Malindi, and Mombasa) on previous pilot research trips to Kenya, primarily to observe in Islamic integrated preschool sites, and had intended to sample the coast in the present study. Again, time and financial limitations necessitated that this more costly travel be scaled back.

Still another challenge, which was resolved in almost all cases, was the qualitative nature of the study, as well as the logistics involved in transcribing, coding, and analyzing interview data from over 460 participants in the study. Although our study was similar in many respects (particularly in topics addressed) to previous research undertaken by NACECE/DICECE, it was the first "qualitative inquiry" or microethno-graphic project, as such, to be completed through this national center. Descriptive quantitative studies had been more frequent, often employing orally administered survey instruments or questionnaires for later statistical analysis. Yet the reasons for keeping the questions open-ended and the dialogue flowing in group interviews became obvious to most of the collaborators—locally and nationally. Moving beyond a forced choice or other type of orally administered survey enabled more locally relevant themes to emerge, and the more conversational tone of the interviews likely contributed to the trustworthiness of the data, or its local validity.

# References

Adams, B., & Mburugu, E. (1994, June). *Women, work and child care*. Paper presented at the Second Early Childhood Collaboration in Training Seminar, Nairobi, Kenya.

Adams, D. (1983). Child care in Kenya. *Day Care and Early Education*, Spring, 11–15.

Adams, D. & Kabiru, M. (1995). *Training for early childhood care and education services in Kenya*. Final report for World Bank consultancy. Nairobi: National Centre for Early Childhood Education.

Adams. D. & Swadener, B. B. (in press). Early childhood education and teacher development in Kenya: Lessons learned, *Child and Youth Care Forum*.

Aptekar, L. (1994). Street children in the developing world: A review of their condition. *Cross-cultural Research, 28* (3), 195–224.

Bali, S., & Kabiru, M. (1992). Needs of children under three in Kenya. *Building on People's Strengths Seminar Report*. Nairobi: National Centre for Early Childhood Education.

Bernard van Leer Foundation (1994). *Building on people's strengths: Early childhood in Africa*. The Hague (Netherlands): Bernard van Leer Foundation.

Bledsoe, C. H. (1980). *Women and marriage in Kpelle society*. Stanford: Stanford University Press.

Boost ailing public health care system. (1999, May 28). *Daily Nation* [Editorial], p. 6.

Bradshaw, Y. W., Noonan, R., Gash, L., & Sershen, C. B. (1993). Borrowing against the future: Children and Third World indebtedness. *Social Forces, 71* (3), 629–656.

Dosnajh, J. S., & Ghuman, P. (1997). Child-rearing practices of two generations of Punjabi parents. *Children and Society, 11* (1), 29–43.

*Embu: District development plan, 1994–96*. Nairobi: Ministry of Planning and National Development.

*Embu District socio-cultural profile*. Government of Kenya: Ministry of Planning and National Development and the Institute of African Studies, University of Nairobi (G. S. Were, Project Director).

Fetterman, D. M. (1989). *Ethnography: Step by step*. Newbury Park, CA: Sage.

Fine, M. (1994). Working the hyphens: Reinventing self and other in qualitative research. In N. K. Denzin & Y. S. Lincoln (Eds.), *Handbook of qualitative research*. Thousand Oaks, CA: Sage.

Fratkin, E. M. (1986). Age-sets, households and the organization of pastoral production: The Ariaal, Samburu, and Rendille of Northern Kenya. *Research in Economic Anthropology, 7.*

Gakuru, O. N. (1992). *Class and pre-school education in Kenya.* Ph.D. dissertation, University of Nairobi.

———. (1995, December). Early childhood care and development: Formative research and quality in the programme for children in Kenya. Paper presented to the Environment of the Child Conference, organized by the Bernard van Leer Foundation, the Hague.

Gakuru, O., & Koech, B. (1995). *The experiences of the young children: A contextualized case study of early childhood care and education in Kenya.* Nairobi: KIE/NACECE.

Gakuru, O. N., Koech, B. G., & Nduti, R. (1995). *Early childhood development services for the under 3 year old children.* World Bank Report. Nairobi: The World Bank.

Gatheru, M. (1981). *Child of two worlds.* London: Heinemann Educational Books.

Gibson, M. A. (1985). Collaborative educational ethnography: Problems and profits. *Anthropology & Education Quarterly, 16,* 124–148.

Glaser, B. G., & Strauss, A. L. (1967). *The discovery of grounded theory: Strategies for qualitative research.* New York: Aldine De Gruyter.

Glesne, C., & Peshkin, A. (1992). *Becoming qualitative researchers: An introduction.* White Plains, NY: Longman.

Goetz, J. P., & LeCompte, M. D. (1984). *Ethnography and qualitative design in educational research.* Orlando, FL: Academic Press.

Government of Kenya and UNICEF. (1998). *The situation of women and children in Kenya.* Nairobi: GOK & UNICEF.

Grant, J. (1993). *The State of the World's Children Report.* New York: UNICEF.

Hancock, G. (1989). *Lords of poverty.* London: Macmillan.

Harkness, S., & Super, C. (1985). The cultural context of gender segregation in children's peer groups. *Child Development, 56,* 219–224.

———. (1987). Fertility change, child survival, and child development: Observations on a rural Kenyan community. In N. Scheper-Hughes (Ed.). *Child survival: Anthyropological perspectives on the treatment and maltreatment of children,* 59–70. Boston: D. Reidel.

———. (1992). Shared child care in East Africa: Sociocultural origins and developmental consequences. In M.E. Lamb, K.J. Sternberg, C. Hwang, & A. Broberg (Eds.), *Child care in context: Cross-cultural perspectives.* Hillsdale, NJ: Lawrence Erlbaum Associates.

Harrison, F. V. (Ed.). (1991). *Decolonizing anthropology: Moving further toward an anthropology for liberation.* Washington, DC: Association for Black Anthropologists, American Anthropological Association.

Herzog, J. A. (1969). *A survey of parents of nursery centre children in four communities in Kenya.* Nairobi: Nairobi University.

Institute of African Studies (1986). *Samburu District Socio-Cultural Profile.* Nairobi: University of Nairobi and Ministry of Planning and National Development.

Jamal, V., & Weeks, J. (1988). The vanishing rural-urban gap in sub-Saharan Africa. *International labour review, 127* (3).

Kabiru, M. (1993). *Early childhood care and development: A Kenyan experience.* Nairobi: UNICEF & KIE/NACECE.

Kabiru, M. (1994). Putting the young child first in the reconstruction of our nation. *Proceedings of the launching congress of the National Organisation for Early Childhood Educare.* March 23–25. Nairobi: KIE/NACECE.

Kabiru, M., & Njenga, A. (1997). *Teenage motherhood: Children raising children (A report of a baseline and needs assessment survey carried out in Mumbuni and Mjini locations in Machakos district)*. Nairobi: Mwana Mwende Project.

———. (1999). *Gender socialization in early childhood: A study carried out in Mung'ala sub-location, Machakos District*. Nairobi: Mwana Mwende Project.

Kabiru, M., Njenga, A., & Mutua, J. (1998). *Policy and programming in early childhood development in Africa*. Nairobi: Early Childhood Development Network for Africa Secretariat. (Proceedings from workshop held in Cape Town, December 1–3, 1997).

Kamerman, S. B. (1989). An international overview of preschool programs. *Phi Delta Kappan, 71* (2), 135–137.

Kenyatta, J. (1938). *Facing Mount Kenya: The tribal life of the Gikuyu*. Nairobi: Heinemann Educational Books.

*Kericho: District development plan, 1994–96*. Nairobi: Republic of Kenya, Ministry of Planning and National Development.

———. Nairobi: Republic of Kenya, Ministry of Planning and National Development.

Kilbride, P., & Kilbride, J. (1990). *Changing family life in East Africa: Women and children at risk*. University Park, PA: The Pennsylvania State University Press.

Kilbride, P., & Njeru, E. (1995, October). *An anthropological perspective on social understanding of street children in Nairobi, Kenya*. Paper presented at Pan African Association of Anthropology, Nairobi, Kenya.

Kilbride, P., Suda, C., Njeru, E., & Kariuki, P. (2000). *Street children in Kenya: Voices of children in search of a childhood*. Westport, CT: Bergin & Garvey.

Kilbride, P. L. (1986). Cultural persistence and socio-economic change among the Abaluyia: Some modern problems in patterns of child care. *Journal of Eastern African Research and Development, 16*, 35–52. Nairobi: Gideon S. Were Press.

———. (1996, November). *Patterns of infant care among Nairobi street girls*. Paper presented at the African Studies Association Meetings, San Francisco.

Kilbride, P. L. (1996, November). *Patterns of infant care among Nairobi street girls*. Paper presented at the African Studies Association Meetings, San Francisco.

Kilbride, P. L., & Kilbride, J. C. (1997). Stigma, role overload, and delocalization among contemporary Kenyan women. In T. S. Weisner, C. Bradley, & P. L. Kilbride (Eds.), *African families and the crisis of social change*. Westport, CT: Bergin & Garvey.

Kipkorir, L. (1994). *Child care: Mothers' Dilemma*. Nairobi: Kenya Institute of Education.

Kipkorir, L., Mwaura, P., Kabiru, M., & Njenga, A. (1988). Innovation in early childhood education and care: The Kenya experience. *Early Childhood Education in Kenya: Implications for Policy and Practice*. Nairobi: Ministry of Education.

*Kisumu: District development plan, 1994–96*. Nairobi: Republic of Kenya, Ministry of Planning and National Development.

Kreimer, A., & Munasinghe, M. (1992). Environmental management and urban vulnerability. *World Bank News, XI* (40), p. 5. Washington, DC: World Bank.

Lefebre, H. (1991). *The production of space*. Oxford, UK: Blackwell Publishers.

Levine, R. A., Dixon, S. E., Levine, S., Richman, A., Leiderman, P. H., Keefer, C. H., & Brazelton, T. B. (1994). *Child care and culture: Lessons from Africa*. Cambridge: Cambridge University Press.

Levine, R. A., & Levine, S. E. (1974). Parental goals: A cross-cultural view. *Teachers College Record, 76*, 226–239.

————. (1988). Parental strategies of the Gusii of Kenya. *New Directions for Child Development*, 40, 27–35.

Linde, C. (1993). *Life stories: The creation of coherence*. New York: Oxford Press.

Lubeck, S. (1987). Nested contexts. In L. Weis (Ed.), *Class, race and gender in American education*. Albany: State University of New York Press.

*Machakos: District development plan, 1994–96*. Nairobi: Ministry of Planning and National Development.

*Machakos District socio-cultural profile*. (1987). Nairobi: Government of Kenya, Ministry of Economic Planning and National Development and The Institute of African Studies, University of Nairobi (G.S. Were, Project Director).

Maillu, D. G. (1986). *The ayah*. Nairobi: East African Educational Publishers Ltd.

Maliyamkono, T. L., & Bagachwa, M. (1990). *The second economy in Tanzania*. London: James Currey.

Mauthner, M. (1997). Methodological aspects of collecting data from children: Lessons from three research projects. *Children and Society*, 11 (1), 16–28.

Mburugu, K. G. (1994). *Family child care as one solution for the care of under threes*. A paper presented at the Second Collaborative Early Childhood Training Seminar, Nairobi: NACECE.

McCarthy, C. (1998). *The uses of culture: Education and the limits of ethnic affiliation*. New York: Routledge.

Mettelin, P. (1987). Activities informelles en Afrique Noire: Les realities urbaines. *Canadian Journal of Developmental Studies*, 8 (1) (as cited in Wallman, 1996).

Mikell, G. (1997). *African feminism: The politics of survival in Sub-Saharan Africa*. Philadelphia: University of Pennsylvania Press.

Ministry of Education and Human Resource Development (MOEHRD) (1994). Preschool enrollment report. Nairobi: MOEHRD.

Mukui, J. T., & Mwaniki, J. A. (1995). *Survey of early childhood care and development*. Nairobi, Kenya: Ministry of Education and the World Bank.

Myers, R. (1992). *The twelve who survive: Strengthening programmes for early childhood development in the third world*. New York: Routledge, in cooperation with UNESCO.

NACECE. (1993). Partnership and networking in the care and development of under threes. Proceedings of Nyeri (October, 1993) conference. Nairobi: KIE/NACECE.

NACECE (1994). *Nyeri Conference on Under Threes Report*. Nairobi: KIE/NACECE.

NACECE/Aga Khan Foundation. (1994). *Survey on the Care of Under Threes*. Nairobi: KIE/NACECE.

*NACECE News*. (1995). NACECE and DICECE mark 10th anniversary: Coordinators reflect on programme growth. Nairobi: NACECE, 4–9.

NACECE/UNICEF. (1995). *Survey on under threes*. (Report). Nairobi: KIE/NACECE.

*Nairobi: District development plan, 1994–96*. Nairobi: Republic of Kenya, Ministry of Planning and National Development.

*Narok District socio-cultural profile*. (1986). Nairobi: Government of Kenya, Ministry of Planning and National Development and the Institute of African Studies, University of Nairobi (G. S. Were, Project Director).

Nyarango, P. M. (1994). *Sunset in Africa: Childhood memories*. Nairobi: East African Educational Publishers.

Nyere, J. K. (1967). *Education for self-reliance*. Dar-es-Salaam: Oxford University Press.

Polakow, V. (1993). *Lives on the edge: Single mothers and their children in the other America*. Chicago: University of Chicago Press.

Polkinghorne, D. E. (1988). *Narrative knowing and the human sciences*. Albany, NY: State University of New York Press.

Reed-Danahay, D. (1997). (Ed.). *Auto/ethnography: Rewriting the self and the social*. New York: Berg.

Rigby, P. (1985). *Persistent pastoralists: Nomadic societies in transition*. London: Zed Books.

Rosaldo, R. (1989). *Culture and truth: The remaking of social analysis*. Boston: Beacon Press.

Rubin, H. J., & Rubin, I. S. (1995). *Qualitative interviewing: The art of hearing data*. Thousand Oaks, CA: Sage.

*Samburu: District development plan, 1994–1996*. Nairobi: Ministry of Planning and National Development.

*Samburu District socio-cultural profile*. (1986). Nairobi: Government of Kenya, Ministry of Planning and National Development and the Institute of African Studies, University of Nairobi (B. E. Kipkorir, Project Director).

Sibley, D. (1995). *Geographies of exclusion: Society and difference in the West*. London: Routledge.

Smith, L. T. (1999). *Decolonizing methodologies: Research and indigenous peoples*. London: Zed Books.

Soja, E. W. (1996). *Thirdspace: Journeys to Los Angeles and other real-and-imagined places*. Oxford, UK: Blackwell Publishers.

Spencer, P. (1973). *Nomads in alliance: Symbiosis and growth among the Redille and Samburu of Kenya*. London: Oxford University Press.

Stren, R., & White, R. (Eds.). (1989). *African cities in crisis*. Boulder, CO: Westview Press.

Swadener, B. B. (1998). Research as praxis: Unlearning oppression and research agendas. In C.A. Grant (Ed.), *Multicultural research: A reflective engagement with race, class, gender and sexual orientation*. New York: Falmer Press.

Swadener, B. B. & Bloch, M. N. (1997). Children, families, and change: Cross-national perspectives in early childhood contexts. *Early Education and Development, 8* (3), 207–218.

Swadener, E. B., Kabiru, M., & Njenga, A. (1995). *Final report of client consultation study: Changing child-rearing and community mobilization for young children and families in Kenya*. Nairobi, Kenya: Ministry of Education, 232 pp.

Swadener, E. B., Kabiru, M., & Njenga, A. (1997). Does the village still raise the child?: A collaborative study of changing childrearing and community mobilization in Kenya. *Early Education and Development, 8* (3), 285–306.

Swadener, B. B., & Marsh, M. M. (1994). Early childhood teacher education in Kenya, Senegal, and the Gambia: Contrasts, common themes, and collaborations. In C. Sunal (Ed.)., *Teacher education in the Caribbean and Africa: Points of contact*. Tuscaloosa: University of Alabama Monograph Series.

Swadener, B. B., & Mutua, K. N. (in press). Mapping terrains of "homelessness" in postcolonial Kenya. In C. Guillean & V. Polakow (eds.). *Homelessness in international context*. Greenwood Press.

Tronick, E. Z., Morelli, G. A., & Winn, S. (1987). Multiple caretaking of Efe infants. *American Anthropologist, 89*, 96–106.

Tsing, A.L. (1993). *In the realm of the Diamond Queen: Marginality in an out-of-the-way place*. Princeton, NJ: Princeton University Press.

UNICEF. (1997). *The progress of nations*. New York: The United Nations Children's Fund.

———. (1992). *The state of the world's children*. New York: The United Nations Children's Fund.

United Nations. (1989). *Prospects of world urbanization*. New York: United Nations.

United States Bureau of the Census (1996). *Report on AIDS/HIV Worldwide.* Washington, D.C.: U.S. Bureau of the Census.

Varkevisser, D. (1973). *Socialization in a changing society: Sukema childhood in rural and urban Mwanza, Tanzania.* Den Haag: Center for the Study of Education in Changing Societies.

Wallman, S. (1996). *Kampala women getting by: Wellbeing in the time of AIDS.* London: James Currey Ltd. (and Kampala: Fountain Publishers).

Walton, J., & Ragin, C. (1990). Global and national sources of political protest: Third world responses to the dept crisis. *American Sociological Review, 55,* 876–890.

Wandibba, S. (1997). Changing roles in the Bukusu family. In T. S. Weisner, C. Bradley, & P. L. Kilbride (Eds.), *African families and the crisis of social change.* Westport, CT: Bergin & Garvey.

Weisner, T. S. (1993). Siblings in cultural place: Ethnographic and ecocultural perspectives on siblings of developmentally delayed children. In Z. Stoneman and P. Berman (Eds.), *Siblings of individuals with mental retardation, physical disabilities, and chronic illness* (pp. 51–83). Baltimore: Brooks.

Weisner, T. S., Bradley, C., & Kilbride, P. L. (1997). *African families and the crisis of social change.* Westport, CT: Bergin & Garvey.

White, M. A., & Epston, D. (1990). *Narrative means to therapeutic ends.* New York: Norton.

Whiting, B., & Whiting, J. (1997). Foreword. In T. S. Weisner, C. Bradley, & P. L. Kilbride (Eds.), *African families and the crisis of social change* (pp. xiii–xviii). Westport, CT: Bergin & Garvey.

Whiting, B. B. (1977). Changing lifestyles in Kenya. *Daedalus, 106* (2), 211–225.

Whiting, B. B. (1996). The effect of social change on concepts of good child and good mothering: A study of families in Kenya. *Ethos, 24,* 3–35.

Whiting, B. B., & Edwards, P. (1988). *Children of different worlds: The formation of social behavior.* Cambridge, MA: Harvard University Press.

Willinsky, J. (1998). *Learning to divide the world: Education at Empire's end.* Minneapolis: University of Minnesota Press.

Woodhead, M. (1996). *In search of the rainbow.* The Hague, Netherlands: Bernard van Leer Foundation.

# Index

Adams, B., 32, 269
Aga Khan Foundation, 27, 38, 110, 137
Aga Khan Hospital, 247
Agriculture: cash crops, 51, 62, 113, 142, 172, 193; dairy farming, 113, 143; dependence on, 169, 175; in Kiambu District, 142; kitchen gardens, 51; mixed, 81–82, 143; in Narok District, 49, 50, 63; in Samburu District, 81–82; sharecropping in, 172; subsistence farming, 23, 110, 169; women and, 23
AIDS crisis, 17, 21, 221, 223, 228, 230, 240, 254
Aptekar, L., 18
Aspirations: children's, 71, 135, 185; parents', 72, 91, 134–135, 155–156, 184, 205, 252
*Ayahs,* 28, 249, 255, 257; characteristics of, 28–29; on plantations, 110; responsibilities of, 30

Bali, S., 23, 31, 32
Bamako Initiative, 259, 282
Bernard van Leer Foundation, 26, 27, 38
Bledsoe, C. H., 18
Bradley, C., 21
Bradshaw, Y. W., 20
Breastfeeding, 24, 69, 180, 201, 271; child spacing and, 94; family planning and, 94; length of, 68, 240; in Maasai group, 57; time for, 117; at weighing stations, 150

Change, social/economic, 2, 3; effect on children, 178–182, 198–202, 206–207, 225, 243; effect on families, 266–269; in Embu District, 178–182; focus groups responses, 58; global context of, 18–19; impact on children, 19; intergenerational continuities and, 22; in Kericho District, 122–126; in Kiambu District, 146–153; in Kisumu Municipality, 245–248; in Machakos District, 198–202; management responses to, 158–159; in Nairobi, 226–230; in Narok District, 58–63; parental responses, 58, 226–230; in Samburu District, 92–95; teacher responses, 95, 226–230
Childbirth: at home, 68; in hospital, 68, 179, 200; maternity leave and, 148, 150, 283; spacing, 244; traditional, 60; traditional birth attendants at, 93, 131, 247
Child care: *ayahs* and, 28, 30; children's responses, 102–103, 158; family change and, 186–190; gender and, 70, 111, 117, 131; goals of, 157,

Child care *(continued)*
234–235; in home, 30, 69, 73, 89,
154, 182–183, 204, 282; in Kericho
District, 130–131; in Kiambu
District, 154–155; loss of support
systems in, 23; Maasai group, 54; in
Narok District, 67–73; parental
responses, 131–133; parents' role in,
31; on plantations, 130–131, 154–155;
in Samburu District, 89–90, 102–103;
shared, 23; by siblings, 18, 53, 66–67,
102–103, 110, 111, 130–131, 154,
158–159, 184–185, 209; for under
threes, 131–137, 157, 189–190, 203–
204, 208, 233–235, 249–250;
traditional, 8; traditional support
systems for, 54
Child Care International, 57, 74, 75
Child labor, 19, 24, 110
Child-rearing. *See also* Child care; as
collective activity, 18; community
leader responses, 257–258; cultural
assumptions in, 3; in Embu District,
180–182; hygiene practices, 62; in
Kericho District, 126; in Kiambu
District, 150; in Kisumu Municipality,
257–258; in Machakos District, 200–
201; in Nairobi, 230; in Narok
District, 62–63, 64–65, 271; pattern
changes, 8; on plantations, 126; in
Samburu District, 94, 271; for single
parents, 110, 125, 149, 150, 224;
social/economic changes and, 2, 178–
182, 198–202, 226–230, 245–248;
teacher responses, 65; traditional
practice in, 18, 24, 57, 64–65, 128,
231–232, 248, 271
Children: aspirations of, 71, 135, 185;
daily activities, 53, 54, 66–67, 156,
188–189, 207; discipline of, 62, 120,
272; effect of changes on, 178–182;
effect of problems on, 121–122, 198–
202, 206–207, 225, 243; emotional
well-being and, 121; family challenge
effects, 56–57, 146, 225, 243, 248–
249; housing effects, 255; hunger
effects, 96; "in debt," 20; memories of
preschool, 71, 104–105, 133–134,
159, 185, 210; neglect of, 111, 120,
121, 146, 225; parental aspirations for,

72, 91, 134–135, 155–156, 184, 205,
252; rights of, 19; in traditional/
pastoralist groups, 53, 54
Children's Trust, 282
Christian Children's Fund, 87, 95, 96,
209
Class: gaps, 201; intersections of, 8;
middle, 176, 226, 246; working, 215
Clinton, Bill, 2
Clinton, Hillary Rodham, 2
Clothing issues: changes in, 94; in
Kericho District, 119, 124; in Narok
District, 57; parental responses, 60
Colonization, 1, 5
Community: feeding programs, 18, 29,
57, 137, 147, 149, 157, 271;
involvement in education, 128–130,
153–154, 182–183, 232–233;
mobilization, 27–29, 87, 95, 169–170,
254; parental roles in, 144, 174, 195,
221; participation, 24, 153–154;
positive actions by, 57–58, 87–88,
122, 153–154, 164–165, 177–178,
198, 226, 243–244, 259–260; rural,
169; services, 63, 68, 125–126, 224,
258, 268; supportive roles for, 31–32
Compassion International, 174
Coping skills: parental responses, 87,
122, 152–153, 187–188, 197–198,
206, 225–226; teacher responses, 56,
152–153, 187, 206
Cost-of-living, 266; birthrates and, 94; in
Embu District, 177; family size and,
229; in Kericho District, 124; in
Kisumu Municipality, 246; in Nairobi,
227–228; in Narok District, 59;
parental responses to, 59, 87, 124,
223, 227–228, 246; in Samburu
District, 93
Crime, 201; gangs and, 268; urban, 268
Cultural: activities, 32; diversity, 126;
heterogeneity, 9; relevance, 64, 88, 97,
110, 118, 126–128, 156, 202–203,
230–231, 251; socialization, 7; taboos,
271; traditions, 31; transmission, 272
Culture: custodianship of, 31–32; home,
128, 155–156, 207, 231; local, 126;
maintenance of, 7, 83, 110, 126–128,
272; of sponsored development, 22;
teacher responses, 64; traditional, 2

Debt crises, 1

Decolonization: donor-recipient dynamics, 5; missionary-convert issues, 5; national/local collaborators and, 5; power/privilege patterns and, 6; of research, 4–8, 35–37, 287

Delocalization, 1

Demographics: Embu District, 171–173; Kericho District, 113–114; Kiambu District, 141–143; Kisumu Municipality, 239–241; Machakos District, 193–195; Narok District, 49–51; Samburu District, 79–84

DICECE. *See* District Centres for Early Childhood Education

Disabilities, 21, 205

Disease: among Maasai group, 51, 55; animal, 86; diarrheal, 19, 21, 55, 114, 228, 268; eye, 51, 55; hepatitis, 21; malaria, 21, 51, 55, 114, 119, 132, 179, 197; respiratory, 21, 51, 114, 119, 125, 132, 197, 223, 228; skin, 51, 55, 114, 119, 197, 228; typhus, 21

Dislocalization, 23

District Centres for Early Childhood Education, 26, 38, 52, 137, 143, 163, 169, 170, 173, 174, 196, 242, 265, 283

Dole, Bob, 2

Drought, 50–51, 79, 175, 177, 178, 197

Early childhood care and education. *See also* Education; background in Kenya, 17–34; community collaboration in, 27–29; community contributions to, 276–277; community involvement in, 65–67, 153–154, 182–183, 232–233; community perceptions of, 270–273; constraints to, 279–281; family involvement in, 65–67, 97–99, 128–130, 187–188, 232–233, 244; feeding programs, 18, 29, 57.18, 137, 147, 149, 157, 271; historical contexts, 22–23; policy implications, 281–284; program planning issues, 270; recommendations for, 31–32, 165, 277–278; resources needed, 136–137; role in cultural transmission/maintenance, 272; sustainability of, 270; in traditional/pastoral settings, 275

ECCE. *See* Early childhood care and education

Economy: cash, 23, 24, 169; global, 17; informal, 216, 240; market, 19, 175; political, 23; wage, 24

Education. *See also* Early childhood care and education; assimilationist function of, 126; attitude toward, 61; community involvement in, 128–130, 153–154, 182–183, 232–233; community leader responses, 257–258; community mobilization in, 27–29; costs, 125; in Embu District, 179; family involvement in, 128–130, 187–188, 232–233, 244; formal, 51; gender and, 69, 70, 179, 186, 195, 241; in Kericho District, 125, 128–130; in Kisumu Municipality, 257–258; management responses, 160, 161; marriage and, 61; mission programs, 24; in Nairobi, 229; in Narok District, 51, 61; national curriculum, 257; parental awareness of, 61, 87, 179; parental levels of, 115; parental responses, 148–149, 200, 229; pastoralist participation in, 47; relevance of, 82, 88, 97, 126–128, 156, 188–189, 202–203, 230–231, 251; segregated, 24; teacher, 52; technology in, 258; Western, 62, 93

Educational involvement: children's responses, 66–67; parental responses, 65–66, 97–98, 153–154, 182–183, 187–188, 232–233, 244; teacher responses, 66, 97, 98, 187, 232–233

Elders: community roles, 195; contact with, 259; Maasai, 57; respect for, 32, 201

Embu District, 171–191; child care in, 180–182, 184–190; Christian Community Services in, 174; Community Welfare Projects Committee in, 174; cooking demonstrations in, 170, 173, 181*fig,* 271; cost-of-living in, 177; demographics, 171–173; family challenges in, 176–177, 183–184; family size in, 179; food issues in, 178; forestry in, 172; health care in, 179; herding in, 172; housing in, 178; intersectoral collaboration in, 185–186;

Embu District *(continued)*
and area, 171; malnutrition/
undernutrition in, 179; market centers
in, 173; parental aspirations for
children, 184; parent contributions to
education, 177–178; population, 171,
172, 173; positive community actions,
177–178; preschools in, 172*fig;*
research sample, 174–176; social
structure in, 180; urbanization in,
176; work in, 174

Family: changes in, 55–56, 231–231,
269; extended, 8, 18, 82, 110, 169,
231, 248; involvement in education,
128–130, 187–188, 244; Maasai
structures, 8; nuclear, 8, 62, 82, 169,
231, 248, 258; planning, 61, 94, 125,
150, 162, 194, 229, 244; policy, 270;
problems facing, 186–190, 242–244;
Samburu structures, 8; single parent,
55, 110, 125, 149, 150, 216, 224,
269; size, 60–61, 94, 125, 150, 162,
179, 200, 229; spacing, 244; structure
patterns, 8; traditional, 8, 64, 202–
203; urban, 216
Family challenges: in Embu District,
176–177; focus group responses, 55;
food issues, 86, 198–199, 227, 245;
in Kericho District, 119–120; in
Kiambu District, 145–146; lack of
time, 120, 126, 201; in Machakos
District, 197–198; in Narok District,
54–58; parental responses, 54, 55,
145–146, 176–177; in Samburu
District, 86–92; teacher responses, 56,
120–126
Famine, 19, 50–51, 79
Feeding programs, 137, 147, 149, 157,
271; community based, 29, 57;
funding for, 18; in Kericho District,
127–128; in Narok District, 57
Feminism, African, 266
Fertility ceremonies, 7
Fine, Michelle, 3, 287
Focus group responses: child-rearing,
257–258; community services, 258; on
family challenges, 55; health care, 60,
164, 253–254; housing, 254–255; on
intersectoral collaboration, 74–75; in

Kiambu District, 164; in Narok
District, 52; preschool participation,
70, 71; social/economic change, 58
Food issues, 267; community leader
responses, 256–257; costs, 123, 227,
245, 256; dietary changes, 58–59; in
Embu District, 178; in Kericho
District, 123; in Kiambu District,
146–147; in Kisumu Municipality,
245, 256–257; for Maasai group, 54;
in Machakos District, 198–199;
management responses, 160, 162; in
Nairobi, 227; in Narok District, 56,
58–59; parental responses, 123,
146–147, 198–199, 227, 245; on
plantations, 146–147; in Samburu
District, 86, 92; scarcity, 92;
security, 114, 267; teacher responses,
120–121

Gakuru, O. N., 8, 20, 21, 22, 30, 32,
271
Gatheru, M., 32
Gender, 8; appropriateness, 89–90; child
care and, 111, 131; education and,
179, 186, 195, 241; enrollment in
school and, 29; equity, 32; marriage
and, 61; preschool participation and,
69, 70; status, 241
Glaser, B. G., 37
Grandmothers, 257; absence of on
plantations, 115, 131; child care by,
67, 73; cultural transmission and, 54;
daily activities, 53, 54, 57, 62;
Maasai, 53, 54, 57; traditional care by,
271, 272
Grant, James, 17, 20
Growth monitoring programs, 29, 122,
132, 170; in Narok District, 58; in
Samburu District, 93

Hancock, G., 20
*Harambee,* 22, 24–26, 27, 30, 75, 85, 95,
143, 177, 244
Harkness, S., 32
Harrison, F. V., 4
Health care: antenatal clinics, 62, 93,
179; availability of, 114; clinic visits,
68; community leader responses,
253–254; distance to, 86; in Embu

District, 179; focus group responses, 60; immunization, 19; in Kericho District, 124; in Kiambu District, 147–148; in Kisumu Municipality, 247–248, 253–254; in Machakos District, 199; management responses, 161, 162; mobile clinics, 62, 86, 93; in Nairobi, 220, 228; in Narok District, 50, 55, 56, 57, 59–60, 68; oral rehydration therapy, 194*fig,* 199, 271; parental responses, 59–60, 93, 124, 199, 228, 247; on plantations, 111–112, 147–148; poverty and, 19; preventive, 271; traditional medicine, 50

Herzog, J. A., 25

Homelessness, 18, 19

Housing: access to, 268; changes in, 123; community leader responses, 254–255; constraints, 267–269; demands for, 255; effect on children, 255; in Embu District, 178; in Kericho District, 123; in Kiambu District, 147; in Kisumu Municipality, 245–246, 254–255; in Machakos District, 199; management responses, 160; modern materials, 178; in Nairobi, 227; in Narok District, 59; parental responses, 59, 147, 199, 227, 245–246; on plantations, 118, 123, 147, 268; safety and, 227, 267–269; in Samburu District, 92; shortages, 255; slum, 219, 220; urbanization and, 268

Hygiene: awareness of, 51, 114, 269; basic, 51; environmental, 51, 60, 170, 179, 199, 268, 269, 271; personal, 60, 94

Immunization, 19, 21, 60, 68, 114, 122, 124, 132, 148, 179, 200–201, 204, 247–248, 253

Infant/child mortality rate, 239; decreases in, 19, 20; as indicator of country concern for children, 20; in Kericho District, 114; in Narok District, 51, 61; nutrition and, 21; structural adjustment and, 20

Infrastructures: failure of, 269; funding, 23; transportation, 79; urban, 220

Intersectoral collaboration: in Embu District, 185–186; in Kericho District, 137–138; in Machakos District, 209; in Nairobi, 235; in Narok District, 74–75; on plantations, 137–138, 163–164; in Samburu District, 101

Islamic Integrated Early Education Project, 7

Kabiru, Margaret, 24, 26, 29, 30, 31, 32, 41, 270, 271, 289–291

Kakamega Seminar on the Care and Educational Needs of Under Threes (1992), 31

Kamerman, S. B., 32

Kenya: birthrates, 19; Christianization of, 5; customs in, 7; dependence on donations in, 22; early childhood care and education changes in, 17–34; educational segregation in, 24; ethnic/racial groups in, 7, 22, 126, 143; independence, 24; infrastructure failure in, 269; internalized oppression in, 5; introduction of preschools, 24; language groups in, 22; mortality rates, 19; population growth, 23; postcolonial history, 22; preschool growth in, 28*fig;* religion in, 22

Kenya Institute of Education, 26

Kenya Railways, 269

Kenyatta, Jomo, 24

Kenya Wildlife Services, 55, 75

Kericho District: child care in, 130–131; clothing issues in, 124; cost-of-living in, 124; County Council, 116, 137; demographics, 113–114; education in, 125; ethnic groups in, 109, 118, 126; family challenges in, 119–120; family size in, 125; food issues in, 123; health care in, 124; housing in, 123; infant/child mortality rate, 114; intersectoral collaboration in, 137–138; lack of land in, 119; malnutrition/undernutrition in, 119, 132; parental aspirations for children in, 134–135; parent contributions to education, 128–130; population, 113; positive community actions, 122; poverty in, 119; research sample, 114–119; social/economic change in, 122–126; social structure in, 125–126

Kiambu District, 141–166; agriculture in, 142; child care in, 150, 154–155; demographics, 141–143; ethnic groups in, 143; family challenges in, 145–146; family size in, 150, 162; focus groups in, 164; food issues, 146–147; health care in, 147–148; herding in, 143; housing in, 147; intersectoral collaboration in, 163–164; migration in, 141; parental aspirations for children in, 155–156; parent contributions to education, 153–154; population, 141; poverty in, 165; preschools in, 148–149; research sample, 143–145; social/economic changes in, 146–153; social structures in, 149–150; work in, 144
Kilbride, P. L. & J. C., 2, 18, 20, 21, 23, 32, 37, 276, 285
Kipkorir, L., 23, 30, 32
Kisumu Municipality, 239–261; child-rearing in, 257–258; Community Development Assistants in, 254; Community Health Workers in, 254; cost-of-living in, 246; demographics, 239–241; District Development Plan, 240; education in, 257–258; ethnic groups in, 240; family challenges in, 242–244, 248–249; food issues in, 245, 256–257; health care in, 247–248, 253–254; housing in, 245–246, 254–255; Maternal and Child Health programs, 253; parental aspirations for children, 252–253; population, 239, 240; positive community actions in, 243–244, 259–260; research sample, 241–242; social structures in, 248–253; urbanization in, 254–255; Village Health Committee in, 254
Kitchen gardens, 51, 53, 88, 114, 119, 147, 267
Koech, Barbara, 8, 20, 21, 22, 32, 271

Labor: child, 9, 24, 110, 143, 151; distribution of, 143; division of, 271; rural, 195; women in, 110, 111, 112, 195
Land: access to, 119, 267; collective ownership, 23; communal, 8; conservation, 194; degradation, 82;

demarcation, 62; hiring out, 172; lack of, 176; ownership, 63; potentials, 113, 171; prices, 172; rental, 178, 267; subdivision, 23, 54, 142, 172; tenure, 8, 169, 269; traditional groups and, 8; use on plantations, 8
Lefebre, Henri, 285
Levine, R. A., 23, 32
Linde, C., 37
Literacy rates, 241
Lubeck, S., 270

Maasai group, 49–77, 50fig; family challenges for, 54–58; family change and, 55–56; family structure in, 8; food issues, 54, 56; health issues, 51; nutrition and, 50–51; traditional diet, 51, 54; traditional medicine and, 50; traditional support systems, 54
McCarthy, Cameron, 288
Machakos District, 193–211; child-rearing in, 200–201; County Council, 196; demographics, 193–195; education in, 200; ethnic groups in, 195; family challenges in, 197–198; family size in, 200; food issues in, 198–199; health care in, 199; housing in, 199; intersectoral collaboration in, 209; land area, 193; migration in, 194; parental aspirations for children, 204; parent contributions to schools, 203–204, 207–208; positive community actions, 197; research sample, 195–196; social/economic changes in, 198–202; social structures in, 201–202; urbanization in, 201
Malnutrition/undernutrition, 21, 151; chronic, 19; in Embu District, 179; in Kericho District, 113–114, 119, 132; in Narok District, 50–51; on plantations, 132; structural adjust-ment and, 20
Marginalization, 3, 8, 9
Maternity leave, 148, 150, 283
Mburugu, E., 269
Medicine: curative, 162; modern, 60; preventive, 162; shortages of, 148; supplies of, 124; traditional, 50, 60, 67
Migration: intradistrict, 83; in Kiambu District, 141; in Machakos District,

194; nomadism and, 83; urban, 18, 219; work and, 24, 194, 269
Mikell, G., 266
Missionaries, influence of, 5
Moi, Daniel arap, 169
Montessori training, 242, 246
Mothers. *See also* Parents; child care by, 68, 73; daily activities, 53; pressures on, 111–112; work roles, 115
Mothers' Union, 248
Mother Tongue Storybook series, 7
Mutua, J., 270, 276
Myers, R., 21

NACECE. *See* National Centre for Early Childhood Education
Nairobi, 219–237; child-rearing in, 230; City Commission Clinics, 228; cost-of-living in, 227–228; demographics, 219–221; education in, 229; ethnic groups in, 216; family challenges in, 223–226; family size in, 229; food issues in, 227; health care in, 220, 228; housing in, 227; intersectoral collaboration in, 235; nongovernmental organizations in, 220; population, 216, 219; positive community actions, 226; poverty in, 220; research sample, 221–223; services in, 219, 224; social structure in, 230
Narok District, 49–77; agriculture in, 49, 50; child care in, 62–63, 64–65, 67–73, 271; clothing issues in, 57, 60; cost-of-living in, 59; daily activities, 53; demographics, 49–51; education in, 51, 61; environment, 49; family challenges in, 54–58; family size in, 60–61; farming in, 63; feeding programs, 57; food issues in, 55, 56, 58–59; growth monitoring programs, 58; health care in, 55, 56, 57, 59–60, 68; health facilities, 50; housing in, 59; infant/child mortality rate, 51, 61; intersectoral collaboration in, 74–75; kitchen gardens in, 53; parental aspirations for children in, 72; parental roles, 51; parents contributions to schools in, 27–29; population, 49; positive community actions in, 57–58; research sample, 51–54; social/

economic change in, 58–63; social structures in, 63; teachers in, 52; transportation in, 55; water issues, 55; work in, 51
National Centre for Early Childhood Education, 22, 26, 169
Neocolonialism, 1, 4, 5, 8, 82
Njenga, Anne, 29, 32, 41, 42–43, 270, 271, 289–291
Njeru, E., 276
Nomadism, 83
Nongovernmental organizations, 6, 22, 95, 282; in Embu District, 174; in Kiambu District, 143; livestock improvement by, 81; in Nairobi, 220; on plantations, 137; school involvement by, 87
Nutrition. *See also* Food issues; awareness of, 113, 256; infant/child mortality rate and, 21; Maasai group and, 50–51; in Narok District, 60
Nyarango, P. M., 32

Orphans, 20, 21, 254, 259
Out-of-School Youth Education Project, 82
Overurbanization, 215
Oxfam, 95

Parental responses: child care, 131–133; child care for under threes, 203–204, 208, 233–235, 249–250; to clothing issues, 60; community roles, 195; coping strategies, 87, 122, 152–153, 187–188, 197–198, 206, 225–226; to cost-of-living issues, 59, 93, 124, 223, 227–228, 246; on education, 148–149, 200, 229; educational involvement, 65–66, 93, 97–99, 128–130, 187–188, 244; to family challenges, 54, 55, 86–87, 145–146, 242–244, 248–249; family size, 200; to food issues, 123, 146–147, 198–199, 245; health care issues, 59–60, 93, 124, 199, 228, 247; to housing issues, 59, 147, 199, 245–246; problems facing children, 150–152, 242–244; social/economic change issues, 58, 226–230
Parents: absent, 31; awareness of importance of education, 61, 87, 179;

Parents *(continued)*
community roles of, 51, 115, 144, 174; contributions to schools, 27–29, 88–89, 97–99, 128–130, 153–154, 177–178, 203–204, 207–208, 276–277; education levels, 115, 196; joys and challenges of, 69, 90–92, 155–156, 183–184, 204–205, 251–252; in Kericho District, 115; multiplicity of roles, 31; in Narok District, 51, 53, 54, 55, 56, 58, 59; perceptions of parenting, 234–235; pride in being, 132; in Samburu District, 88–89, 97–99; school fees and, 52; single, 20, 55, 110, 117, 125, 149, 150, 216, 224, 269

"Partnership and Networking in the Care and Development of Under Threes," 31

Plan International, 143

Plantations, 39, 109–139. *See also* Kericho District; Kiambu District; absence of grandmothers on, 115; alcohol abuse on, 118, 146; *ayahs* on, 110; child care on, 130–131, 150, 154–155; corporate ownership of, 110; ethnic mix on, 109, 118, 126; health care on, 111–112, 147–148; housing on, 118, 147, 268; intersectoral collaboration on, 137–138, 163–164; land use in, 8; loss of traditions and, 149–150; malnutrition/undernutrition, 132; management contributions, 112, 114, 118, 148, 153–154, 160–163; parental aspirations for children on, 134–135, 155–156; permanent/casual work on, 109–110, 117–118, 147, 150; poverty on, 110; preschools on, 110–111, 113–139, 148–149, 273–274; recreational facilities, 118, 125, 126; salary deductions by management, 118–119; self-help groups on, 149; social/economic changes on, 146–153; teachers on, 115–116; weighing stations as child care setting, 149–150

Polakow, V., 4, 21

Political: corruption, 17; economy, 23; instability, 17

Portraits: Embu boy, 176; Embu casual laborer, 175; Kericho student, 117; Kericho tea worker, 116; Kiambu girl, 158; Kiambu single father, 145; Kisumu mother, 248; Lchorolelerai mother, 86; Loltulelei girl, 102; Maasai grandmother, 52; Maasai mother, 53; Machakos boy, 209; Machakos teacher/mother, 196; Naiborkeju boy, 102; Narok primary student, 53; single mother, 223

Postcolonial theory, 266

Poverty: absolute, 169; effect on children, 207, 221, 225; effect on families, 266; health issues in, 19; homelessness and, 19; increases in, 19; in Kericho District, 119; in Kiambu District, 165; in Nairobi, 220; on plantations, 110; rural, 24, 201–202; single parent families and, 241; urban, 24

Preschool Education Project, 26–27

Preschools: alternatives to, 28; children's memories of, 71, 104–105, 133–134, 159, 185, 210; community funded, 24–25; cultural relevance, 64, 88, 97, 118, 126–128, 156, 188–189, 202–203, 230–231, 251; curriculum in, 26; enrollment factors, 188; enrollment growth, 29–30; funding for, 18, 25; gender and participation in, 69, 70; goals of, 70, 99; home-based, 75; introduction of, 24; in Kericho District, 127*fig;* in Kiambu District, 148–149; in Nairobi, 220*fig;* participation factors, 69–71; planta-tion, 110–111, 148–149; as preparation for primary school, 272–273; reasons for non-enrollment, 29; role in rural/agricultural societies, 274–275; role on plantations, 273–274; rural, 30; urban, 30, 275–276

Privatization, 23

Quality-of-life issues, 2

Reed-Danahay, D., 35

Reform, welfare, 2

Refugees, 21

Research: "Africanization" of, 35–37; Africanization of, 35–37; collaborative,

32–43, 287–291; cross-cultural, 3;
cultural relevance, 6; decolonizing, 4–
8; design and methodology, 37–38,
295–306; ethical issues, 4–8;
methodological issues, 4–8; micro-
ethnographic design, 36–37; narratives
in, 37; sampling procedures, 38–39;
sites for, 39–40
Resources, allocation of, 75–76
Respect: for adults, 259; for elders, 32
Rights, workers, 268
Rosaldo, R., 288
Rural/agricultural groups, 39. *See also*
Embu District; Machakos District;
intersectoral collaboration and, 209;
involvement in education, 186–190;
relevance of education to, 188–189,
202–203; role of preschool for, 274–
275; social/economic changes and,
178–182

Salvation Army, 74, 75
Samburu District: agriculture in, 81–82;
area of, 79; child care in, 89–90, 94,
102–103, 271; cost-of-living in, 93;
demographics, 79–84; description of,
79–84; ethnic groups in, 83; family
challenges in, 86–92; family size in,
94; family structure in, 8; food issues
in, 86, 92; growth monitoring
programs in, 93; herding in, 81, 83;
housing in, 92; intersectoral
collaboration in, 101; land potential
in, 81; land use in, 81–82; Out-of-
School Youth Education Project in, 82;
parental aspirations for children in, 91;
parents' contributions to schools in,
88–89, 97–99; population, 82–83;
positive community actions by, 87–88;
research sample, 85–86; social/economic
change in, 92–95; social structures in,
94; tourism in, 82; transportation in,
79; water resources in, 81; Women's
Development Committee in, 85; work
in, 85, 87
Sanitation, 21; awareness of, 269;
environmental, 255; lack of, 31;
latrines, 92, 179, 255, 271; toilet
training, 68, 94, 132

Schools, primary: drop-outs, 110, 111,
151; entry postponement, 117
Self-help groups, 7, 149, 195; church,
230; economically supporting, 180;
growth of, 230; local, 22; in Narok
District, 32; on plantations, 125, 149;
in Samburu District, 85; women's, 32,
85, 175, 197, 225, 282
Shamba cultivation, 52, 53, 68, 85, 94,
115, 118, 172, 179, 183, 271. *See also*
Kitchen gardens
Sibley, D., 4, 285, 288
Siblings: care responsibilities, 102–103;
caring for sick children, 67, 103–104,
159, 184, 210; child care and, 18,
66–67, 110, 111, 117, 130–131, 154,
158–159, 184–185, 209; daily activities, 53; household responsibility, 53
Single mothers, 20, 110, 117, 125, 149,
150, 216, 224, 269
Sisters of Mercy, 228
Smith, L. T., 4
Social: change, 2, 3; contexts, 37;
environment, 2; policy, 270; strata,
112; structures, 63, 94, 125–126, 149–
150, 180, 201–202, 230, 248–253
Socialization: cultural, 7; traditional, 47
Soja, E. W., 11, 266, 285, 288
Squatters, 268
Street children, 19, 20, 216, 240, 241,
267
Structural adjustment, 215; austerity
measures in, 8, 17, 24; debt
restructuring and, 20; impacts of, 8;
malnutrition/undernutrition and, 20;
mortality and, 20
Super, C., 23, 32
Swadener, E. B., 18, 20, 25, 30, 32, 276

Teacher Assistance Centre, 37
Teacher responses: caring for under
threes, 72–73, 133, 135–137, 157,
189–190, 208, 233–235, 249–250;
child-rearing, 65; on coping strategies,
56, 152–153, 206, 225–226; to cost-
of-living issues, 93; on cultural
relevance, 127; on cultural transmission, 64; educational involvement,
66, 97, 98, 187; to effects of hunger

Teacher responses (continued)
on children, 96; to family challenges, 56, 120–126, 145–146, 242–244; on family change and child care, 186–190; to food issues, 120–121; on intersectoral collaboration, 74–75, 101, 163–164, 209; preschool participation, 69, 70; to problems facing children, 96, 150–152, 242–244; to social/economic changes, 95, 226–230

Teachers, preschool: attitudes toward under threes, 72–73, 135–137, 157, 189–190, 208, 249–250; discipline of children by, 62–63; experience with under threes, 72–73, 99–101, 133, 233–235; marital status, 116, 145, 174, 222; salaries, 52, 86, 116, 144–145, 196, 222; support panels, 173; training for, 22, 26, 52, 85, 115–116, 174, 196, 222, 241–242

Teachers Advisory Centre, 242

"Thirdspace," 266, 285–286

Toileting, 68, 94, 132

Traditional/pastoralist groups, 39, 47–77, 79–106. See also Narok District; Samburu District; family structures in, 8; intersectoral collaboration for, 74–75, 101; involvement in preschool education, 65–67; land tenure and, 8; relevance of education to, 64, 88, 97

Transportation, 122; infrastructures, 79; lack of, 269; in Narok District, 55; in Samburu District, 79; urbanization and, 269

Tronick, E. Z., 32

Tsing, Anna Lowenhaupt, 2, 3, 9, 35, 288

Unemployment, 1, 20, 23, 171

United Nations: Convention on the Rights of the Child, 19, 283; Labor Organization, 19

Urban groups, 40, 215–217, 219–237, 238–261; intersectoral collaboration and, 235; involvement in education, 244; relevance of preschool education to, 230–231, 251

Urbanization, 1, 23, 24, 201, 215; in Embu District, 176; housing and, 268; in Kisumu Municipality, 254–255; transportation and, 269

U.S.-Kenyan Early Childhood Collaborative Training Seminars, 33

Varkevisser,, 32

Violence: ethnic, 19; religious, 19

Wallman, S., 2, 21

Wandibba, S., 23

Warfare, 21

Water: access to, 21, 56, 57, 60, 118, 246, 255, 269, 271; illness and, 199; lack of, 51, 86, 148, 228, 269; risk awareness, 199; safe, 21, 32; shared use, 86; shortages, 55; tap, 118

Weaning: bottle feeding and, 182; early, 201, 267, 271; foods, 51, 62, 68, 92, 117, 131, 132, 147, 170, 173, 178, 181, 201, 240, 271; practices, 24, 180

Weisner, Thomas, 2, 18, 21, 23, 32, 265

White, M.A., 37

Whiting, B. B., 3, 23, 32

Willinsky, J., 4

Women: in cultivation, 82; in development activities, 195; discrimination against, 143; health of, 21; in labor force, 23, 110, 111–112, 195; in Narok District, 55; rural predominance, 23; self-help groups, 7, 22, 32, 85, 175, 197, 225, 282; status of, 21, 241; traditional roles, 23; in urban settings, 216

Women Bus Unions, 143

Woodhead, M., 21, 22, 23

Work: in Embu District, 174; in Kiambu District, 144; in Kisumu Municipality, 241; migration and, 194; in Nairobi, 221; in Narok District, 51; in Samburu District, 85, 87

World Bank, 8, 215; Early Childhood Development Mission to Kenya, 270

World Health Organization, 254

World Summit for Children (1990), 19, 283

World Vision, 209